Used Boat Notebook

From the pages of Sailing Magazine, reviews of 40 used boats

plus a detailed look at ten great used boats to sail around the world

JOHN KRETSCHMER

SHERIDAN HOUSE

This book is dedicated to Carl Wake and Dave Morrison, Good Shipmates

First published 2002 by
Sheridan House Inc.
145 Palisade Street
Dobbs Ferry, NY 10522
www.sheridanhouse.com

Copyright © 2002 by Sheridan House Inc.

Part 1 is reprinted from articles published
under the title "Used Boat Notebook"
in SAILING Magazine

All rights reserved. No part of this publication
may be reproduced, stored in a retrieval system
or transmitted in any form or by any means, electronic,
mechanical, photocopying, recording, or otherwise,
without the prior permission in writing of Sheridan House.

Library of Congress Cataloging-in-Publication Data

Kretschmer, John.
Used boat notebook : from the pages of Sailing magazine, reviews of 40 used boats plus a detailed look at ten great used boats to sail around the world / John Kretschmer.
p. cm.
ISBN 1-57409-150-6 (alk. paper)
1. Used boats—Catalogs. 2. Sailboats—Catalogs. 3. Sailing ships—Catalogs. 4. Yachts—Catalogs. I. Title.

VM321 .K723 2002
623.8'223—dc21

2002021188

Production Management: Quantum Publishing Services, Inc., Bellingham, WA
Composition/Design: Jill Mathews

Printed in the United States of America

ISBN 1-57409-150-6

Contents

Part 1 — Forty Great Used Boats

Sailboats 23'–30'

Sailboats 31'–36'

Sailboats 37'–42'

Part 2 — Ten Great Used Boats to Sail Around the World

"The love that is given to ships is profoundly different from the love men feel for every other work of their hands."—Joseph Conrad

"As she rode at her ancient, rust eaten anchor, she sat upon the water like a swan."—Joshua Slocum

"There was room to lie and sleep, and room to sit, what more does any man want?"—Arthur Ransome

INTRODUCTION

Like most magazine columns "The Used Boat Notebook" sprang to life brimming with optimism and a bit of naiveté. Former SAILING Magazine Editor Micca Hutchins suggested I write a column about boats that would attempt to fill a void in the sailing press, and at the time, seemed anything but novel. What was different about her vision was the concept of writing about used boats. And it wasn't to be skimpy watered-down articles, but thoroughly researched, hard-hitting reviews of used boats.

"Let's present the good, the bad and the ugly, the information we all really crave," she said. "Kretschmer, you're ideal for this project. Who else has sailed as many different kinds of boats as you and has had as many problems along the way?"

I wasn't sure if that was a compliment or an insult, but the first column, a review of the Ted Brewer-designed Morgan 38, appeared in March 1996. It may seem odd to those outside the magazine publishing business, but the column was considered something of a risky venture. We were aware of the fact that many of our readers had purchased used boats, but we thought most were more interested in reading about the shiny new ones. After all, the sailing press is the major showplace for the latest in boats and equipment. To a lesser degree, we also worried about alienating SAILING's new-boat advertisers. Our fears, as it turned out, were ungrounded. There was plenty of room between the magazine's oversized covers for new and used boat aficionados. In fact, boatbuilders have been generous and helpful in supplying information about their old boats, some of which even compete with their new models in the marketplace.

It seems we had the right idea with "Used Boat Notebook," and many other publications have followed our lead. Only Practical Sailor was regularly offering used boat reviews when we began. Now most sailing periodicals offer some type of used boat news and evaluations. Today, six years and more than 50 reviews (and counting) later, the "Used Boat Notebook" has become one of SAILING's most popular regular features.

The Nuts and Bolts of Each Review

The reviews are a combination of my sailing experience aboard a wide variety of boats, in-depth research and invaluable information provided by owners. I work closely with Greta Schanen, SAILING's managing editor. An experienced sailor, having sailed a variety of boats the world over, she steers me in the right direction, especially when I'm tackling a performance boat. (She actually likes today's blunt-nosed, flat-bottomed rocket ships.) She is not only responsible for wrestling my words into shape every month but also suggests many of the boats profiled. Added into the mix is my experience conducting several boat buying workshops and working briefly as a yacht broker, which may not have been a noble calling, but it was a terrific way to learn about boats. As a yacht delivery skipper and a reviewer of new and used boats, I have sailed more than 100 different boats.

In general, the column targets affordable, good-quality, fiberglass production boats, steering clear of wood and metal boats. Most sell for less than $100,000 and some even sell for less than $10,000. Naturally, some of the boats larger than 40 feet and some of the higher quality boats sell for more. The bulk of the reviews, however, examine boats in the 30- to 40-foot range, with prices falling from $30,000 to $70,000. For the most part, the column covers boats that are popular and have had long production runs, making them widely available in the North American marketplace.

Each review follows the same basic format, while revealing the unique personality of the boat reviewed. A general overview of the boat, the designer and the builder opens the review, which is followed by **First Impressions.** This section is an initial glance as though I have just spotted an intriguing boat lying to a mooring or sitting on the hard in a boatyard and am struck by the profile.

I provide some design parameters and some statistics in this section, but the reviews are not all about numbers. I leave number crunching to yacht designers because practical experience has made me skeptical of the numbers listed on a spec sheet. Over the years I have found glaring inaccuracies between paper and fiberglass for statistics like displacement, draft and sail area. Accepting the design premise for what it is, be it a coastal cruiser, sport boat, casual daysailer or bluewater voyager, my objective is to analyze each boat for what it is meant to be and whether it hits the mark. This method is more valuable than simply putting a boat through a litmus test of what I consider to be desirable traits in a boat. We all have our own ideas of what we desire and need in a boat, I help by pointing out what works and what doesn't.

Under the heading **Construction,** the review answers such questions as, Is the hull solid glass or cored? Is the ballast internal or external? How is the hull and deck joined? Are molded liners used or are the bulkheads and furnishings fiberglassed to the hull? At the end of the day, the construction quality determines more about a boat's value than almost any other feature. Of course, boats can be overbuilt as well as underbuilt, depending upon the design premise. The ultralight Olson 30 has a displacement of just 4,000 pounds and the construction quality is excellent. The double-ended Westsail 32 tips the displacement scales at more than 30,000 pounds and was also built to a high standard. In between these two extremes are plenty of examples of poorly constructed sailboats, some turning up in these pages.

The next facet of the review, **What to look for,** may be the most important. What common problems have been documented by current or previous owners and how can they be avoided or repaired? I am always impressed by the candor of most owners. Although they invariably love their boats, they're not blind to their boats' faults and are willing to share them with other sailors. It is always enlightening to see what problems turn up in each review. Some problems are common to most boats, yet each one has its own quirks. The water tanks are a source of problems on the Whitby 42 center-cockpit cruiser, while the teak decks on the Swan 38s are problematic and expensive to repair. Certain hull numbers of Valiant 40s were plagued with blisters, and the aluminum toerail on the lovely C&C 39 corrodes around the stainless fasteners. The list goes on and on. Rarely do these problems eliminate a boat from consideration for used boat buyers, but they give you a heads up on what to look for when shopping. One of the Used Boat Notebook readers wrote that after reading a review he knew more about the boat he was looking at than the marine surveyor he had hired.

The reviews next take the reader **On deck,** examining the sail controls, spars and standing rigging, fittings and safety features. The layout of the cockpit receives scrutiny, both from a sailing and comfort point of view. Even a one-design rocket ship has to accommodate the crew with some measure of civility. Next we drop **Down below** and explore the interior. From layouts to storage, from joinerwork to engineering details, I point out various features of the cabin. Are the bunks actually long enough to sleep in? Will the sinks drain on both tacks? Are there fiddles, do the lockers latch securely, are the handholds accessible for short people?

Finally we move into propulsion and examine the **Engine.** I list the types of engines put into the boat during its production run and describe what kind of access there is for both routine maintenance and major repairs, including just how big a job it is to repower. **Underway** looks at a boat's sailing characteristics through a range of conditions. I have sailed many of the boats reviewed, but I also rely heavily on owner feedback. How high can the boat point? Does it make much leeway? At what wind range would you need to reef and shorten the headsail? How does the boat handle heavy weather and light air? These and more questions are answered.

After a brief **Conclusion,** which invariably includes a discussion about the boat's value on the market, I provide a unique quick reference **Value Guide.** This feature rates the boat in 10 categories, giving it from one to five sailboats in each category, with a five-boat rating being the best and extremely rare. The Value Guide also provides useful, updated resources for support and refits. The Value Guide lists the overall rating for the boat, with most of the boats reviewed falling between 2 and 3$^1/_2$ sailboats. The **Boats for Sale** guide is a list of current prices, both from the BUC Book (an industry standard guide to pricing used frequently by brokers) and from an analysis of boats listed on the open market

The "Used Boat Notebook" reviews are the next best thing to actually sailing the boat and are designed to help readers zero in on a specific boat before committing funds to sea trials, haul outs and surveys.

The 10 Best

The second part of the book, **Ten Great and Affordable Used Boats to Sail Around the World,** features reviews of quality boats that prospective world cruisers should seriously consider. These reviews are a bit longer and more in-depth. In addition to my observations and research, there are comments from owners, many of them circumnavigators and all bluewater sailors. They openly explain what they like and don't like about their boats, changes they made for offshore sailing and what they would look for if they were buying a boat all over again. These 10 boats merely scratch the surface of all the great bluewater boats afloat. Indeed, some of the boats that have been profiled in The Used Boat Notebook like the Valiant 40, Tayana 37 and Whitby 42 would have certainly made the 10 Best list if not for the fact that they have already been reviewed. Some choices on the 10 Best list seem predictable. The Camper Nicholson 35 is a classic small cruiser with a proud pedigree, and the Peterson 44 and Mason 43 are well-respected passagemakers. However, some of the boats on the list may raise some eyebrows. The Beneteau First 38 may surprise a few readers, as will the Gulfstar 50 ketch. Don't be too quick to judge. The boats were chosen for a combination of their seaworthiness and value in the marketplace.

The list is anything but definitive.I omitted the Contessa 32, one of my all-time favorite boats, for instance. The diminutive Contessa has carried me across the Atlantic, from south to north in the Pacific and to the bottom of the world and back. It is a terrific oceangoing boat, sure-footed in a blow. With its lovely lines and affordability, it meets all the criteria except for one thing—it is miserably uncomfortable. For every day at sea during a typical circumnavigation, 10 or more are spent in port at the dock or at anchor. The interior of the 32 is just too small for two normal sized people to live with any style.

The choices for the 10 Best reflect the changing nature of cruising. Boats are getting bigger. Recent surveys show that the average bluewater cruiser is more than 40 feet long. It is easy to conjure up the dream to sail around the world, and rather straightforward to put together a plan to accumulate the funds for the voyage. Choosing the right boat to head off into the blue unknown, however, can be most confusing. The task is easier if you have 20 years of hard won experience and an unlimited budget. While this book won't offer investment advice to enhance your budget, it can hasten your exodus if you are willing to consider an affordable boat instead of waiting for that perfect yet more expensive boat.

The key to **Ten Great and Affordable Boats,** and the **Used Boat Notebook** in general, is that this book is about specific boats. You won't find a laundry list of what makes for a perfect boat and how to choose the one right for you. This book is for sailors farther along the learning curve. It is for those sailors who are ready to take the plunge and need information about specific boats. "The Used Boat Notebook" is a collection of honest and informed reviews covering a wide range of boats. Ten Great and Affordable Boats offers invaluable details and insights on boats that can carry you safely around the world.

I have spent the past two decades sailing all over the world in an assortment of sailboats. Ironically, I haven't actually sailed around the world—there is a little chunk in the East Indian Ocean that I've missed. I have crossed the Atlantic 14 times, the Pacific three times and sailed most of the way across the Indian Ocean. I have sailed to near 60 degrees both north and south, from Stockholm to Cape Horn, and spent years plying the Mediterranean and Caribbean Seas. As a professional delivery captain I have logged 200,000 miles and spent more than 1,600 days and nights at sea. I recently compiled a list of the different boats I have sailed 1,000 miles or more in a single stretch. It's 35 and counting.

During all this sailing I have learned that boats come in all shapes and sizes, with individual personalities to match. Somewhere between these pages there is a boat that will not only fit your cruising budget, but more importantly, will fit your dreams.

PART 1

Forty Great Used Boats

O'Day 23

This inexpensive trailerable cruiser is a good choice for protected waters

A frequent complaint about sailing is that it's too expensive. The argument has merit. The cost of buying a boat is just the opening volley when it comes to the overall expense of sailing.

First, there is new equipment to purchase. Then comes haulouts and maintenance, which tap the credit cards every spring, followed by insurance and other fees that must be paid year after year. A hidden back breaker is the monthly payment for dockage or moorage that arrives as regularly as the morning tide. And if you live where it's cold, add the expense of winter storage, a particularly mean-spirited tax levied on our fun. Even a small boat slip can set you back more than $200 a month. All these costs add up over the course of a year and the calculation of cost per hour on the water can be downright depressing.

One alternative that will help keep sailing costs under control is to consider buying an older, inexpensive, trailerable boat.

Thirty years ago, trailerable weekenders represented a sizeable chunk of the sailboat market. I remember as a kid, passing a bright yellow Venture 23 as we headed "Up North" on I-75 and insisting that my dad slow down so that I could study every detail of that salty looking trailersailer. The rather silly wooden cockpit railing stirred my heart, and although we were somewhere near Midland, Michigan, I was dreaming of Tahiti.

The 1960s may have been the Age of Aquarius, but the 1970s were the age of trailerable weekend boats. Shiny new Catalinas, Paceships, Balboas and Ventures could be found at small marinas and launching ramps all over the country. The undisputed king of the trailerable builders was O'Day, with the O'Day 23 as one of the company's most successful models.

O'Day was the brainchild of 1960 Olympic sailing gold medalist George O'Day and was one of the country's leading production builders for more than 30 years. Although the company was later assimilated by the conglomerate Bangor Punta and began to produce larger boats before folding in the late 1980s, O'Day is still best known for building sprightly daysailers and trailerable weekend boats. The 19-foot O'Day Mariner is considered a classic, and at one time a complete line of trailersailers up to 25 feet poured off the assembly line at the O'Day plant in Fall River, Massachusetts. C. Raymond Hunt and Associates designed most of the O'Day fleet, including the 23.

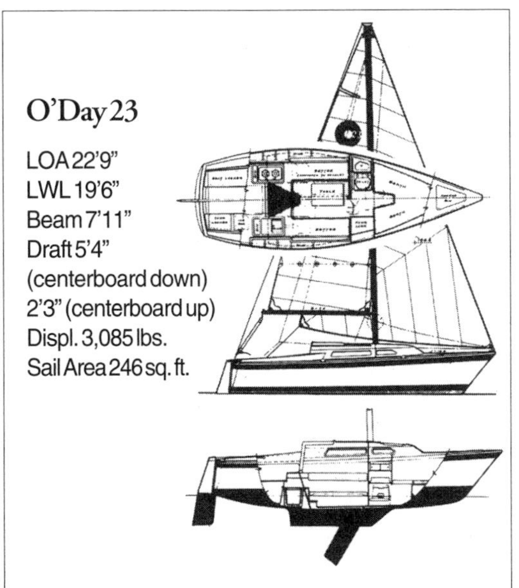

First impressions

Several thousand O'Day 23s were launched during a production run that began in 1972 and lasted approximately 13 years. The exact figures are not known, as most of the O'Day records are lost. One of the reasons for the 23's enduring popularity is that it is a handsome boat that looks more at home bobbing in the water than riding behind an SUV.

The profile is classic 1970s with little sheer and a pronounced bow overhang. The flat stern features an outboard rudder with the result being a fairly long LWL. One note about outboard rudders is that they often show signs of collision damage along the aft edge, usually the result of an unexpected kiss from a dock or piling. The designers did a good job of blending the height of the coachroof into the overall lines of the boat, resisting the urge to improve upon the "sitting headroom" below.

Unlike many trailersailers of the period, the O'Day 23 is a keel-centerboarder. Many boats, like the O'Day 22, for example, came with fixed stub keels that resulted in their making more leeway than forward progress in any kind of upwind breeze. Other trailerables were swing keelers, which meant that all the ballast was contained in the centerboard, making them both tender and prone to centerboard problems. The O'Day 23, on the other hand, carries 1,200 pounds of encapsulated lead ballast in a stub keel, and the centerboard is only lightly weighted to make it easier to deploy when sailing upwind. The board-up draft is just 2 feet, 3 inches, while draft with the board down is 5 feet, 4 inches. The biggest drawback to the keel-centerboard O'Day 23 is that the overall displacement of 3,085 pounds makes it a substantial load to tow and launch.

O'Day 23 Price Data

		Low	High
BUC Retail Range	1972	$ 2,950	$ 3,400
	1978	$ 3,400	$ 3,950
	1984	$ 5,200	$ 6,000

		State	Asking
Boats For Sale	1976	FL	$ 4,000
	1981	ME	$ 4,500
	1982	MA	$ 4,200

Construction

The O'Day 23 was built like most boats of the day, with a solid fiberglass hull and a balsa-cored deck. While these boats were designed for rapid construction and the scantlings are on the light side, O'Days have held up well in comparison to other boats of this era. The hull-to-deck joint is mechanically fastened and lapped with a vinyl rubrail. The outboard rudder is quite light, being foam cored and covered with gelcoat. Even so, the pintles and gudgeons are on the small side.

A molded pan incorporates the cabin sole and supplies most of the structural support. A fiberglass liner is also used overhead and the combination of the two makes it difficult to access the hull. Some boats were fitted with a pop-top, which increases the headroom in the galley area to 6 feet, 4 inches, but also increases the likelihood of leaks. The centerboard assembly appears to be well done, and few owners report the usual problems with the pivot pin and pendant.

What to look for

The first thing to remember when you start looking at O'Day 23s is that most boats will be at least 20 years old, and some will be nearing 30. Naturally, some will be in rough shape. There are plenty of common problems to be aware of. Check for deck delamination, especially in the foredeck and around the base of the mast. The gelcoat is often crazed and cracked, a good indicator of delamination below. The hull sections forward have been known to oilcan, or flex, so check the pan for cracks. As mentioned earlier, the rudder is lightly built as are the gudgeons and pintles, so these should be carefully inspected. It is likely that they will have been replaced, so check the installation.

The 1978 model that I inspected in Miami had several access points cut in the overhead liner to get at the underside of deck fittings. Obviously these fittings had leaked, and in fact, the boat had caulk dripped lavishly around the ports, hatches and toerail, a clear indicator of leaks. In addition to the boat, also check the trailer. Most of the original trailers will be piles of rust unless they have been properly maintained. You

O'Day 23

Sailing Magazine's Value Guide

PRICE: The O'Day 23 is an affordable alternative to newer, more expensive boats. Its trailerability further reduces costs associated with sailing.

DESIGN QUALITY: The overall design is very effective. The keel centerboard is the best compromise for a trailerable boat and the cabin is surprisingly roomy.

CONSTRUCTION QUALITY: There is nothing exceptional about the build of the 23, but the boats have held up well over the years. The rudder is a known weak spot.

USER-FRIENDLINESS: The 23 is simple to sail and comfortable, which makes it user-friendly by most accounts. The sitting headroom however, can be a bit annoying.

SAFETY: The 23 was designed and built to be a weekender and sailed in relatively protected waters. There is a fair amount of freeboard that lends a feeling of security but the boat is not overly stiff. You need to shorten sail early.

TYPICAL CONDITION: Despite ranging from 17 to nearly 30 years old, most 23s I've inspected are in decent shape. The basic simplicity of the design and better-than-average initial construction have stood the test of time.

REFITTING: Working on the 23 is a challenge because of molded liners and tight access in general. Replacing leaky deck fittings requires cutting through the liner.

SUPPORT: O'Day is out of business and unfortunately there is no company support. However, there are several active Web sites for O'Day owners, including www.odayowners.com.

AVAILABILITY: There were thousands of O'Day 23s launched and at any given time there are many boats for sale.

INVESTMENT AND RESALE: It is hard to spend more than $5,000 on an O'Day 23 so your initial investment is rather modest. The used market is lively and if you maintain the boat in decent condition, you will get a good portion of your money back out of the boat.

OVERALL 'SVG' RATING

can manage with a suspect trailer if you only use it twice a year: once to the water and once to your driveway. If you plan to transport the boat frequently, or any great distance, an investment in a new trailer will be well worth the money. After all, one of the great advantages of an O'Day 23 is that you can move it to far-flung sailing sites.

On deck

The cockpit is fairly roomy, and the outboard rudder allows the tiller to be moved out of the way when not under way. The mainsheet arrangement is a bit awkward for the person at the helm, as it angles from the transom up to the rather short boom. Still, this is better than leading the sheet to the cockpit sole or cluttering up a small boat with a traveler across the cockpit. Remember, this isn't a performance boat.

If you are used to bigger boats, the pulpits, stanchions and lifelines will seem undersized. However, when compared to other trailerables of a similar size and era, the O'Day 23 is probably the best equipped, with standard equipment including Barient sheet winches.

The mast is set in a tabernacle for raising and lowering, and the O'Day owners' Web page is full of advice on stepping the mast. One owner was adamant that you should only step and unstep the mast twice a season. But the consensus seemed to be that once you have the process down, it is possible to do it yourself in about 20 minutes. One 23 owner suggested adding rollers to the bow and stern pulpits to allow the mast to slide forward easier. Others stressed the importance of having a four-wheel-drive vehicle for low-end power when hauling the boat out of the water.

Down below

The interior is surprisingly roomy and includes a few innovations that enhance the useable space. First is the pop-top, which not only adds headroom in the aft end of the saloon but creates instant ventilation below. The stove and sink are each fitted into molded drawers that slide out from under the cockpit seats. The small galley also includes an icebox.

The standard arrangement includes a V-berth forward followed by a small head with a sink. The head is often a Porta-Potti, which is actually quite practical in a small boat. The saloon includes long, sleepable settees and a fold-out table. Except for the limited headroom, it is hard to believe that the boat is just 23 feet and I suspect that the well-thought-out interior was a big reason for the 23's popularity.

Engine

The O'Day 23 can be powered by a variety of outboard engines, although you will likely need at least a six-horsepower engine to push into a chop or against a foul current. The engine mounting bracket is off center on the transom and there is a convenient tank locker beneath the starboard cockpit seat. Used outboards are about as reliable as free advice, and unless the engine was fairly new, I would consider purchasing a quiet, environmentally friendly four-stroke model. One handling advantage of an outboard is that you can steer the engine directly when backing down, which is more efficient than using the boat's tiller.

Underway

It is safe to say that the O'Day 23 is a good first "big" boat, or an entry-level boat, and the performance reflects accordingly. Like all trailerables, the 23 is a bit tender and needs to be reefed early. The mainsail becomes more efficient if you add a traveler, allowing the main to be dumped a bit to flatten the boat while maintaining sail shape. However, a traveler really crowds the cockpit.

Most owners report that the boat is fairly well balanced under working sail with little weather helm. The boat I inspected in Miami had been retrofitted with CDI roller furling on the headsail. I was a bit surprised at the size of the furling-line lead blocks, as they looked to me like they wouldn't support a decent size burgee. Roller furling also complicates stepping the rig.

The sheeting angles are quite wide and the 23 is not very close-winded. If you really want to improve performance you can tighten the leads, although you may actually have to add some ballast if you want to beat efficiently in a stiff breeze. I don't think it is worth the effort.

Conclusion

It is important to remember what the O'Day 23 is and is not. It is an inexpensive, roomy boat built to sail in relatively protected waters. It's not a performance boat that should be pushed hard and put away wet. It is an ideal boat to explore the rivers and reaches of the Chesapeake Bay, the mangrove islands of the Florida Keys and the clear waters of Grand Traverse Bay. And, unlike other small boats, you can hitch the O'Day 23 behind the family SUV and head off toward any or all of those destinations.

Stone Horse

A weekend cruiser with loads of charm and sailing sensibility

The Stone Horse transcends fiberglass mat, woven roving, epoxy resins, teak and stainless steel. It is difficult to picture this boat beginning life like every other fiberglass boat, as a bucket of smelly chemicals and a pile of fittings in a warehouse. A winsome raised-deck, double-headsail sloop, the Stone Horse was created and crafted around a philosophy, not a business plan. Built by the Edey & Duff yard in Mattapoisett, Massachusetts, the Stone Horse is a fiberglass recreation of a 1931 classic Sam Crocker design that stands apart from the other plastic boats at almost any marina.

The first Stone Horses were built by William Lee at Harwich, Massachusetts, and named after a lightship anchored off the eastern end of Nantucket Sound. Lee launched 38 boats before World War II interrupted production, and many of these 23-foot, 4-inch, LOD wooden cruisers are still afloat and revered by their owners. In fact, Peter Duff and Mait Edey owned a 1938, engineless model called *Little Slipper*, which they used as the prototype for their fiberglass version.

The first modern Stone Horse was built in Peter Duff's living room and backyard herb garden. Now, nearly 30 years later, Edey & Duff has produced 1,200 boats, including the distinctive Dovekie and Shearwater shoal-draft sailboats. Overall, 150 Stone Horses have been built and although not actively in production these days, it wouldn't take much cajoling to convince the company to build a custom boat. The tools are still available. The bulk of the production run was in the 1970s.

There were plenty of small sloops on the market in 1969 but Edey & Duff were convinced that no other boat met what their company's 24-page brochure describes as the "five essential characteristics" of a small cruising boat, which were ease of handling, comfort at sea, seaworthiness, speed, and last but certainly not least, beauty. Idealistic to be sure, but with these objectives in mind, Edey & Duff went into production. From the beginning, the Stone Horse caught the attention of sailors already weary of fiberglass boats that for the most part looked the same. Of course, any boat built to these five guidelines is bound to be a fine boat indeed.

First impressions

Sam Crocker was a master of creating small raised-deck boats that maintained handsome, well-balanced lines. The raised deck is quite practical, especially for small boats, but it can also make the freeboard seem excessive and destroy the look of a boat. This certainly is not the case with the Stone Horse. The sheer stripe does a good job of blending the flow of the deck into the lower cockpit, and the boomkin and bowsprit stretch the lines and emphasize the springy sheer. From the cockpit you feel close to the water. No wonder, with a maximum freeboard of just two feet.

The Stone Horse has a long keel of moderate draft, typical of the many small boats that were designed for the windy, shoal waters south of Cape Cod. The Stone Horse displaces just over two tons and with 2,000 pounds of lead and cement, the ballast/displacement ratio is 44 percent, higher than usual for a full-keel boat. However, the Stone Horse is not a slow boat. Its displacement/length ratio is a respectable 326 and it carries a generous 339 square feet of sail, giving it a sail area/displacement ratio of 19.6. The Stone Horse may not be sporty, but it's a lively sailer that keeps way on through a chop and can carry sail in a breeze.

Stone Horse Price Data

		Low	High
BUC Retail Range	1974	$ 8,350	$ 9,600
	1980	$11,300	$ 12,800
	1986	$16,800	$ 19,100
		State	**Asking**
Boats For Sale	1977	FL	$ 14,000
	1979	MA	$ 12,500

Construction

Edey & Duff was convinced that by building a sandwich or cored hull it was closer to replicating the nature of a wooden boat. And it cites many advantages of cored construction, including better sound insulation, less condensation below, overall strength and stiffness of two skins, and, of course, less weight. As regular readers of this column know, I have my complaints with cored hulls, especially balsa cores. But in this case, it seems to have worked. The Stone Horse is cored with Airex PVC foam composite, which has two advantages as a core: It is somewhat resistant to rot when water penetrates the skin, and its flexibility can absorb impacts, returning it to its original shape. The deck is also cored with Airex but the molded interior liners are solid fiberglass.

The hull and deck are joined on an internal flange with 3M's 5200 as the strong but flexible bonding agent. For good measure the joint is also mechanically fastened with $^{3}/_{16}$-inch monel or stainless rivets. A teak toerail covers the rivets and a stout rubbing strake also protects the hull-and-deck joint. The internal ballast is lead, in the form of 80 individual pigs, weighing 20 pounds each that are encapsulated in the keel cavity and covered with 400 pounds of cement. A molded liner of sorts rims the interior and is tabbed to the hull near the waterline. Additional moldings include the fiberglass water tank and engine pan.

What to look for

"If you are considering a Stone Horse," says Joseph Keogh, long time general manager at Edey & Duff, "you have to be prepared to keep the brightwork up, otherwise, the boat can look bad in a hurry."

Vin Falcigno, who sails a 1975 Stone Horse on Long Island Sound, agrees. "Don't underestimate how much wood there is on this boat," he said. Falcigno, who keeps his boat in pristine condition, has reached a maintenance compromise. "I keep everything bright except the rails, the toerail, rubbing and sheer strakes. These are the back breakers, so on these I use Cetol by Sikkens," he said.

Still, brightwork is a cosmetic issue. If you are on a tight budget, you might be better off buying a boat that needs a lot of elbow grease and spend the money saved on the purchase price upgrading other parts of the boat.

Structural problems seem few and far between. Check the spruce spars, including the spreaders, for signs of rot. Wooden spars need annual maintenance if they are varnished. Painted spars don't look as nice, but they resist the elements better. Check the bronze fittings on the rudder gudgeon and pintle below the waterline for signs of electrolysis. Also, there may be small pockets of delamination in the core, both in the hull and the deck. There isn't much that can be done short of major surgery, and unless the delamination is widespread, I wouldn't worry about it, although one boat that I know of in Marblehead had a saturated core and needed a lot of work.

Look for a boat with an inboard diesel. The vast majority were built this way, although the first inboards were gasoline engines, and a precious few were set up for outboards. Various diesels were used over the years.

On deck

Remember Edey & Duff's five essential characteristics? Numbers one and two were ease of handling and comfort, and both of these features describe the Stone Horse cockpit. Nearly 8 feet long, the company made no excuses for the cockpit

Stone Horse

Sailing Magazine's Value Guide

PRICE: With asking prices from $8,000 to $19,000, the Stone Horse is relatively expensive compared to other 23-footers. But it is a good buy when looking at value per dollar.

DESIGN QUALITY: The design is dated, but timeless. What gives this Crocker-designed boat such value is that it is in a league of its own.

CONSTRUCTION QUALITY: There is little to fault with in the original construction, although any cored hull is a potential problem. Wooden spars need to be checked carefully.

USER-FRIENDLINESS: The premise of the Stone Horse was to make it easy to handle, and within the design parameters, comfortable. It succeeds brilliantly.

SAFETY: The Stone Horse was designed for coastal cruising. The large cockpit could be dangerous offshore, and raised decks in general are less friendly than a lower side deck.

TYPICAL CONDITION: Most owners lavish love and care on their boats. However, the Stone Horse is a demanding mistress; the brightwork can look old quickly.

REFITTING: Many owners visit the Edey & Duff yard regularly for refits and repairs. Parts and fittings are still available.

SUPPORT: There isn't an active owner's group or Web page. However, Joe Keogh at the yard is extremely knowledgeable and helpful. You can reach him at (508) 758-2743, or at www.by-the-sea.com/edey&duff.

AVAILABILITY: Although 150 Stone Horses were built, they don't change hands frequently. The majority of boats are in New England.

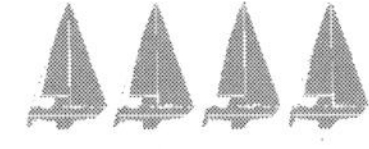

INVESTMENT AND RESALE: The Stone Horse has a cult following and to some is considered a classic. There will always be a market for used boats, and the boat has held its value nicely over the years.

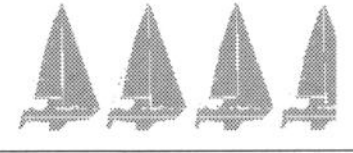

OVERALL 'SVG' RATING

dominating much of the human space aboard. The brochure states, "The cockpit must be spacious. You spend most of your waking hours there. Nothing is more ludicrous than the boat which sleeps four and sails two!" If you lash the tiller out of the way, you really open it up.

All running rigging is led aft, along the raised deck to the forward end of the cockpit. A great advantage of a small boat is that everything is within the quick grasp of the helmsman. The mainsheet traveler runs across the transom, completely out of the way. Most Stone Horses are not fitted with sheet winches; the two small headsails can be controlled by hand. The cockpit features two lockers and a lazarette. The portable fuel tank is stored to port. Also, there is a teak bridgedeck hatch that gives good access to the engine and to the quarterberths. The boomkins and bowsprits were offered in either teak or mahogany and possibly spruce.

It takes a moment to realize there are no stanchions and lifelines. The nature of a raised deck doesn't really permit their use without drastically changing the look of the boat. However, on a 23-foot boat, especially one with an 8-foot cockpit, it only requires a step or two to reach the security of the shrouds. The Stone Horse has terrific nonskid that was designed to look and feel like the canvas used on wooden boats. The wooden spar is keel stepped. All the spars, booms and wishbones, when used, are Sitka Spruce. Edey & Duff called the boat a double headsail sloop, not a cutter. The company makes the distinction by claiming that a true cutter carries less than 50 percent of total sail area in the mainsail, while the Stone Horse has a proportionately larger main. Originally most boats had tanbark sails.

Down below

At first glance it doesn't look like there can be much of an interior in the Stone Horse. However, this is where the advantage of a raised deck comes into play. Although the headroom is only 4 feet in the saloon, the interior is surprisingly livable for one or two people out for a couple days of coastal cruising. The woodwork below is nicely finished and the boat has a distinct New England feel. Most boats have kerosene lamps.

Beginning up forward is a watertight bulkhead that seals off the chain locker, followed by a large V-berth. There is quite a bit of storage below the bunk. In the bunk cutout area, which is aft of the spar, there is a comfortable, molded-in seat, only half jokingly called "the throne." Of course this seat covers the Porta-Potti. Although Edey & Duff does its best to defend the advantage of Porta-Pottis in its brochure, I hate them. Of course my prejudice stems from a spill in the saloon of my little Bristol 27 that rivaled the *Exxon Valdez* disaster.

Next forward is what might be called the saloon. A two-burner Primus stove is to starboard, followed by another molded-in seat. Instead of settees, the Stone Horse interior has two seats that are comfortable to sit in. The galley is to port, with a Rubbermaid bowl serving as the sink and a large icebox. Aft are two small quarterberths, or as the brochure describes them, 3/16 berths. They are small, but I know my young daughters would happily claim them for their own. Another clever feature is a tool storage area, forward of the engine, beneath the bridgedeck.

Engine

Almost every Stone Horse built came with an inboard engine. During the first years of production a Palmer gas engine was standard, but the majority of boats have diesels. The original diesel was a single-cylinder Westerbeke 5, which was later changed to the Westerbeke 7 and later still to the BMW 7. Late in production, a two-cylinder Westerbeke 10, which became the 12, was used. Westerbekes are preferred over the BMW 7s, due to price and availability of replacement parts.

Access to the engine is terrific, and it can be removed through the bridgedeck hatch. The fuel tank is plastic and portable.

Under way

The Stone Horse is well balanced under sail. From close-hauled to a beam reach, it is possible to leave the helm to slip below. Owners report very little weather helm, just enough to make the boat self-steer. The main provides most of the horsepower, and despite the long keel, the boat can maneuver away from the dock under main alone.

The Stone Horse likes a fresh breeze. Falcigno claims that he happily carries full sail to about 20 knots, before putting in a reef. Above 25 he puts another reef and rolls up the jib. In a near gale, the boat rides steadily with a deeply reefed main and club staysail, or under staysail alone. For light air, Falcigno has an asymmetrical cruising chute, which he says has greatly enhanced his sailing pleasure. "I can make my way upwind at 4 knots on a light day, and reach back with the chute at the same speed," he said.

Conclusion

I find myself looking wistfully at the lovely Stone Horse moored not far from my boat on the New River in Ft. Lauderdale, Florida. Simple, strong, capable, and lovely to look at, Edey & Duff achieved its ideals. When I finally grow weary of bluewater passages, I am going to find a used Stone Horse and enjoy puttering about Biscayne Bay and the Keys. Who knows, I might even sneak up to New England and . . . Oops, I guess I'm not quite ready.

Cal 25

Low-cost solution for a first family boat that delivers good performance

Browse around any sizable marina, it doesn't matter where, from the Great Lakes to the West Coast, from the Chesapeake to Florida, wherever your dockside rambles lead. There is a very good likelihood that you'll stumble across a Cal 25 suspended between the pilings.

With its distinctive raised deck and long cockpit, the innovative Bill Lapworth design evolved from the highly successful pocket ocean racer and well-known San Francisco Bay boat, the Cal 20. Built by Jensen Marine, which at one time in the 1960s was the largest production builder in the country, and later by Bangor Punta Marine and others, the Cal 25 had a long production run through all its incarnations. From 1965 through 1983, a couple thousand Cal 25s were launched. (Don't confuse this original Cal 25 with a later Cal 25 that was beamier and did not have a raised deck. It was in production for only a short time.)

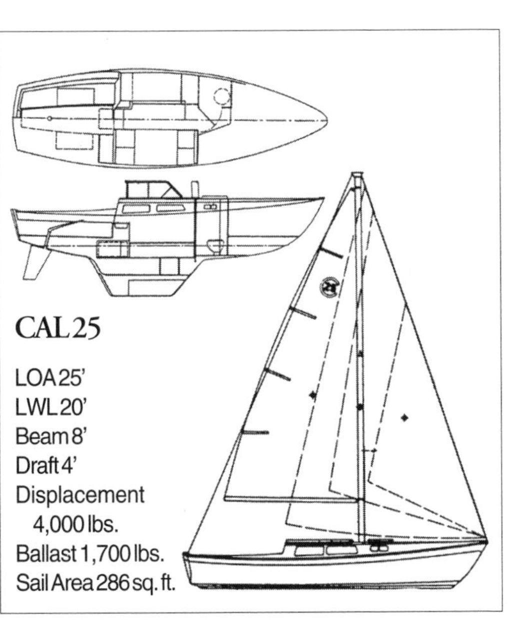

The Cal 25 was originally marketed as an ocean racer that could occasionally double as a cruiser during the golden age of fiberglass boats when a 25-footer was considered big. The prospect of serious cruising in a Cal 25 these days seems almost comical. However, it can be done. In fact, Dave and Jaja Martin and their two young children completely rebuilt a stock 25 and then proceeded to log 45,000 miles while circumnavigating. That, however, is taking things to extremes. The Cal 25 is actually a fine first boat that delivers pretty good performance while graciously tolerating learning miscues. And most importantly, you can find an assortment of decent 25s on the market for around $5,000 while late model boats can be had for around $10,000. The Cal 25 is a logical boat to test the waters of family sailing before committing to a newer and bigger boat with its bigger monthly payment.

First impressions

Aficionados of 1960-era designs quickly recognize the Cal 25 as a classic collaboration of Bill Lapworth and Jack Jensen. From the spoon bow to the flattish transom, from the wide cove stripe to the raised deck with long rectangular portlights, the 25 cuts a handsome profile. Lapworth usually saved his best work for what was below the waterline and the 25 is no exception. Like a miniature Cal 40, the 25 features a long fin keel and spade rudder, which was a radical concept in 1965, and a relatively long waterline of 20 feet. The displacement of 4,000 pounds was considered quite light, although the cast lead ballast of 1,700 pounds certainly helps keep the 25 on its feet. In fact, the Cal 25 is a remarkably stiff boat, as numerous ocean passages attest, and is by no means overcanvassed with 286 square feet of sail area. By comparison, the Cal 25, yesterday's nimble racer, is heavier and has less sail area than a typical modern pocket cruiser like the Catalina 250.

Construction

The Cal 25's hull is solid fiberglass, and typical of the construction methods of the day, it is rather thick and resin rich. As a result, it's often not very fair with occasional hard spots and "print throughs," which means that the underlying glass fabric is visible in the surface of the hull.

The one-piece molded deck was reinforced with plywood. The hull-and-deck joint, which is set on a small flange, is riveted and covered with a 6-inch fiberglass tape from the inside. It is covered with a rubber rubrail and therefore is subject to damage from impact.

The lead keel is externally fastened and the spade rudder is draped over a robust stainless steel stock. The forward bulkheads, which are usually mahogany-faced plywood and tabbed to the hull, front a deck beam, which was actually molded into the deck and supports the deck-stepped spar. The inboard chainplates are bolted through the bulkheads as well.

Cal 25 Price Data

		Low	High
BUC Retail Range	1968	$ 4,550	$ 5,250
	1974	$ 5,300	$ 6,150
	1980	$ 8,600	$ 9,900

		State	Asking
Boats For Sale	1969	PA	$ 4,500
	1970	CA	$ 5,300
	1981	WA	$ 8,600

What to look for

As with any older boat, especially one that has been raced hard and put away wet, there are many problems to be aware of before purchasing. With Cal 25s, however, it is difficult to comment on general problems because the boats have usually been refit by previous owners along the way and one can't always be sure what has and hasn't been upgraded. Still, there are some common flaws to be on the lookout for. A lot of old Cal 25s have soft and sometimes spongy decks. Invariably the plywood has rotted, usually the result of a deck leak, and needs to be replaced. At least the plywood is accessible in most places. Although it is a big job, it is possible to stiffen weak deck sections with new marine-grade plywood, although the purchase price should certainly reflect this time-consuming repair project. If the deck is soft, it's likely that the main deck beam may be sagging or worse, delaminating. Again, this is not a task for the mechanically challenged, yet it is certainly a do-it-yourself-type task if you have adequate woodworking and fiberglass skills. John Hall, who owns the 1970 Cal 25 *Lady Marion* suggests adding a new mast compression post at the same time.

The forward bulkheads may also need attention. If the bulkheads are pulling away from the hull, they can usually be wrangled back into place, especially when the rig is out of the boat, and refiberglassed. If they have begun to rot, usually caused by leaking chainplates, it may be necessary to replace them. Unless you are literally stealing the boat, you should probably look for another 25.

Another common problem is leaking portlights. Originally, they were safety glass, and if you need to replace them, use Plexiglas or Lexan. Also, the rubrail is often in sad repair and needs to be replaced. Fortunately, Steve Seal of Seal's Spars and Rigging in Alameda, California, has new rubrails available. When hauled, check the rudder for any signs of cracking. The original rudder was of light sandwich construction, subject to cracking, especially after a cold winter on the hard. Seal, who was a rigger with Jensen Marine in the 1960s, is an excellent resource for Cal owners. He can help you track down a new rudder if necessary. Also, Cal 25s have a tendency to blister, although they are certainly not unique in this category.

One item to inspect carefully is the electrical system. The original boats came with an "optional" electrical system that was basic to say the least. Most boats have some type of owner-installed electrical system that can vary wildly in quality. Carefully check the panel and wiring, being alert to twisted wire and taped-over connections. These are not only a nuisance and cause electrical instruments to fail, they can be dangerous.

One final item to check carefully is the companionway hatch on older boats. The original

Cal 25

Sailing Magazine's Value Guide

PRICE: Most Cal 25s, especially those built before 1978 when inboard diesels were first offered, can be purchased for around $5,000. Any way you look at it, theCal 25 is a lot of boat for the money.

DESIGN QUALITY: Lapworth's design was innovative and has stood the test of time well. Used as a weekender, the Cal 25's design is still quite functional.

CONSTRUCTION QUALITY: Although the initial quality was good, the boat has not aged well. Problems with the deck and rudder are not uncommon.

USER-FRIENDLINESS: The Cal 25 is an easy, responsive and forgiving boat to sail. Routing the halyards aft on the flush deck is easy. Below, a lack of headroom makes the boat cramped.

SAFETY: The Cal 25 lacks some basic safety features. The cockpit is vulnerable to swamping, the companionway is dangerously large and the deck is tricky to work.

TYPICAL CONDITION: Most Cal 25s on the used boat market that I have inspected are in pretty rough condition—a factor of age, hard use and neglect.

REFITTING: The Cal 25 is certainly a boat that can be brought back to life, though finding parts is not always easy. Finding information can be even more difficult. Fortunately, the boat was built and fitted out in a simple, stout fashion.

SUPPORT: Steve Seal of Seal's Spars and Rigging in Alameda, California, is a good reference for Cals. He can be reached at (510) 521-7730 or on the Web at www.Sealsspars.com. There is no active class association. A loose organization has a Web page at: http://www.cal25.com

AVAILABILITY: There are a lot of 25s on the market. The challenge is to find the good ones. Most seem to be in Southern California and on the Great Lakes.

INVESTMENT AND RESALE: The Cal 25 is not a boat that you invest in; it is a boat you sail for fun.

OVERALL 'SVG' RATING

design was a three-piece model that not only slid on tracks but also popped up. Many of these hatches were retrofitted at some point, so be sure to check the construction carefully.

On deck

The cockpit is the most distinctive feature on the Cal 25. It is 7 feet, 6 inches long, which represents 30 percent of the LOA, and is quite comfortable. It can easily accommodate four adults. Hall remembers a time when he had 12 people aboard on the Columbia River. In a way it is surprising that the 25 has such a proud record of offshore sailing because the voluminous cockpit and huge companionway are certainly not designed for bluewater sailing. The 25 is a tiller boat, and although I'm sure some have probably been retrofitted with wheel steering, I have never seen or heard of one.

Although pulpits and lifelines were options, most boats on the market have them. Be sure to carefully check that they are through-bolted with backing plates, as owners often undertook this upgrade themselves. As with any boat more than 10 years old, carefully inspect the standing rigging and consider replacing it. One item that Seal suggests replacing on older boats is the lightweight cast aluminum spreader brackets. Also, although there are stout mooring cleats forward, there is often no provision for anchoring. You may need to add a small anchor roller of some kind.

Down below

When you consider the lack of headroom, the interior of the Cal 25 is surprisingly comfortable. The V-berth forward is a genuine double with decent storage below and a large hatch above. The head compartment, aft to port, is large enough to do your business without feeling too cramped. Although if it hasn't been done already, you will have to plumb a holding tank.

The saloon has a dinette to port and a long settee opposite, which makes a good sea berth. The galley, which was also an option, usually has an icebox, a small alcohol stove and a sink tucked beneath the companionway. The idea behind the pop-top hatch was to create standing headroom for the cook. Although I wouldn't want to live aboard, the Cal 25's cabin is cozy and comfortable for weekend sailing.

Engine

Although an inboard diesel was offered in 1979, which was toward the end of the production run, the vast majority of boats on the used boat market have outboard engines. Old outboard engines are invariably trouble; I hate them and strongly suggest that, unless the outboard is relatively new and runs perfectly, you factor the cost of a new engine into the equation from the start.

Lapworth recommended at least 6-horsepower engine and not more than 10 for the boat. Hall's *Lady Marion*, which has a new Honda 9.9, steams along smartly at 5 to 6 knots under power.

One of the original design innovations of the Cal 25 was an "outboard transom," or removable stern section permitting low, supposedly effective mounting of the outboard. However, most 25s that I have seen recently have opted for folding outboard motor brackets permanently mounted astern.

Underway

The reason for the Cal 25's enduring popularity is simple: It is still a nice boat to sail. While that may sound trite, I think it accurately defines the boat. Hall enjoys sailing his 25 so much he has actually spent more than the boat is worth shipping it from Oregon to Texas and on to Florida as his newspaper career dictated his moving about the country.

With a well-balanced sloop rig, the 25 can carry a full main to 20 knots, according to Ed Williamson, who sails his 25 along the East Coast. Although several owners report that the keel actually moves slightly from side to side when under way, none seemed concerned. Hall, who sails in the Florida Keys, notes that even when an occasional squall catches him off guard, the 25's forgiving nature keeps the boat upright while he scrambles forward to drop the headsail.

"I could buy another boat," Hall says, "but why should I? The Cal 25 is simple to sail, has a shallow-enough draft to go anywhere I want and doesn't cost much to maintain. It's all the boat I need."

Conclusion

If you have been frustrated trying to find an affordable used boat, the Cal 25 offers a wonderful, low-cost solution to one of life's important quests, namely: How to get out on the water and experience the unique combination of elements that make a sailboat glide through the water and a spirit soar.

MacGregor 25 and 26

Inexpensive, simple-to-sail trailerable cruiser

Roger MacGregor has been an iconoclast in the sailboat industry—something of a black sheep in a business with blue (and often bankrupt) blood lines. An original thinker, MacGregor has focused almost exclusively on trailerable boats. In fact, in his literature he claims to have started the trailer-sailer market. Only an offbeat 65-foot ULDB sled and a 36-foot catamaran varied from a line of inexpensive boats aimed at the first-time sailboat buyer.

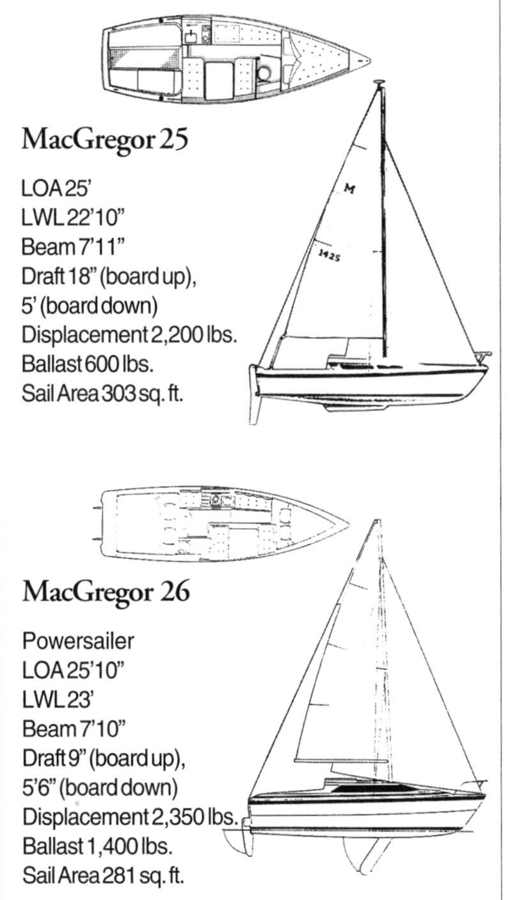

MacGregor 25

LOA 25'
LWL 22'10"
Beam 7'11"
Draft 18" (board up),
5' (board down)
Displacement 2,200 lbs.
Ballast 600 lbs.
Sail Area 303 sq. ft.

MacGregor 26

Powersailer
LOA 25'10"
LWL 23'
Beam 7'10"
Draft 9" (board up),
5'6" (board down)
Displacement 2,350 lbs.
Ballast 1,400 lbs.
Sail Area 281 sq. ft.

According to MacGregor lore, his company began in 1964 as a class project when he was a graduate student at Stanford's School of Business. The premise of the project was simple: If sailboat manufacturers would build boats more efficiently, they could sell them cheaper and make more money. Now, 37,000 sailboats later, you could say MacGregor has proven his hypothesis.

Although the company built a full range of small boats for many years, the 25-foot and 26-foot models have been the most popular. The new MacGregor 26 Powersailer, which the Costa Mesa, California, factory is turning out at a clip of 60 per month, is the only boat currently in production. The various MacGregor 25/26 incarnations, including the Venture 25, MacGregor 25, MacGregor 26 and 26X, total around 20,000 boats. With prices ranging from about $3,000 for an old 25 to near $20,000 for a late-model 26 Powersailer, there is a used MacGregor 25 or 26 floating somewhere in the right condition and at the right price to fit the needs of most first-time sailboat buyers.

First impressions

MacGregor designed boats with an emphasis on efficient production, low cost and practical ownership. The 26 was designed to ride four on a truck trailer, making them efficient to ship to dealers around the country. It also has a sterile interior that can be hosed clean. This mass-production mentality may strike some as sacrilegious, however, MacGregor's large-scale production runs have allowed for experimentation and innovation. The 26 Powersailer was one of the first boats to effectively use water ballast and MacGregor's bilge tank system has often been copied.

The MacGregor 25 and 26 are daysailers, with comfortable, no-frills decks and cockpits and spartan interiors. The 26 Powersailer, which is not as handsome as the older boats, is very innovative and

offers sailors an unusual option: the ability to motor at 20 knots. A new planing hull design coupled with the ability to jettison the water ballast and to hang a 50-horsepower outboard on the transom allow usually considerate sailors the unique opportunity to become as obnoxious as some powerboaters.

Construction

The MacGregor 25s and 26s are lightly constructed for two reasons. First, the logistics of mass producing small boats and selling them at affordable prices dictate the need to keep material costs to a minimum. Nobody has ever accused MacGregor of overbuilding his boats. Secondly, the demands of trailering require that boats be light enough to be pulled by midsize cars. It is one of the keys to MacGregor's success that a family doesn't need to buy a truck or a sport utility vehicle just to haul the boat to the lake. The old Honda Civic will do just fine.

The hull is a solid, though rather thin, fiberglass laminate. On newer boats, the deck is balsa-cored in high-stress flat sections. Older boats were cored with plywood. The hull-and-deck joint is surprisingly strong, through-bolted on a narrow, internal flange. Many small boats use screws or rivets for this critical joint. Although some of the hardware on newer boats is backed with washers, no backing plates are used to support stanchions, pulpits and cleats. A molded hull liner provides the bulk of the boat's structural support and is fiberglassed to the hull in exposed vertical sections.

The MacGregor 25 features a 600-pound retractable centerboard. The newer 26-foot models eliminated the need for a heavy centerboard by using water ballast. Unlike movable water ballast used by high-performance offshore racing boats, MacGregor's system uses a single fiberglass bilge tank. When filled, the tank adds roughly 1,200 pounds of ballast to the older 26s and 1,400 pounds to the 26-foot Powersailers. The tank, which actually forms the bottom of the boat, is well baffled to keep the water from sloshing around too much while under sail and can be inspected from inside the boat. It also serves as a false floor if the boat is accidentally holed, although at that point the boat will lose stability with no ballast. One of the best features about all MacGregors is that they have positive foam flotation and are essentially unsinkable.

What to look for

When shopping for a MacGregor 25 or 26, it is important to understand how the models evolved and

MacGregor 25 and 26 Price Data

		Low	High
BUC Retail Range (25)	1975	$ 2,250	$ 2,600
	1985	$ 3,600	$ 4,200
(26 Power-sailer)	1995	$10,100	$11,500
	1999	$15,000	$17,100
		State	**Asking**
Boats For Sale	1984	TX	$ 3,900
	1997	FL	$18,000

MacGregor 25 and 26

Sailing Magazine's Value Guide

PRICE: Price is a prime motivation for buying a MacGregor 25 and 26. It is possible to find older 25s for almost nothing and even two-year-old 26 Powersailers sell for less than $20,000. Though lightly built, they are still a lot of boat for the money.

DESIGN QUALITY: MacGregor designs combine innovative concepts with the need to keep the boat light and inexpensive.

CONSTRUCTION QUALITY: The boats are very lightly built and poorly finished.

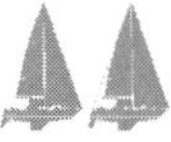

USER-FRIENDLINESS: They are simple and easy to sail, though frustrating from a performance sense.

SAFETY: The boats are light, and the rails and lifelines are poorly supported. They do have positive foam flotation, and with the water ballast tank, a watertight false floor.

TYPICAL CONDITION: The boats do not age well and owners are often not very committed to maintaining their boats. Luckily there isn't that much that can go wrong.

REFITTING: Working on the boat is not all that easy, according to Paul Evans of Dunedin Marine Systems. Don't buy a MacGregor 25 or 26 as a refit project but as a boat to use and enjoy.

SUPPORT: Most support comes through an extensive dealer network. A good reference is Paul Evans at Dunedin Marine Systems, at (727) 733-5067 www.dunedinsystems.com. You can reach MacGregor Yachts directly at (949) 642-6830 and at http://www.macgregor26.com.

AVAILABILITY: There are thousands of 25s and 26s for sale around the country. New Powersailers are more difficult to find.

INVESTMENT AND RESALE: Secondhand MacGregor 25s and 26s don't represent much of an investment. But, for the low original price, they aren't so bad after all.

OVERALL 'SVG' RATING

when changes occurred. Here is an encapsulated history according to MacGregor Sales Manager Bill Snedeker. In 1981 the Venture 25 was replaced by the MacGregor 25. The primary change: The deck was extended to the gunwale, which eliminated any side deck area. This resulted in more interior volume and the raised-deck look that is still evident in today's Powersailer. MacGregor replaced the 25 with the 26 in 1987. Although the boats looked similar, the 26 used ballasting instead of the centerboard. The 25 also featured a revamped interior, including a double bunk aft under the cockpit. In 1995 the Powersailer was introduced, which included many new features including twin, kick-up rudders for sailing, direct engine steering for motoring and forward-facing ports for a brighter interior.

Common problems that result from lightweight construction include gelcoat crazing and cracks, and occasional fiberglass delamination. Older 25s on the market will undoubtedly suffer from gelcoat crazing. Plywood-cored decks should be carefully checked for signs of rot, although replacing the coring, which is accessible from inside the boat, is not an insurmountable task.

The chainplates, which are a bit flimsy, are bolted to the hull at the turn of the deck and often leak. The standing rigging is very light and undersized, and the Nicopress sleeves and eyes on older boats should be carefully inspected for cracks. Although the electrical system is simple—bordering on primitive, most boats came with just two lights below—the wiring is often suspect and a new owner should consider rewiring the boat and adding a new breaker panel.

Paul Evans, of Dunedin Marine Systems on the west coast of Florida, has refitted several 26 and 26Xs (the original model name of the 26 Powersailer) recently, and offers a complete electrical update package. Most used boats on the market do not include any electronic instruments. Evans warns buyers to be wary of bungled attempts at rewiring, including broken wires and taped-over connections.

On deck

The rig of the old 25s and 26s is remarkably light. Still, several dealers that I spoke with noted that they knew of no rigging failures, a statement that may say more about how MacGregor owners use their boats than about the structure of the rig. Fractionally rigged sloops with swept-back spreaders, most older boats had simple plate adjusters instead of turnbuckles for tightening the rigging. It is important to remember that you don't buy a MacGregor 25 or 26 for offshore sailing; the boats are lightly built for coastal and lake daysailing and are rigged accordingly. If your plans include any offshore work, this is the wrong boat.

In some ways, the cockpit of the older 25 is more comfortable than that of a newer 26. On the new boats the cockpit floor was raised to accommodate the aft bunk. The 26 Powersailer has wheel steering, which connects to twin rudders when sailing and by Morse cable directly to the outboard engine when motoring. Clever cockpit cushions attach to stainless grabrails, making for comfortable seat backs. The cockpit seats are long enough for napping. Bow and stern pulpits and single lifelines lend some security to moving about the deck. The cleats are small and not well-supported.

Down below

Considering that the MacGregor 25 and 26 must be light and narrow enough for trailering, the interiors are quite spacious. The older 25s featured a good-sized double bunk forward, an enclosed head compartment, a convertible dinette to starboard with a settee opposite, a slide-away galley and a pop-top companionway for headroom. When the 26 was introduced, the double berth aft, stretching under the cockpit, was added. Although it would be possible to spend a weekend on the boat, pray it doesn't rain. The 26 Powersailer has a more refined interior, featuring a larger head aft of the dinette, a bit more of a galley and a huge aft bunk. There are also forward-facing plastic ports that give the interior more light.

Boats on the used market usually have carpeting on the sole. This often needs to be replaced. Also, despite the head compartment, many boats do not have heads and, if they do, they are invariably Porta-Pottis, which are not very pleasant. Also, be prepared for joinerwork down below that borders on crude, although, with the new 26 Powersailer, MacGregor has upgraded the overall quality of the boat.

Engine

On older MacGregors, the engine was typically a small outboard, ranging from 6 to 10 horsepower. As I have stated before, I don't like old, secondhand outboards and strongly suggest that you consider a new engine when purchasing an old boat. The outboard mounts to a cutout directly on the transom instead of a bracket, and when tilted up, it can be left in place while trailering.

The engine arrangement on the new Powersailer is more interesting. By redesigning the hull to plane, the Powersailer can carry a 50-horsepower outboard and cruise along at 20 knots. While under power, the twin rudders pivot out of the way and steering is direct to the engine, like on any small powerboat.

Underway

One of the first "big" boats I ever sailed was a MacGregor 25 on Higgins Lake in northern Michigan. The 25s and 26s were not only underrigged but were also undercanvassed and I remember the futility of trying to make the boat move in the light air of summer. With that said, however, my two brothers and I had a most enjoyable summer, sailing the boat all over the lake.

Most 25s and 26s on the used market have just a main and a working jib, although occasionally you'll see one with a genoa. The genoa doesn't sheet cleanly for any kind of upwind sailing as the leads are fixed—it is strictly a reaching sail. Spinnakers are rare. Sheet winches are Lewmar No. 6, tiny but adequate. An improvement that was added to the 26 was slab reefing.

The new Powersailer is a completely different animal than the older boats. According to several owners I communicated with on the Internet, it is not surprising to sail at more than 10 knots, and when the boat achieves a plane under power, it really can fly along at nearly 20 knots. Although MacGregor has built more than 2,000 of the new 26s, very few turn up on the used boat market.

Conclusion

The older MacGregor 25s and 26s are inexpensive, lightweight boats designed for simple sailing and minimal maintenance. If you want to see if sailing is indeed a pursuit you want to follow and you plan to sail in friendly waters, a MacGregor 25 or 26 is a logical boat to buy. The initial expense is low, and by storing it in your driveway on a trailer, ongoing expenses are also quite low. The MacGregor 25s and 26s have introduced thousands of us to sailing and for that they are to be commended.

Contessa 26

Rugged and affordable, this little cruiser has a proven ocean pedigree

The diminutive Contessa 26 was a highly regarded bluewater boat long before Tania Aebi and B.J. Caldwell elevated it to classic status with their epic circumnavigations. Patterned closely after the Scandinavian Folkboat, Contessa 26s competed successfully in the rugged Round Britain Race and the OSTAR, back when the race was still primarily a small-boat affair. The Contessa 26 was designed by David Sadler and first built by Jeremy Rogers in Lymington, England.

At one time, Rogers' Contessa Yachts company was one of Europe's premier builders of a range of boats. A Contessa 43 won two legs of an early Whitbread Race and the Contessa 32, big sister to the 26, became famous for its seaworthiness after the infamous 1979 Fastnet Race. I confess I am partial to the Contessa 32, having sailed a 1982 model from New York to San Francisco by way of Cape Horn. Several years ago I had a wild sail across the English Channel in a Contessa 26 and came to appreciate its seakindly nature.

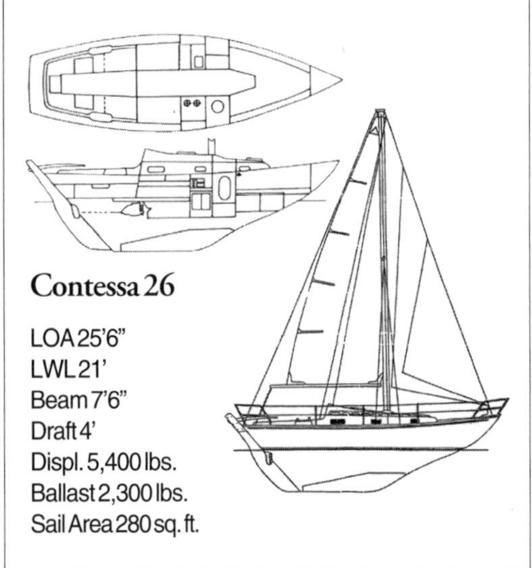

The Contessa 26 was introduced at the London Boat Show in 1966 and was an immediate success. After building 350 boats in just three years, Contessa retooled and shipped the molds to Canada. The North American Contessa 26s were built by J.J. Taylor and Sons in Toronto. A venerable Canadian boatbuilding firm, J.J. Taylor and Sons was looking to convert its operation from wood to fiberglass boats. The company picked a good boat, as the Contessa 26 also proved popular on this side of the Atlantic. By 1983, 300 Contessa 26s had been built and sold in Canada and the United States. A legal battle with the English company that had bought the molds from Jeremy Rogers' bankrupt Contessa Yachts forced the Canadians to change the name to the J.J. Taylor 26 in 1984. Another 100 boats were built before J.J. Taylor and Sons closed its doors for good in 1990.

While this column will discuss both English and Canadian Contessa 26s, the emphasis will be on the J.J. Taylor boats, the most prevalent boats on the U.S. market. Interestingly, both Aebi and Caldwell sailed in Canadian-built boats, although purists contend that the English version is a slightly better seagoing boat. And while English-built Contessa 26s do occasionally turn up for sale in this country, most boats on the used boat market are Taylor boats.

First impressions

Anyone familiar with wooden Folkboats—and you still see them in the Pacific Northwest, San Francisco Bay and Great Lakes—will immediately recognize the similarity to the Contessa 26. The Folkboat has served as an inspiration for many fine fiberglass boats, including Carl Alberg's legendary Pearson Triton. Sadler is an underrated designer and has a knack for drawing handsome boats. The Contessa 26 is no exception.

The Contessa 26 has very low freeboard (although a tad more than the original Folkboat) and a proud bow with an overall sweet sheerline. The 26 was never influenced by that all-too-pervasive IOR rule that created pinched ends. Instead, the flat transom, which hosts a distinctive and rather massive outboard rudder, contributes to good off-the-wind performance. While wooden Folkboats were usually fractionally rigged, the Contessa 26 has always been a masthead sloop.

Below the water, the 26 has a classic Folkboat long keel and attached rudder. Although there is a sizable overhang forward, the rudder essentially extends the waterline aft. With an LOA of 21 feet and moderate displacement (the 26 weighs about half of what the Pacific Seacraft Dana 24 displaces) the 26 is deceptively fast. Unlike the other small boats, it is able to maintain way in a lumpy sea. The Contessa 26 has a stately bearing in the water, and despite the low freeboard, stealthlike beam and low-slung coachhouse, it looks like a bigger boat when viewed in profile.

Contessa 26 Price Data

		Low	High
BUC Retail Range	1974	$ 9,150	$10,400
	1978	$10,500	$11,900
	1982	$13,200	$15,000

		State	Asking
Boats For Sale	1975	FL	$18,000
	1979	CAN	$12,500
	1984	PR	$13,500

Construction

The strength of the Contessa 26 lies more in the design than it does in the construction scantlings. Like all good offshore designs, the Contessa 26 rarely takes a direct hit from a wave and almost never pounds when sailing upwind. This is not a heavily constructed boat, with bronze portlights, massive hardware and that foolhardy, I'm-stronger-than-the-ocean mentality. The layup is solid fiberglass, including the deck. Don't be misled by the spring in the foredeck, especially on the English-built boats. It is not that the deck is weak. It just has more flexibility because it lacks a core.

The interior features molded liners, pans and plywood veneered bulkheads, which is the most practical way to build strong yet small boats. The ballast in the English boats is iron and encapsulated in the keel cavity. In 1983 J.J. Taylor initiated a partial redesign that included changing the ballast to cast lead. The hull-and-deck joint is on a flange and includes a caprail, and in the amidships area, the genoa track. The mast is stepped on deck and supported by an overhead stringer and the main bulkheads. Part of the Contessa lore is the claim that no 26 has ever lost its stick.

What to look for

The British Contessa has a slightly smaller cockpit and a large lazarette aft, hence its reputation as a better bluewater boat. Except for the early boats, the Taylor boats have a more comfortable cockpit, which of course is where you spend most of your time on any boat. The notion that a cockpit has to be tiny to be safe offshore is a bit outdated.

As much as I like English boats, I'd probably look for a Taylor Contessa first. The 1983 changes in the Canadian boats also included more headroom by lowering the saloon floor, the addition of amidships hatch and an anchor locker forward.

The early Contessas came with 6.6-horsepower Petter diesel, which was later changed to 7-horsepower Farymann. Neither of these engines offer anything to cheer about, and if you can find a boat with a retrofitted small Yanmar, seriously consider it.

Considering the fact that many Contessa 26s have been sailed hard and have logged thousands of offshore miles, there are precious few structural problems to be on the lookout for. Check out the rudder carefully as some owners have reported the need to add an extra pintle and gudgeon, or at least beef up the standard ones. Also, it is not unusual for the spreader sockets to be cracked. If this is the case, they will obviously need to be replaced.

The original mainsheet arrangement called for a single-point tack on the cockpit sole. Many owners have opted to install traveler systems and unfortunately, there is no easy way to accomplish this without sacrificing cockpit space. One additional note: the early boats have trouble draining the side decks because the scuppers were not located at the low point.

Contessa 26

Sailing Magazine's Value Guide

PRICE: You can buy cheaper 26-foot boats, but not a 26-footer that can cross oceans. Prices range from $9,000 for an early boat that needs a bit of love, to around $15,000 for a later model. Oftentimes the boats are well-equipped for offshore sailing.

DESIGN QUALITY: David Sadler is a talented designer and his adaptation of the classic Folkboat in fiberglass was superb.

CONSTRUCTION QUALITY: The Contessa 26 is not overbuilt, but it is intelligently engineered and constructed. A seakindly design built to proportion is eminently more seaworthy than a poor design built massively.

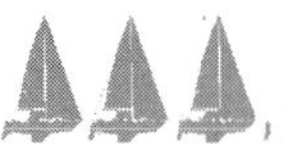

USER-FRIENDLINESS: Easy to handle in a variety of conditions, the Contessa 26 is a sweet sailing boat. The interior, however, is really small and not very comfortable. This is an ideal singlehander's boat.

SAFETY: It is hard to imagine a safer pocket cruiser. Like it or loathe it, the Contessa 26 has a most impressive bluewater track record.

TYPICAL CONDITION: Many Contessa 26s have been fitted out for bluewater sailing, and like most boats, only a few really achieve the dreams their owners have for them. Consequently there are some well-equipped, lightly used boats for sale.

REFITTING: The Contessa 26 is not an overly convenient boat to work on simply because you must squeeze into some small places. But the engine can be removed through the cockpit hatch if repowering.

SUPPORT: J.J. Taylor and Sons is out of business as is Contessa Yachts in the U.K. However, Aebi's book **Maiden Voyage** was a bestseller and Caldwell's voyage was well-documented in the sailing press.

AVAILABILITY: Although something of a cult boat, there are enough Contessa 26s about to allow for a bit of shopping. Boats seem to be concentrated in Canada and the Great Lakes, and oddly enough, along the Gulf Coast.

INVESTMENT AND RESALE: As its reputation as a capable bluewater boat grows, so does its resale value. There is a pretty strong market for the 26.

OVERALL 'SVG' RATING

On deck

Both versions of the Contessa 26 cockpit are meant for going to sea—with little overall volume if an errant wave should come aboard. There are a few problems, though. Because of the low freeboard, the cockpit doesn't drain efficiently. More seriously, there really isn't much of a bridgedeck.

Indeed, the Contessa 26's companionway arrangement is a bit strange. There is a bubble at the end of the coachroof instead of a sliding companionway hatch. This creates a stronger, more waterproof opening, but it makes entering the cabin more challenging. A bridgedeck would require more stooping, especially for tall people. The solution is simple and timeless: leave the bottom washboard in place when sailing offshore.

The outboard rudder and tiller assembly takes up less space than you might think, and the tiller can be moved out of the way once in port. There are two decent-size cockpit lockers and access to the diesel is from a cockpit sole hatch.

Naturally the side decks are narrow, with an overall beam of just 7 feet, 6 inches. There are grabrails on the coachroof to lend a hand as you make your way forward. I looked at several J.J.Taylor Contessas recently in Fairhope, Alabama, of all places, and without fail the nonskid was worn nearly smooth.

After 1983, the Taylor boats included an external anchor locker forward, but the owner has usually added a custom anchoring arrangement. Check this installation carefully. The older boats feature a single but stout mooring cleat fore and aft, and the leads are completely encapsulated by the teak caprail.

The stern rail is husky, but you would need X-ray vision to see the loom of the tiny stern light mounted on the aft deck. Also, many owners have opted to lead the halyards aft to the cockpit. I have mixed feelings about this, as the leads take up precious deck space on a small boat.

Down below

I can't imagine anybody buying a Contessa 26 because of its interior; more likely, it is in spite of the tunnel-like space below. The layout includes a decent-size V-berth forward followed aft by a small head compartment with a hanging locker opposite. The galley of sorts is located just aft, with a sink and icebox to port and a small stove top opposite. Two quarter berths, which make excellent sea berths, round out the interior plan.

The J.J. Taylor boats have a slightly more comfortable interior than the English boats. The additional headroom that makes it full-sitting helps, as does the midships hatch. I strongly recommend adding this hatch to open up the boat. Yet, for all of its lack of creature comforts, the space below is safe and secure at sea. Caldwell and Aebi have both remarked that they felt very secure in their tiny cabins.

The joinerwork is quite nice and complements the white molded pieces. There is also a surprising amount of storage.

Engine

Neither of the single-cylinder British diesels that were fitted on the Contessa are famous for reliability, and they only provide just enough oomph to power the Contessa 26 at 5 knots. One advantage is that they can be easily hand cranked for starting. It is not uncommon to find boats on the used market that have been repowered, and small Yanmars seem to be the engine of choice.

The cockpit sole hatch dramatically improves access to the engine room. The fuel tank is poly plastic and the whopping seven gallons offers a range of nearly 100 miles.

Underway

The records of Aebi and Caldwell speak volumes about the sailing nature of the Contessa 26. Aebi in particular was woefully inexperienced when she began her voyage, and she relied on the boat to take care of her when the weather turned nasty. Caldwell survived a capsize in the Indian Ocean and several subsequent knockdowns. He was amazed at the 26's ability to endure the near-constant battering he faced.

The Contessa tracks very well and is surprisingly close-winded. The boat can carry sail in a blow, although the first reef should be tucked in when the wind is around 20 knots. There is just enough weather helm to make the 26 respond brilliantly to windvane self-steering.

I remember leaving the picturesque harbor of Yarmouth on the Isle of Wight in a 1972 British Contessa 26 called *Whitehawk*. Within hours we were battling a full gale in the channel. With two reefs in the main and the storm jib, we clipped along toward Cherbourg, France. My two English companions were completely unperturbed by the weather, and despite frequent dousing by gray walls of water, we had a pleasant sail. There was simply no stress, no worry that the boat was in trouble. That's pretty impressive for a 26-foot boat.

Conclusion

The Contessa 26 is well deserving of its classic status, having proved itself in the only manner that counts, out on the ocean. If you have less than $15,000 to spend and you want to cross oceans, you owe it to yourself to consider a Contessa 26.

Tartan 27

Thin-water cruising, singlehanded sailing and rocking reaches make this plastic classic fantastic

The Tartan 27 keeps good company. One of Sparkman & Stephens' first fiberglass designs, the Tartan 27 belongs to a select group of early fiberglass boats that can justifiably be called classics. Introduced in the early 1960s when the stench of styrene was just beginning to supplant the sweet aroma of fresh-cut cedar and mahogany, this group of classics includes the 28-foot Pearson Triton, the Hinckley Bermuda 40 and the Cal 40. The Tartan 27 was launched in 1961, and by the time production stopped in 1979, more than 700 had been built.

The boat traces its lineage to a similar S&S design, the New Horizon 25, which was first built in 1957 by early fiberglass innovator Ray Greene. Dan Spurr noted in his outstanding book, **Heart of Glass**, that Greene was miffed that S&S would sell rival Douglas & McLeod Plastics, the predecessor to Tartan Marine, a design that was essentially the same boat, just a couple feet longer. Douglas & McLeod was the original builder of the Thistle, the International 14 and the Great Lakes 21, now called the International 21. Its first foray into fiberglass construction was the Tartan 27, which was done in partnership with Charles Britton.

Britton was both a sailor and a businessman, having completed a 20,000-mile voyage in 1959 from Japan to the West Indies via the Indian Ocean and Cape of Good Hope. After the Tartan 27 was launched, Douglas & McLeod introduced the Ted Hood-designed Black Watch 37 (which became the first version of the Tartan 37) and another S&S classic, the Tartan 34. Unfortunately, a fire completely wiped out the Douglas & McLeod plant in Grand River, Ohio, in 1971. After the fire, D&M sold Britton the Tartan division.

During the 1970s Britton introduced the popular Tartan 30, the well-known S&S designed 37, and an innovative one-design, the 33-foot Tartan Ten. Tartan was one of the largest production builders in the country during this decade. Britton sold the company in 1983, and although the ownership has changed several times since, Tartan's only production hiatus was when it had to rebuild after the fire.

Tartan 27

1979 Model
LOA 27'
LWL 21'5"
Beam 8'7"
Draft board up 3'2"
Draft board down 6'4"
Displ. 7,400 lbs.
Ballast 2,400 lbs.
Sail Area 376.2 sq. ft.

First impressions

After recently climbing aboard a 1964 model that was in still fine condition, I had to remind myself that the Tartan 27 was considered a big boat in its day. Although the interior may seem cramped by today's standards, it was clearly finished to a higher standard than the Alberg-designed Triton and other comparable production boats.

The 27's handsome lines have worn well. Like other early fiberglass boats, the design blends a narrow, slack-bilge hull with a long keel and attached rudder. The molded cabintrunk originally had a step, similar to many of Alberg's early designs. The overhangs are relatively short, resulting in a fairly long LWL and good turn of speed when reaching. The Tartan 27 has an LWL of 21 feet, 5 inches; in comparison, the Triton's LWL is just 20 feet, 6 inches despite an additional foot and a half of LOA. Like many of Sparkman & Stephens' early fiberglass boats, especially those built by Tartan, the 27 is a keel centerboarder. Board-up draft is just 3 feet, 2 inches, a feature that is still a major attraction for buyers.

The Tartan 27 is not a lightweight, with a displacement of 7,400 pounds. To put this into perspective, the fin-keel Tartan 26, which was launched in 1972, was a foot shorter than her older sister but weighed 2,200 pounds less. Tartan 27s, at least those launched after 1966, have 2,400 pounds of encapsulated lead ballast, which translates into a ballast-to-displacement ratio of 32 percent—a typical number for early keel centerboarders. Before 1966 the ballast was external and approximately 350 pounds lighter. The vast majority of 27s are low-aspect masthead sloops with a long boom. Sail area is 376 square feet, which is comparable to the Triton. A yawl rig was an option, although very few were sold.

Construction

Like most early fiberglass boats the Tartan 27 was built to heavy scantlings. Early glass laminates were not sophisticated. Laid up with woven roving and mat, the hulls are invariably resin-rich and thick. Almost all Tartan 27s built are still sailing more than 40 years after the launch of hull No. 1. The 1964 model I was aboard had an incredibly sturdy feel to it. The hull plug from a recent depthsounder transducer installation showed the hull to be almost 3/4-inch thick just up from the turn of the bilge.

The deck on the 27 is balsa cored and joined to the hull on an outward turning flange. This type of joint is more prone to damage than the more common inward turning hull flange and it is something of a mystery why Tartan built it this way. Even so, hull-and-deck-joint leaks do not seem to be a common, hard-to-repair problem that plagues many older boats. I spoke with several owners and none of them mentioned a leaking hull-and-deck joint. The centerboard on the very early boats was made of bronze. It was changed to glassed-over steel on later models. As already noted, after 1966 the ballast was encapsulated inside the keel cavity, which is a good situation in full-keel boats.

Tartan 27 Price Data

		Low	High
BUC Retail Range	1961	$ 8,300	$ 9,550
	1964	$ 8,550	$ 9,850
	1967	$10,900	$12,400

		State	Asking
Boats For Sale	1969	NY	$15,000
	1970	FL	$11,500
	1978	NY	$17,000

What to look for

Naturally, any boat with a long production run will have changes along the way. As mentioned earlier, the first dozen or so boats had bronze centerboards, which were maintenance-intensive to say the least. In 1966, around hull No. 200, 350 pounds of ballast was added and it was encapsulated. That same year Tartan switched from wooden to molded dorade boxes and changed the galley stove so that it was flush with the counters.

In 1973 Tartan introduced the Tartan 27 II, which had a new deck mold that lengthened the cockpit and added a bridgedeck. In 1975, Tartan began offering a 12-horsepower diesel as an option to the standard Atomic 4 gasoline engine.

In 1977, beginning with hull No. 649, the Tartan 27 III was offered. This version included a new deck design that eliminated the step in the doghouse. The interior was also completely revamped, exchanging the dinette and amidships galley arrangement for a more modern aft galley with settees in the saloon and a drop-leaf table. Approximately 65 type IIIs were built.

In addition to the production variations, there are a few common problems to be on the lookout for. First, the balsa-cored deck will likely have some level of delamination. If the decks are spongy, it can be a difficult and expensive repair and you might be better off looking for a different 27. If the delamination is isolated to certain areas, you can probably live with it. Check around the chainplates; two owners reported

Tartan 27

Sailing Magazine's Value Guide

PRICE: Prices seem to range from $8,000 to around $15,000 for an excellent late-model edition. However, most boats on the market are priced around $10,000, which translates into a lot of boat for the buck.

DESIGN QUALITY: The S&S pedigree bumps the Tartan 27 up a notch from many production boats. While the design seems dated today, it was both original and functional in 1960.

CONSTRUCTION QUALITY: Time is the test of a boat's original construction and the Tartan 27 has held up well. Bulkheads were securely tabbed, the laminate was heavy and materials were well chosen.

USER-FRIENDLINESS: The 27 is an easy boat to sail, has little weather helm and balances easily. However, the cockpit can become uncomfortable after a while and the interior is cramped in the older models.

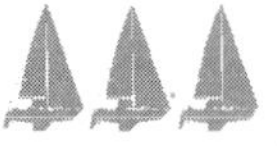

SAFETY: The addition of a better bridgedeck in later models added to the safety factor for offshore sailing. The lifelines are low and led to the base of the bow pulpit, and the nonskid is likely to be worn. Still, the original sturdy construction and sweet motion in a seaway contribute to overall safety.

TYPICAL CONDITION: Most owners have cared for their 27s, but because of their age, some boats will need a bit of love to regain their luster.

REFITTING: Although the Tartan 27 is worthy of the time and money required for a complete refit, like many older, small boats, it is not easy to work on and parts can be hard to come by.

SUPPORT: Although Tartans are still produced by Fairport Marine in Ohio, the Tartan 27 has been out of production for 22 years. There are a couple of strong owner organizations in the Northeast.

AVAILABILITY: More than 700 boats were built and virtually all are still sailing. There are plenty of boats on the market at any one time. The Northeast, Great Lakes and Chesapeake Bay have the heaviest concentrations.

INVESTMENT AND RESALE: Like most older glass boats that have become classics, the Tartan 27 has held its value well over the years. You won't pay a lot when you buy, and chances are you will get your money back when you sell.

OVERALL 'SVG' RATING

problems in that area. As with any old centerboard boat, carefully inspect the board, the pivot and the pennant. The rudder post can also become sloppy in the rudder tube due to the lack of bearing support, and the tiller head fitting is prone to wear and tear. Down below, it is likely that many owners will have made modifications with varying degrees of skill. Many boats have been converted from alcohol to propane stoves—check this installation carefully.

On deck

"She has a lot of deck space," said Neville Doherty, who sails hull No. 83 along the rocky Maine coast, "and that's something I really like about the boat." There is no doubt that the cockpit of the later boats, after the last changes were made, is more comfortable than those of earlier boats, although the coaming boards on both versions are tough on the lower back. The cockpit is functional, however, and several owners note that they singlehand their boats frequently.

The long boom allows the mainsheet to be led aft for good purchase, which also keeps the cockpit clear. At anchor the tiller can be lifted out of the way. The original winches were of the knife-blade-handle type and it is difficult to find replacement parts for them.

There is a slight bulwark with a teak toerail on deck, although the nonskid surface is likely worn. Also the stanchions and lifelines are low and not particularly well supported. The forward lifelines angle down to the base of the bow pulpit. This set-up was common in the 1960s, which allowed for low-cut genoas to set cleanly. In this day of roller-furling headsails it is easy to route the lifelines to the top of the pulpit. The aluminum spar is keel-stepped and leaks are common around the mast.

Be sure to check the standing rigging carefully. The original maststep was wood and may need to be replaced. A handful of Tartan 27s were built as yawls, inspired no doubt by the CCA rule, which didn't penalize added sail area from a mizzen. Unfortunately this is too small a boat for a split rig and the mizzen mast really crowds the cockpit.

Down below

The original interior arrangement features an amidships galley with a dinette opposite. There is a V-berth forward. A small but enclosed head and a quarter berth are aft to port. This was a common arrangement for the period. My 1965 Bristol 27 had the same layout, complete with cockpit access to the icebox, which didn't help preserve my precious ice. Two large portlights in the saloon let in a fair bit of light, although ventilation is not very good. Some owners have added opening portlights forward. The original workmanship was nicely done with plenty of teak splashed about.

In 1976 the interior arrangement was completely updated. In these boats, the small L-shaped galley is aft to starboard with the nav station opposite. The relatively useless quarter berth is also eliminated. Two settees replaced the dinette in the saloon, giving the boat a bit more space for moving about and a couple of sea berths, although the starboard-side berth is definitely designed for short people. On the plus side there is decent storage, including cabinets above the portside settees and under the seats. The last boats were beautifully finished.

Engine

The vast majority of Tartan 27s came down the ways with Universal Atomic 4 gasoline engines. These venerable machines give the boat plenty of pop while being inexpensive to maintain and repair. Indeed, a completely rebuilt Atomic 4 can usually be found for less than $500. Around 1975 a 2-cylinder, 12-horsepower Farymann diesel was offered. I know the Farymann well and can attest that it is reliable, but vibrates to the point where it will shake the fillings out of your teeth. Still, being predisposed to diesels for their overall reliability, simplicity and safety, I'd look for a boat with a diesel first. Many Tartan 27s have been repowered over the years. Engine access is adequate, although you'll have to be something of a contortionist to do any serious work on-site. Be sure to check the fuel tank—especially if the boat has an Atomic 4—for signs of fuel leaks, which are not uncommon.

Underway

The primary reason the Tartan 27 has maintained its stellar reputation is simple: it is a lovely sailing boat. Richard Crockford, who sails *Antares*, hull No. 22, concedes that the boat isn't close-winded but sails exceptionally well when you foot off a bit. "Just put the old girl on a reach and hold on, because that's her best point of sail," Crockford said. "In a race she's hard to beat if there is a lot of reaching."

Crockford has changed to a loose-footed main, added inside headsail tracks and two-speed sheet winches in the cockpit. The boat balances easily, he claims. "When trimmed right she will sail herself, which is great for daysailing," he said. The boat is well-known for its lack of weather helm.

Neville Doherty has sailed *Cimbria* along the Northeast Coast from Long Island Sound to the St. John's River in New Brunswick, New Jersey. He also said the boat is fast, especially on a reach. "She is phenomenal under spinnaker in not-too-strong airs. That's my favorite time with her," he said. Doherty, who likes the flexibility offered by the shoal-draft centerboard arrangement, noted that the board doesn't drop easily when beating. "It is wise to adjust up or down either when tacking or while running." Doherty singlehands often, and also likes the easily achieved balance. "I never felt the need to get a larger boat," he said. "This summer I'm heading for Nova Scotia."

Conclusion

The Tartan 27 appeals to sailors of different experience levels. It is a perfect small family boat that can be purchased for around $10,000. The boat is well constructed and is indeed capable of extended coastal cruising. With a board-up draft of just over 3 feet, it can also explore thin waters that modern, deeper-draft boats can't. The Tartan 27 offers another intangible element: pride of ownership. There is something special about sailing a fiberglass classic.

Pearson Triton

Stiff-sailing cruiser from the early days of fiberglass boatbuilding

In the early days of fiberglass boatbuilding, skeptics often asked, how long will these plastic boats last? Can they really stand up to serious sailing? Won't they become saturated when the fibers and resins break down? Of course everyone predicted a short life span for these characterless boats that were ignominiously slapped together from a bucket of chemicals. They were wrong. The Pearson Triton and I both turned 40 in 1999, and we're doing just fine, although most Tritons are probably in better shape than me. Introduced by the Pearson brothers, Everett and Clint, at the New York Boat Show in 1959, the Carl Alberg-designed Triton attained classic status long ago and maintains a devoted following today. More than 700 boats were built before production stopped in 1967.

Alberg was Swedish, and the Triton, which conveniently fit the then all-powerful CCA rule like a glove, was the first of many designs that were patterned, in one form or another, after the Scandinavian Folkboat. Low freeboard, narrow beam, long overhangs—the look is familiar in most Alberg designs, from the Bristol 27 to the Alberg 30 to the later Cape Dory line. Pearson was a great American sailboat company for more than 30 years. Pearson built a wide variety of boats, and its early boats, including the Ariel, Wanderer, Vanguard, Invicta and of course the Triton, are the most fondly remembered and were an important bridge between wood and fiberglass boatbuilding.

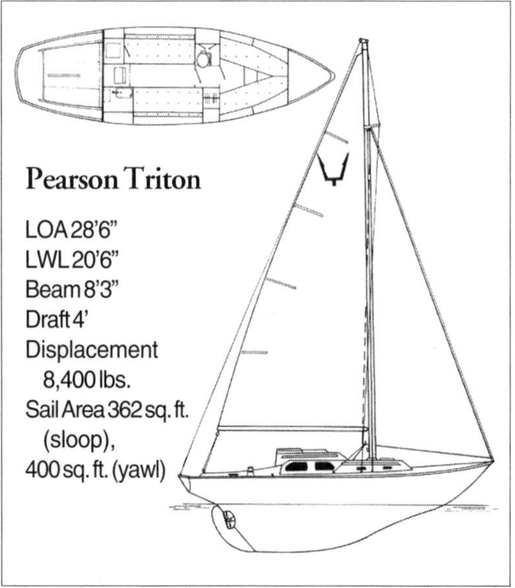

First impressions

From a distance, the Triton has a stately bearing in the water and looks larger than it is. It has a handsome, pronounced sheer, and although the lines are spoiled a bit by a rather large, stepped trunkhouse, Alberg realized that 6-foot-plus headroom in the saloon was worth the aesthetic compromise. Most Tritons were 3/4-rigged sloops with distinctive jumper struts, although a few masthead sloops were also built. Early boats were often yawls, a rig favored by the CCA rule.

It is not quite right to call the Triton a full-keel shape, at least in the traditional sense. The keel is cutaway forward and aft, and in fact, the leading edge of the rudder is directly under the cockpit sole. The Triton has long overhangs, with a 20-foot, 6-inch length waterline on a 28-foot, 6-inch LOA, giving the boat a very generous PHRF rating.

Construction

While it is true that early fiberglass boats were heavily laid-up, the hulls are not quite as thick as some owners claim. The glass work was unsophisticated, resin rich and often times full of voids. Still, it is impressive how well most Tritons have endured, and there have been few reports of structural hull damage. The boat has been thoroughly tested and many Tritons have made extensive bluewater voyages, including at least one circumnavigation. The ballast in early boats was iron, which was later changed to lead. In either case it is encapsulated in a molded keel cavity. The original rudders were wooden, usually mahogany, with a bronze shoe and drift pins.

The decks were balsa cored, at least in the boats built at Pearson's Rhode Island plant. I was surprised to learn that Tritons were also built in Sausalito, California, by Aeromarine Plastics. In some ways the West Coast boats are superior. Ralph Beauregard, a longtime Triton owner, writes in the National Triton Association Web page that West Coast boats had solid-glass decks, a great advantage in any old boat. West Coast boats are distinguishable by fiberglass cockpit coamings. The more common East Coast boats have mahogany cockpit boards. Aeromarine built 150 boats in the early 1960s and many are still sailing on San Francisco Bay.

Pearson Triton Price Data

		Low	High
BUC Retail Range	1961	$ 8,300	$ 9,550
	1964	$ 8,500	$ 9,850
	1967	$10,900	$12,400

		State	Asking
Boats For Sale	1960	RI	$ 8,000
	1965	OR	$14,000
	1966	MA	$11,500

What to look for

It is difficult to pin down specific changes to model years because so many changes were made during the Triton's eight-year production run. The first thing I would look for is probably a West Coast boat just to avoid the problem of deck delamination. Also, West Coast boats were built a little bit beefier to cope with blustery San Francisco Bay.

Of course most Tritons have cored decks and a little delamination is common. An area of concern is the mast support arrangement. If the deck area around the mast is depressed, then the step support needs to be beefed up. The Triton has centerline access to the forward cabin, which eliminates a convenient place for a compression post. A wooden beam, tied into the bulkhead, and framed around the door, often needs to be sistered with fresh wood. Some owners have replaced the beam with aluminum and others have actually added a compression post right smack in the middle of the forward walkway.

The rudder is another item to check carefully. It is not surprising to find the original wooden rudders glassed over, but it is better if a new fiberglass rudder has been fabricated, using the old rudder for a mold. The standing rigging of any old boat should be suspect. And while the spars themselves usually hold up well, tangs, toggles and old bronze turnbuckles should be thoroughly inspected. On some boats the spreaders were wood and should be checked for cracks and delamination. Also note the spreader sockets; they were made of aluminum and the metal is often fatigued.

Old Tritons seem to be selling between $10,000 and $13,000 regardless of condition. Look for a boat that has been upgraded with newer winches, sails, a professional paint job and possibly a new engine since the improvements will not be proportionately reflected in the asking price. It makes more sense to pay $15,000 for a boat with many recent and significant upgrades than $10,000 for an old tired model.

On deck

The cockpit is quite spacious and there is room forward and aft of the helmsman, an advantage of tiller steering. There is a stout bridgedeck and a narrow foot well making the cockpit safe in a seaway. The mainsheet traveler is aft, and the angle from the boom is not particularly efficient. Some owners have converted to wheel steering, and there is a good explanation of just how to do this on the association Web page. I think it is a mistake and wastes valuable space in the cockpit. Money would be better spent upgrading to self-tailing winches and replacing the standing rigging. Early boats had side opening (sure to leak) cockpit lockers. A common feature of Alberg's was a clever hatch from the cockpit into the icebox.

Most Tritons came from the factory with the 3/4 rig. The first 120 boats had single lower shrouds. After that, double-lowers were standard and Pearson offered rigging kits to owners of earlier boats. Surveying the deck of a 40-year-old Triton that has not

Pearson Triton

Sailing Magazine's Value Guide

PRICE: It is hard to imagine a better boat for the money. However, every Triton is at least 35 years old, meaning that they all need work.

DESIGN QUALITY: Carl Alberg keelboats have stood the test of time simply because there is nothing extreme about them. The boat seems small and slow by today's standards.

CONSTRUCTION QUALITY: Tritons are typical of early glass boats. The layup is heavy but not sophisticated. Look for a West Coast boat without cored decks.

USER-FRIENDLINESS: The 3/4 sloop rig is preferred, both for simplicity and for space in the cockpit. Most Tritons are refreshingly free of complicated systems.

SAFETY: While the structural integrity and seakindly motion provide a measure of safety, deck fittings need to be upgraded.

TYPICAL CONDITION: Although most Triton owners are conscientious, the boats are old and unless retrofitted recently it may be time to do it all over again.

REFITTING: Tritons have often been refitted at least once, and sometimes more, which is both good and bad. Sometimes redoing or replacing what a previous owner changed is more work than replacing original parts. Parts and suggestions are available through the National Triton Association. The web page can be found at pw1.netcom.com.com/~suter/triton.html

SUPPORT: Although Pearson has been out of business since 1990, the owner's association is very supportive.

AVAILABILITY: With more than 700 boats built and almost all still in service, there are always Tritons for sale all over the country. There seem to be more boats on the East Coast.

INVESTMENT AND RESALE: With prices steady near $10,000 Tritons don't fluctuate much. A known commodity, Tritons are brought and sold without too much trouble, which can't be said for many boats less than 30 feet.

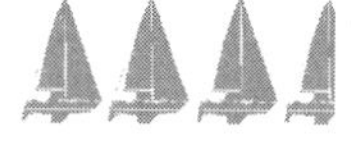
OVERALL 'SVG' RATING

been upgraded reminds you just how far sailboat design has come. From the totally inadequate stemhead fitting, to deck-mounted running lights, to low lifelines that bend to the deck aft of the bow pulpit and just forward of the cockpit coamings, the boat can seem archaic and somewhat unsafe on deck.

Down below

When you step below you realize just how small a Triton really is, especially when contrasted with modern interior designs. Although there isn't an aft cabin squeezed under the cockpit, or a separate shower stall hidden away somewhere, the arrangement is practical, especially at sea, and not completely uncomfortable at anchor. I know. I lived aboard a 1966 Bristol 27 (which has a nearly identical interior) for a year and a half.

A standard V-berth is forward, with shelves above. It takes a large filler piece to make this berth into an acceptable double. The athwartship head is next aft with a small hanging locker opposite and linen locker behind. While it is conceivable to close the doors to both the V-berth and the saloon for privacy, it is not very comfortable. The saloon had two fairly long settee berths with shelves above and a drawer below. A portable table was offered for the saloon but rarely used. An icebox is to port and a small sink is to starboard. The box has terrible insulation and unfortunately there isn't much room for improvement. Most owners have added some kind of cooking arrangement. Mike Davis, who is retrofitting *Falcon*, a 1984 Triton, for extended Caribbean cruising, added a one-burner Origo nonpressurized alcohol stove.

The interior finish is drab, with teak grain formica bulkheads and unfinished fiberglass. Later boats had a gelcoat liner in the saloon and many owners have painted the fiberglass. The cabin is bright, however, with four large side ports and two forward-facing portlights that can be opened for ventilation.

Engine

Except for the first few years of production, when outboards were standard, most Tritons came with Universal Atomic 4 gasoline engines, which many of the boats still have. "I bought a spare engine," explained Skip Kendrick, who sails his 37-year-old *Sorceress* out of Pensacola on the Florida Panhandle. Kendrick paid $450 for an engine in good shape and now has a complete set of spare parts.

Access is from behind the companionway ladder and the front end is well-suited for working. However, you will need to be extremely thin and have long arms and powerful fingers to repack the stuffing box. The 15-gallon fuel tank is mounted below the cockpit and can usually be removed through a hatch in the port locker. The 22.5-gallon water tank is mounted beneath the starboard cockpit seat. Kendrick reports that his Atomic 4 pushes the boat along at 5 knots without much of a problem. Despite the economic advantages of a gasoline engine, I would look for a Triton that had been repowered with a diesel. Universal made a diesel replacement for the Atomic 4 with the same footprint.

Underway

Davis, who sailed *Falcon* south from the Chesapeake, said he is impressed with how much sail the Triton can carry. "I usually reef the main pretty early, mostly to ease the helm, but I keep my No. 2 up in 20 knots all day long." Like many Alberg and CCA designs of this vintage, the long boom and small fore triangle produce weather-helm. The Triton heels readily to about 15 to 20 degrees and then stiffens up significantly. The cockpit stays rather dry, even hard on the wind.

Speaking of windward sailing, Skip Kendrick said that his Triton is not closewinded. He noted that the boat tracks extremely well, however, and most importantly, has a smooth motion even in rough conditions. "The boat never pounds, she just slices through the water." For those who prefer to race every now and then, the Triton will sail better than its PHRF rating would lead you to believe.

Conclusion

The Triton is an admirable, enduring and forgiving boat that once again proves that sailing does not have to be an expensive undertaking. An upgraded Triton costs less than half of a new sport utility vehicle and can take you a lot farther away from the daily grind.

Sabre 28

High-quality, small coastal cruiser with strong resaleability

The Sabre 28, in its own quiet way, changed my life. I was a teenager when my father unsuspectingly announced to the family one winter morning that we were going to buy a sailboat. In a snowy boatyard in Mt. Clemens, Michigan, we narrowed the choices down to two boats: an Irwin Competition 30 and a Sabre 28. My father finally selected the Sabre for the simple reason that it had a wheel instead of a tiller. That spring we launched the boat, and I have literally been sailing ever since.

When we purchased *Our Way* in 1973, Sabre Yachts of Casco, Maine, was a small builder, producing this single model. Although we didn't know it at the time, the 28 was destined to become a very successful boat. In all, 588 Sabre 28s were built during a 16-year production run stretching from 1970 to 1986. Like most boats that have long runs, the 28 evolved with many changes and improvements made along the way. The one consistent feature of the boat, however, has always been quality construction. Sabre was, and continues to be, perceived as a high-quality builder, and for the most part, it has lived up to the perception.

There are three versions or series of the 28. Series 1 ran through 1976. Series 2 introduced a new deck mold and included a T-shaped cockpit, which was a great improvement over the straight seats that required a very small wheel or a cramped steering station. Series 3, which commenced with the 1982 models, introduced several significant changes, including a taller spar, a deeper fin keel and the traveler was moved from the transom to the trunkhouse.

Quality usually means pricey and the 28 was a relatively expensive boat when purchased new. Although the 28 has held its value better than most boats, the wide array of 28s available and the general malaise of the small-boat side of the used boat market have made the 28 an attractive option for buyers of used boats in the $20,000 to $30,000 range. And because the original design was rather progressive, with a swept-back fin, a partial skeg rudder and relatively long waterline, even the older models deliver good performance, making the 28 seem less dated than other boats of the same vintage.

First impressions

True to their Down East heritage, founder Roger Hewson and the Sabre design team created a rather conventional-looking boat, but one that has aged gracefully. With only a slight sheer, a straight-raked stern and a modest bow overhang, the Sabre 28 still looks relatively modern today. Its amidships sections are rounded and it was beamy for its day. The cabintrunk is a little boxy but the resulting headroom and light below from good-sized portlights is a nice trade-off. From the teak toerail to nicely framed aluminum ports to stout deck fittings, it is obvious that this is a small boat that was put together like a big boat. Three years ago, I sailed a 1976 Sabre 28 from Freeport in the Bahamas, across the Gulf Stream to Ft. Lauderdale, Florida, and was reminded then of how responsive the Sabre 28 is as we completed the 80-mile run in about 14 hours.

Construction

From the beginning, the Sabre 28 was a well-engineered boat. The hull is not an overly heavy layup of mat and roving, but the workmanship is good, and strict attention was paid to designed thicknesses, which gradually decrease from eight layers at the turn of the bilge to four layers at the sheerline. The deck is cored with 3/8-inch endgrain balsa for stiffness. Additional reinforcing with marine plywood is used for high-load areas like the maststep, rudder post and stanchion bases. While you should always check for any deck delamination, especially in older boats, Sabres are not historically prone to this malady. The hull-to-deck joint is on an internal flange and is through-bolted on 6-inch centers. Aluminum backing plates support most through-deck hardware.

Unfortunately, some deck hardware is hard to access because of a fiberglass liner below. I have never liked liners but I do understand the practical application for small boats, and Sabre does a good job of encapsulating the top of the bulkheads in ribs in the liner. The keel is external lead, supported by cast stainless steel bolts that extend through a heavily reinforced molded fillet. The nuts and washers are accessible in the bilge and should be checked for tightness and corrosion.

While you're down there, look for signs of keel impact via stress cracks in the floors. Also, when the boat is out of the water check the draft; on Series 1 and 2, the standard draft was 4 feet, 4 inches, but on Series 3 the draft was increased to 4 feet, 8 inches. The shoal-draft version was 3 feet, 10 inches for all models. For some reason draft is often misstated on listing sheets, so be sure to actually measure the keel of the 28 you are considering. Also, it is worth noting that on deeper keelboats, built after 1982, the ballast was increased to 3,100 pounds for an increased ballast-to-displacement ratio of 40 percent.

What to look for

One thing not to look for is a ketch rig. Sabre actually produced eight of these over the years, but the boat just doesn't lend itself to a split rig. Also, if you are considering a pre-1975 model, be sure that the forward lower shrouds have been retrofitted. The 28 originally came with single uppers and lowers and the mast was prone to pumping in strong winds. And while the chainplates are well-supported through the deck to the main bulkhead, one owner I spoke with in Solomons, Maryland, told me that chainplate leaks eventually caused delamination of the bulkhead. If the bulkhead shows signs of damage, be sure to check the integrity of the teak compression post that is incorporated in the bulkhead. Although 90 percent of the 28s came standard with an Edson wheel, don't necessarily follow the lead of my dad and discount a boat with a tiller. The original design called for a tiller and it does open up the cockpit.

Pearson Triton Price Data

		Low	High
BUC Retail Range	1975	$14,800	$16,800
	1979	$19,600	$21,800
	1983	$24,400	$27,100

		State	Asking
Boats For Sale	1979	CT	$ 26,000
	1982	FL	$ 24,000

On deck

Speaking of the cockpit, it is certainly comfortable for a 28-foot boat designed more than 25 years ago. The seats are long and wide enough to sleep on and up to five people are manageable while under way. The locker to starboard serves as a sail locker with a clever rack for holding the hatch boards, while the port locker is a shallow catch-all. If it hasn't been done already, it is possible to convert the large locker under the helmsman's seat to a propane locker for a new gas cooker to replace the original alcohol model. Just be sure the job is done professionally so that it is vented overboard. If the original winches, which are very handy for the helmsman, haven't been updated, they will probably need to be.

The side decks are quite narrow and the lifelines could be taller. However, the molded nonskid is superb and seems to age very well, and the teak grabrails on the cabintop are well-placed and secure. After 1976, a small anchor locker was added on the foredeck. There is a single dorade vent forward and a hatch over

Sabre 28

Sailing Magazine's Value Guide

PRICE: New 28s were considered pricey, but the used market has driven prices down. It is hard to find a quality boat in the $20,000 range.

DESIGN QUALITY: While there is nothing striking about the design, it has endured well. The design represents a good blend of performance and comfort, which is rare in boats less than 30 feet.

CONSTRUCTION QUALITY: Sabre Yachts built its reputation on quality, and the 28 is one of the best-built small production boats available on the used boat market.

USER-FRIENDLINESS: The 28 is an easy boat to sail, although it can be overpowered and can become overloaded with more than four people. The galley needs to be improved.

SAFETY: The side decks are hard to negotiate and the stanchions could be higher. The bridgedeck is adequate and there are good handholds on deck and below. The overall quality is a safety feature.

TYPICAL CONDITIONS: Older 28s seem to be holding up well. Also, Sabre has had remarkable owner loyalty over the years and the owners, in general, seem to have taken good care of their boats.

REFITTING: Repowering the boat is a challenge. Also, the liner makes it difficult to change deck fittings. Parts, including molded pieces, are available.

SUPPORT: Sabre is back in business and Mike Plourde in the customer service division is most helpful. The original owner's manual is available for $40 and would be a good purchase for anyone considering a secondhand 28.

AVAILABILITY: With a production run of more than 500 boats, there is always a good selection of 28s on the market. The Northeast and Chesapeake areas have the largest concentration of used 28s.

INVESTMENT AND RESALE: The Sabre 28 has maintained its value very well over the years, and despite a tough market for boats less than 30 feet, still sells well. Most of the depreciation is already out of the older boats; their price won't fall much lower.

OVERALL 'SVG' RATING

the forward cabin. Most Sabres seem to have been originally northern boats, meaning that added ventilation is required for southern sailing, although some later boats did have opening portlights as an option.

The mast height was increased from 41 feet on Series 1 and 2, to 43 feet above the water on Series 3 boats in 1982. This added about 10 feet of sail area. The mast, which on some boats was Awlgripped, featured internal halyards and the boom had an internal clew outhaul and topping lift.

On Series 3 boats, the traveler was moved from the transom to just forward of the companionway. And while midboom sheeting places a lot of load on the boom and mainsheet fittings, the stern-mounted mainsheet was annoying and surely kept the helmsman on her toes, especially during jibes. If you are looking at a pre-1982 boat with a midboom traveler and sheeting arrangement, be sure that the jib was done right.

Down below

Although the interior arrangement is quite standard, the level of finish is very nice. Teak-faced bulkheads and solid-teak trim give the boat a warm feeling below. There is just about 6 feet of headroom throughout. The V-berth has a filler for a large double and a couple of good-sized drawers for storage. The head is full width when closed off, and on later models, the holding tank was increased from 14 to 24 gallons.

The saloon has a bulkhead-mounted, fold-down table. An owner I spoke with on the west coast of Florida told me that he replaced the wooden dowel with a screw fitting to keep the table from clanging while underway. There is a large quarter berth to port and the galley is to starboard. If there is one drawback to the interior it is the galley, which is quite compact. A two-burner alcohol stove was standard and it is challenging to retrofit a full-sized stove and oven in the space available. The single sink is just off the centerline under the companionway and I remember accidentally stepping into the sink more than once when going below while heeled hard to starboard in the Gulf Stream.

Engine

Sabre used four different engines on the 28. The old standby Universal Atomic 4 gas engine was standard until 1975 when a 10-horsepower, single-cylinder Volvo diesel was added as an option. In 1978, a Volvo MD 7A, a 2-cylinder, 13-horsepower diesel became standard, and in 1981, Sabre switched to a 13-horsepower Westerbeke. If you are considering repowering an older boat, note that the shaft for the Atomic 4, which is a right-hand turning engine, is offset to port. The shaft is offset to starboard on the left-hand turning Volvo, so when replacing the engine be sure to replace it with one that turns the same way. This is one reason why there are still a lot of old 28s with gas engines.

Engine access is terrible for the Atomic 4 and only slightly better for the smaller diesels. Also, reaching the stuffing box is a job for an extremely thin contortionist—the Sabre 28 is a good candidate for a new mechanical shaft seal. The boat I sailed from the Bahamas had the Volvo diesel and it pushed the old girl along at 5.5 to 6 knots, although there was a lot of vibration. Fuel capacity on the later models was 22 gallons.

Underway

The Sabre 28 is a graceful boat under sail. Although it is easily driven and can be tender, it still has the feel and bearing of a bigger boat. With the older transom-mounted mainsheet, the sail controls are in easy reach of the helmsman. By leading the halyards aft, and especially with the addition of self-tailing winches, the 28 can be set up for singlehanded sailing.

The chainplates are set well inboard, which allows for an optional inboard genoa track in addition to the standard track set on the toerail. This, coupled with the deep keel and taller rig, makes later model 28s good performers to weather. As mentioned earlier, the 28 is not overly stiff, but with a versatile furling headsail, you can control sail area easily enough—and besides, it is always possible to shorten sail, but not always possible to keep a sluggish boat moving in light air. The 28 is a good light-air boat. And although the Sabre 28 is primarily a coastal cruiser and club racer under PHRF, over the years some owners have sailed far and wide, including passages to Bermuda and the Caribbean.

Conclusion

The Sabre 28 offers an excellent blend of quality construction, lively performance and value with prices ranging from less than $20,000 for an early boat to around $30,000 for late models.

S2 9.2

Solid construction and timeless styling provide good value

S2 Yachts surprised many sailing purists by proving that a powerboat builder could successfully make the transition to sailboats. S2 was created by Leon Slickers after he sold his eponymous powerboat company, Slickcraft. A noncompete clause prevented Slickers from building powerboats for a few years, so he focused his production talents on sailboats instead. The first S2s rolled off the line in 1974, looking a lot like powerboats with masts. In a word, they were unsightly. A couple of years later, the Holland, Michigan-based company found its stride and created a line of boats that were well-designed, well-built, stylishly appointed and very popular.

S2 was one of the few American builders to take the metric system seriously, and it classed boats accordingly. The 9.2, which is 9.2 meters or 29 feet, 11 inches LOA, was introduced in 1977, enjoyed a 10-year production run and was available in two very different models: the 9.2A, a conventional aft-cockpit model, and the 9.2C, an innovative center-cockpit version. More than 700 9.2s of both types were launched before S2 stopped all production.

S2 9.2A

LOA 29'11"
DWL 25'
Beam 10'3"
Draft 4'11" (standard), 3'11" (shoal)
Displacement 9,800 lbs.
Ballast 4,000 lbs.
Sail Area 468 sq. ft.

First impressions

The 9.2 (A and C) was the brainchild of Arthur Edmunds, a versatile naval architect who designed several S2s and other boats ranging from the utilitarian Allied Princess to high-speed power catamarans. The hull shapes of both 9.2 models are identical, featuring healthy beam and freeboard, fairly short overhangs, a flat sheerline and a slightly reversed transom.

Under the water, Edmunds opted for a moderately deep forefoot to reduce pounding, a long fin keel and a spade rudder. An optional 3-foot, 11-inch shoal-draft model was popular, although the standard 4-foot, 11-inch draft model is stiffer and points higher. The 9.2A featured a rakish, sloping trunkhouse with large Lexan portlights and nice moldings that gave the boat an ultramodern appearance 20 years ago and a contemporary look today. Inevitably, the 9.2C appears a bit cramped on deck, with the cockpit squeezed between two boxy trunkhouses, but the livability below equals that of a 36-foot boat, especially one of this age and for this price. S2's original fiberglass work, particularly the gelcoat layer, was extremely well-done, and from a cosmetic standpoint, S2s have aged better than many other boats.

Construction

S2's plant was state of the art in the mid-1970s, and the company eventually developed a reputation for efficiently producing quality boats. The 9.2 hull is solid, hand-laid-up fiberglass. The deck is balsa-cored and married to the hull on an inward flange. An aluminum T-rail is incorporated in the joint. The 4,000 pounds of lead ballast is internal and well-secured in the keel cavity. It is important with encapsulated ballast that the bilge seal remain watertight. One way to check if this seal is intact is to fill the bilge area above the keel cavity with a measurable amount of water. Check the next day to make sure the level hasn't decreased noticeably.

S2 did not use many molded liners in the 9.2. Bulkheads and furniture fittings are tabbed to the hull, usually on both sides of each surface, which increases hull panel stiffness. Bulkheads are plywood with teak veneers and solid teak trim, and the cabin sole is teak and holly. The deck-stepped mast is well-supported with a stout compression post.

S2 9.2 Price Data

		Low	High
BUC Retail Range	1978	$20,100	$22,400
	1981	$23,500	$25,500
	1984	$27,200	$29,000

		State	Asking
Boats For Sale	1979	MI	$18,000
	1980	WI	$25,900
	1982	FL	$24,000

What to look for

Be sure not to confuse the 9.2 with a later model, the 9.1, a performance boat designed by Graham and Schlageter and a different animal altogether. Adding to that confusion, S2 eventually gave up on the metric system. During the last years of production, both boats were called S2 30s; be certain to specify the 9.2 model when tracking down used boats.

I spoke to several owners of both A and C model 9.2s. It's interesting to note that those with A models would never consider Cs, and vice versa. As a group, they were extremely pleased with the boat. After a bit of chatting, however, a few common problems surfaced. Below the waterline, hull blisters seem to be prevalent, although this is by no means unique to the S2. Like all older fiberglass boats, the level of osmosis varies from a few thumbnail-sized blisters to cases requiring a bottom peel. Another frequent complaint was that the boat was underpowered by its auxiliary. During the first two years of production the Universal Atomic 4 gas engine was standard, but by 1979, the two-cylinder, 13-horsepower Yanmar was the engine of choice. Roger Nicholas, who sails a 1982 9.2C called *Bosa Nova* on the Chesapeake, admits frankly, "At times, especially powering into a stiff breeze, the boat needs more oomph." While adding a three-bladed prop helps, the best solution if you intend to power a lot is to look for a boat with a larger engine. Some owners specified the three-cylinder, 23-horsepower Yanmar 3GM from the factory, and others have retrofitted larger engines. In 1985, the larger engine became standard. One last note on the engine: 9.2C owners report that there is little access to the starboard side of the engine, making simple tasks like checking the oil and changing the impeller difficult.

Other reported problems include leaking chainplates, problems with the plastic portlights (the knobs break off) and a small holding tank. Although some S2s have had problems with delamination of the balsa-cored decks, it does not seem to be much of a problem with the 9.2. Of course, as with any used boat more than 10 years old, it is important to carefully check the standing rigging. Also, the 9.2 came with North Sails, which have held up so well that many 9.2s on the market still have the originals. These will probably need to be replaced.

On deck

It is apparent from the moment you step aboard that S2 used good gear in fitting out the boat. From the bow fittings and anchor locker to the more-than-adequate chocks and cleats, to the well-supported stanchions and double lifelines, S2 chose to beef up deck hardware. The side decks are not very wide, although a very good nonskid surface lends security when going forward under way. Most 9.2s came standard with Kenyon spars and Lewmar winches. Also, Harken seems a popular choice for the headsail roller-furling system. The traveler is all the way aft, providing good purchase on the boom and keeping the mainsheet out of harm's way.

The cockpits of both models are well-laid-out, and the two boats that I examined in South Florida had all sail controls led aft. The view from the helm, especially in the center-cockpit model, is excellent. Larry Jensen, who sails a 1979 9.2A called *Valkyrie*, likes the fact that he can trim the main from the helm while his wife Peggy takes care of the headsail sheets. Mike Williams, who owns a 1982 9.2C, told me that, like most center-cockpits, the boat is wet when sailing to weather in a blow—a dodger is a great addition.

S2 9.2

Sailing Magazine's Value Guide

PRICE: The 9.2 is rather expensive for its LOA, but in many ways, the boat is more comparable to a 32- or 33-foot boat.

DESIGN QUALITY: While the 9.2A is a rather conventional design, it has aged gracefully and performs adequately. The very innovative 9.2C, on the other hand, is a boat you either love or hate.

CONSTRUCTION QUALITY: Time is the test of original construction, and 20-year-old 9.2s still look good and report few serious problems.

USER-FRIENDLINESS: Ease of handling and comfort were important criteria in the development of the 9.2. The boat can be easily sailed by one or two people and the interiors of both boats are more comfortable than those of most 30-footers.

SAFETY: The 9.2 has solid construction and first-rate deck equipment, but is a tad tender and requires sail to be shortened early.

TYPICAL CONDITION: Because the fiberglass and gelcoat have stood up well, it is rare to find a painted 9.2 on the market. Owners have paid a price for the boat and tend to maintain it.

REFITTING: The 9.2 is not the easiest boat to work on; the interior uses every nook and cranny. Repowering can be done, but it is a big job.

SUPPORT: Most owners report cordial relations with Tiara Yachts, the new parent company of S2. Tiara makes it clear that it is no longer in the sailboat business, but it has some parts remaining for the 9.2. Fax requests for parts or information to (616) 394-7473.

AVAILABILITY: A long, successful production run has resulted in plenty of 9.2s for sale all over the country. Although more 9.2As were built, the 9.2C seems more in demand and fetches a bit more money.

INVESTMENT AND RESALE: The 9.2 has held its value quite well. However, if you are willing to accept a smaller diesel and an aft cockpit, you should be able to find a deal simply because there is a good selection of boats to choose from.

OVERALL 'SVG' RATING

Down below

There is no question that the well-appointed interior was a huge part of the 9.2's initial success and continuing popularity as a used boat. Typical of the times, the interior woodwork is teak, and although it is a bit dark by today's standards, the workmanship was quite good and seems to be holding up well. The overhead liner is fabric, not my favorite because sooner or later the adhesive gives out and it starts to droop. The galley countertops were done in Formica and often show signs of wear.

The 9.2A has a conventional layout, with a V-berth forward, followed by a large head and hanging locker. The saloon has a convertible dinette and a settee opposite. There is a good amount of storage under the berths because the 40-gallon poly water tank is forward and the 20-gallon aluminum fuel tank is aft. The galley is L-shaped, and most boats on the market have converted the original alcohol stove to propane or natural gas. The chart table and quarter berth are opposite the galley.

The 9.2C has a very innovative interior that never fails to impress; indeed, it is hard to believe that you are in a 30-foot boat down below. The saloon is forward, just aft of a small V-berth cabin. The surprisingly spacious aft cabin is devoted to a large athwartship bunk and good-sized hanging locker. The huge head and shower stall are aft to starboard in the main cabin. The in-line galley is opposite the head, and the nav station is neatly tucked under the cockpit in the walkway leading aft. The 9.2C interior spawns dreams of living aboard, and several owners that I corresponded with do just that for months at a time.

Engine

As mentioned earlier, most 9.2s have two-cylinder Yanmar diesels. Although these two-bangers thump and shake while running, they are highly reliable, stingy on fuel and relatively inexpensive to repair. However, times have changed. Everyone is in a hurry and most sailors, including myself, motor more than we used to. It is tough to accept 4.5 to 5 knots. Dick Barclay, who sails a 1984 9.2C with the 23-horsepower 3GM notes that he can power easily at 6-plus knots in flat water and can also cut through a moderate chop at 5 knots.

While repowering is an expensive option, removing the old diesel from both models is possible without major surgery. Larry Jensen also told me that his engine panel, standard from the factory, has idiot lights only, no gauges. Overall access is marginal on both models, but that is the nature of small-boat engine rooms. One improvement on the 9.2C would be to cut another access hatch through the head compartment.

Underway

Dick and Bunny Barclay sail close to 1,000 miles every summer exploring the Maine coast aboard *Windseeker*, a 9.2C. The Barclays have been surprised and delighted by the good performance, which they view as a bonus. The accommodation plan was their primary reason for buying a 9.2 seven years ago. Dick slaps the first reef in the main when the wind touches 18 knots and shortens his 140-percent roller genny to around 100 percent. "I like to keep the boat on her lines to ease the helm, and she sails easier and just as fast. Upwind, without too much of a sea, we can hit 7 knots," he said. The Barclays also carry a cruising spinnaker and pop it every chance they can.

Roger Nicholas has a shoal draft model 9.2, which suits him perfectly for the thin waters of Chesapeake Bay. He often tucks in a reef at 15 knots, and notes that he is able to keep the boat moving around 6 knots in most conditions. "I use the boat for cruising, I don't push the boat," he said. "I have a 'StackPack' on the main and a Harken roller-furling genoa, and I like to sail the boat flat." Mike Williams reported that his boat can develop a fair bit of weather helm, and he added a backstay adjuster to help cope. "In the end, however, there is really no way to ease the helm without shortening the main," he said.

Conclusion

With prices generally ranging from the low 20s to the high 30s, the S2 9.2 has held its value and is an intriguing used boat option. Although it is perched at the high end of the market, the 9.2 still delivers a lot of boat for the buck, especially when compared to new or even newer used boats. In fact, after surveying the market, Larry and Peggy Jensen have decided to spend money upgrading their 20-year-old 9.2A instead of buying a bigger boat. Two different deck arrangements and good quality construction should put the S2 9.2 on the short list if you are looking for a good coastal cruiser in a 30-foot package.

Catalina 30

Inexpensive, refit-friendly coastal cruiser

By the time you read this report, nearly 7,000 Catalina 30s will have been christened. In terms of sheer numbers, the Catalina 30 is arguably the most successful cruiser-racer ever built. Designed by Frank Butler, the Catalina 30 was first launched in 1975 and the Mark III model is still in production today. Catalina has always been a company without pretenses; it builds affordable boats with high-volume interiors designed for families. Catalina, which has produced more than 60,000 boats in 26 years, never suffered the trauma of converting from traditional to modern designs. From the beginning, it built moderate-displacement, fin-keel boats that perform relatively well. One of the keys to its considerable success has simply been that Catalina keeps its boats in production longer than most builders.

After the second year of production, Catalina added two options—a tall rig that added 2 feet to the spar and 50 square feet to the sail area and shoal draft, which clipped 11 inches off the keel. The Mark II, which was introduced after hull No. 4,276, included a T-shaped cockpit, an aluminum-framed forward hatch, a sit-down nav station and better access to wiring and batteries. The Mark III, which came out recently—after hull No. 6,250, to be precise—incorporates the de rigueur boarding/swim platform in the transom and a further modified cockpit with observation seats built into the stern rail. In addition, the interior styling has been considerably upgraded.

Catalina 30

LOA 29'11"
LWL 25'
Beam 10'10"
Draft 3'10" (wing)
Draft 5'3" (standard)
Displ. 10,200 (standard) lbs.
Displ. 10,300 (wing) lbs.
Ballast standard 4,200 lbs, wing keel 4,300 lbs.
Sail Area 446 sq. ft.
Sail Area tall rig 505 sq. ft.

In some ways, Catalinas are difficult boats to evaluate, especially when compared to its competitor's boats. Catalina owners are fiercely loyal and often trade up to the next size model, be it new or used. Yet, it's fair to say that there are invariably better quality boats within a class or size parameter for the used-boat buyer to consider. Still, as thousands ofCatalina owners know, it is nearly impossible to get more boat for the money. A 15-year-old Catalina 30 in good shape with a diesel will sell for just over $20,000. An 8-year-old Mark II in average condition should be available for around $35,000. Granted, these boats are not designed or built to sail across oceans, but they are boats that are very comfortable for weekend cruising and are easy to maintain, simple to sail and fun to race.

First impressions

Catalinas are recognizable in any marina. The styling is modern, yet the appearance does not completely put off traditionalists. Catalina prides itself on consistency and the changes from the first 30 to the last have been subtle. In fact, the latest Mark III boats can still compete in one-design events with the early boats. The sheerline is rather straight and there is a fair amount of freeboard, which, when seen in profile, tends to make the cabintrunk appear lower than it really is. A nearly 11-foot beam, which is carried well aft, helps create the spacious saloon below. The ends are rather short, the waterline is 25 feet, the ballast is lead and the displacement is 10,200 pounds on deep-draft models.

Construction

The Catalina 30 has a hull of solid fiberglass with plywood-cored decks. As with any cored deck, the used-boat buyer needs to carefully check for signs of delamination. Plywood is not an ideal coring material, although Catalina completely encapsulates the coring, and deck delamination is not a common problem. To test this, stomp heavily in high-stress areas around the mast, the chainplates and on the foredeck. The 30's hull-to-deck joint incorporates an overlapping deck flange, fiberglassed to the hull. The joint is covered by a plastic rub rail and an aluminum strip. While adequate for coastal cruising, this is not a hull-and-deck joint for offshore work. The lead keel is externally fastened to the hull. On very early models, iron keelbolts were used and if they have not been replaced, they will need to be imminently. On most boats, the keelbolts are stainless steel.

Like so many small boats, the Catalina 30 has a molded liner that makes it difficult to examine the undersides of deck fittings. The liner not only makes for a clean appearance below, it also allows the bulkheads to be mechanically fastened, which means that they can be easily replaced if necessary. In fact, all of the wood below is mechanically fastened and can literally be unbolted or unscrewed and taken out of the boat to be worked on. And yes, every piece fits through the extra-large companionway hatch.

Catalina 30 Price Data

BUC Retail Range		Low	High
	1976	$16,300	$18,500
	1982	$22,400	$24,900
	1988	$32,500	$36,100

Boats For Sale		State	Asking
	1976	FL	$18,000
	1982	WA	$31,000
	1988	CA	$34,000

What to look for

Every used boat has certain flaws that were either inherent from the beginning or evolved with time. Used Catalina 30s have a few quirks to be checked. The aft chainplates had two problems on early models. First, on the very early boats, the chainplates were fastened solely to the deck and needed beefing up. In the neighborhood of hull No. 200, aft knees were added for this purpose. Also, early boats had chainplates that tended to rotate when tightened. A simple lock fitting eliminates the problem.

Up until approximately hull No. 800, wooden spreaders were used. There is nothing wrong with wooden spreaders if they have been maintained. If they haven't, they can rot, especially around the tips, and cause much grief. Catalina sells an aluminum spreader replacement kit. One huge advantage of purchasing a secondhand Catalina is that Catalina Yachts has an extensive parts inventory, primarily because it manufactures so many of its own fittings. The customer service department is most helpful. Also, check the steering system. On some early boats, a rod-and-pin system (direct drive with universal joints) was offered as an option. I spoke to an owner who had this system on his 1978 model.He liked it but noted that, initially, the alignment was way out of whack.

On deck

Catalinas are user-friendly by nature and nowhere is this more apparent than on deck and in the cockpit of the Catalina 30. The side decks are easy to navigate, going outside the shrouds and the nonskid provides good footing. The stanchions, which are closely spaced and through-bolted, could certainly be taller. Catalina was one of the first companies to make double lifelines standard. Forward, there is a small anchor well but there isn't room to mount a bow roller of any reasonable size. Consequently, you must lift the anchor over the pulpit to launch it. An alternative is to clip-mount a Danforth type on the pulpit. There are stout mooring cleats fore and aft but no chocks.

The mast is stepped on deck, and be sure to check for deck depression around the base of the mast. The compression post below is a wooden boxed column and it is not uncommon to find slight depressions

Catalina 30

Sailing Magazine's Value Guide

PRICE: Without a doubt, the most attractive feature of the Catalina 30 is its low price.

DESIGN QUALITY: There is nothing particularly innovative about the design. Despite interior and deck upgrades, under the water the design is dated.

CONSTRUCTION QUALITY: Catalina 30s are mass-produced and not built for offshore sailing. They are more than adequate for lake and coastal use.

USER-FRIENDLINESS: The 30 is an easy, forgiving boat, but can be unmanageable in a stiff breeze. Below, the boat is comfortable and easily accommodates four people for a short cruise.

SAFETY: The extra large companionway is a safety hazard. There are good grab rails on deck but not below. Short stanchions and lack of an anchoring system are safety problems.

TYPICAL CONDITIONS: Older 30s should be carefully inspected before purchasing. Because the design is rather basic, there really is not that much to go wrong. Often, problems are just cosmetic.

REFITTING: The 30 seems designed with refitting in mind. Everything can be removed through the companionway. Parts are readily available fromCatalina, as is advice from owners through the company's publication *Mainsheet.*

SUPPORT: Catalina has an excellent customer service department. Because so much of each boat is built in-house, a ready inventory of parts is available. For information on the Web: www.CatalinaOwners.com; www.catalinayachts.com; www.catalina30.com.

AVAILABILITY: With nearly 7,000 boats floating around, availability is excellent.

INVESTMENT AND RESALE: Owner loyalty has kept the Catalina used boat market healthy. The boats are inexpensive to purchase, but there is a ready market when it comes time to sell. Most get their money back out of the boat.

OVERALL 'SVG' RATING

around the mast. If, however, the deck has dipped more than 1/4-inch and there are obvious stress cracks, then the situation is more serious and may require attention. The mainsheet traveler on most boats is set on the cabintop with a midboom sheeting arrangement.

The cockpit of all three versions of the Catalina 30 is remarkably comfortable. Again, this is not a cockpit for serious offshore sailing. It is too large, has only two small scuppers and the companionway simply invites water below. But we must remember: The Catalina 30 was designed for fun, not for ocean passages. Also, the standard wheel is a little small.

Down below

The interior of the Catalina 30 is another selling feature; it is roomy and well laid out. The V-berth forward is good sized, especially with the filler in place. The overhead hatch, however, which is incorporated into the forward slope of the trunkhouse, is almost certain to leak on older boats. The new, aluminum-framed hatch is a great improvement. The head is large and includes a shower and opposite is a hanging locker and bureau. Be sure to check the plumbing on the shower; on most early models it drained into the bilge.

The saloon seems spacious because the table folds up against the bulkhead, which is a good idea in any boat 30 feet long or less. There is good storage throughout and despite the molded liner, there is adequate access to the hull from behind the settees. A huge double quarter berth extends beneath the cockpit.

The U-shaped galley is immediately to port and includes double sinks. On most older models, an alcohol stove was standard. The icebox does not have enough insulation, especially for warm-water sailing and drains directly into the bilge. There is, however, a lot of storage throughout. The nav station is opposite the galley and batteries are usually mounted below the small chart table.

Engine

The standard power plant on the early 30s was that old workhorse, the Universal Atomic 4 gas engine. A diesel was also available, a puny 11-horsepower Universal that had a hard time pushing the boat along at 5 knots. Also, some early models had a 12-horsepower Yanmar. By 1983, gas engines were a thing of the past and most 30s were fitted with 25-horsepower Universal diesels.

The engine is located in the saloon on the centerline beneath the L-shaped settee cushion. Access is excellent, when you remove part of the galley counter. Also, there is a hatch in the galley directly above the stuffing box. The insulation on the engine box is inadequate and the cabin is quite loud when motoring. However, the Catalina 30 handles extremely well under power—an advantage of a fin keel and spade rudder. With a 21-gallon tank, it has a range of 150 to 200 miles.

Underway

Bob Beck, who sailed a Catalina 30 tall rig on Lake Texoma for years, observed clearly the performance differences between the tall and standard rigs while competing in the nationals off San Pedro,California. The two rigs were raced in the same fleet. In 15 knots of wind, the tall rigs dominated. But with the sea breeze kicked in at 20 knots, the tall-rig crews struggled to tuck in a reef and the standard rigs surged ahead. Beck, who was a tall-rig national champion, emphasizes that you should know your local sailing conditions before selecting a tall or standard rig.

Typical of most beamy, flat-bottomed boats, the Catalina 30 sails best with little heel and when you do lay it over, it develops a mighty weather helm. If you do go with a larger, lapping genoa, you will need to add turning blocks aft for a proper lead to the sheet winches. The standard main has only one set of reef points.

Conclusion

The Catalina 30 is a perfect first "big boat" for a family on a budget. It is easy to write glowing reviews about the shiny new 30s at this year's boat shows. But the stark reality is that a new 30-footer can easily cost more than $150,000, while you can buy a used Catalina 30 in good condition for around $25,000. Now that is something to think about.

Olson 30

The ULDB that showed the world light is fast and fast is fun

The Olson 30 was a part of the Santa Cruz revolution that permanently altered the face of sailing. A small but progressive group of builders (the most well-known is Santa Cruz 70 designer Bill Lee) began designing and manufacturing incredibly light and fast boats in the mid-1970s. These new boats were dubbed ultralight displacement boats. The phrase "fast is fun" became part of the sailing lexicon and 6 knots went from being a standard of performance to being simply slow. George Olson's 30-footer rocket ship is a classic example of early ULDB design that has stood the test of time. Although it has been out of production for more than a decade, it is still considered a very fast boat and routinely surfs at 15-plus knots and claws upwind at 7.

Olson built one of the first ULDBs, the 24-foot flyer *Grendel*, which later became the prototype for the popular Moore 24. Olson worked briefly with Lee and together they developed another legendary West Coast flyer, the Santa Cruz 27. The two parted ways when Olson formed his company, Pacific Boats, located in Santa Cruz. His first and ultimately most successful project was the 30, introduced in 1978. In all, 244 boats were built before production stopped in 1986.

Olson 30

LOD 30'
LWL 27'6"
Beam 9'
Draft 5'1"
Displacement 3,600 lbs.
Ballast 1,800 lbs.
Sail Area 380 sq. ft.

First impressions

The Olson 30 looks fast even when it's tied to the dock. Olson masterfully created a long 27-foot, 6-inch waterline without the stubby, blunt-nosed, wide-body look of today's vertically ended sport boats. The profile view reveals a bit of sheer, and the relatively long tapered deckhouse, low freeboard and reverse transom combine to give the boat deceptively soft, sexy lines. The numbers, however, jump off the page. The Olson 30 displaces just 3,600 pounds with 1,800 pounds of ballast in the keel. To put that in perspective, the 21-year-old Olson 30 weighs nearly 1,000 pounds less than the Mumm 30 and nearly 2,000 less than the J/92.

Construction

In the early days of ULDB construction many predicted that the boats would never hold up, that they were just too light to take the relentless pounding of wind and waves. What the experts didn't realize was that lighter boats are subject to lighter loads, and by dramatically increasing speed when sailing off the wind, the apparent wind is much less, reducing loads even further. ULDB manufacturers also introduced new building techniques and higher standards of construction. Many of these techniques, which included vacuum bagging, have become common even among cruising boatbuilders.

The Olson 30 has a balsa-cored hull and the vacuum-bagged method of construction of the 30's hull has proven to be not only light and strong, but durable. Vacuum bagging is the process of placing the core against a wet mat or cloth and then covering it with a plastic bag. A vacuum is applied, causing the bag to collapse onto the core. The even pressure created across the entire surface draws resin through the cloth, removing any excess. The vacuum also sucks out air pockets or bubbles, eliminating the voids between the skin and the core. The result is a well-saturated laminate using as little resin as possible. This produces a light, stiff and extremely watertight sandwich hull. The balsa-cored deck is also vacuum bagged.

The hull has a 3-inch inward-turning flange to support the deck, which is bolted through an aluminum toerail on 4-inch centers. Two plywood structural half-bulkheads below are well tabbed to the hull and support the chainplates. A tie rod and turnbuckle connects the deck to the keel-stepped spar. The early boats had an inadequate wooden maststep. The lead keel section is quite narrow, approximately 5 inches, and held in place with nine $^5/_8$-inch bolts and a single 1-inch bolt that doubles as the lifting ring. This ring is accessible through a deck hatch, making it rather easy to lift the boat in and out of the water when it is dry stored. Interestingly, the rudder stock is solid fiberglass.

What to look for

There are a few common problems in Olson 30s. The original wooden maststep didn't hold up very well although chances are that it has already been replaced with an aluminum I-beam athwart. Be wary of a fore and aft retrofitted maststep that might make it difficult to access keel bolts. Also, be sure to examine the bulkheads for cracks or delamination. Because these are half-bulkheads, replacing them is not a huge job. These structural members often carry high loads and need to be strong. Also carefully check the keel-to-hull joint at the stub—some boats have leaked, especially if the wrong sealant was used when the keel was last removed.

The key to buying an Olson 30 is to honestly assess how you plan to sail the boat. This will help you to accurately determine how much of the inventory is useful. Larry Rota, who recently bought a 1981 Olson 30, sails out of Santa Cruz and doesn't plan to race the boat, at least not initially. He was happy to find an older boat that had few modifications over the years. "It was almost like buying a stock boat," Rota said. "This way I can make the changes I want."

Steve Maseda, who sailed his 1980 Olson 30 *Holy Guacamole* out of Southern California, advises prospective racers to have a sailmaker check the value of the sails. "While the purchase price for the boat might be $15,000, if the sail inventory has to be completely updated, you can easily spend $7,000 to $10,000 to be competitive," Maseda said. He suggested looking for lightweight polyester chutes as opposed to the heavier nylon ones. The boats that win the most races have been retrofitted with a double-spreader spar, which can add another $3,000 to $4,000 to the price.

Another potential problem area is the bottom. While many Olsons have been dry-sailed, those that haven't might well have blisters. Having a fair bottom affects speed over ground, and a complete bottom job can add an additional $2,000 to $4,000. Over the years, certain key deck and rigging changes have become critical to successful racing. If you want to race at a high level, look for a boat that has an adjustable tackle for headsail leads, Kevlar halyards, and additional backstay purchase.

Olson 30 Price Data

		Low	High
BUC Retail Range	1980	$ 9,650	$10,900
	1983	$13,000	$14,800
	1986	$16,600	$18,900

		State	Asking
Boats For Sale	1982	CA	$14,000
	1984	WA	$15,500

On deck

The Olson 30 cockpit seems outdated when compared to the open-style sport boat cockpits of today's boats, but when racing offshore, (Olson 30s were designed for offshore racing and cruising) the companionway sill and large lazarette astern lend a feeling of security. The mainsheet traveler cuts across the aft end of the cockpit, which provides good end-boom sheeting but doesn't help an already small working area. There are two decent-sized drains, and because the actual well is quite small, they are more than adequate. Some owners have removed the small teak coamings, which isn't a bad idea. Coupled with

Olson 30

Sailing Magazine's Value Guide

PRICE: Although the days of the super cheap Olson 30s may be behind us, with prices generally still less than$20,000 the boat is a great value.

DESIGN QUALITY: The boat is what it is, an ULDB that offers blistering off-the-wind performance. The Olson 30 was very innovative in its day and the design has stood the test of time.

CONSTRUCTION QUALITY: Considering that these boats have been sailed hard, it is a testament to their original construction that they have endured so well. The original construction was sophisticated.

USER-FRIENDLINESS: You need to be a skilled sailor and stay one step ahead of the boat to get the most out of sailing a ULDB.

SAFETY: Olson 30s often sail offshore, but the lack of comfort is fatiguing, which is a safety concern. The motion isn't very friendly in rough seas. The deck features secure handholds and aggressive nonskid, but I wouldn't want to put a lot of weight on the stanchions.

TYPICAL CONDITION: Like most race boats, Olson 30s show signs of wear and tear and much of the inventory must be upgraded. But because 30s were well built and cared for, Olson 30s are still viable used boats.

REFITTING: The changes to keep the boat competitive are well documented and not difficult to achieve, but finding original parts is a bit of a challenge.

SUPPORT: Pacific Boats is no longer in business, but the Olson 30 class association, www.olson30.org, is well organized.

AVAILABILITY: The demand for the Olson 30 has outstripped the supply. The West Coast is the best place to find used Olsons.

INVESTMENT AND RESALE: It can be costly owning an Olson 30 if you plan to race. But because the initial cost is so low, it's less painful with an Olson 30.

OVERALL 'SVG' RATING

the aluminum toerail, there is no comfortable place to sit when at the helm or on the rail. The primary winches were Barient 22s, but there is a good chance that these have been upgraded. A man-overboard pole tube in the stern is standard.

Maseda strongly recommends replacing the Schaefer headsail leads and the T-track with an adjustable ball bearing system. Remember, you need to be able to adjust everything from the windward side, which is made easier by the Olson's narrow beam. Maseda also notes that the trend among competitive Olsons is to make the foredeck person self-sufficient by leaving headsail and chute controls at the base of the mast. Most leads originally led back to the cockpit with the winch controls on the aft end of the doghouse.

The nonskid is aggressive and the standard boat came with double lifelines. Be careful to check the lifeline hardware; these were often loosened to allow the crew to sit farther outboard on the rail. The stanchion bases are set into molded deck sockets and not very well supported. The yoked backstay can use all the purchase you can give it. A Headfoil II came standard with later model boats. The tapered mast is a fairly beefy aluminum section. The standard standing rigging was Navtec rod.

Down below

"You can cruise the boat," Maseda admits with a wry laugh, "but any way you look at it, it is glorified camping." The headroom below is less than 5 feet. The arrangement includes a V-berth forward, with a Porta-Potti underneath. There is a tiny galley to port, usually with a nonpressurized alcohol stove and a small nondraining essentially useless sink. A nav station of sorts is opposite. Two quarter berths make good sea berths and there are small ice chests at the head of each bunk. There is not much storage in the boat. The wood and painted finishes are all designed to be hosed down after sailing—not a bad design concept. The furniture in the boat is all extremely well tabbed, which is more for structural support than for human comfort. Several Olsons have been sailed from California to Hawaii.

Engine

There is even less to say about auxiliary power since only a few 30s came from the factory with an inboard. A seven-horsepower, lightweight BMW diesel was offered as an option but few checked it on the purchase order. The Olson 30 is light enough to be pushed along adequately by a very small outboard. A six-horsepower is required to achieve a 6-knot minimum. Mounting the outboard on the 30's reverse transom is a bit of a challenge, and as a result, the bracket must be fairly low on the hull, making it difficult to reach the controls. It doesn't make any sense to leave the engine astern for racing and it's usually removed, schlepped below and placed on the cabin sole: another good reason for choosing a small, lightweight outboard. The only time you will really need an engine is for close maneuvering in congested marinas or for motoring back home on utterly calm days.

Underway

It takes a while to get used to the fast motion of an ultralight-displacement boat. The boat rides on top of the water, not in it. While "fast is fun" became the market slogan for ULDBs, "flat is fast" is the sailing mantra for the Olson 30. "You have to keep the boat on its lines," Maseda said, "even if it means flattening the jib and flogging the main upwind. Be ruthless about keeping the boat flat and you will be fast." The Olson 30 shines in light air, accelerating rapidly after tacks. But in moderate air, especially upwind, it is vital to put weight on the rail and shorten to a No. 2 headsail to keep the boat flat. Otherwise the boat makes a lot of leeway.

The Olson 30 comes to life when it turns the weather mark in heavy air. The boat planes in 20 knots and easily surfs in big seas. Speeds in excess of 20 knots are not uncommon. Maseda remembers an offshore race from San Francisco south to Los Angeles, screaming before the wind and routinely burying the speedo. "It takes tremendous concentration to keep the boat under the spinnaker," Maseda said. "About 30 minutes was all we could take at the helm. You have to remind yourself that you are in control of the stern, it is not in control of you." In fact, slowing down after a wild surfing ride requires skills that many heavy boat sailors don't have as you steer off waves and through troughs.

While the Olson can certainly sail to its PHRF rating, which ranges between 96 on the West Coast to 112 in Florida, one-design racing is the most fun. The class association keeps the rules simple and there are lively Olson 30 fleets on San Francisco Bay, in the Pacific Northwest and Lake Ontario.

Conclusion

With prices ranging from $10,000 to $20,000, the Olson 30 offers exhilarating sailing at truly affordable prices.

Cape Dory 30

This traditional cruiser inspires confidence with its forgiving nature

The Cape Dory 30 offers few surprises, and in a sailboat, especially a used boat, that's usually a good thing. Designed by the late Carl Alberg, the Cape Dory 30 is loaded with the enduring characteristics that marks all his designs.

In our age of flash and splash, when so many cruising boats are shamelessly promoted as "performance cruisers with luxury interiors," there is refreshing humility in Alberg's narrow, full-keel boats. The Cape Dory 30 is certainly not a performance cruiser, and it's anything but luxurious. It is a stout, capable cruiser that will stand up to the sea and handle well in a variety of conditions.

Andrew Vavolotis founded Cape Dory in 1963, setting up shop in East Taunton, Massachusetts. The company, which began by building a 10-foot dory, found its stride when it introduced the Alberg-designed Typhoon in 1969. More than 2,000 Typhoons were launched during a long production run. In many ways the winsome, 19-foot weekender set the agenda for most of the ensuing Cape Dory line.

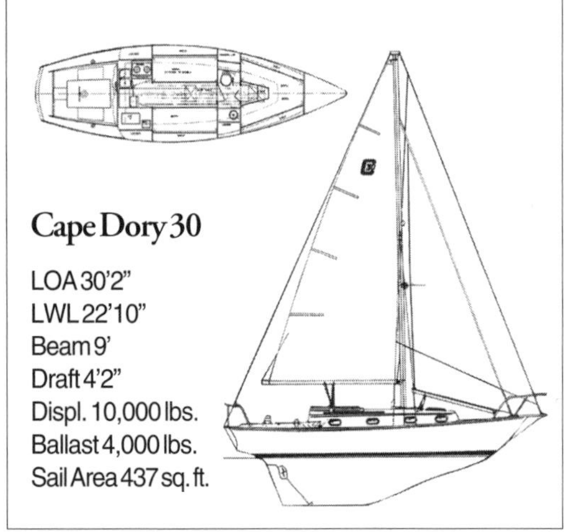

Like the Typhoon, most models were designed by Alberg and featured full keels with attached rudders, a cutaway forefoot, narrow beam and traditional styling and finish. In the early days, Cape Dory was primarily a small-boat builder. When the company launched the 30 in 1976, it was the queen of the fleet. Inspired by the 30's popularity (367 boats were ultimately built during a 10-year production run) Cape Dory went on to build larger boats, including a popular 36 and an ill-fated 45.

The 1980s were tough times for all sailboat builders and Cape Dory tried to stem the tide of red ink by adding a line of powerboats. It didn't work, and in 1991, Cape Dory folded.

Interestingly, the molds were scattered among different builders and several sailboat models are still available on a semicustom basis. Vavolotis ended up in Georgetown, Maine, where he runs Robinhood Marine. He builds a 36-, 40-, and 45-footer, all from the original Cape Dory molds. Nauset Marine on Cape Cod has the molds for the Typhoon weekender and Typhoon senior and will build boats on request. It also has the molds for the Cape Dory 30 MK II, although there are no plans for production. Check the Web site listed in the Value Guide for a complete list of other models available.

Cape Dory 30 Price Data

		Low	High
BUC Retail Range	1975	$21,100	$23,400
	1980	$25,700	$28,600
	1985	$38,500	$42,700
		State	**Asking**
Boats For Sale	1979	NY	$24,500
	1980	VA	$31,000
	1982	SC	$37,000

First impressions

"Traditional" is the word that springs to mind when you see a graceful Cape Dory 30, either under sail or tied to a dock. Yet, in some ways, Cape Dory's styling makes Alberg's design seem more traditional than it really is. If you took away the beefy bronze portlights and deck hardware, changed the salty ketch rig to a sloop, eliminated the short bowsprit and added a step to the coachroof, you would have a hard time telling the Cape Dory 30 from the Alberg 30, or even the old Pearson Triton. Now of course you could say those boats are traditional too, yet in their day, they were considered rather modern. I remember reading an early review of the Alberg 30 that questioned the length of the keel, as the reviewer thought it was dangerously short for offshore work.

Below the water Alberg's boats all look the same. The Cape Dory 30's full keel has the signature cutaway, and the attached constellation rudder slants forward, ensuring a bit of weather helm. The boat offered an appealing compromise to many sailors. A draft of just 4 feet, 2 inches kept thin-water areas viable. The long keel and 40-percent ballast-to-displacement ratio assured skittish sailors that the boat would be able to handle a blow. Also many sailors like the optional sailplans. About halfway through the 30's production life, the cutter rig replaced the ketch as standard. With either rig, the profile is pure Alberg—a handsome sheer accentuating the long overhangs, tapered ends and a low freeboard.

Construction

The Cape Dory 30 was solidly and conservatively built. The hull is solid glass and the deck is balsa-cored. Interestingly, the hull-and-deck joint is not through-bolted, at least not on uniform centers. Several owners that I spoke to noted this shortcoming and yet none mentioned any associated problems. A joint that is fiberglassed is likely to be just as strong as a bolted joint and is much less likely to leak. In fact, the prime reason hull-to-deck joints are bolted is to allow the interior to be assembled during production without having to work around the deck.

Cape Dory didn't skimp on fittings above or below the waterline. All the through-hull fittings are bronze seacocks and the bronze deck hardware, ranging from opening portlights to stout mooring cleats, is oversized. There is also a lot of teak on deck and below—a good supply of sandpaper will be vital.

Naturally the ballast is internal, encapsulated low in the keel cavity. The spars are deck-stepped and well-supported below. Just like internal or external ballast, there will always be an argument over whether deck- or keel-stepped spars are better in extreme conditions. Some claim that a keel-stepped spar might rip open the cabinhouse during a knockdown

Cape Dory 30

Sailing Magazine's Value Guide

PRICE: While the Cape Dory is more expensive than an Alberg 30, or an old Bristol 30, it is better finished and usually better fitted out.

DESIGN QUALITY: This rating really varies on personal preference. Alberg's designs have endured, and have been thoroughly tested. I suspect full-keel boats will still be built 100 years from now.

CONSTRUCTION QUALITY: Cape Dory built solid hulls and while some techniques may be questioned, the boats have held up well. The company used quality materials.

USER-FRIENDLINESS: This rating would be higher except for the rather uncomfortable cockpit, especially on the ketch model. Otherwise, the boat is easy to sail and looks after itself. The interior is small but comfortable.

SAFETY: The overall construction and hull design make the boat inherently safe. However, the lifelines are short and not well supported and the cockpit is shallow.

TYPICAL CONDITION: Most Cape Dory owners maintain their boats to a high level and the good original construction helps the boats hold up well.

REFITTING: The nature of the hull shape makes certain areas of the boat difficult to work on, particularly the engine.

SUPPORT: Although Cape Dory is out of business there are several active owner's groups. Also, several models are offered on a semicustom basis, so this provides another level of support. A good Web site can be found at www.toolworks.com/capedory.

AVAILABILITY: There were 367 30s built, which means there are always many boats on the market. Boats seem to be concentrated in the Northeast and Chesapeake. There is an active class in California as well.

INVESTMENT AND RESALE: Cape Dorys have held their value well over the years despite an expensive original price. Full-keel boats have gradually waned in popularity, but Cape Dory's reputation is secure.

OVERALL 'SVG' RATING

or a capsize, while a deck-stepped stick will just be carried away, leaving the boat intact. For what it's worth, the Contessa 32 in which I sailed around Cape Horn had a keel-stepped mast that survived a rollover. My mother's Jeanneau 37 sloop in which she sailed around the world also had a keel-stepped mast, and it survived two vicious knockdowns in the Indian Ocean.

What to look for

There were a couple of changes during production that buyers should be aware of. First, don't confuse the Cape Dory 30 with the later 30 MKII, which was introduced in 1986. Although similar, the Mark II was updated in-house (not by Alberg) and is more expensive. As earlier noted, around 1981 the standard rig changed from a ketch with a club-footed jib to a cutter with a club staysail. Most 30 owners, whether they have a ketch or cutter, abandoned the small headsail/sails, in favor of a large genoa. If there is one consistent complaint about the boat it is that it doesn't sail well in light air, especially the ketch. Some owners converted the cutter to a sloop by eliminating the staysail. A better idea is to set up the staysail with a babystay adjuster like the Wichard pelican.

During the first year of production, the standard engine was a single-cylinder 12-horsepower Yanmar. In 1977 Cape Dory switched to a two-cylinder Volvo rated at 13 horsepower. Either way, most owners report that the boat is underpowered. Tad McDonald, who sailed a 1982 model on Chesapeake Bay, told me that even with a three-bladed prop it was difficult to attain 5 knots in anything but flat seas. As a result, many boats have been repowered. While a boat with a larger engine is preferred, be sure to check the installation carefully. Late in the production run, Cape Dory switched to a larger Universal diesel.

Few reports of construction problems have been reported, although early boats had an odd tank arrangement. There were two original tanks and one was plumbed to the galley sink and the other to the head sink, without any way to join them. On some early boats you had to fill the tanks from below.

On deck

The Cape Dory 30 ketch featured Edson worm-gear steering with a small raked wheel. The cutter allowed the option of tiller steering. Most boats seem to have the worm-gear arrangement, which is nearly bulletproof and eliminates the need for a pedestal. However, the mizzen mast forces the helmsperson to either sit prone on the steering box, or awkwardly next to the wheel. Also, there is little feel with worm-gear steering. Given the choice, I'd opt for the cutter rig and tiller steering.

The cockpit is shallow and not quite comfortable with teak coaming boards that hit you in the small of the back. There is a bridgedeck, with a small cutout that makes climbing in and out of the companionway easier. The mainsheet traveler spans the companionway, keeping the cockpit clear, but the midboom sheeting isn't very efficient.

The main spar on the ketch rig has an air draft of 38 feet, 6 inches while the cutter model is two feet taller. The mast section is beefy and well supported. Naturally the ketch's mast is stepped farther forward. The original ketch sailplan included a club-footed working jib that made an undercanvassed boat even slower. Even many cutter owners who have converted the boat to a sloop have often set up the boat with a roller furled genoa. The headsail leads are not very tight and windward sailing is not the 30's strongest suit. Like almost all the hardware, the chainplates are bronze and give the appearance of being corroded when in fact they just need to be cleaned up.

Down below

The short waterline on older designs becomes immediately apparent when you drop below. The Cape Dory 30 loses nearly 25-percent of its LOA to overhangs, leaving limited interior volume to work with. Former owners Tad McDonald and Peter Wolf both note that the lack of space below was the major reason for moving up to larger boats.

Alberg's interior arrangements are fairly predictable and functional. The 30 is no exception. There is a V-berth cabin forward with drawers and lockers below. There are also opening portlights on most boats and a decent-sized overhead hatch. The head compartment is just aft, with the toilet to starboard and the sink opposite. This is a much better arrangement than trying to squeeze the head into one side or the other. Most owners have added pressure water by this point and there is a grate for a shower. However, both the head sink and shower originally drained into the bilge, which of course needs to be remedied if it hasn't already.

The saloon has opposite settees with small shelves above and limited storage. Thirty-gallon water tanks are located beneath each settee. A centerline table opens up to seat four. The finish is all in teak and characteristically dark. However the joinerwork is tastefully done without a lot of fanfare.

The galley occupies the aft end of the cabin with a two-burner stove to port and the icebox and nav station is to starboard. It was common for boats of this era to use the top of the icebox as the chart table, an arrangement I have never liked. The two sinks are aft of the stove and a bit difficult to reach. There are fiddles and handholds throughout.

Engine

Alberg always struggled with squeezing inboard engines into his small boats because of the narrow beam and slack bilges. The Cape Dory 30 originally came with a 12-horsepower Yanmar but that was quickly changed to a 13-horsepower Volvo. Both engines are too small for a 10,000-pound-plus boat. Worse still, the engine is mounted quite far aft, literally under the cockpit, necessitating the need for a V-drive transmission, which complicates maintenance. Engine access is tight at best. Late in production a 21-horsepower Universal diesel was offered. Fuel capacity is 20 gallons, which because all three engines are stingy with fuel, provides a cruising range of around 200 miles.

Underway

Few dispute that no matter what original sailplan, the Cape Dory 30 needs help when the wind is less than 10 knots. Wolf, who owned a 30 for 10 years, said that performance really improved when he stripped the bottom, added a spinnaker and, most importantly, converted his cutter to a sloop. McDonald kept the staysail but changed the high-cut yankee for a 140-

percent roller-furling jib. McDonald gradually furls the headsail as the wind increases, and notes that with 25 to 30 knots, the boat is well balanced and behaves nicely with a single reef in the main and the staysail.

There is a bit of weather helm, a function more of the hull shape than anything else. The boat also tends to heel easily initially, before hardening up. Both the cutter and ketch rigs are easy to balance and take nicely to self-steering. The cutter points a bit higher and, with less weight aloft, is a bit stiffer. However, one great advantage of a ketch is the option to drop the main and sail jib and jigger in a blow. This is also a very efficient rig to heave-to with. The motion through the water is very comfortable, with little tendency to pound. However, choppy conditions can set up a pitching or hobbyhorsing motion.

Conclusion

The Cape Dory 30 continues to have a strong following and is a genuine coastal cruiser. The boat inspires confidence and is forgiving by design. With prices ranging from the low $20,000s for an old boat that needs TLC, to around $40,000 for a top-of-the-line late model, this is a perfect boat to test your cruising dreams.

Nonsuch 30

Cat-rigged cruiser with a devoted following

It was an idea that only a couple of sailors could conjure, and most likely it was first sketched on a cocktail napkin in someplace dark and smoky. Eavesdropping, the conversation might have gone like this: "Let's build a new boat, you know, something completely different. Let's combine a traditional Cape Cod catboat look with a modern underbody, state-of-the-art cored construction and an unconventional rig. And, for good measure, we'll add a great interior, make it incredibly easy to sail and give it a really strange name." The result was the Nonsuch line of sailboats built by Hinterhoeller Yachts in Ontario, Canada. Be honest, would you have predicted a long shelf life for a fleet of modern-day catboats with unusual rigs? Not many people did when the first Nonsuch 30 was launched in Lake Erie in 1978. Yet the quirky, commodious, easy-to-handle Nonsuch touched a nerve and became one of the industry's surprise success stories of the 1980s. More than 1,000 were built, including 522 30s, before production ground to a stop in the early 1990s.

Nonsuch 30

LOA 30'4"
LWL 28'9"
Beam 11'10"
Draft 4'11½"
or 3'11½"
Displacement 11,500 lbs.
Sail Area 540 sq. ft.

The Nonsuch 30 was the brainchild of Gordon Fisher, one of Canada's leading racing yachtsmen. Fisher was ready to change course and wanted a boat for family cruising that was simple to sail. He took his ideas to Mark Ellis, a versatile naval architect not bound by convention. "Gordon admired the Lundstrom rig from the early 1930s. With a free-standing mast and no boom, this rig was perfect for singlehandling," Ellis said. Ellis and Fisher eventually modified the rig by adding a windsurfer-style wishbone boom for better sail control.

Ellis and Fisher took their drawings to George Hinterhoeller's shop in St. Catherine's, and the German-born boatbuilder was, to put it mildly, unimpressed. He didn't like the look of New England catboats and was well aware of the biceps-building weather helm that is an unfortunate catboat feature. Ellis and Fisher convinced Hinterhoeller that with a fin keel, spade rudder and symmetrical balanced hull shape, their catboat would be a different animal. They were right.

Nonsuch, the name they chose, was the original flagship of the once mighty Hudson's Bay Company.

First impressions

The Nonsuch 30 takes some getting used to, at least from an aesthetic point of view. The unique rig overshadows the soft, springy catboat lines, with their wide beam, large cockpit and rounded trunkhouse. The tapered aluminum spar seems massive and set too far forward, and the unfamiliar wishbone looks more intimidating than a conventional boom. These misgivings, however, are quickly allayed after your first sail when you discover the Nonsuch 30's turn of speed. The 30-foot, 4-inch Nonsuch has a plumb bow and a wide, flat stern that results in a 28-foot, 9-inch

Nonsuch 30 Price Data

		Low	High
BUC Retail Range	1980	$30,800	$34,200
	1983	$44,700	$49,600
	1987	$60,100	$66,100

		State	Asking
Boats For Sale	1980	NY	$45,000
	1984	MD	$55,000
	1987	FL	$57,000

LWL. Combine this with 540-square-feet of sail area, moderate displacement and shapely proportions below the water, and you have a recipe for lively sailing. In fact, out of the water it's a bit surprising to see a catboat with a turn of the bilge that looks more like a Finn. Back in the water, however, it doesn't take much of an adjustment to realize that tacking consists of simply turning the wheel.

Construction

The Nonsuch 30 has a balsa-cored hull and deck. This building technique may remind you of another Canadian boatbuilder of the period, C&C. This comes as no surprise since Hinterhoeller was the president of C&C before launching his own company. I am no fan of cored hulls, especially in cruising boats, but I understand the necessity of keeping the Nonsuch 30 hull light. The wide beam and subsequent structural support needed for a free-standing spar seems a natural for a long keel, heavy-displacement boat. But that, of course, would spoil the good performance. If I had to pick a used boat with a cored hull, I'd choose one built by Hinterhoeller. The hull is solid fiberglass around the through-hulls. The fin keel is externally fashioned to a small stub with stainless bolts.

The deck is also balsa cored and it is not uncommon to find stress cracks around the deckhouse and along the cockpit seat backs. There are no chainplates, obviously, and the forward section of the hull is beefy to support the spar. The aluminum maststep is on the keel, and there is also a turnbuckle tie down. A stout aluminum casting, with 12 wedge channels, is deployed at the partners, typical of the overall high quality of construction.

What to look for

The Nonsuch 30 has proven to be a good investment for most owners and the reason is simple: the boat has held up quite well over the years. The common problems that exist are, for the most part, minor and an active owner's association provides information and support. Bill Spencer, who is on the owner's association board, sails hull No. 352, a 1986-vintage 30 called *Lion Heart* out of Hyde Park, New York. Spencer suggests that prospective buyers, especially of older boats, carefully inspect turning blocks, cheek blocks and halyard sheaves, as the early Garhauer blocks did not have ball bearings. Garhauer's new blocks are well-engineered and affordable. Spencer also notes that the rudder bearing occasionally leaks, but can usually be stopped up with a simple adjustment. The rudder quadrant stops are sharp and exposed and have been known to cut into the exhaust line if the rudder drops slightly. Both of these problems are caused when the bearing retaining bolt works loose.

Early boats were fitted with gate valves on through-hull fittings, including those below the waterline, but these have likely been changed to ball valves or seacocks. The original aluminum water and holding tanks are prone to pitting and may need to be replaced. As Spencer says, "a leaking water tank is an irritation, a leaking holding tank is a problem." There are apparently no off-the-shelf tanks that can be retrofitted simply, but the owner's association is organizing an effort to produce replacement tanks. While researching the market for a Nonsuch 30, I found that somewhere around hull No. 120, the original Volvo MD 11 diesel with a saildrive unit was replaced with a 27-horsepower straight shaft Westerbeke.

On deck

I once asked a Nonsuch owner if he ever stopped reaching for the shrouds as he moved about the deck. A former owner of a Valiant 47, he laughed and said, "I've

Nonsuch 30

Sailing Magazine's Value Guide

PRICE: With used prices reaching the mid 60s, the Nonsuch 30 is relatively expensive. But it is not accurate to compare this to other 30-footers.

DESIGN QUALITY: MarkEllis made an original statement by merging old ideas with new ones. You either become a Nonsuch convert or you don't; there is little room for indifference.

CONSTRUCTION QUALITY: Hinterhoeller Yachts did an excellent job of building these boats. These are boats that have stood the test of time. I'm still not crazy about balsa cored hulls.

USER-FRIENDLINESS: The basic premise of the Nonsuch 30 was to make it user-friendly.From simple sailing to comfortable and functional interior space, the boat is appealing to sailors and nonsailors alike.

SAFETY: There are some safety concerns, especially for heavy weather offshore. There is no bridgedeck, and lack of standing rigging makes clawing forward on deck less secure. The mainsheet can also entangle the helmsman.

TYPICAL CONDITION: Most owners seem to take good care of their boats. There are many Nonsuch 30s on the Great Lakes, where a short season and sweet water combine for less wear and tear.

REFITTING: The Nonsuch 30 is an easy boat to work on, and the systems appear to be well-thought-out. Nonsuch is out of business, but the boats are still being built on a custom basis. Parts are widely available.

SUPPORT: The Nonsuch Owner's Association is one of the largest non-manufacturer supported groups in existence. It publishes a quarterly newsletter and has a great Web page. Reach them at www.nonsuch.org.

AVAILABILITY: With more than 500 boats afloat, there is always a good selection. They don't linger on the market, however. The best selection seems to be on the Great Lakes and in the Northeast.

INVESTMENT AND RESALE: The Nonsuch 30 is comparatively expensive, yet it holds its value extremely well.

OVERALL 'SVG' RATING

had the boat five years and I still reach for them." The absence of standing rigging certainly makes the side decks easy to navigate.

When looking at used Nonsuches, try to find one with both the optional bowsprit/anchor platform and bow pulpit. The mooring cleats and chocks are stout and the stanchions and double lines are well-supported. The nonskid seems to hold up well, although a friend's boat on Lake Texoma had quite a bit of gelcoat crazing.

The Nonsuch 30 has a huge cockpit, and the few sail controls are led aft. Unfortunately the cockpit is not particularly comfortable, at least not without cushions, as the seat back angles are acute. You need to be tall to see well from the helm, and there is no bridgedeck to speak of. There are large lockers port and starboard, and a lazarette propane locker. The mainsheet arrangement, which uses a centerline double block on the aft coaming, is good at knocking off the helmsman's hat.

Down below

The long waterline, high freeboard and wide beam carried well forward and aft, translate into a voluminous interior. Stepping below it is hard to believe you are on a 30-foot boat. The original interior arrangement, coined the "classic," is quite functional. Ellis did away with the V-berth forward. Instead, he devoted the bow area to storage, with two hanging lockers and several smaller storage bins. The rest of the interior is wide open. Next aft is the saloon, which has opposite settees with a centerline table. The interior is the dark teak popular in the 1980s, but the joinerwork is well done. Ventilation is excellent with several opening portlights, two overhead hatches and a couple of Dorades.

Continuing aft, the L-shaped galley is to port. The single sink is nearly on the centerline, which is good for drainage. A two-burner propane stove was standard. The icebox is well-insulated, especially for a boat built in northern climes. Opposite the galley is the head, and anyone prone to seasickness will appreciate its amidships location. Two aft quarter berths complete the arrangement. The starboard side is considered a double with a single to port. A measure of privacy can be had by a folding door that sections off the saloon from the rest of the boat. Later in the production, the "ultra" interior plan was offered, featuring an offset double forward, followed by the head and galley with the saloon aft.

Engine

With either engine, the Volvo or the Westerbeke, maneuvering the Nonsuch 30 under power can be tricky. There is a lot of freeboard, and with the mast so far forward, the bow tends to blow off. Spencer suggests adding a Max Prop, or another brand of feathering propeller to add control, especially in reverse. While my saildrive biases are fading, I would still choose the Westerbeke straight-shaft for its dependability, although as long as you periodically check the lower unit seal, a saildrive eliminates the hassle of the stuffing box. Thirty gallons of fuel provide a realistic motoring range of about 200 miles.

Underway

The Nonsuch 30 is a delight to sail. I first sailed the boat on Lake Texoma and later off Ft. Lauderdale. Several years ago, I delivered a 30 from St. Martin in the Dutch Antilles to Marsh Harbor in the Bahamas, an 800-mile off-the-wind romp that convinced me that with a few modifications, the Nonsuch 30 would be a surprisingly capable offshore boat.

If Nonsuches took over the world, sailing schools would be obsolete. Once the sail is hoisted, tacking consists of turning the wheel, with the boat tacking cleanly through about 85 degrees. Jibing can be a lot more interesting, especially if it is breezy.

The few sail controls—namely the halyard, the reefing lines and the choker line—are led aft. The choker gives a measure of sail shape control by trimming the wishbone like a clew outhaul. Tightening the choker pulls the wishbone aft, which flattens the sail. Easing the choker lets the wishbone slide forward, putting a bit more draft in the sail. Slab reefing is the order of the day, and the permanently mounted lazy jacks gather up the sail beneath the wishbone.

The Nonsuch 30 carries plenty of sail to move smartly in light air, but it is also a fairly stiff boat in a blow. The tapered spar tends to spill air, even when reefed, and this helps keep the boat on its feet. The bane of most catboats is weather helm, but Ellis and Fisher were right, the modern underbody really helps. Even in a stiff breeze the Nonsuch 30 isn't too bad, and with a little coaxing, the helm balances nicely.

One great advantage of owning a Nonsuch is that you don't need much of a sail inventory.

Conclusion

Although the Nonsuch 30 is no longer available as a production boat, the boat remains popular and rarely lingers on the used boat market. When you add up the pluses—simple to sail, a nice turn of speed, spacious interior, quality construction, active owner's association—you can see why.

Pearson 30

Well-built all-around sailboat that offers a lot of fun for the dollar

The Pearson 30 is a textbook example of a 1970's production boat. Moderate in proportion, there is certainly nothing offensive about the boat, yet there is little that stirs you either. It was designed by Pearson's then in-house designer and future president Bill Shaw, and nearly 1,200 boats were built during an incredibly successful 10-year production run that ended in 1981.

In the original brochure the boat was touted as a capable coastal cruiser that was easy to handle for impromptu family outings. It was also said to be lively enough for spirited yacht club racing. With today's boats tending to fall into more specialized categories, it's easy to fault the basic premise of the Pearson 30. It was conceived as a racer-cruiser or cruiser-racer, depending upon how you wanted to look at it. Like most boats of the times, the P30 was meant to be nearly all things to all sailors. However, considering the way most of us sail, there really is nothing wrong with an all-around boat, especially for new sailors.

In many ways the Pearson 30, which replaced the long-keeled Wanderer, continued the decisive course change away from the company's more traditional designs of the early and mid-1960s. The Wanderer, Triton, Vanguard and Alberg 35 were all cutaway full-keel cruisers, while the P30 and her popular sistership, the Pearson 26, had swept-back fin keels and spade rudders.

What was more of a departure from the earlier boats was the actual shape of the hull. While the Carl Alberg-designed long-keel boats had typical slack bilges, short waterlines and often sluggish performance, the P30 had more of a dinghy-shaped underbody. There is no denying that the P30 is a bit tender, but it is also easily driven in light to moderate breezes and well balanced on most points of sail.

Don't confuse the Shaw-designed 30 with the Wanderer, which was mothballed in 1970, or the one-design PearsonFlyer. All three boats are sometimes called Pearson 30s.

Pearson 30

LOA 29'10"
LWL 25'
Beam 9'6"
Draft 5'
Displ. 8,320 lbs.
Ballast 3,560 lbs.

First impressions

I began sailing around the same time the Pearson 30 came into existence. I remember the fleet that formed quickly on Lake St. Clair and was always disappointed when a P30 from the North Star Sail Club outfooted our Sabre 28. When sailed well, the P30 was a successful racer. In fact, a P30 won the 3/4-ton North American Championships in 1972.

In many ways the Pearson 30 looks like the Sabre and the boats were occasionally confused. The sheerline is nicely drawn, with a swoop aft and a handsome rake to the bow. The cabintrunk was built a bit boxy in order to achieve 6-foot headroom without a deep bilge. But then the boat's decent headroom was one of the key reasons for the boat's enduring popularity.

The P30 displaces 8,320 pounds and carries 3,560 pounds of lead for a ballast-to-displacement ratio of 43 percent. The air draft is 42 feet, 3 inches above the waterline and total working sail area is 444 square feet. The numbers reveal the moderation of the

Pearson 30 Price Data

		Low	High
BUC Retail Range	1972	$11,300	$12,900
	1975	$13,100	$14,800
	1978	$15,400	$17,500

		State	Asking
Boats For Sale	1971	IL	$ 9,999
	1976	MO	$15,900
	1978	NY	$13,500

design. The displacement-to-length ratio is 238 while the sail area-to-displacement ratio is 17.3 making it a prototypical racer-cruiser. The 5-foot draft is on the deep side. But of course those were the days when the Great Lakes still had water. Deep draft has never been a problem in the Northeast, the other area where the boat was widely sailed.

Construction

The hull is classic Pearson construction, solid and conservative. Pearson resisted the temptation of cored hulls and stuck with hand-laid-up laminates, alternating plies of 1 1/2-ounce mat and 18-ounce woven roving. The hull thickness tapers from around a quarter inch at the deck edge to more than a half inch at the turn of the bilge. The deck is a fiberglass-and-balsa sandwich. The deck is actually fiberglassed to the hull on a rather narrow external flange and further reinforced with stainless steel self-tapping screws every four inches. The flange, which is vulnerable to docking miscues and wayward pilings, is covered by a vinyl rubrail.

The Pearson 30 made use of molded liners, including a floor pan and a headliner, which in this case provide good structural support, but as always, limit access to the hull. An oak compression post supports the deck-stepped mast, although the boat I examined in Ft. Lauderdale had retrofitted an aluminum section. The keel has internal ballast, meaning the lead is encapsulated in a molded cavity that is part of the original mold and then covered over with a resin slurry.

The debate over internal or external ballast continues unresolved. But in an older boat I see some advantages to internal ballast, since it is fairly easy to inspect a hull for any damage while it is difficult to assess the condition of old, metal keel bolts.

What to look for

Owners report a few recurring problems that prospective buyers should be aware of. Foremost is the condition of the rudder stock and bearings. The original stock was aluminum, which was completely inadequate, and Pearson recalled the first couple hundred P30s and replaced the stock with stainless steel. The stock is supported by two bearings that tend to wear excessively and need frequent replacement. Also, the fitting for the tiller end frequently develops excessive play and needs to be shimmed. Many P30s have been retrofitted with wheel systems, so be sure to check the installation carefully. Also check the condition of the rudder blade.

Pearsons are not immune to osmotic blisters and you should be sure to find out if and when a blister job was done. The P30 was one of the few fiberglass boats I have ever seen "written off" because the laminate was so wet that the surveyor felt the cost of repairs exceeded the market value of the boat. It was an extreme case and I should note that nearly every Pearson 30 ever built is still sailing. If there is a problem with the laminate, it is more likely to occur in the balsa-cored deck.

Other items to look for include signs of a leaking hull-and-deck joint and leaks around the chainplates that can cause delamination in the bulkheads. Also, be sure to check the through-hull fittings. Early boats had gate valves below the water, and even if the boat is fitted with seacocks, you should probably replace them if they are more than 15 years old. Also, check the compression post for signs of rot. As with any older boat, carefully check the swage fittings on the standing rigging.

Most boats were originally fitted with Atomic 4 gas engines. While these venerable engines have given good service over the years, several owners report problems with the exhaust manifold. Many boats have also been retrofitted with small diesels, so be on the lookout for sloppy owner-installed engines.

On deck

The Pearson 30 has a large, fairly comfortable cockpit, although the sweep of the long tiller limits space when under way. I'm not normally a fan of retrofitting wheel steering on boats this size, but I admit that a wheel and small pedestal certainly opens up the cockpit. Of course, when dockside or at anchor, the tiller can be tied back out of the way. Tillers and wheels have advantages and disadvantages even on Pearson 30s. There is an enormous cockpit locker to starboard and a lazarette aft. Unfortunately, the engine exhaust hose runs through the lazarette taking up valuable space.

A mainsheet traveler was an option on early boats, but it is almost a necessity for effective sail trim, as the large main is an integral part of the drive system. Also, the original sheet winches are a bit undersized if you plan to do more than cruise or daysail.

It is always interesting to see what 20 to 25 years have wrought in owner innovations. Some owners have followed the trends by routing halyards and sail controls aft and fitting headsail and occasionally even mainsail furling systems. Others have left things in near-original condition. My inclination is to choose a boat in original condition and then make only the changes I want.

It is likely that you will find some alternative to the original stemhead fitting, which was inadequate for anchoring and anchor stowage. The side decks are rather narrow, and the shrouds are usually passed by stepping on the trunkhouse. The molded nonskid will likely have lost its edge, either by new coats of paint or wear. The stanchions have adequately supported bases but could be taller. Late in the production run, double lifelines became standard.

Down below

The interior is surprisingly spacious for a boat of this vintage. The bulkheads came standard with teak veneer, and painting them white with just teak trim really brightens the cabin. The layout is predictable, but the space has been well used. The V-berth forward has both the water tank and decent storage space underneath, with shelving along side. The head compartment is athwartships with the toilet to port and a small wash basin and locker opposite.

The saloon has a lot of storage, although it isn't always convenient to reach under the settees to retrieve items. The table folds up against the bulkhead enhancing the elbow room below but still leaving the option of a sit-down dinner and a place to navigate. The galley is to starboard and quite functional, although retrofitting a propane stove with an oven takes a bit of work. Also, the original insulation in the fridge is not good enough for tropic-bound boats. A large quarter berth is to port.

Engine

The Atomic 4 pushes the boat along smartly according to several owners, and aside from a common exhaust problem, is quite reliable. A 10-horsepower Farymann diesel was an option beginning in 1975, followed by the 10-horsepower Westerbeke in 1976. In 1978 a Universal 11-horsepower diesel was offered and it became standard during the last two years of production. One note about handling the boat under power—be careful when in reverse. The swept-back rudder is forward facing in reverse and easily swings hard over, sending the tiller flying in the process. It takes a strong arm to handle it when in reverse.

Engine access is behind the companionway steps and as one owner put it, "a high-degree of flexibility is required just for routine maintenance. You need to be a monkey to really work on the thing." Just to check the oil of the Atomic 4 requires that you reach behind the engine and find the dipstick by feel. The hard part is replacing it, especially if the engine is hot. The 22-gallon fuel tank is located behind the engine, and like the stuffing box, is accessed from the large cockpit locker.

Underway

Tad Sheldon and Rick Leeds sail their P30s on San Francisco Bay. Sheldon notes that his 1978 boat is easy to handle, and "turns on a dime." But he said that the boat is tender and "buries her rails on a breezy day." Sheldon noted that the primary sheet winches are behind the helmsman, crowding the cockpit a bit.

Leeds is the original owner of his 1978 model. He also commented on the boat's initial tenderness, but

Pearson 30

Sailing Magazine's Value Guide

PRICE: The Pearson 30 is one of the few diesel-powered, good-quality coastal cruisers that can be purchased for under $15,000.

DESIGN QUALITY: There is nothing spectacular about this Shaw design, but like many Pearsons, it has stood the test of time.

CONSTRUCTION QUALITY: Pearson had a well-earned reputation for building quality boats, especially for a production builder. Some hulls blistered, a common problem with boats of the era.

USER-FRIENDLINESS: The P30 is easy to handle, with a surprisingly spacious interior. Handling in reverse takes a bit of getting used to, and you need to shorten sail early.

SAFETY: The P30 is well built but the decks are narrow and the nonskid worn. The lifelines and stanchions could be taller. There are well-placed handholds below and the cockpit has coamings and a stout bridgedeck.

TYPICAL CONDITION: Considering the age of the boats and the toll multiple ownerships can take, the condition of many boats on the market is impressive. Still, time takes its toll on all production boats.

REFITTING: The Pearson is not a particularly easy boat to retrofit. The molded liners limit access and some working conditions are in tight spaces.

SUPPORT: Although Pearson has been out of business for quite a few years, the owner's association is almost like having the company active. You can reach the group at www.Pearsoncurrent.com. *The Current,* the group's newsletter is an excellent source of information.

AVAILABILITY: There are P30s for sale all over the country, especially in the Chesapeake, theGreat Lakes and the Northeast.

INVESTMENT AND RESALE: The Pearson 30 has held its value well over its long life and will likely not sell for much less than current prices, with an active market for the boat.

OVERALL 'SVG' RATING

claims that with a bit of reduced sail, the P30 handles a stiff blow without much trouble. Leeds improved the performance of the working jib by extending the jib tracks forward. He also added a rigid vang and has beefed up his sail inventory by purchasing used sails, including a 150-percent genoa from a Ranger 29. Leeds has owned and enjoyed his *Grand Jete* for 22 years. That says a lot about a boat.

The P30 comes through the wind easily and accelerates quickly. It attains hull speed of 6.5 knots without much fuss. The boat is in its element in breezes under 15 knots. Mark Jones, who sails his 1975 P30 in Biscayne Bay, reefs the main when the wind is near 20 knots. He also claims that it is a mistake to carry a large genoa. "The boat has a good-size main and a 120-percent genoa is all you need," he said. "Get a cruising chute for downwind work."

Conclusion

The Pearson 30 is a well-built all around sailboat that offers a lot of fun per dollar. With prices ranging from $10,000 to $20,000, there is no excuse for not being on the water.

Gemini 3000

Comfortable coastal cruising multihull that's user-friendly

In some ways, it seems like the phenomenon of cruising catamarans emerged out of thin air. Beamy, bulbous and full of double staterooms, they suddenly snapped up entire docks and generated the longest queues at fall boat shows. After years of occupying the fringes of the sailboat market, multihulls and the people who sail them changed like a capricious summer wind. Multihull sailors were no longer California hippies in home-built plywood boats. Suddenly they were software designers in $500,000 floating palaces, vying for the heads of T-docks everywhere.

This, like most stereotypes, is not quite right. Cruising catamarans have evolved slowly, gaining popularity in Europe long before establishing a beachhead on this side of the Atlantic. Nobody has done more to bring catamarans into the American sailboat mainstream than Tony Smith. Performance Cruising, Inc., his Annapolis-based company, has been building innovative, affordable cats for almost 20 years. Revered by his many clients, the British-born Smith introduced the first American-made production cruising cat, the Gemini 31, in 1981. The

successes of Smith, a research engineer, have been hard won.

"I was the cruising-cat pioneer in this country," he confesses with a wry laugh, "and the times have just caught up with me." He built 28 Gemini 31s, which led to what became one of the most successful multihull productions ever, the Gemini 3000. Around 250 Gemini 3000s were built between 1983 and 1990, when the 3000 was replaced by the Gemini 3200.

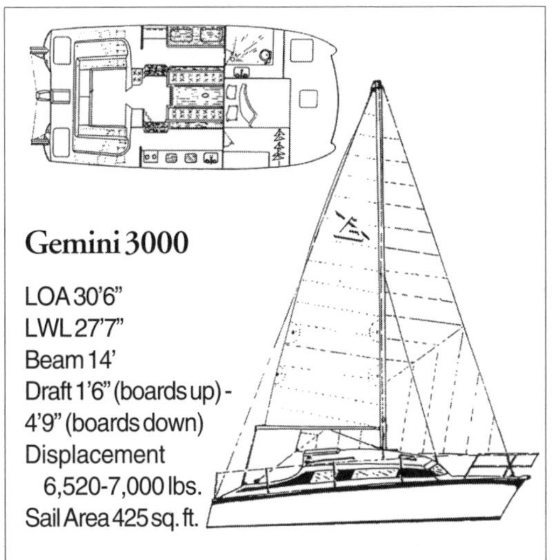

First impressions

Unlike other small cruising cats, the Gemini is not excessively beamy. Compared to most cruising monohulls of the same length, the 3000 offers excellent performance, especially off the wind.

However, you quickly realize that the Gemini was designed more for cruising comfort and ease of handling than high-performance sailing. The

Gemini 3000 Price Data

		Low	High
BUC Retail Range	1985	$32,700	$36,400
	1987	$37,900	$42,100
	1989	$44,200	$49,100

		State	Asking
Boats For Sale	1984	FL	$39,500
	1988	MD	$45,000
	1988	MD	$49,900

bridgedeck forward is solid, adding a bit of weight and windage but offering a wide, secure foredeck platform. A swept-back hard dodger, often tied to an expansive bimini top, encloses the huge cockpit. The companionway is more akin to a patio door than a hatch. Large portlights, which are neatly blended into the trunkhouse by a stylish deck stripe, flood the interior with light.

Each hull is proportionately wide, nearly $3^{1}/_{2}$ feet, which gives the 3000 a higher load capacity than other cats of similar size. Unlike most cruising cats, the Gemini 3000 features centerboards instead of fixed keels in each hull, which, to maintain modest draft, tend to be stubby and low-aspect. The centerboards serve two functions that account for much of the 3000's popularity. First, unlike many of its competitors, the 3000 tracks well to windward when one or both boards are deployed. Second, with the boards up and a draft of less than 2 feet, the 3000 can nose its way into all but the thinnest waters.

Construction

The Gemini 3000 hulls are solid fiberglass and laid up in a large, one-piece mold. The deck is also a one-piece mold, with all flat sections balsa-cored. The hulls are married on a flange and through-bolted. The layups are not heavy, but a vital factor in catamaran performance and seaworthiness is to keep the boat relatively light. Although a few Gemini 3000s have crossed oceans, the boat, for the most part, is a coastal cruiser and has been constructed accordingly. You will feel a bit of flex as you make your way around the deck, but this does not necessarily reflect a lack of strength in the laminate. Remember: Fiberglass is a flexible material. This does, however, make maintaining a craze-free gelcoat difficult. Many older 3000s on the used boat market have crazes and spider cracks in the gelcoat. A boat that has flexed beyond the capacity of the gelcoat to cope will be covered with stress cracks and should be checked for subdeck delamination.

The centerboard trunk is molded into the hull and the boards are high-grade marine plywood. A simple line-and-block system operated from below controls the centerboards, which are designed to kick up in unexpected shallows. The rudders are wooden blades encased in stainless steel cages. The deck-stepped mast is supported by a compression post that in turn is supported by a metal thwart that spans the hulls. The large portlights are Plexiglas.

What to look for

A big allure of the Gemini 3000 is the overall simplicity of the boat. There are few complicated systems and most owners are content to keep it that way. "Simplicity attracted me to the boat," says hull No. 252 owner John Munzel. "The aft hatches slide up and down and are secured with a peg. I like that. I can fix a peg." But while most owners, like Munzel, are unabashedly pleased with their boats, when pressed they will reveal a few common problems to watch for when considering a used Gemini 3000.

The Plexiglas portlights are prone to leaking and crazing. If they haven't been replaced, they will probably need to be at some point. Plexiglas was changed to Lexan in the later models. Smith advises prospective buyers to inspect the stainless steel cages on the rudders. "We know now that stainless is not immune to corrosion." John Sykes, who has probably sold more Gemini 3000s than any other dealer in the country, suggests that buyers carefully check the steering systems. The rudders are driven by simple teleflex cables that corrode over time. Gelcoat crazing and occasional stress cracks can also show up on deck. A common problem, but one by no means unique to Geminis, is the fabric headliner, which can get droopy and eventually fall down.

Most Gemini 3000s are at least 10 years old and some are approaching 20. Be sure to check all age-related ailments, including the standing rigging, condition of sails and if the boat ever had osmotic blisters.

On deck

The wheel is mounted on the starboard bulkhead and appears marginal. To see forward, the helmsman must peer through the portlights or around the side of the trunkhouse. This isn't a problem when at sea but I imagine close-quarters maneuvering takes some getting used to. The sail controls are logically placed with the mainsheet traveler aft and the sheet winches on the coaming. The genoa tracks are outboard, making it difficult to attain tight sheeting angles upwind. Placing the inboard tracks on the coachroof was another improvement on later Gemini models. Few Gemini owners have opted to lead all control lines aft—probably because working the foredeck is a pleasure on this boat. There are large lockers under the aft cockpit seats, including the propane locker.

The side decks are quite narrow and it's a squeeze going forward from the cockpit. Once there, however, there is plenty of room to work and lounge. The solid bridgedeck may not be as sporty as trampolines, but it is certainly more practical on a small cruising cat. The deck hardware, including cleats and leads, is too light, especially the anchor roller and the lead to the chain locker. This is not a good place to pare weight. Beefing up the anchoring system would be money well spent. There is a good-sized lazarette on the port bow.

Down below

The interior of the 3000 is amazingly spacious and, more importantly, well-thought-out, which is not always the case with cruising cats.

The Gemini 3000 offers a forward centerline owner's cabin with a legitimate queen-sized bunk and a great view. "When I want to check the anchor at night," Munzel says, "I just lean forward and look around. Then I lie down and go back to sleep."

The in-line galley occupies the starboard hull, which has a huge storage and hanging locker all the way forward. The long nav station and large forward head with shower reside in the port hull. There are two almost-double cabins in the aft sections of each hull, which makes the Gemini 3000 perfect for a family with two children.

As you step into the saloon there is full headroom, which then tapers at the dinette. The small electrical panel is immediately to port, with a double battery box below. Opposite is a three-way, household-style fridge that runs on propane, 12 volts or 110 volts when dockside. The finish work, featuring teak trim, is simple and friendly. In addition to the saloon's bright and airy feeling, fore and aft ventilation is good. Some owners have added side-opening portlights by mounting them into the larger Plexiglas ports. While this certainly helps generate a cross breeze below, I question the structural ramifications. Plexiglas isn't all that strong to begin with and cutting large holes in it won't make it any stronger.

Engine

Although some Gemini 3000s were offered with optional inboard diesels, few buyers were willing to pay for them, and for good reason. An outboard engine powers the Gemini along smartly. It's also light, fuel-efficient, and is in keeping with the "keep it simple" philosophy. If the outboard breaks down, you simply remove it, throw it in the trunk and take it to the mechanic. Originally the 3000 came with a 35-horsepower, long-shaft Mercury, but this engine, complete with a 25-inch shaft, is no longer made. Later boats came with a 40-horsepower Tohatsu. Many boats on the used market appear to have further retrofitted the engine to a 4-stroke Honda 25. It is not necessary to have a big outboard on the boat. Munzel powers his 3000 with a 9.9-horsepower Yamaha and claims to ease along at 5.5 to 6 knots while burning around a half gallon of gasoline per hour. Today's diesel outboards offer an interesting alternative power source. Two 15-gallon fuel tanks are mounted aft in the cockpit bridge.

Under power, the 3000 handles fairly well, primarily because the outboard turns with the rudders via a simple line system. Under sail, the outboard pivots up, reducing drag and saving wear and tear on the engine's lower unit. One problem with outboards, however, is their inefficient charging system. Keeping the batteries topped up is difficult, even with a large outboard's small alternator. Most Gemini owners solve the problem by keeping electrical loads to a minimum. Because the boat stays level, the fridge runs on propane at sea, as does the on-demand hot-water system. A few solar panels help maintain the amps required for lights, pumps, autopilots and navigational electronics.

Gemini 3000

Sailing Magazine's Value Guide

PRICE: With prices ranging from the low$30s to the $50s, the Gemini 3000 is an excellent value, one of the few affordable cruising catamarans.

DESIGN QUALITY: Newer Geminis have refined hull shapes offering better performance. Its comfortable interior and load-carrying ability are important elements in a small cruising cat.

CONSTRUCTION QUALITY: The Gemini 3000 is certainly not overbuilt. However, hundreds of boats have stood up well over the years.

USER-FRIENDLINESS: Prime attractions of the Gemini 3000 are comfort, ease of handling and simple systems. The 3000 is very user-friendly.

SAFETY: The boat is better-suited for coastal cruising. Narrow side decks, exposed cockpit and lack of a companionway bridgedeck are limiting factors.

TYPICAL CONDITION: Most owners take pride in the boat; the 3000s that I inspected were in good condition. The gelcoat crazing is a cosmetic negative.

REFITTING: Spaciousness and ease of access make the 3000 an easy boat to work on. Refit projects include replacing the portlights, steering cables and rudder cages.

SUPPORT: The support system is excellent. For more information on the owner's association and to receive the newsletter, contact: John Munzel, 548 Roanoke Ave., Riverhead, NY 11901, or wanderer@ieaccess.net.

AVAILABILITY: With several hundred boats around, there are always several Gemini 3000s on the market. A good source for used boat information is John Sykes of 2 Hulls at: (954) 525-3326, or www.2hulls.com

INVESTMENT AND RESALE: Geminis hold value very well over the years. Strong factory-owner support contributes to the investment value.

OVERALL 'SVG' RATING

Underway

Gemini 3000s that are not overloaded are nimble in light air. The Gemini, with its single-spreader, modest sailplan, thrives on flat seas and may need to be shortened up early when the wind pipes up. Munzel shortens the headsail first and reefs the main when the winds touch 20 knots. Tracy Dell, who recently purchased a 3000 in Georgia and trucked it to Sandy Hook Bay, is delighted with the way the boat handles under sail. "The boat is better upwind than I suspected," Dell told me. "I can point to 40 degrees apparent without losing too much speed. Coming through the wind, it is hard to keep forward momentum, but because the boat accelerates so quickly, it doesn't matter." Most 3000s on the market will have just two or three sails: a main, with or without full battens, a roller-furled genoa and possibly a cruising spinnaker.

Conclusion

The Gemini 3000 forces us to consider our sailing priorities carefully. It is a boat that would make frustrated sailors hold off on buying a noisy trawler. If comfortable coastal cruising is the objective, sailors, even hard-core monohull sailors, owe it to themselves to take a close look at the Gemini 3000. It is difficult to imagine a better boat for gunkholing in the Florida Keys or Bahamas, or anywhere, for that matter.

Island Packet 31

Roomy, well-built cruiser that holds its value

When the Island Packet 31 was introduced in Annapolis at the United States Sailboat Show in 1983, it was crunch time for the small Florida boatbuilding firm. Designer Bob Johnson had launched his company four years earlier with the introduction of a beamy 26-footer called the Bombay Express. This later became the Island Packet MK II and sold well. Yet the expense of tooling up for the new 31, coupled with the consumer skittishness of the early 1980s, pushed the company to the brink. However, when the dust settled after the show, Johnson and company returned to Largo, Florida, with 13 new orders and Island Packet Yachts has never looked back.

With 265 boats sold from 1983 to 1989, the Island Packet 31 is, for the moment anyway, the company's best-selling model. Used 31s epitomize the design philosophy that continues to drive Island Packet Yachts today. Traditional lines, solid construction and voluminous interiors are features consistent with every Island Packet.

Excellent value can also be added to that list because used Packets have held their resale value as well as any American-made sailboat in the last decade. A new 1984 Island Packet 31 had a fairly complete base price of $58,950 and that same model, in average to above-average condition, today will sell for somewhere around $50,000. A 1988 model originally sold for $73,950 and a nice one today will bring around $65,000.

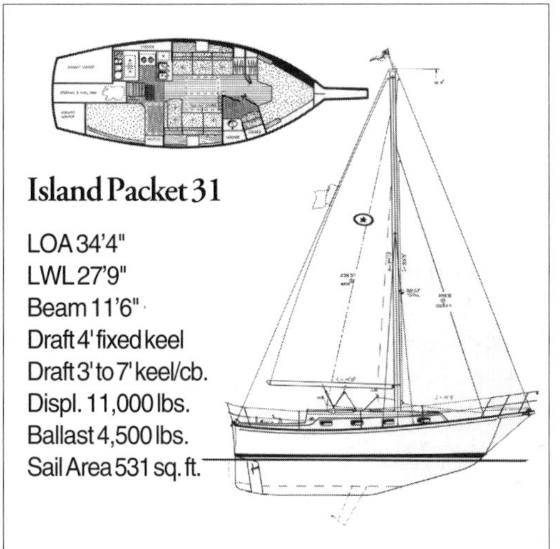

First impressions

The success of Island Packet Yachts proves that traditional styling still appeals to many sailors. The Island Packet 31 is a nice blend of traditional appearance joined with modern amenities and construction techniques. The 31 has short overhangs, a slight flare in the bow sections, a sweeping sheerline accentuated by a stubby bowsprit and a wide, vertical transom. In profile, the straight coachroof and nearly plumb bow reveal Johnson's affinity for New England catboats. Like a catboat, the 31 has a considerable 11-foot, 6-inch beam that it attains before the midships mark and carries well aft. There is no secret that the spacious interior of the 31 is largely a result of carrying the beam in the hull shape and stretching out the waterline.

Below the water, the 31 features a full keel with a cutaway forefoot. Johnson describes the 31's hull as U-shaped, which translates into a broad-in-the-bilges, shoal-draft cruiser. About 10 percent of the 31s came off the line as centerboarders, which reduced the standard draft from 4 feet to 3 feet.

Island Packet 31 Price Data

		Low	High
BUC Retail Range	1984	$48,900	$53,800
	1986	$56,000	$61,500
	1989	$70,000	$76,600

		State	Asking
Boats For Sale	1984	MD	$59,000
	1987	FL	$69,500
	1988	MA	$65,000

Despite the keel shape, the 31 is not excessively heavy with a design displacement of 11,000 pounds. This is about the same displacement as the Pacific Seacraft 31 and the Catalina 320. Interestingly, the Island Packet 32, which replaced the 31, has a waterline just 1 foot longer but has a displacement of 13,500 pounds. The rudder is unique for a full-keel boat in that it is essentially a balanced spade. The foot of the rudder is strapped to the trailing edge of the keel only to prevent prop wraps, not to provide structural-bearing support.

Construction

The hull of the 31 is solid hand-laid-up glass and the deck is cored with Island Packet's own material called Polycore. This mixture of resin and microballoons is an excellent alternative to traditional end-grain balsa because it is much more resistant to rot and subsequent delamination. Very few used Packets report deck problems, which, of course, are a common malady of older boats. This core material on early Island Packets was called Polycel, but the company was forced to change the name when they started selling to the European market. It seems that Polycel is the name of a well-known spackling paste in England—good for fixing holes in plaster walls but not a great material for coring decks. The hull-to-deck joint is on an internal flange, and there are few, if any, reports of leaks.

The IP 31 relies on several molded liners for structural support inside the boat. I am no fan of liners, yet I must admit that the molded Polycore linings used by Island Packet are extremely well-made and sensibly installed. Liners often block vital access to critical areas in the hull. However, on the 31 the hull liner ends at seat-back height and there is decent access to the bilge through the hatches in the molded sole. There are also access panels in the headliner to get at the undersides of deck hardware. Whenever liners are used as structural members, be sure to check for cracks and twists, especially in the bow area. The iron ballast is fully encapsulated in the robust keel cavity and the rudder stock is beefy $1\,^1/_2$-inch stainless steel.

What to look for

From the beginning, Island Packet Yachts has consistently updated and improved its boats and responded to owner input. There is no question that the high level of organizational support is a continuing factor in the success of Island Packet. Just ask any Island Packet owner; they love the company. As a result of this, however, older Packets sometimes seem outdated on the used-boat market by newer sisterships.

The year 1986 seems to be a breakthrough year for the 31. Late-1985 and newer models featured a 27-

horsepower Yanmar instead of the 22. Although it was the same engine, Yanmar increased the horsepower rating and changed the model number from 3GM22F to 3GM30F.

In 1986 plastic portlights were replaced by aluminum ones which, incidentally, were upgraded to stainless in 1987. Also, 1986 models featured a hatch over the head, a stern gate, swim ladder and a cockpit shower. Because Island Packet has always marketed a fairly complete standard boat, many 31s on the used boat market are just that, standard boats. Therefore, noting each model year's engineering changes is quite important. Some major updates to standard features included self-tailing winches and wheel break in 1987. A second anchor roller, single-line reefing, gel cell batteries and gas stove with oven were added in 1988. In 1989 the head was upgraded and the company issued a 10-year, transferable hull warranty.

On deck

The 31 has a spacious cockpit of more than 7 feet long, although by today's standards the seat backs seem a little abrupt and the pedestal and wheel seem a bit undersized. Yet the cockpit is full of clever features, including an icebox and an access hatch to the engine in the cockpit sole, which is a great feature in a small boat—as long as the seal around the hatch stays watertight. Like most Island Packets, the 31 has rack-and-pinion geared wheel steering, which is virtually bulletproof. The only problem with this steering system is that in the unlikely event of something going wrong, it is almost impossible to rig an emergency tiller of any kind. There are also two good-sized lockers and a stout bridgedeck.

Moving forward on deck, I find it hard to believe that this is only a 31-foot boat. A molded bulwark provides firm footing and Island Packet has always done an outstanding job with its diamond-pattern nonskid. Older 31s reveal a few gelcoat crazes and cracks. Johnson is a big believer in bowsprits and I am not. Johnson cites the advantages of increased sail area, better sheeting angles, handy anchor stowage and deployment, as well as pleasing aesthetics. I admit that bowsprits are pretty, but structurally they make little sense. I recommend that you carefully check the fittings on the bobstay as well as the sprit itself.

Most 31s on the used boat market are cutters, although the boat was also sold as a sloop. The 31 is really more of a double-headsail sloop than a true cutter, and the staysail boom tends to clutter up the foredeck. Owners of sloops report better overall performances by flying an overlapping genoa, but cutter owners are stalwart in proclaiming the merits of that rig. I think the solution is to have a hanked-on, loose-footed staysail set on a removable stay and a decent-sized genoa in addition to the yankee, giving the option of sailing the boat either way. The standard deck hardware is consistently good quality. Everything that should be is through-bolted with aluminum backing plates and locking nuts.

Down below

"The Island Packet 31 is about the smallest boat that I felt I could live aboard comfortably," said Jon Bickel, owner of a 1986 IP 31 called *Papillion*. Bickel, who has recently formed the Island Packet 31 owners' association, has lived aboard for several years along the Mississippi coast. The interior of the 31 is simply huge. The arrangement is fairly straightforward with a V-berth forward followed by a head with a hanging locker opposite. The saloon features a fold-down bulkhead table that helps open up the saloon area and also reveals a handsome bar, magazine and spice rack behind it. There is ample storage throughout and good ventilation with eight opening portlights and several overhead hatches.

The nav station and quarterberth can be completely enclosed for privacy by flipping up the chart table desk and pulling shut a folding pocket door. This is a clever design feature for a 31-foot boat. The galley is a legitimate U-shaped galley with large double sinks, a big icebox, and at least on later models, a two-burner stove and oven. The only common complaint about the interior accommodations is that the forward shower sump drains into the bilge. This, of course, is not a difficult situation to correct.

Engine

As mentioned earlier, the original engine was a 22-horsepower Yanmar that was later upgraded to a 27-horsepower engine. This change began with the late 1985 models and was a result of Yanmar upgrading the horsepower. The block and components of the engine were unchanged, which makes retrofits easier. Access to the engine is excellent both below and from the cockpit. I am partial to these small Yanmars and over the years have found them to be very reliable. The 31 carries 25 gallons of fuel in an aluminum tank. The 27-

Island Packet 31

Sailing Magazine's Value Guide

PRICE: The IP 31 isn't cheap; used boat buyers must be willing to pay around $50,000 for even the earliest models. Yet in terms of liveaboard coastal cruisers, the IP 31 is one of the few real animals in this price range.

DESIGN QUALITY: The traditional design of the 31 is either a positive or a negative, and most sailors have strong feelings either way. Designer Bob Johnson is very talented at marrying traditional concepts with modern materials and engineering.

CONSTRUCTION QUALITY: The IP 31 is a well-built cruiser with high-quality gear, although some construction techniques, like the use of molded liners throughout and iron ballast, might be better done in other ways.

USER- FRIENDLINESS: Island Packet excels at making its boats easy to handle under sail. The nature of the design makes close handling under power a little tricky. The interior is well-thought-out, spacious and comfortable.

SAFETY: The bulwark, long grabrails, stout stanchions and double lifelines lend security to deck work. The large cockpit could be dangerous in a seaway. Shoal-draft boats have a harder time clawing off a lee shore.

TYPICAL CONDITIONS: Used IPs as a general rule seem to be in excellent condition.

REFITTING: The factory can make parts available or recommend solutions to most refitting problems. The interior construction does not lend itself to major changes.

SUPPORT: It must be noted that this is the first five rating ever doled out in the Value Guide. Island Packet is probably the best-run sailboat company in the business and this service extends to its used boat customers.

AVAILABILITY: With a production run of 265 boats, there will always be a few IP 31s on the market. These boats don't linger, however.

INVESTMENT AND RESALE: The IP 31 has held its value as well as any used boat over the last 10 to 15 years. In fact, recent figures indicate that sales of 1989 models brought in more than the original base price.

OVERALL 'SVG' RATING

horsepower auxiliary, the 3GM30F, will push the boat at 6 knots without much trouble and will consume about $^1/_2$ gallon per hour in the process, if the bottom is clean and the boat is swinging a three-blade prop.

Underway

The sailing performance of the IP 31 is deceptive. With 531 square feet of working sail area and a long 27-foot, 9-inch LWL, the boat moves along easily at 6-plus knots on a reach. Upwind is another story. There is no disputing that windward work is not the 31's forte. However, Bickel said that he routinely sails his sloop-rigged 31 at 45 degrees of apparent wind, and with a bit of fussing, can do better than that. He claims that off the wind his 150-percent genoa drives the boat at more than 7 knots in 15 knots of breeze or higher. "And the boat is stiff," he said. "I don't pull the 150-percent down until there is more than 20 knots."

Bickel also likes that the boat is easy to singlehand. Although he has not led all sail controls aft, he finds that the forgiving nature of the boat accounts for the ease of handling. When in reverse under power, close-quarter maneuvering is a bit of a challenge, having to contend with the long keel and bowsprit. But these are trade-offs inherent to traditional designs.

Conclusion

If you are the type of used boat buyer who makes lists of positives and negatives in a boat and you are looking for a roomy, well-built, coastal cruiser, chances are the Island Packet 31 is going to rank very high on your list. And when you factor in the strong factory support and solid resale value, the case for the Island Packet becomes even stronger.

Allied Seawind II

A genuine seagoing boat wrapped in a small, plain envelope

The Allied Seawind II was the heir apparent to the original Seawind, a capable, salty, 30-foot ketch designed by Tom Gillmer. The Seawind was a tough act to follow. In the early 1960s, *Apogee* was the first fiberglass boat to circumnavigate. Several other Seawinds have also made their way around the world, including Scott and Kitty Kuhner's well-known *Bebinka.* In 1975, Allied introduced the Gillmer-redesigned and modified Seawind II, and although it was only a foot longer and wider, it was 2,700 pounds heavier, making it seem like a much larger and more comfortable boat. The Seawind II was produced until 1981, when Allied Yachts went out of business for the last time.

Allied Yachts was as infamous as some of its boats were famous. The company went into bankruptcy four times before the doors closed for good on its factory in Catskill, New York, an unlikely boatbuilding location on the Hudson River. The company, known for a while as Wright/Allied Yachts, was better at building boats than marketing them, as the lead copy on the original Seawind II brochure reveals: "Challenge the Lee Shores of the World With the Seawind II." Also, although its boats were always robustly constructed, the level of finish below varied considerably, earning Allied a sketchy reputation. Like many builders of the time, Allied used copious amounts of wood-grain formica, and workmanship was average at best.

Allieds were built to shine at sea, not at the boat shows, which unfortunately were becoming the prime marketing venues of the industry. Along with the original Seawind and other husky cruisers including the 36-foot Princess and 39-foot Mistress, Allied also built a handsome 33-footer designed by Bill Luders that some consider a classic, and a 42-foot keel/centerboarder designed by Sparkman & Stephens that bears a striking resemblance to the Hinckley Bermuda 40. The company made a desperate attempt to upgrade its interior styling after Brax Freeman took over the company in 1980, but by then it was too late; 15-percent interest rates and an indifferent market would soon finish off the company.

Allied Seawind II

LOA 31' 7"
LWL 25' 6"
Beam 10' 5"
Draft 4' 6"
Air Draft 43'
Displacement 14,900 lbs.
Ballast 5,800 lbs.
Sail Area 555 sq. ft. (ketch), 512 sq. ft. (cutter)

First impressions

The Seawind II was built to go to sea and it certainly looks the part. The profile shows a pronounced sheer emphasized by a plucky bowsprit and low-slung deckhouse. The standard ketch rig seems squeezed into a small package—the LOD is only 31 feet, 7 inches—and toward the end of production, more owners were choosing the optional cutter rig. Other than teak hand rails, a caprail and cockpit coaming boards, there isn't much wood on deck. At first glance the boat seems a bit sterile; we have been trained to expect traditional cruising boats to be laden with teak, from decks to deck boxes, which also translates into unrelenting maintenance. I don't think it would take long to come to admire the austere deck appointments. After all, molded Dorade boxes let in just as much air as teak ones, but they don't require varnish.

Below the waterline, the Seawind II has a long keel with a cutaway forefoot and 4-foot, 6-inch draft. The underbody shape is not unlike Gillmer's other well-known small cruiser, the Southern Cross 31. The attached rudder is the large, barn door variety, with a

Allied Seawind II Price Data

		Low	High
BUC Retail Range	1976	$30,900	$34,400
	1978	$32,800	$36,500
	1980	$40,300	$44,800

		State	Asking
Boats For Sale	1976	FL	$32,000
	1979	MD	$30,000
	1980	NY	$35,000

stainless steel stock. The boat can be wet on a beat, but it also has sweet motion in a seaway. The ketch rig has 555 square feet of sail area while the cutter carries 512. The air draft of both models is 43 feet.

Construction

The hull is solid fiberglass, heavily laid up by hand. Horizontal areas of the deck are cored with balsa, except around the base of the deck-stepped mast where the sandwich deck is filled with epoxy. An improvement from the original Seawind, the Seawind II hull-and-deck joint is fiberglassed from the inside. This is a good but time-consuming way to build a boat because you must do a significant amount of interior work with the deck already in place. While manufacturers may tout the strength of mechanically fastened hulls and decks, the method is primarily used because it dramatically speeds up the building process. The Seawind II's hull and deck have outward-turning flanges that are also bolted on 7-inch centers and covered with an aluminum extrusion that doubles as a rubbing strake.

The lead ballast is cast to size, dropped into the keel cavity, then fiberglassed over. The deck-stepped mast is supported by deck beams and a stout compression post. The bowsprit is a teak platform, bolted to the foredeck and secured with a bobstay. While I admire the look of bowsprits, I question their structural integrity. With a traditional sprit such as the Seawind II has, the fittings on the bobstay are ultimately responsible for keeping the mast standing. Bowsprits do have advantages, however: Weather helm is reduced by pushing the sail area forward, and they make great anchoring platforms and nice perches in a trade wind breeze.

Beefy bronze seacocks bolted to the hull were standard issue and typical of the robust original construction.

What to look for

Considering that many of the Seawind IIs on the market have been cruised extensively, most used boats that I have inspected have held up remarkably well. It is safe to say that the later models have better-finished interiors, but it should be noted that Allied offered customized interiors early on. Don't assume a Seawind II for sale has the exact arrangement you want. Also, many second, third or fourth owners customized the boats themselves, and as we all know, some people are better with tools than others. A common change was to expand the area behind the settees into more locker space.

Henry Roesner, who sails his ketch *Poseidon* on ChesapeakeBay, has spent the past two seasons completely updating the boat. He advises potential buyers to check the chainplates, forward hatch and portlights for leaks. If they haven't been recently rebedded, put the job at the top of your to-do list. Roesner eventually replaced the opening portlights.

Other items to check relate more to the age of the boat than to the original design or construction. Most Seawind IIs came with a two-burner alcohol stove that has likely been replaced by a propane model. Check this installation carefully. Consider changing the hose and fittings just for peace of mind. Roesner chose the new nonpressurized alcohol stove by Origo, eliminating both the installation problems and dangers associated with propane.

Boats that came with factory diesels may need repowering. Today's engines are smaller and quieter, and they deliver more horsepower while using less fuel. They are also expensive. Another option would be to rebuild the standard engine, a four-cylinder, 27-horsepower Westerbeke. By the time you dismember the engine, rebuild it and then reinstall it, however, costs could come close to that of purchasing new. Roesner retrofitted a new, three-cylinder, 38-horsepower Yanmar that pushes the boat along at 6.5 knots.

Allied Seawind II

Sailing Magazine's Value Guide

PRICE: You can buy less expensive cruisers than the AlliedSeawind II, but you won't find this much quality for the money.

DESIGN QUALITY: While the design is timeless, it is also rather conservative. You know what you are getting with a Gillmer full-keel cruising boat: a decent performer with a good motion that usually can stand up to foul weather.

CONSTRUCTION QUALITY: If basic seaworthiness were the only issue, this would be a higher ranking. However, the interior work is inconsistent.

USER-FRIENDLINESS: The ketch rig is not particularly user-friendly, especially on a smaller boat. The sails are not large to begin with.

SAFETY: The good sailing motion, robust construction, molded bulwark, tall lifelines, stout bridgedeck and well-placed handholds above and below make the boat quite safe.

TYPICAL CONDITION: Although many Seawind IIs have been extensively cruised, they seem to hold up well.

REFITTING: The boat is not easy to work on and finding original parts is a challenge. Good original construction helps.

SUPPORT: There is not much support from Allied. There is a Web site for the boat at www.geocities.com/TheTropics/Paradise/1131/a-pracsailsw2.html. Also, good information can be found from other owners through Sailnet's Boat Check at Sailnet.com.

AVAILABILITY: The Seawind had a six-year production run. Quite a few boats were built, but they don't linger on the market.

INVESTMENT AND RESALE: The Seawind holds its value quite well. It has a well-earned reputation as a capable cruiser.

OVERALL 'SVG' RATING

Be sure to check the condition of the bowsprit; the teak platform may have stress cracks. Also, carefully check the swage fittings on the bobstay. If they are more than 10 years old, you will need to replace them. The same warning applies to the standing rigging.

On deck

Although the side decks are narrow and the nonskid is often worn, especially on older boats, the Seawind II still has a very secure, oceangoing deck. A molded toerail, 30-inch stanchions with double lifelines and well-placed grabrails make going forward safer and easier, even in heavy weather. Most bowsprits were set up with double anchor rollers, although the anchor rodes can chafe on both the pulpit and bobstay. Also, a system usually has to be devised to stow the anchors underneath. The cleats are massive and the dock lines are led through hawsepipes in the toerail. The deck hardware is almost all oversized and is well-supported with fiberglass doublers serving as backing plates.

The shrouds are just inside the toerail, so on the ketch rig, with the main mast forward and the genoa tracks on the caprail, the sheeting angles are not very tight to say the least. The mainsheet is led to a traveler on a bridgedeck in the cockpit, and the mizzen is usually sheeted to a single block on the transom. The cockpit is large and fairly comfortable. There are good-size lockers, formerly sail lockers before furling headsails became ubiquitous, and there is a raised helmsman's seat. The steering is an Edson rack-and-pinion model that is close to bulletproof. Of course, the helmsman has to adjust to looking past the mizzen mast on the ketch. Also, from behind the wheel it is a long stretch to any sail controls other than the mizzen sheet.

Down below

The most common arrangement featured a V-berth forward with a wash basin, a hanging locker, drawers under the berth and shelves above. The small head, usually with a shower, is to starboard. It was a good idea to move the basin to the forward cabin. The main cabin came with either a fixed-table dinette or, more commonly, with a table that folded down from the bulkhead. I would choose the bulkhead table, as it opens up the cabin area considerably.

There is ample storage behind, below and above the settees, especially for a 32-foot boat. As previously mentioned, the quality of the interior joinerwork was workmanlike on early boats. The teak-and-holly cabin sole has utilitarian but unsightly aluminum rings on access hatches. When areas were not covered with dark wood-grain formica, they were often left unfinished. Later models were vastly improved, so if interior aesthetics are important to you, try to find a 1980 or '81 model. If you are handy, or just want a capable cruiser, the early boats often represent an excellent value.

The galley is to starboard, with the sink and icebox aft and the stove outboard. Again, for a small boat, the galley is functional, although a fold-up counter top would be a useful addition. The nav station is either a desk that incorporates the end of the settee as a seat, or a dresser with the top surface usable as a chart desk and with drawers below. The electrical panel and three-way battery switch are directly behind the companionway steps, and there is room to expand to a larger panel.

Engine

The standard engine was a four-cylinder Westerbeke. It was rated anywhere from 25- to 30-horsepower depending on the boatbuilder. It was actually a very good engine for the boat because it was fairly light and compact. Access is not particularly good; the companionway steps must be removed just to check the oil. The stuffing box is checked through the cockpit locker. Roesner was able to squeeze his new Yanmar through the companionway. The 40-gallon fuel tank is either Corten steel or, in later models, aluminum, and it is located in the bilge. A 60-gallon stainless water tank is also in the bilge.

Underway

The Seawind II was designed and built for bluewater sailing. Mike Harrison, who sails a 1979 ketch out of Pensacola, Florida, has crossed the Gulf of Mexico more than once and doesn't think twice about heading out to sea when a cold north wind is blowing. Roesner, an experienced sailor and an avid racer, is surprised how well the boat sails in light air. "I knew it would handle the rough stuff, but I never expected it would sail so well in a typical light summer breeze on the bay," he said.

Carol Dean, who sails with Roesner, likes the way the boat balances. "You can leave the helm and the boat will steer herself," she said. "There is virtually no weather helm, and when the wind does pipe up, we just drop the main and sail under jib and jigger."

The mizzen sail, much maligned these days, especially in small boats, does offer unique advantages. In addition to being able to just drop the main, a mizzen makes a great riding sail at anchor, and it allows for better efficiency when heaving to. The cutter rig, of course, offers different options, including double headsails for downwind sailing, a less-cluttered cockpit and much less weight aloft.

Conclusion

The Allied Seawind II is a genuine bluewater boat, albeit in a small package. With prices ranging from $30,000 to $45,000, the option of taking a bluewater sabbatical may be more affordable than you thought.

Westsail 32

The boat that launched a thousand cruising dreams

"The Westsail 32 changed everything," Bob Perry told me. "Cruising came out of the closet and became a lifestyle." I know exactly what he means. I remember as a high school kid, slipping the well-worn Westsail brochure into my book bag and studying it instead of algebra. Inspired by the genius of Colin Archer and William Atkins, the double-ended Westsail, complete with bowsprit and boomkin, was the perfect synthesis of tropical-island romance, American-style marketing and the fiberglass hull.

"Westsail the world," the brochure screamed. Anybody could do it, even a landlubbing kid from the Midwest. I'll never forget the picture of a 32 anchored off Moorea, or was it Bora Bora? It doesn't matter. I can still visualize the tanned family of four, in the buff, diving off the boom into crystalline waters. I knew then that I had to sail to the South Seas one day, and of course, a Westsail 32 was the only boat for me. While my thinking on boats has changed—changed quite a bit in fact—there is no denying the influence of the Westsail 32, or at least the beautiful brochure. And I'm not alone. Despite its many flaws, the Westsail 32 is the Helen of sailing—the boat that launched a thousand dreams.

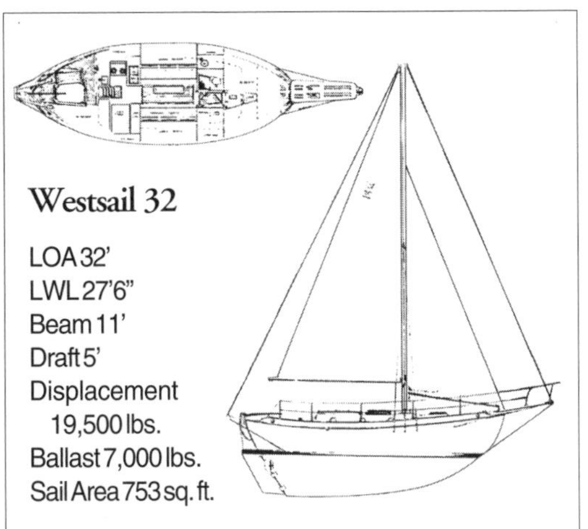

Westsail 32

LOA 32'
LWL 27'6"
Beam 11'
Draft 5'
Displacement 19,500 lbs.
Ballast 7,000 lbs.
Sail Area 753 sq. ft.

First impressions

Although there is no way to tally how many cruising sailors were first inspired by the Westsail 32, we do know that about 840 boats were built between 1970 and 1981. The first incarnation was a flush-deck edition, adapted by Bill Crealock for fiberglass from the original Atkins design. It was called the Kendall 32 and about 30 were built. In 1972 a cabintrunk was added and something about the boat touched a nerve. Production skyrocketed. Westsail added a plant in Wrightsville Beach, North Carolina, because its main facility in Costa Mesa, California, was backlogged and buyers had to wait almost two years for a boat.

The Westsail 32 pushed all the right buttons. It was just what we thought a cruising boat should be and look like in the early 1970s. In addition to the fullest of full keels, the 32, in an age of the sloop rig, was one of the first boats to tout a traditional cutter rig. The rig was considered preferable for ease of handling two small headsails instead of one overlapping genoa. The cockpit was appropriately small and uncomfortable—or as we called it then, seaworthy. There was plenty of teak on deck to keep idle hands from worshipping the devil. Ironically, although many of these concepts seem out of date, take a hard look at today's new heavy-displacement cruising boats and you will find lingering features that evolved from the Westsail idea.

Westsail was a victim of its own success, as many cult products are, and the 32 spawned many imitators. The dismal economy during the late 1970s and early 1980s didn't help. The company went bankrupt in 1981. The molds were acquired by P&M Worldwide and another 15 Westsail 32s were sold in kit form before production stopped for good.

Construction

Westsail 32s have been criticized for poor light-air performance, but few have questioned their robust construction. Although many 32s were sold as

Westsail 32 Price Data

		Low	High
BUC Retail Range	1972	$38,300	$42,500
	1975	$42,400	$47,100
	1979	$52,500	$58,000

		State	Asking
Boats For Sale	1973	CA	$49,900
	1975	NY	$39,900
	1976	MD	$54,500

unfinished hulls and decks or as kits (60 to 65 percent) to be completed by the owner, all the hulls were molded in similar fashion. If you want to know which boats were factory-finished and which were kits, check the hull ID number stamped on the stern. Numbers that begin with WSSF were factory-completed, while those starting with WSSK were kit boats. The next four digits are the hull number and the last four are the month and year of lamination.

The two-piece hull is a solid laminate, bonded together from the inside and extremely thick. In fact, Bud Taplin, who was Westsail's first general manager and today operates Worldcruiser Yacht Co. in Newport Beach, California, a company that supplies Westsail parts, notes that osmotic blisters that would be considered structural on most boats are not even a problem on the 32. The hull is about $1^1/_8$ inches thick at the turn of the bilge and tapers to $^3/_4$ inch at the gunwale.

The deck and cabintrunk are plywood, and quite a few boats have teak decks as well. The original teak decks were $^{13}/_{16}$-inch—unbelievably thick, not to mention heavy. The 7,000 pounds of ballast apparently varied in makeup in early boats. Some contained 2,000 pounds of lead and 5,000 pounds of steel punchings, and others had 5,500 pounds of steel. From 1974 onward, cast-lead ballast was used and dropped into the keel cavity in three pieces. The boxed hull-and-deck joint incorporates the substantial bulwark, and while strong, is not immune to leaks.

What to look for

Unlike many boats, most Westsail 32s have done bluewater duty. Many have been sailed thousands of miles. Because all the boats are at least 20 years old, there are some common problems to look out for. Without doubt, the prime source of information about used 32s is Taplin. Eileen Oelschlager, who along with her husband, Frank, heads up the active Westsail Owners Association, calls Taplin "the midwife." Taplin, who is quite busy flying around the country surveying used Westsails for prospective buyers and attending rendezvous, has prepared extensive information sheets that detail common problems and their solutions. This material is available in a complete manual. Taplin can also deliver almost any replacement part in a matter of days. "A big part of the value of owning a Westsail is Bud Taplin," says Scotty Allen, who with his wife, Marguerite, has lived aboard for 20 years, crossed the Atlantic four times and extensively cruised in northern and southern climes.

Allen, who owns a 1976 kit boat named *Robin*, noted that anyone considering buying a Westsail 32 should be prepared to do all the refitting and maintenance work himself. "The first so-called expert you hire blows the value in buying a used boat," Allen said. Allen advised prospective buyers to look closely at the fuel tanks, especially if they are black iron. Allen recently replaced his diesel tank. "I called Bud," he said, "and he told me that he was making up some new tanks and would put me on the list." Taplin's price for a new, 30-gallon, thick-walled aluminum tank built from the original patterns was just $250.

Taplin said that the 32 has had few, if any, serious structural problems over the years. He does, however, suggest that buyers check the bottom fittings, or tangs, on the boomkin and the bobstay. Although they were originally stainless, 20 years of life at the waterline takes its toll. Taplin warns buyers to check for signs of rot and to look closely at the base of the deck-stepped mast for any signs of fiberglass compression.

On deck

The molded bulwark, fairly wide side decks, stout grabrails on the trunkhouse, and teak decks on many boats lend security when going forward. Deck delamination does not seem to be a common problem, probably because the fiberglass subdeck is unusually thick and well-supported. If you do find delamination, the plywood core is easily accessed from below by removing a thin plywood liner. Hatches and portlight leaks are a bit more common; 20-year-old sealant doesn't have much resilience left. If ports are leaking, take the time to remove and completely rebed them. It will be time well-spent.

Many 32 owners have retrofitted the wooden bowsprit section with an identical, stainless-steel, boxed version. Taplin has also designed a tubular stainless pipe sprit that is now available. Check for cracks at the original bronze hawsepipes that run through the bulwark. Mast rails are often retrofitted. Make sure that these are well-supported.

Also, as with any old boat, if the standing rigging is original, consider replacing it. Look closely at the chainplates for hole elongation or hairline cracks and consider removing one to check the condition of the carriage bolts. Many boats have retrofitted split backstays that are mounted directly to the hull, replacing the need for a boomkin. Be sure to check this installation carefully.

The cockpit of the 32 is small, especially when the sweep of the large tiller is considered. It is also quite exposed. The original boats did not have a stern rail, and if the boat you're considering doesn't have one, it should be high on your project priority list. Naturally, a stainless rail is available through Taplin. Check the wear and tear on the pintles and gudgeons supporting the massive outboard rudder. Most boats have fiberglass fittings that have held up well.

Down below

It is impossible to generalize about the quality of the 32's interior. Many of the kit boats are finished superbly but some are disasters. The factory finish varied over the years, but the focus was on utility more than on beautiful joinerwork. The interior layout, however, seems to be fairly standard. There is a double berth forward, either V or Pullman style, followed by the head and hanging locker. The saloon usually has a dinette table to port and a long settee and pilot berth to starboard. With the tanks in the bilge, there is ample storage beneath and behind the settees. In fact, one of the most appealing aspects of a Westsail 32 for long-range cruising is the amount of storage.

The U-shaped galley, which came standard with a two-burner stove with oven and a single sink, is to port. There is a large nav station and wet locker opposite. Many owners have converted to propane cooking systems, while reporting that the standard icebox needs more insulation when refrigeration is added. The 32's interior is voluminous because its volume is carried well forward, the cabintrunk stretches aft and the cockpit is short.

Engine

The type of diesel engine is an important factor when considering a Westsail 32. The standard engine was a saltwater-cooled, two-cylinder Volvo. It was undersized when new and is probably useless today. An option was to upgrade the engine to either an MD3B, a three-cylinder saltwater-cooled Volvo or the venerable Perkins 4108. Taplin noted that horsepower, which cannot be accurately compared between manufacturers, is less important than the cubic inches of displacement. For example, the MD2B is rated at 25 horsepower but has just 66 cubic inches of displacement. The MD3B, rated at 35 horsepower, has 99 cubic inches. The Perkins 4108, rated at 50 horsepower, has 108 cubic inches of displacement. Naturally, the freshwater-cooled 4108 is the original engine of choice.

Repowering is not a nightmare on the 32 for the simple reason that the cockpit floor is completely removable on the early boats. Later models have a hatch that the engine can fit through. Taplin recommends the new Perkins M-50, which is lighter and more powerful than the old 4108. Most 32s carry approximately 80 gallons of fuel, which means a realistic range under power of 400 to 500 miles.

Underway

"The Westsail 32 is a miserable boat for daysailing," Allen said with a laugh. "It's not even good for weekending; this is a cruising boat." Allen's point is valid. It really doesn't make sense to give performance parameters for various conditions, and it is better to note passage times. Allen is proud of two tradewind transatlantics when he averaged better than 140 miles a day for 20-plus days. My friend Dave McGowan sailed from the Galapagos to the Marquesas, a distance of 3,000 miles, in 21 days, averaging close to 150 miles a day, which translates into more than 6 knots day in and day out.

"The Westsail 32 had a terrible reputation for sailing," Taplin explained. "But that isn't the case anymore. Many of the people who bought 32s were not sailors. They were dreamers and didn't understand how to make a heavy-displacement boat

Westsail 32

Sailing Magazine's Value Guide

PRICE: Selling at $40,000 to $55,000, price is one of the attractions of used Westsail 32s.

DESIGN QUALITY: The design, though traditional and romantic, was dated from the beginning. This was very much a wooden-boat design.

CONSTRUCTION QUALITY: The original construction was heavy. The quality of finish varied from boat to boat because of the many kits. Even heavily built boats age; just about every 32 is more than 20 years old.

USER-FRIENDLINESS: The 32 is cumbersome to sail, and requires practice and skill to generate tolerable performance. It is not easy to maneuver under power; many were underpowered. The motion on passages is kind to the crew.

SAFETY: The 32 has proven itself a world-class cruiser. Current safety features like stern pulpit and mast rails should be retrofitted.

TYPICAL CONDITION: Although most Westsail owners are devoted to their boats, most Westsails have seen a lot of water and have some wear and tear.

REFITTING: Bud Taplin's Worldcruiser Yacht Co. is a godsend for Westsail owners. Taplin can track down just about any part and is very knowledgeable about these boats. Contact him at (800) 310-WORLD, or on the Web at www.westsail.com

SUPPORT: The owner's association is very supportive.

AVAILABILITY: There are always 32s for sale. Lately they are not lingering on the market as people realize the value in the boat. Type of engine is related to price.

INVESTMENT AND RESALE: If you bought a Westsail in 1978, today you could sell it for more than you paid for it. It is hard to imagine Westsails selling for much less or more than they do today.

OVERALL 'SVG' RATING

move. Also, the rig wasn't right in the early days. The mainsail was too big and the headsails were too small."

Any way you slice it, the Westsail 32 is not a great performing boat, but then nobody who buys a 32 expects a thoroughbred. It is a marathon runner. Just ask Molly and Roger Firey on *Sundowner*. Currently in Southeast Asia, they have been cruising their 32 for 20 years and are now on their fourth circumnavigation. Although the 32 is famous for weather helm, the boat has a nice motion offshore. Once balanced, it copes well with wind-vane self-steering gears, both important factors for happy bluewater sailing.

Conclusion

How many boats can you buy for around $50,000 and sail around the world with confidence? Not many. The Westsail 32 is not only a sound value but is also a unique boat on the secondhand market. With prices ranging from $40,000 to $55,000, the original Westsail premise is still valid. Anybody can Westsail the world.

Ranger 33

Solid, inexpensive and quick

The Ranger 33 was designed by the late Gary Mull with hull No. 1 hitting the water in 1969. Ranger was originally the performance division of Jensen Marine, which also built Cals. Later, Ranger became part of the conglomerate Bangor Punta. For a time in the 1970s, the behemoth marine operation, which included Cal and O'Day, was the largest sailboat company in the country.

Although both boats are long out of production, the Ranger 33, as well as the 26, have enjoyed enduring popularity. More than 450 Ranger 33s were built before production ground to a halt in 1978. Ranger 33s have followed the conventional evolution of older fiberglass boats, going from "a high-performance racing machine," as an original brochure said, to PHRF club racer and then coastal cruiser. Although every Ranger 33 afloat is at least 20 years old, with some approaching 30, lively sailing ability, solid original construction and reasonable prices make the Ranger 33 an interesting used boat option.

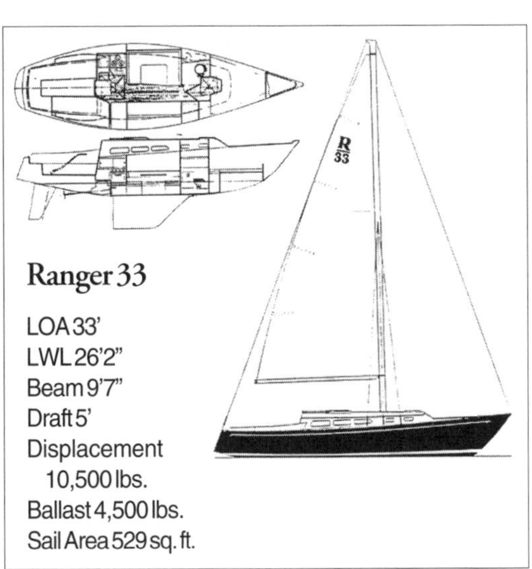

First impressions

The Ranger 33 fell between the cracks when it came to racing rules. Ironically, it is probably better off. It was designed before the IOR completely ruled the waves, avoiding the fate of other mid-1970s boats that were bent around IOR's sometimes cranky parameters, but after the stodgy influence of the CCA rule. Mull's objective was simply to draw a boat that would sail fast. By all accounts, he succeeded. Many early Rangers were successful in IOR racing. The Ranger 33 now normally carries a PHRF rating between 150 and 155, and often gives time to newer and larger boats.

The 33 was sleek for its time. Although it doesn't look like a race boat by today's standards, it has aged gracefully. The sheer is more pronounced than you

Ranger 33 Price Data

		Low	High
BUC Retail Range	1971	$18,300	$20,300
	1974	$20,300	$22,500
	1977	$22,100	$24,500

		State	Asking
Boats For Sale	1973	NY	$19,900
	1975	MI	$25,000
	1976	CA	$23,000

might expect for a performance boat, even one designed in 1969. The overhangs are fairly long, as a 26-foot, 2-inch waterline on a 33-foot LOA reveals. The cabintrunk appears lower than it really is and has a subtle slope. The cockpit has prominent molded coamings for the sheet winches and teak coaming boards that run aft. The handsome stern has a reverse transom.

Below the waterline, the 33 has a moderate-aspect fin (which is the ratio between the keel depth to fore and aft width), with a 5-foot, 3-inch draft and a semibalanced spade rudder. The bottom is quite flat, especially the aft sections, which no doubt contributes to the 33's excellent off-the-wind performance. Displacing 10,500 pounds, the 33 was light for its day, but by no means radically so. With a masthead rig and a moderately long boom, the 33 carries 529 square feet of working sail.

Construction

Rangers were built similarly to Cals and O'Days, and except for a few common problems, they have held up well over the years. The hull is solid fiberglass and proportionately thick like most early fiberglass boats. Of course, these early layups were resin-rich, making them thick but necessarily strong. The lead keel is encapsulated in the keel cavity.

The decks were first cored with plywood and later balsa.The hull-and-deck joint incorporates the toerail, which was originally teak and then aluminum on later boats. Ranger used fiberglass liners and furniture modules to stiffen the hull and make production more efficient. I don't like liners on used boats because they make accessing components behind them, particularly electrical wiring, difficult and occasionally impossible. There are fiberglassed, encased wooden floors in the bilge for athwartships support and a deep sump area.

What to look for

Although most owners, including some original owners, have few complaints with the boat, there are some common problems to look for in a used 33. Bill Bartz, who sails *Corsair*, a 1976 model, on Lake Michigan, advises prospective buyers to carefully inspect the mast compression post and general support area of the deck-stepped spar. Although he has not had the problem on his boat, he knows of sisterships where the 2-by-6-foot oak compression post has been bowed out from the bulkhead by compression loading. It is easy to spot this because the compression post bends into the forward walkway. Other signs of this problem include deck depressions and gelcoat cracks around the base of the mast, saggy forestay tension that can't be taken up with the backstay and obvious misalignment (or removal) of the joiner cover pieces on the bulkhead below. Sometimes the bulkhead is actually adrift and needs to be retabbed to the deck after the compression post has been resupported.

Another problem that should be checked is the rudder tube, especially on tiller-steered boats. The original bearing supports were inadequate and it is not uncommon for the rudder stock to feel quite sloppy in the rudder tube. The solution is to drop the rudder and add new Teflon bearings. Hull-and-deck joint leaks are not uncommon, but Ranger 33s have no exclusive claim on this malady. The interim solution is to rebed the toerail fasteners and buy more time. Also, check the aft chainplates, which sometimes cause the deck to lift because they are bolted directly through the deck with only small backing plates for support.

Most Ranger 33s have been raced, sometimes extensively. This is a mixed blessing. While boats that have been raced have usually been upgraded, including sails and electronics, they have also been used hard. Boats that haven't been raced likely have not been upgraded and may require extensive retrofits. Try to find a 1975 or later model because that is when the Atomic 4 gas engine was changed to a 16-horsepower Universal diesel and the interior styling was upgraded. Ranger 33s came sparsely equipped. Many boats have been extensively retrofitted, from electric pumps for fresh water to rewiring to accommodate today's electronics. Be sure to check these installations carefully.

On deck

A small molded bulwark is capped with a teak toerail on older pre-1975 boats, with the genoa track mounted on top. Newer boats have an aluminum railing. The narrow side decks, where the lack of beam really becomes obvious, have a distinct camber. This keeps them from collecting water, and more importantly, makes for a level surface when going forward while sailing to weather. Cambered decks have gone out of style though they are quite practical. The deck hardware is rather small, especially the chocks and cleats. The stemhead fitting is also undersized, and if you plan to cruise the boat seriously, some provision for anchoring must be made. Long teak grabrails line each side of the cabintrunk. Most older boats have single lifelines with rather stubby stanchions. The nonskid surface does not seem to hold up well. When it comes time to paint the deck, nonskid should be added to the paint.

The original mast section was beefy but the long boom extrusion was undersized. It is quite likely that the boom has been retrofitted, but you should verify this on the used boat you are considering. A giveaway is if the boom is still set up for roller reefing with a small worm gear, which was originally specified. Obviously, if the standing rigging is original, or for that matter, more than 10 years old, consider replacing it.

The cockpit of tiller-steered boats seems larger than those with wheels because the pedestal, which takes up a lot of room, is not there. Of course, when sailing, the sweep of the tiller must be considered. But when tied up at the dock or at anchor, the tiller can be swung out of the way. There is a large sail locker to port and coaming compartments on each side. There is not much of a bridgedeck so it wouldn't take much for green water to slosh below. With the mainsheet traveler aft (where it is on most 33s), the angle of the sheet led from the boom is not optimal.

Down below

For a boat designed in the 1960s, the interior layout is well-thought-out. Starting at the bow is the standard V-berth. Going aft, a deceptively large molded head complete with sink is to port, with a big hanging locker opposite. The saloon has either settees to each side, or more commonly, a U-shaped dinette to port. This can be dropped and converted to a double berth. There isn't much storage in the boat. The slim 9-foot, 7-inch beam hits home down below. There are small shelves behind the settees.

The galley is way aft and to port. There is decent counter space, a deep icebox and room for a good-sized stove and oven. It is likely that the cooking system has been changed from alcohol to propane. You should carefully inspect the installation. I have encountered propane tanks installed in the sail locker. This is dangerous and not a good idea. The best feature of the interior is the forward-facing navigation station opposite the galley. The navigator sits on the foot of the quarter berth, but the chart desk is good-sized.

Fortunately, the six large portlights keep the saloon light because the woodworking, typical of the era, is dark and heavy. Unfortunately, the ventilation below is terrible. There is not an opening hatch or opening portlights to be found in the saloon. The forward fiberglass hatch is flimsy and needs to be replaced or rebuilt. An excellent off-season project would be to add opening portlights and an overhead hatch in the saloon.

Engine

The Ranger 33 was first fitted with the ubiquitous Atomic 4 gas engine. There is nothing wrong with these timeless engines, most are still running. However, I prefer diesels for their safety and ruggedness. Diesel-equipped boats are invariably more desirable on the used boat market. In 1975 the Universal 16-horsepower diesel became an option. Engine access is good, as the engine sound box extends well into the cabin from the companionway. The stuffing box is tougher to inspect and must be reached through the cockpit sail locker. The original design called for a miserly 20 gallons of fuel and water, although many boats are likely to have augmented the freshwater-tank capacity. Be sure to check the condition of the prop when you haul the boat for survey. Many 33s are fitted with folding props.

Underway

"The boat screams off the wind," said Sandy Curtiss, who raced his 1976-built *Rocking Horse* for a dozen years on Lake Michigan. *Rocking Horse* won class

Ranger 33

Sailing Magazine's Value Guide

PRICE: The value would be even higher but there are a lot of other boats of this vintage priced in the same ballpark.

DESIGN QUALITY: The Gary Mull design began as a hot racer and continues as a performance cruiser.

CONSTRUCTION QUALITY: A typical production boat of its time, the 33's construction was pretty good. Problems with the mast compression post and steering systems may have been dealt with.

USER-FRIENDLINESS: An easy boat to sail and obtain good performance from. The cockpit is not comfortable by today's standards and the interior lacks volume and ventilation.

SAFETY: Single lifelines, poor nonskid and no bridgedeck compromise safety.

TYPICAL CONDITION: While the boats seem to generally hold up well, they are often a mess cosmetically.

REFITTING: For its vintage, the 33 will be some work, as is to be expected. Extensive use of interior moldings makes interior work more difficult.

SUPPORT: There is not much support when it comes to an owner organization, although there are nearly 500 boats afloat.

AVAILABILITY: At any given time, there are numerous Ranger 33s on the market. There are more boats for sale today in the Great Lakes and on the West Coast.

INVESTMENT AND RESALE: With a purchase price likely below $30,000 and mainly cosmetic repairs, the Ranger 33 represents a sound value that holds up.

OVERALL 'SVG' RATING

honors twice and was second overall in the 1985 Chicago to Mackinac race. "The 1985 race was windy and a reach, which suited us," Curtiss said. "When the wind really piped up, we power-reached with double headsails. We carried the No. 2, with a high-cut clew and staysail as well." The 33 is a bit tender and most owners report that it is necessary to shorten up early. Curtiss learned that by dressing down to the No. 2 first, he could carry the main longer when sailing to weather. "At 20 knots, however, the main was usually reefed," he said.

According to some owners, the 33 develops a lot of weather helm when heeled. Like most flat-bottom boats, the 33 should be sailed close to its lines. The 33 is easily driven in light air, although it also pounds a bit and makes some leeway when beating into a moderate breeze.

Like almost all Gary Mull designs, the Ranger 33 really shines off the wind. "The boat surfs easily," Curtiss said. "And even when running in big seas, it's easy to control." Bartz likes the feeling of security the boat gives him. "I never feel like the boat will let me down."

Conclusion

Though it had its heyday more than 20 years ago, the Ranger 33, like many other boats developed in the late 1960s, is still appealing today. Well-designed and well-built, it remains an extremely satisfying boat to sail. Considering that you can buy a Ranger 33 in decent condition for less than $25,000, sailing can be affordable for many more people.

Irwin Citation 34

Inexpensively built coastal cruiser with great potential

Ted Irwin is an enigma in the sailing industry. As a designer and builder, he has produced a vast and diverse collection of boats that total more than 6,000 during a career that has spanned more than 30 years. As a sailor, he has won more than his share of races, particularly during the glory days of the SORC in the late 1960s and early 1970s, and he has cruised all over the world in an innovative 65-foot ketch of his own design.

At one time, in the mid-1980s, Irwin Yachts had more than 300 employees and was building 13 different models. At that time, Irwin's company was the largest privately owned sailboat manufacturer in the country. He was the first builder to recognize the trend toward larger cruising boats, and he has built more boats longer than 50 feet than anyone in the world.

Still, there remains a stigma attached to Irwins because they are not usually considered quality boats. Aside from the larger Irwins, the boats haven't held their value well over the years. This is likely because most of Irwin's production was targeted toward the lower end of the market, at least from a price standpoint. And there is no disputing that quality control was not what it could have been. It is revealing, though, to chat with Irwin owners, for while they openly admit some nagging problems with their boats, they also lavish them with praise. Irwin had a natural talent for drawing handsome boats, and aesthetically at least, most of his designs have aged well. Regardless of how they're built, they sail well. Irwin didn't build slow boats.

Irwin spent a few years working as a draftsman for Charlie Morgan, cutting his teeth in the business at the right hand of the master. During his off hours he rented a Quonset hut on St. Pete Beach and built his first boat, a 31-foot sloop called *Voodoo*. Irwin had great success with the boat, winning 24 of 28 races in the old Florida

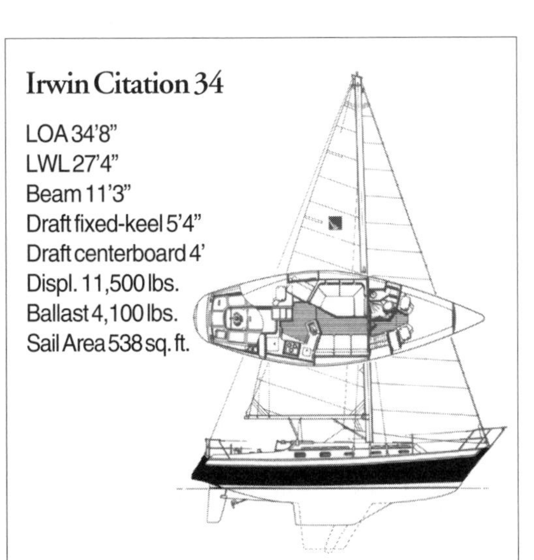

Irwin Citation 34 Price Data

		Low	High
BUC Retail Range	1979	$24,100	$26,800
	1982	$29,300	$32,600
	1985	$35,600	$39,600

		State	Asking
Boats For Sale	1979	MI	$37,500
	1980	FL	$29,900
	1984	FL	$34,900

Ocean Racing Association. In 1966, at the ripe old age of 26, Irwin moved to Clearwater, Florida, and started his own company. Although Irwin's heart was in performance boats, he soon recognized that if he was going to make a living he needed to produce boats that appealed to a broader sailing public, and most importantly, were affordable.

His original plant was just 12,500 square feet, but would grow to 75,000 square feet before production ground to a halt in the early 1990s. Irwin's designs were often innovative and ranged from the fat but roomy 10/4, which became Bob Johnson's inspiration for the Island Packet 26, to the luxurious 65, which featured a deck saloon arrangement long before Oyster supposedly invented the concept. In the end, however, it was the thousands of boats built between those extremes that more accurately define the long run of Irwin Yachts. Of these, the Irwin Citation 34 is a good example.

First impressions

Introduced in 1978, more than 300 Citation 34s were built during a seven-year production run. The "Citation" signature indicated that the boat was finished with a bit more flair than standard models—a slick marketing trick gleaned from the auto industry.

Like the bulk of Irwin's designs, the Citation 34 is a stylish boat with a comfortable cockpit and well-thought-out interior. Although modern for its times, there is still a subtle sheer, and the coachroof blends nicely into the overall lines. A bold, molded covestripe, which was a common feature on most Irwins, tends to accentuate the sheer. The bow has a concave curve—also something of an Irwin trademark—and a moderate overhang. The stern is pinched with the raised sections favored by the IOR.

By the numbers, the Citation 34 is moderate in its proportions, displacing 11,500 pounds with 4,100 pounds of ballast.

Although the Citation was offered with a few different hull designs, most were the keel centerboard arrangement. Irwin was one of the first builders to realize the importance of a shoal draft. The fixed keel model has a draft of 5 feet, 4 inches. The keel section is a modified fin and the semibalanced rudder has a small skeg. The rig is a masthead sloop. A healthy working sail area of 538 square feet keeps the boat moving in light air.

Construction

The construction is typical of the period with a solid fiberglass hull and a balsa-cored deck. For the most part the hulls are laid up well, although a recent survey of an Irwin Citation 34 in Ft. Lauderdale revealed a few hull voids and a less than sparkling gelcoat application. The boat also had a bad case of blisters, but as we all know, this malady spared few builders. The cored deck showed a few signs of delamination, but the teak-faced plywood bulkheads were still adequately tabbed to the hull and glassed-over wood floors offered athwartship support.

The hull-and-deck joint, however, is not a strong point of the boat. Although it is chemically joined with 3M 5200 (or something comparable), it is fastened mechanically with sheet metal screws, both from the top and sides, incorporating an aluminum toerail. Through-bolts would be better because a hard impact to the toerail might result in a hull-to-deck joint leak, which by several accounts is not uncommon.

While the overall construction is not unlike other production boats of the period, the lack of attention to details has earned Irwin its less than enviable reputation. From undersized cleats, to pulpits and stanchions that are not through-bolted, to poor quality through-hull valves, the Citation 34 came from the factory with several shortcomings. The good news for the used boat buyer is that often these problems have already been corrected by previous owners.

What to look for

I have mixed feelings about keel centerboarders, and unless shoal draft is an important consideration, I would look for one of the rare deep-keel models. These boats are usually less desirable and cheaper. They also sail better and don't have any centerboard problems like broken pennants, leaks and wobbling. That said, I wouldn't hesitate to buy a board boat after careful inspection.

Most owners that I talked with mentioned leaks as the most common and most annoying problems with the Citation 34. Robert Benton, who sails a centerboard model near Savannah, Georgia, said that the stanchions frequently work loose, causing leaks below. Other owners mentioned leaking hatches, portlights and chainplates. Mike Herman of Ft. Lauderdale complained about hull-and-deck joint leaks and how he has tried unsuccessfully to remedy the situation.

Thomas Wright, who sails a 1979 model, noted that there is no adequate provision for an emergency tiller. Because most of the boats you will be inspecting will be around 20 years old, check the standing rigging carefully. If it hasn't been rerigged, factor that project into your calculations. Irwin finished its own masts and booms, and they often need to be repainted.

On deck

The Citation 34 has a large, comfortable cockpit. It can accommodate six adults and has an icebox, two lockers and a propane locker. Wheel steering was standard, although some owners complained that the wheel is loose on the pedestal and too large. The view from the helm is good, even with a dodger and bimini in place. There is not much of a bridgedeck, just a small sill above the companionway, but this can be remedied by leaving the bottom hatch board in place. The 34 was not intended to be a bluewater boat, and most coastal cruisers prefer the easy access to below decks. Incidentally, the two cockpit scuppers are quite large.

The side decks are wide and easy to navigate, although the molded nonskid does not seem to hold up well. There is an external anchor locker forward, but the anchoring hardware is undersized. The standard mooring cleats are almost comical, and small as they are, may not be through-bolted.

The mainsheet traveler is located over the companionway, and the sheet fixes in the center of the boom, which causes a lot of load and trim friction. It does, however, free up space in the cockpit. Despite some poor outfitting, the Citation 34 has the potential to be an excellent boat with a few modifications and upgrades.

Down below

The 34 has a conventional interior presented in an unconventional way. Irwin was one of the first builders to realize that interiors sold boats. He used angled, partial bulkheads to make good use of the space below. A double V-berth is forward, followed by a large head to port. The saloon has a wraparound settee to port, which allows easy access to the seats behind the table and a settee opposite.

Tankage takes up most of the space below the settees, but there is adequate storage above and behind. The teak veneer finish of the 1980 model I examined was unfortunately stained from leaks. The teak-and-holly veneered sole also showed evidence of water damage, likely caused by the shallow bilge that allows small amounts of water to slosh onto the sole when heeled. Ventilation was excellent with three overhead hatches and seven opening plastic portlights, which unfortunately had broken dogs and obvious leaks.

An angled nav station is to port, and although the desktop is a bit small, it does allow easy access to the quarter berth. The galley is the best feature of the interior. The large single sink angles toward the middle of the boat, which allows good drainage on either tack, something rarely achieved in 1980s aft cockpit boats. A three-burner propane stove was standard, and many boats came with factory-installed refrigeration. There is plenty of counter space, although the Formica tops may need to be replaced.

Engine

The standard engine was a 16-horsepower, two-cylinder Yanmar diesel. Irwin was one of the first builders to offer Yanmars, which have since come to dominate the industry. A 22-horsepower model was offered as an option, but it was not a popular choice. Like any 20-year-old boat, it may be time to rebuild or repower. If you do decide to upgrade, opt for more horsepower.

One of the best features of the Citation 34 is engine access. Part of the cockpit sole lifts up to allow

Irwin Citation 34

Sailing Magazine's Value Guide

PRICE: With prices ranging from $24,000 to $39,000, the Citation 34 is one of the best-priced 34-footers on the market.

DESIGN QUALITY: Ted Irwin's designs invariably look good, perform well and have comfortable accommodations. The centerboard makes for a desirable shoal-draft.

CONSTRUCTION QUALITY: The main drawback to the Citation 34 is the inconsistent construction quality. Although the basic fiberglass work is adequate, the details and outfitting leave something to be desired.

USER-FRIENDLINESS: Lots of features make it easy to handle and comfortable—from a midboom sheeting arrangement that keeps the cockpit clear, to wide side decks and easy access to the quarterberth.

SAFETY: It is the details that keep this rating low. The pulpits and stanchion bases are not through-bolted, there are poor-quality valves below the waterline and the deck hardware is undersized.

TYPICAL CONDITION: Although most owners seem to maintain and upgrade their boats, the poor initial quality is still apparent.

REFITTING: The Citation is easy to work on and has great engine access. Irwin used many proprietary parts and the company is out of business. Still, parts are available and until recently, Irwin maintained a supply.

SUPPORT: Although Irwin Yachts is out of business, a new company has been formed that is building large 56-foot-plus boats. There is also an Irwin e-mail discussion group that can be found through SailNet.com. Also, Gene Gammon, www.irwinyacht.com, a longtime associate of Ted Irwin's, is running the new company and is very knowledgeable about the old boats.

AVAILABILITY: With a fairly large production run and a once-broad distribution network, you will find a good selection of Citations for sale. The Gulf Coast of Florida probably has the most boats.

INVESTMENT AND RESALE: The Irwin stigma affects all models to some degree. Original 34 owners took a hit on their boat, but the used market for the boat has been fairly steady for years. It is a lot of boat for the buck.

OVERALL 'SVG' RATING

access from above. I think you might be able to squeeze the engine through if you needed to repower.

"Regular maintenance is a breeze, and from the cockpit hatch you can also inspect the steering system," Benton said. You can also reach the engine from a hatch in the quarterberth and from behind the companionway steps. The standard fuel tank is 30 gallons, providing a range of 700 miles.

Underway

Like almost all Irwin designs, the Citation 34 is balanced under sail, easily handled and fairly fast. Wright, who sails on Lake Michigan, loves the way his boat handles, especially when the wind pipes up. Benton admits to learning to sail while learning to race, and is justly proud of his Citation's results. During a recent Carolina Ocean Challenge, he encountered 35-knot winds and 10-foot seas and finished first in class.

The Citation is relatively close winded, although the midboom sheeting arrangement on the main may require a vang or barberhauler. Some owners report the boat to be a bit tender and list its best point of sail as a broad reach, but that's not much of a surprise. Herman, who takes his boat to the Bahamas every year, refutes the tender tag and said he has encountered rough going in the Gulf Stream several times without any problems. In fact, he said the boat has a nice sea motion, which is interesting because the hull shape was fairly modern for its time.

Conclusion

The Irwin Citation 34 offers many advantages if you are looking for an inexpensive coastal cruiser. Overall performance is quite good, and the interior comfortable. Another advantage of buying a second, third, or fourth-hand Citation 34 is that most of the problems will likely have been remedied.

Beneteau First 345

A spirited well-built racer-cruiser

It was 18 years ago and I still remember being nervous about picking up a Beneteau First 38 in Bermuda. I was young, new to the delivery business and filled with the straight dope gleaned from books by Hal Roth and Don Street. According to the masters, it was downright dicey to take a fin-keel, spade-rudder boat offshore, especially one built in France and rigged with, dare I say it, running backstays. But I needed the money and shoved off anyway. It was August and of course we had a brush with a tropical storm. Not only did the Beneteau stand up to 40-plus-knot winds and big seas, but we blasted along on a screaming reach and raised the Chesapeake Bay Bridge after three days of spectacular sailing. That little jaunt forever changed my perception of the First Series.

The First 345, designed by versatile naval architect Jean Berret, was the third boat in the series and introduced in 1984. It was one of Beneteau's most successful production runs. In all, nearly 500 boats were built before the model was replaced by the 355 in 1988. Today, Beneteau is the largest sailboat manufacturer on the planet, but in the early '80s, the company was just gaining a firm toehold in the U.S. market. The sleek First series, emphasizing performance boats that were also comfortable enough to cruise, was a smashing success on this side of the Atlantic, so much so that by 1987, Beneteau opened a plant in Marion, South Carolina. Nearly 50 First 345s were built in the United States.

Beneteau First 345

LOA 34'6"
LWL 28'8"
Beam 11'6"
Draft 6'4"
Displacement 12,000 lbs.
Ballast 4,651 lbs.
Sail Area 546 sq. ft.

First impressions

From the splashy orange-and-black racing stripes on the angular cabintrunk, to the triple boot tops, the First 345 made a vivid impression when delivered new from the factory. Unfortunately, those same gimmicks look a bit dated today, although the clean entry and overall fine lines have aged well. In fact, the rake of the stem looks nicely proportioned, especially when contrasted to today's vertical bows. The wide reverse transom helps extend the waterline to 28 feet, 8 inches on an LOA of 34 feet, 6 inches. The First 345 had a masthead sloop rig stepped on the keel. Today's First series models feature fractional rigs.

Below the water the deep fin results in a draft of 6 feet, 4 inches. A 4-foot, 10-inch shoal-draft option was popular on U.S. boats, especially those not destined for a race course. The iron keel is externally fastened, and the spade rudder is balanced. The First 345 was definitely not a lightweight for its day, with a displacement of 12,000 pounds. By comparison, the Hunter 34 and Catalina 34 both displace slightly less, and a true performance boat of the same period, the J/35 for example, weighs in at 10,000 pounds.

Construction

Because of the high volume of production, it is easy to underestimate Beneteau's quality construction. The 345 has a solid fiberglass hull married to a balsa-cored deck on an inward-turning flange. The joint also incorporates an aluminum toerail that is riveted to the hull. Beneteau used a grid pattern of floors in the bilge that provides great structural integrity. The 345 was built to France's Bureau Veritas standards for offshore sailing. I closely examined a 1985 First 345 recently

Beneteau First 345 Price Data

		Low	High
BUC Retail Range	1984	$30,400	$33,800
	1985	$32,000	$34,200
	1986	$33,500	$37,000
		State	**Asking**
Boats For Sale	1984	CT	$42,000
	1985	TX	$44,500
	1986	FL	$39,900

and was impressed by the lack of gelcoat crazing on deck. The molded nonskid pattern is intricate and holds up well over time. This particular boat had been used in the Caribbean charter fleet, and aside from expected wear and tear, the boat appeared structurally sound.

A laminated backing plate in the bilge supports the cast-iron keel, although the keel bolts are a source of confusion. While the bolts themselves are stainless, apparently the nuts are not, and corrosion is often evident. The bolts and nuts are completely covered with a sealing solution, but it seems to lose its water-resistance after time. The maststep is on a small bridge in the shallow bilge. The rudderstock is stainless steel, and the rudder blade is fiberglass.

What to look for

It must be noted that in the early 1980s, particularly between 1983 and 1985, Beneteau had serious blister problems with several of its models, including the 345. However, the company did the right thing and corrected the problem at its own expense. Many of the 345s on the market in the United States have had professional blister jobs in the past that carried transferable 10-year warranties. These warranties are out of date now, but fortunately the blisters don't seem to return. The original source of the problem was a catalyst applied to the resin.

When looking at 345s, carefully examine the keel bolts and the top nuts in the bilge. While the keel bolts are usually fine, the nuts may need to be replaced. This is not a huge project, but it may best be left to a boatyard; if you have any worries, have the bolts x-rayed. (It seems to be more of a problem with early boats.) Also, check the deck area around the chain locker where a few owners have reported minor delamination. Other items to look for include droopy fabric headliners that are difficult to put back up and a mess to replace. This seems to be a problem caused by heat and humidity and is more commonly found on southern boats. The bladder water tanks were prone to leaking and should be checked. Early boats built in France came from the factory with gate valves on through-hull fittings. If these haven't been changed, they should be. One thing to look for is a 345 with the 28-horsepower Volvo diesel instead of the more popular 18-horsepower 2002 model. Several owners reported that the 18-horsepower was just barely adequate for pushing the boat through a chop or headwind.

On deck

The wide side decks, low-slung cabintrunk and large comfortable cockpit make the 345 seem like a larger boat on deck. The stemhead fitting can accommodate two anchors and the chain locker is large and can stow a fair amount of chain and rode. The Goiot cleats and fairleads are husky, although the aluminum stanchions could be taller and better supported. The aluminum toerail, while practical for all matter of tie downs and sheet leads, is not friendly on bare feet. A single piece of smoked Plexiglas, externally bolted in place, takes the place of portlights on the cabin side. The standard spar was built by Isomast, and most owners have opted to lead all control lines aft to the cockpit. Originally, the 345 came in two versions: The racing version had a one-foot taller mast, a tiller, load-bearing adjustable genoa leads and the mainsheet traveler located across the bridgedeck. The cruising package included a shorter stick, wheel steering and the mainsheet traveler above the companionway. It seems to me that most owners opted for the racing setup.

The cockpit is spacious, especially on the tiller boats, and the seat backs are well angled for comfort and support. Gary Bielekjeski, who sails *Namaskar,* a 1984 French-built 345 out of Bellhaven, North Carolina, noted that the teak slats on the cockpit seats keep you from sliding, especially when stepping from

Beneteau First 345

Sailing Magazine's Value Guide

PRICE: When compared to Hunters and Catalinas, the old First series boats are a bit pricey, but you also get more boat.

DESIGN QUALITY: Jean Berret's design was not extreme and has stood the test of time. The boat performs well and is capable offshore. The interior arrangement is clever. Different rig and interior options give you plenty of choices.

CONSTRUCTION QUALITY: Beneteaus, especially the older First Series, were better built boats than they get credit for. The blistering problem was unfortunate, but the company handled it well.

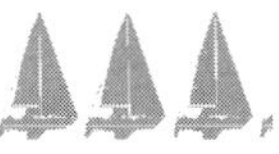

USER-FRIENDLINESS: Most boats on the market seem to have the racing package, with the deep draft. The boat is rewarding to sail, although the tiller can be a chore in heavy air. The interior is comfortable.

SAFETY: Wide side decks make moving about easy, but the lifelines won't do much to stop you from falling overboard. The boat could use more handholds below.

TYPICAL CONDITION: This rating would be higher, but some boats spent time in the charter trade, which is hard on equipment. Look for boats that were not chartered.

REFITTING: The First 345 can be tough to work on below where foam and fabric liners make for tough access. Parts are available in the United States and France.

SUPPORT: The Beneteau owners group maintains a great web page at www.beneateau-owners.com. The company's page, www.beneateauusa.com is also helpful and has information about previous models.

AVAILABILITY: With a large production run there is always a good selection of 345s on the market, and they seem to be spread across the country. They are also widely available in Europe.

INVESTMENT AND RESALE: The price has held steady on the First 345 as the market recognizes that the boat provides a lot of bang for the buck. The fact that Beneteau is still in business and prospering helps maintain the value of its used boats.

OVERALL 'SVG' RATING

the cockpit to the deck. Bielekjeski said he also likes the tiller steering, both from a performance and practical standpoint.

"The tiller lets me feel what's happening with the boat much faster than with a wheel," he said. "I wouldn't, however, want a tiller on a much bigger boat, it can get tough to handle when the wind kicks up." He also said that he likes how the tiller frees up the cockpit at anchor, making it easier to move around the cockpit and creating more party room.

Down below

European boatbuilders, especially the French, were the first to break with conventional wisdom on interior design layout. While American builders were still offering cramped quarter berths on most boats under 40 feet, the Europeans were offering aft cabins tucked cleverly under the cockpit. The 345 is a good example of this kind of innovation. The interior includes two private cabins, a functional galley, a large chart table and a comfortable saloon—all this in a 34-foot boat. There is also the charter version with two small double cabins forward.

In the noncharter layout, the forward stateroom has a large V-berth with a hanging locker to port and a bureau opposite. The saloon has settees straddling a lovely teak table with a handsome wine rack in the middle. Bielekjeski noted that his boat has additional storage above the port side settee, although the bladder water tanks take up all the storage under the settees. I am not a great fan of bladder tanks and would look at converting this space to rigid tanks.

The U-shaped galley is to port and most boats have a three-burner stove and double sinks. Refrigeration seems to be a retrofit item on most boats, and the icebox is not very well insulated. Pressurized hot and cold water seemed to be standard. The chart table is opposite the galley, and in typical Beneteau fashion, it's huge, although there isn't much headroom when seated. The aft cabin is behind the chart table. The double bunk is large, but there isn't much headroom there either. This isn't a spot for the claustrophobic. The head is aft to port, which is a great place for a head when under way, and includes a shower arrangement.

Engine

As mentioned earlier, two different engines were available, either a three-cylinder, Volvo 28-horsepower or a two-cylinder 18-horsepower model. Most of the boats built in France have the smaller engine, and by all accounts, the boat is underpowered. One solution is to add a variable pitched prop like a Max Prop. Engine access is good, although you have to dismantle the aft cabin in order to reach the back of the engine and the stuffing box. The engine room insulation is adequate and the Volvo is a quiet engine.

Underway

The reason most people chose a new Beneteau First 345 was because they loved the way the boat sailed. That is still a pretty good reason to buy the boat secondhand. The 345s are weatherly and surprisingly stiff. Willfried Eggmont, who sails a 1985 First 345 off the Belgian coast, told me that the boat is very close winded and, even when pinching, can usually make 5 to 6 knots in a moderate breeze.

Eggmont noted that while he can stay with larger boats upwind, on a close reach the 345 is not as fast. He flies his spinnaker as soon as he can when reaching. Eggmont said that what he likes best about the boat is that it is easy to handle in heavy weather. He described how he singlehanded the boat in Force 8 conditions while crossing the English Channel, and the boat never gave him an anxious moment.

Bielekjeski agreed that the boat is close winded, and while it sails well enough in light air, it finds its stride in moderate to strong breezes. Bielekjeski club races the boat on the Neuse River and Pamlico Sound, and with a PHRF rating of 144, he is usually the scratch boat.

Some owners mentioned a bit of weather helm, especially when carrying a large headsail. Eggmont said he thinks the standard Lewmar 48s are a bit undersized. It is worth noting that many of the French boats in this country came over on their own bottoms.

Conclusion

The Beneteau First 345 packs a lot of boat into a small package. Prices range from \$30,000 to around \$45,000, and seem to be holding steady. If you are looking for a lively, well-built boat and your budget is in this range, you owe it to yourself to check out the First 345, it may surprise you.

Niagara 35

Handsome, high-quality cruiser that's capable of crossing oceans or coastal cruising in style

The Niagara 35 is, according to its designer Mark Ellis, "a moderate design." Moderate, however, does not mean uninspired and certainly not unpopular. The Niagara 35 is highly valued for its moderate proportions. Although more than 300 of the 35s were built, it's hard to find one on the used boat market because they are so highly sought after.

Built by George Hinterhoeller in St. Catherines, Ontario, the Niagara 35, like many C&C models of the same era, was well-received on both sides of the border. Hinterhoeller, who at one time was president of C&C, is probably best known for building the distinctive line of Nonsuch catboats. However, the Niagara 35 and its larger sistership, the Niagara 42, are excellent examples of a talented and often underrated builder.

Ellis is a designer of great originality. His designs include the surprisingly popular Nonsuch boats and the innovative Northeast 37 motorsailer. The Niagara 35 was really his baby from the inception, and he told me that he actually designed it on spec. He opted for a traditional look above the waterline and a bit more modern shape below. His intent was to create a capable cruiser that could be, in his words, "occasionally passaged."

He exceeded his own expectations as several notable ocean voyages have been completed in 35s. A few years ago I met a Canadian family in the Azores who had been cruising on their 35 for years and spoke highly of the boat's seakindliness. Of course, credit also has to be attributed to Hinterhoeller and his crew, who consistently turned out a high-quality product.

Niagara 35

LOD 35'1"
LWL 26'8"
Beam 11'5"
Draft 5'2"
Displacement 15,000 lbs.
Ballast 5,500 lbs.
Sail Area 598 sq. ft.

First impressions

In certain respects the Niagara 35 is similar in concept to Bob Perry's Valiants. Looking at the springy sheer, handsome bow overhang, short bowsprit and boxed coachhouse, you might expect a long keel and attached rudder below the water. Instead, the fin keel is a standard NACA foil of moderate draft, and the rudder is a balanced spade. It's not that the 35 is a flyer in disguise, but it does perform surprisingly well through a wide range of conditions.

When you step aboard you immediately realize the 35 carries a lot of freeboard. This freeboard, however, blends nicely into the overall lines, thanks in part, to the pronounced sheer. The 35 has a solid, big boat feel and the quality of the construction is readily apparent. The freeboard combined with an unusual yet functional interior arrangement makes the 35 seem like a larger boat despite a moderate beam of 11 feet, 5 inches. The overall displacement is 15,000 pounds with 5,500 pounds of external lead ballast, giving the boat a 37-percent ballast-to-displacement ratio. The single spreader, sloop rig carries just under 600 square feet of working sail area.

Niagara 35 Price Data

		Low	High
BUC Retail Range	1980	$47,500	$ 52,200
	1985	$68,300	$ 75,000
	1990	$98,200	$108,000

		State	Asking
Boats For Sale	1980	FL	$ 60,000
	1986	CT	$ 99,500
	1988	ME	$125,000

Construction

Ellis, who cut his teeth designing at Hood and C&C, insisted on a balsa-cored hull and deck. Naturally, Hinterhoeller, who built thousands of balsa-cored boats at C&C, had no problem with this request. Ellis told me they were careful to preplan the hull and provide areas of solid glass where necessary. The centerline is solid glass, as are the areas around through-hull fittings and around high-load areas on deck like those found under the winches and steering pedestal. The hull-and-deck joint incorporates the bulwark for a watertight joint.

The external ballast is bolted to a keel stubby. The 1983 model I recently inspected in Ft. Lauderdale, Florida, had keel bolts in near-perfect condition. Stout floors provide athwartship support. The bulkheads are securely tabbed to the hull, and there is evidence of attention to small details. For example, the mast base rests on an aluminum bridge that keeps it out of the bilge and free of corrosion. Quality construction is always a mix of proper workmanship, a sound design and good planning.

What to look for

Both a standard model and the Encore version, introduced around 1985, were built. The Niagara 35 went into production in 1979 and more than 250 hulls were built before the Encore became available. The only difference between the two is the interior arrangement.

The standard (sometimes called the Classic or Mark I) arrangement is quite innovative. It includes two large quarter berths aft, a head and galley amidships separated by a bulkhead, a large saloon and a small area forward often used as a workroom. The Encore version offered a more common arrangement with a double cabin aft and a double cabin forward.

The Niagara 35 has held up very well over the years, and the owners I spoke with simply loved their boats. Even when pressed, they could only come up with a few things about the boat that have caused any problems or they would like to have changed. The most common complaint concerns the engine, a Volvo two-cylinder saildrive that owners like Colin Campbell in Toronto said is reliable but leaves the boat underpowered. In some ways Ellis and Hinterhoeller were ahead of their time by using the saildrive. Although it is widely accepted today, in the late 1970s saildrives met market resistance. In 1982 a four-cylinder Westerbeke with a V-drive transmission became the standard engine.

Other problems to look out for are primarily age-related. Check for delamination on deck and make sure that the rig has been updated if it is more than 10 years old.

On deck

The 35's cockpit is shallow and quite large, with good-sized lockers port and starboard. The helmsman sits on the propane locker, which is slightly elevated to improve visibility, although it is still tough for short sailors to see over the coachroof. Also, the seatbacks are a bit abrupt. Cockpit seating is one aspect of yacht design that has really improved in the last decade.

The Niagara 35 is an easy boat to sail shorthanded. The primary winches are within reach of the wheel, and a mast deck collar makes it convenient to lead sail controls aft to the cockpit. If I have one criticism it is that, on the boat I examined, I found it difficult to squeeze around the wheel.

The foredeck is extremely well thought out. The short bowsprit is made from tubular stainless and the bobstay is a stainless rod. There are two husky anchor rollers and two hawsepipes, features every cruising sailor appreciates. The nonskid is aggressive, the teak handholds are strong and well placed, and the molded bulwark provides a sense of security when moving about. The stanchions and lifelines could be a little taller, but this is a common complaint with boats of this

Niagara 35 — Sailing Magazine's Value Guide

PRICE: The high asking price is the main drawback of the boat, but that old cliché usually rings true: you get what you pay for. Although the Canadian dollar is weak against the U.S. dollar, the boat may be even more expensive in Canada where it is considered a classic.

DESIGN QUALITY: The design is moderate in proportion, but overall it is a very nice combination of traditional and modern. The interior arrangement of the Mark I is quite innovative and functional for passagemaking.

CONSTRUCTION QUALITY: Although I am not a fan of cored hulls, especially balsa-cored hulls, few did it better than George Hinterhoeller. Time is the test, and old 35s have held up very well.

USER-FRIENDLINESS: The boat is easy to sail and handles well under power. The systems are well-thought-out without being overengineered.

SAFETY: Quality construction makes the boat inherently safe. Bulwarks make the deck secure. Lifelines could be taller and the spade rudder adds vulnerability.

TYPICAL CONDITION: The Niagara 35s that I have seen on the used market are really in nice shape as a general rule. This speaks to the care their owners have lavished on them and the overall high quality of the design and construction.

REFITTING: Designer Mark Ellis planned for access right from the beginning, which makes refitting much easier. The overall spaciousness of the boat makes working less aggravating.

SUPPORT: Although Hinterhoeller is out of business, there is still good information about the 35. The best source is designer Mark Ellis, who can be reached through Harris and Ellis Yachts at (905) 825-0036, or on the Web at www.harrisellis.com.

AVAILABILITY: There were more than 300 Niagara 35s built, but they don't linger long on the used market. The best place to find boats is in the Great Lakes area, particularly near Toronto.

INVESTMENT AND RESALE: The Niagara 35 has held its value now for many years and there is no reason to think that it won't well into the future. You pay a premium for these cruisers but you usually can get your money back out when you sell.

OVERALL 'SVG' RATING

era. The deck hardware is oversized, from the mooring cleats to the Skene chocks.

The original running rigging came with swage end fittings, but many boats will have been changed to mechanical terminals by now. Inboard and outboard headsail tracks are a nice touch on a cruising boat. The mainsheet traveler spans the companionway, the result being that the mainsheet is routed to a point approximately one-third from the end of the boom, providing better purchase than a midboom sheeting setup.

Down below

The standard interior is the one you will most likely find on the used boat market. According to Mark Ellis, all but 70 or 80 boats had this interior. Dropping below, you are almost immediately faced with a fore-and-aft bulkhead and quickly realize you've dropped into an aft cabin of sorts. There are large quarter berths port and starboard. The stand-up nav station is to starboard, at the head of the bunk, and a large hanging locker is to port. The aforementioned bulkhead separates the galley and head. This is a practical arrangement. The cook is well supported and plumbing fittings can be shared, limiting through-hull fittings. The saloon is next, with its large settees. There is no table, or at least there wasn't on the boat I looked at. The V-berth area can be used as a workroom or stateroom, or as in the boat I looked at, a child's cabin.

Ellis told me that this interior was designed for passagemaking. The plan provides four excellent sea berths. The off-watch can remain undisturbed sleeping in the saloon, while the deck watch can work at the chart table or heat up coffee. The centerline bulkhead provides good support for the cook in a seaway, and the amidship head is much more civilized than slogging forward to relieve yourself, especially if it is rough.

The Encore arrangement was a result of owners telling Ellis and Hinterhoeller that they wanted a forward cabin. This plan has a head and shower aft of the V-berth followed by the saloon. A U-shaped galley is to port, and a quarter cabin and nav station are starboard. Both interiors are nicely executed. The joinerwork is not ornate, but there is plenty of teak around. Ventilation is excellent with opening portlights standard and three hatches. Storage is limited by size and by the poly water tanks located under both settees in the saloon.

Engine

The original power plant was a Volvo 21-horsepower two-cylinder saildrive. As mentioned earlier, saildrives were not popular 20 years ago, and with some justification as the lower units tended to corrode. Still, I would prefer a saildrive to a V-drive, although Ellis said that when the company converted the boat to the 33-horsepower Westerbeke in 1982, he specified the V-drive to keep the prop forward. "These boats really handle well under power and a big part of that is because the prop is located quite far forward," Ellis said. Access to the engine, located behind the companionway, is good.

The fuel tank is made of aluminum and holds 30 gallons, which should provide a range of around 200 miles. The Canadians I met in the Azores had jerrycans with extra fuel sprinkled around the deck. The boat in Ft. Lauderdale had a Yanmar diesel that was retrofitted using a V-drive transmission.

Underway

Colin Campbell sails *Stowaway*, hull No. 111, on Lake Ontario. He noted that the boat sails well under headsail alone and easily balances with the spade rudder. He also claims that the boat is dry in heavy going, which he attributes to the freeboard. He claimed the boat has never given him an anxious moment. He lists the 35's speed through a range of conditions at 5.5 to 7 knots. Mark Gesiurer, who sails his uncle's Niagara 35 on Lake St. Clair, claims that the boat sails closer to the wind than most people think and tracks well, especially in choppy conditions. The Canadian couple I met in the Azores had completed the 1,800-mile passage from Bermuda in the same time it took me on a 40-foot Jeanneau, less than 14 days, which equates to a daily average of more than 130 miles.

Conclusion

The Niagara 35 is a handsome, high-quality all-around cruiser that appeals on many levels. It is capable of crossing the Atlantic or providing years of easy sailing on the Chesapeake Bay, Great Lakes or Puget Sound. It isn't cheap, with prices ranging from $50,000 to around $100,000 for a late model, but it will likely hold its value well into the future.

J/35

Groundbreaking one-design keelboat that is still a great performer

The J/35 radically changed the way many of us looked at big-boat one-design racing. When the Rod Johnstone-designed 35 was introduced in 1983, it offered more flat-out boat speed than most larger grand prix boats selling for twice the money. The allure of ultracompetitive one-design racing combined with a reasonably affordable boat to own and campaign, and one that guaranteed extraordinary performance, was an irresistible combination.

Like earlier J Boats, the 35 was designed with little regard for ratings and, ironically, that only contributed to its popularity. First to finish has always been more fun than first on corrected time, and the 35 was a major force in reviving the popularity of larger one-design boats. The J/35 class is the largest one-design class for boats longer than 30 feet in the world. This is not to say that J/35s are not competitive under PHRF or IMS. It is just nice to know that nothing in the design was compromised for a set of rules. In all, 320 J/35s were built before production ceased in 1995.

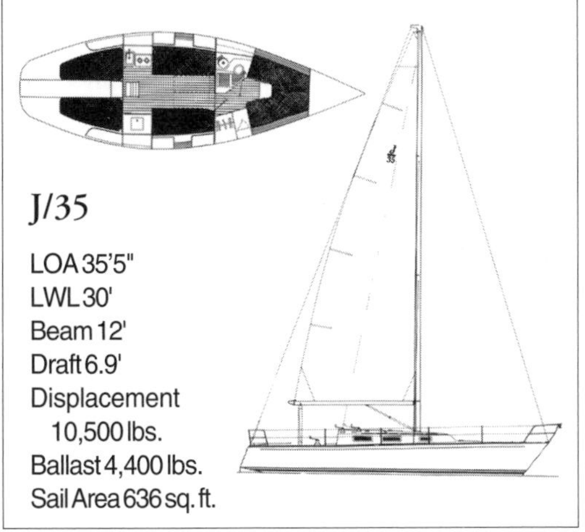

J/35

LOA 35'5"
LWL 30'
Beam 12'
Draft 6.9'
Displacement 10,500 lbs.
Ballast 4,400 lbs.
Sail Area 636 sq. ft.

First impressions

The intriguing thing about J Boats and their amazing proliferation is that their general appearance is rather understated; there is nothing showy about J Boats. While the boat is handsome in a spartan way, peering down at a J/35 tied to the dock, you wouldn't suspect that it can sustain surfing spinnaker runs of 15-plus knots and can easily track upwind at 8 knots. You also wouldn't guess that the boat is a veteran of several rugged offshore races, including the OSTAR, and renowned sailors like Francis Stokes and Tony Lush chose J/35s to race solo across the Atlantic.

The J/35 has the prototypical Johnstone profile. It has very short overhangs—although its bow is far from plumb by today's standards—and a slight reverse transom. The LWL stretches out 30 feet from an LOA of 35 feet, 5 inches. The sheerline is almost straight, which is another way of saying that there isn't much sheer. The freeboard is modest and the sleek, short cabintrunk blends into the deck just behind the forward hatch. The double-spreader rig is moderate in proportion.

You don't have to be a yacht designer to realize that speed results from a combination of hull shape and weight. Clearly, Johnstone has a keen sense of what makes a boat go fast. When asked several years ago, he modestly claimed that there is no secret to the 35's design. "Keep the weight down, especially in the ends, keep the center of gravity low with a deep lead keel and avoid hull-line distortions." (Johnstone told me recently that the statement is still valid except that today's shoal-draft keels can be just as efficient as the 35's nearly 7-foot fin.)

This of course oversimplifies what is, in fact, a very sophisticated underwater profile. With a displacement of 10,500 pounds, the J/35 is not radically light anymore. For example, the more recently designed J/105, which has a 34-foot, 6-inch overall length, displaces 7,750 pounds. However, the J/35 is very well-balanced and seems to attain great

J/35 Price Data

		Low	High
BUC Retail Range	1984	$43,100	$47,900
	1988	$59,500	$65,400
	1992	$72,500	$79,700

		State	Asking
Boats For Sale	1984	NY	$54,000
	1986	OH	$69,900
	1989	TX	$80,000

boat speed without a lot of fanfare. The J/35 has 633 square feet of working sail, and a sail area/displacement ratio of 21.

Construction

From the beginning, Johnstone brothers Rod and Bob decided to concentrate on the design and marketing aspects of the business and leave the building to the crew down the street at Tillotson-Pearson. TPI Composites, as the company is known today, is one of the premier boatbuilding concerns in the world and its client list has included, at one time or another, Freedom, Alden, Pearson and others.

When you build light boats, you have to build them intelligently. The 35's hull and deck are cored with end-grained balsa sandwiched between layers of unidirectional and biaxial fibers, which makes a stiffer hull than one laid up with conventional cloth and woven-roving laminates. Obviously, balsa-cored hulls pose more potential problems than solid laminates, especially below the waterline. However, TPI has been successfully coring hulls for many years and I have not heard of any problems with J/35 hull cores.

The J/35 has an unusual fiberglass main bulkhead that supports the rig load and provides athwart ships support. The bulkhead is constructed much like the hull except that it is solid laminate around the edges and in high-stress areas, like around the chainplates. In fact, Johnstone told me of a 35 that washed up on the rocks and still failed to break up the main bulkhead. Although cored boats are inherently stiffer than uncored ones, the 35 also has a series of fiberglass floors. These floors support the maststep and the keel bolts. The lead keel is externally fastened. The hull-to-deck joint is bonded and through-bolted. In examining older J/35s that have been sailed hard and put away wet for years, it is impressive that there is very little evidence of any structural problems. Later models were offered with ABS certificates.

What to look for

Look for a boat built after 1988 because that is when TPI began to use vinylester resin in the first layer of fiberglass as a barrier coat behind the gelcoat to prevent blistering. TPI was so confident that this resin prevented blisters they issued a 10-year, transferable hull warranty. Some of the early 35s had blister problems, so be sure to check with the seller to find out if and when a bottom job was done and what type of epoxy barrier coat was used.

Check the area around the genoa track on the gunwale. Owners are always looking for ways to pare weight, so many owners shortened these tracks and some didn't fill the bolt holes very well. Probe around the old hole; looking for signs of leaks and delamination. Check the bottom of the mast. Although top-quality spars were used and the mast is stepped on an I-beam that spans a couple of floors above the bilge, there may be spider cracks in the aluminum. Michael Kennedy, former president of the J/35 Class Association, suggests that potential buyers examine how well the boat is set up. This will tell you much about the boat's competitiveness and the seller's attention to detail.

Be sure you don't confuse the J/35 with the J/35C. The 35C evolved from the J/34C, which was J's version of a cruising boat. Also, there are a handful of shoal-draft models. Johnstone told me that retrofitting a modern, high-performance shoal keel is an option.

The outside-fitting portlights usually have to be replaced or rebedded, so check for signs of leaks. Also, a few owners told me that while the keel is usually quite fair, the rudder often has a dimple or two and may need fairing. One other item to mention: When you begin searching for a used J/35, be wary of listings. Bags of sails look impressive on the inventory sheet but many may be worn out. There is also nothing older than high-tech electronics that aren't high-tech anymore.

J/35

Sailing Magazine's Value Guide

PRICE: The J/35 is pricey, considering there is not much interior. However, if you want great one-design racing, you have to pay the price.

DESIGN QUALITY: The J/35 is a wonderful design that offers outstanding performance and ease of handling. The boat is not beautiful, but has a neat, clean profile.

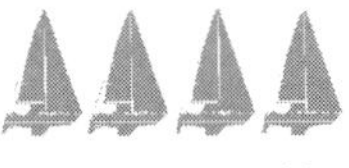

CONSTRUCTION QUALITY: TPI builds good boats. The overall quality of the J/35 is excellent. There are annoying problems, like leaky portlights, but few structural problems.

USER-FRIENDLINESS: The J/35 is a relatively easy boat to sail. However, if you do serious ocean racing, you need a good crew. The interior is not very comfortable.

SAFETY: The stanchions could be taller and better supported and the nonskid loses its bite after time.

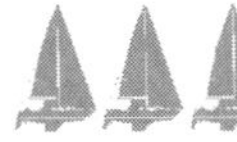

TYPICAL CONDITION: Most J/35s on the used boat market are in pretty good condition. Owners are obligated to keep up the boat to stay competitive. Sails and electronics are often outdated.

REFITTING: The lack of complex systems makes the task easier although access to certain areas is not great.

SUPPORT: J Boats is helpful. It is not difficult to get the president on the phone. TPI is good at finding, fabricating and sending parts. You can find the J/35 Class Association Web page at sailingsource.com/j35.

AVAILABILITY: There are more than 300 35s in existence, but there are often less than 10 for sale at any one time.

INVESTMENT AND RESALE: While J/35s hold their value pretty well, they are relatively expensive compared to the other high-performance boats on the used boat market.

OVERALL 'SVG' RATING

On deck

Most J/35s came with tiller steering, roughly 85 percent. Anybody contemplating serious racing should definitely opt for a tiller boat. However, today more 35s have wheels because some owners retrofitted a pedestal system after discovering that they just were not racing as much as expected. Either way, the J/35 cockpit is very workmanlike. Early boats featured both a Harken Hexacat mainsheet and vang, while later boats went to Hall Quick Vangs. Barient 28s were the standard primaries.

The molded nonskid was excellent when new but can be worn near smooth on older boats. Unless nonskid was added, painting only makes the situation worse. Newer J/35s have a Hall Spars mast and Navtec rod rigging. The deck hardware was all first-rate when new, but 10 or more years of racing takes its toll, and if the hardware has not been upgraded, factor that cost into your offer. The same can be said for the running rigging.

Down below

While early J/35s had a spartan interior at best, by the end of the production run, J Boats was touting the 35's "cruising yacht" interior, but this was a stretch. Early boats had the option of having a V-berth or just sail bins and the galley consisted of a sink and ice chest. Later boats had a finished forward cabin, head with shower and teak cabinetwork throughout. Ironically, because the J/35 Class uses float lines, you can't make the boat too light, and 35s with full interiors can do quite well.

The interior arrangement is the standard V-berth forward, followed by a head with a hanging locker opposite. The saloon has two settees, which make good sea berths, and an optional bulkhead-mounted table. The galley is to port with the ice chest and nav station opposite. There are two good-sized quarter berths. Later boats had eight opening Bowmar hatches for excellent ventilation.

Engine

Prior to 1985, the 35 had a 22-horsepower Yanmar. In 1985 Yanmar increased the horsepower of what became the 3GM series. Although the block and other components were the same, the engine became a 28-horsepower. Watching a J/35 under power reveals much about why the boat is fast under sail—there is hardly a trace of wake. The 20-gallon fuel tank gives the 35 a range of around 200 miles. A Martec folding prop is standard. Access to the stuffing box is adequate.

Underway

Of course, under sail is where the J/35 shines. Few boats are so universally admired by their owners. The 35 is well-balanced under all points of sail and is surprisingly easy to sail. Many 35s are sailed by couples or families who don't race. The 35 is fast upwind, especially in light to moderate seas, although she can be wet in heavy air with a chop. Off the wind, the 35 surfs easily. Kennedy, who sails a 1985 model on Lake Michigan, told me that he once had the boat out in 30 knots and was surfing down waves at 11 to 12 knots with good control. Kennedy also advises new 35 owners not to waste money buying new electronics. "Listen to your boat, not the little black boxes, your competitors tell you when you're not doing well soon enough."

Wayne Hargis, who sails his 1986 35 out of Ft. Lauderdale, says that even in heavy air the 35 stays on its feet and keeps moving. "We were doing the Key West Race a few years ago and the wind was steady at 40 knots. We had a reefed main and the blade set. Suddenly, out of nowhere, a line squall hit us and we did a hard standing jibe. One minute I was on the high side steering, the next I was on the low side in three feet of water. Amazingly, we didn't break a thing and quickly we were back on course." Hargis' only complaint with the boat is that it requires a big crew for serious racing.

Conclusion

With prices ranging from around $50,000 for an early boat to nearly $90,000 for a late model, the J/35 is certainly not cheap. However, the quality is good and the pedigree proud. If one-design racing is what you desire, or if you simply insist on great performance, you should look seriously at the J/35—you won't be disappointed.

Bristol 35

Don't forget about this robustly built classic that keeps improving with age

The Bristol 35 was designed more by eye than by ratio. Introduced in 1966, the Alden-designed 35 had a relatively long production run that stretched into the mid-1970s before Bristol mothballed the boat and replaced it with the more modern, Hood-designed 35.5. Like most boats of this vintage, its design was shaped around the Cruising Club of America Rule. By 1966 the CCA Rule seemed more a look than a rule, and this look—long overhangs, narrow beam, low freeboard and a sweet sheerline—dominated sailboat design for nearly 40 years. Early fiberglass boats dutifully emulated wooden boat designs until 1970, when the IOR Rule radically, and forever, changed the relationship between the two materials.

First impressions

When introduced 30 years ago, it was promoted as "a racing yacht with fine accommodations." And while the original factory brochure touted "gracious spaciousness," most of today's sailors will be shocked by the 35's spartan quarters below. By comparison, a 10-foot beam seems pretty skinny these days, and coupled with a short waterline of 23 feet, 9 inches, the Bristol 35 probably has less room than most new 28-footers. In fact, the Catalina 30, introduced only eight years after the Bristol 35 and nearly 5 feet shorter overall, seems dramatically more roomy. But you don't buy a Bristol 35 for the accommodations.

Bristol 35

LOA 34'8"
LWL 23'9"
Beam 10'
Draft: keel 5',
centerboard 3'9"
Displacement 12,500 lbs.
Ballast 5,200 lbs.
Sail Area 531 sq. ft.

Construction

The 35 was originally available as a sloop or yawl, with a 5-foot deep-draft version. The sailaway price was $18,000. When we think of Bristol Yachts today, we think of big, high-quality, expensive boats. But in the early days, Bristol was a middle-of-the-road builder, aiming for the mass market that the magic material of fiberglass was rapidly creating. The fact that the Bristol 35 has endured so well structurally over the years has less to do with Bristol's high standards than with the generally robust fiberglass construction techniques of the time.

The 35's hull was solid fiberglass, mainly woven roving and heavy on the polyester resin. And it was thick. Bristol 35 owner Bob Pierce showed me a hull plug from where he had installed a new depthsounder and it was nearly an inch thick. While this hull sample does not stack up well on a glass-to-resin ratio, there is a lot of strength simply from the amount of material involved. The deck and stair-stepped cabintrunk are balsa- or plywood-cored. The underbody has a cutaway forefoot tapering into a long keel with an attached rudder. The 5,200 pounds of lead ballast are encapsulated in the keel cavity.

What to look for

While it is risky to generalize about older boats because so many changes may have occurred, it is safe to assume that if you find an older 35 and the hull has not been painted, it soon will need to be. Pierce's *Dragon Lady*

Bristol 35 Price Data

		Low	High
BUC Retail Range	1968	$27,700	$30,800
	1973	$32,900	$36,500
	1975	$35,300	$37,200

		State	Asking
Boats For Sale	1967	FL	$29,900
	1970	ME	$30,000
	1973	NY	$35,000

was painted in Awlgrip 10 years ago and the hull still has a nice sheen. He recently painted the decks with Sterling and used Easypoxy on the cabintrunk. The Bristol 35 has a fair amount of tumblehome and one of Pierce's first projects after he acquired the boat was to protect his painted hull by mounting a teak and bronze rubrail. But before you start painting or building rubrails, you should check carefully for leaks.

Leaks on older boats can cause untold aggravation. The bedding compound around the portlights and other fittings may well be 20 to 30 years old and quite possibly has hardened. Unfortunately, water usually takes a circuitous route down below, making it difficult to pinpoint the leaking fitting. Although it represents a lot of work, rebedding all portlights and deck fittings with fresh 5200 is invariably time well spent. When you look at older 35s be sure to investigate for signs of hull-and-deck joint leaks. There are many areas below—such as inside lockers—where you can see the joint clearly. A leaking, hull-and-deck joint, while certainly repairable, might be cause to look at a sistership, or, at the least, should be reflected in the price. Also, look carefully at the molded nonskid on deck. Although it may be worn nearly smooth, it is not easily noticed until the decks are wet.

On deck

The shallow cockpit on theBristol 35 is quite large; the seats are more than six feet long. There are two good-sized lockers and a big lazarette, all with scuppered edges to prevent leakage. The sole has two scuppers and these could stand to be made a bit larger. Typical of this vintage, no provision was made for the helmsman to sit behind the wheel because the boat was also offered with a tiller. *Dragon Lady* was fitted with a wheel, so Pierce added a shapely teak seat. The area underneath the helmsman's seat became a handy place to install the propane tank after converting the original alcohol stove. The winch bases are molded and both primary and secondary winches are within reach of the helmsman. It is likely that these winches will need updating.

The rig came either as a single spreader masthead sloop or a yawl. I admit that I like the look of a yawl and it is a great place to mount antennas, but functionally speaking, it does not enhance the Bristol 35's sailing characteristics, especially upwind—not its strong suit to begin with. A furling headsail is a nice addition because the 35 tends to be a little tender initially, and by controlling headsail size, you can stay on top of the puffs. The original boom was fitted with roller reefing and if this has not already been converted to slab reefing, don't hesitate to do so.

Down below

Down below, the 35's saloon came with either a convertible dinette to port with upper and lower berths to starboard, or a centerline table with berths on both sides. The galley is to port. Again, by today's standards, there is not much counter space, but in 1966 this galley was considered fit for a gourmet. Pierce has added additional locker space behind the sink. The original stove was alcohol and I would not hesitate to convert this to propane or natural gas. The icebox/refrigerator is to starboard, under the chart table. While a separate navigation station is common on 35-footers today, in the 1960s it was standard for the chart table to be on top of the icebox. The box is quite large and has plenty of room for cold plates when updating to a modern refrigeration system.

The saloon came with either the preferred mahogany veneer or the ubiquitous teak-grained Formica bulkheads of the 1960s. The Formica bulkheads can be painted white, which will lighten up the interior and set off the rest of the teak trim. The cabin sole is teak and fiberglass with a huge 130-gallon fiberglass (some boats had stainless) water tank under it. The athwartships head is large when closed off, and with an unusual dash of luxury for the times, came

Bristol 35

Sailing Magazine's Value Guide

PRICE: Ranges from mid to high-20s to the high-30s, the Bristol 35 represents a good value.

DESIGN QUALITY: Early fiberglass designs were quite handsome and the Alden pedigree will endure. However, modern designs really spotlight some shortcomings of the CCA boats.

CONSTRUCTION QUALITY: There is still something to be said for early fiberglass construction techniques. They were heavily laid up and constructed more like wooden boats. Old Bristols seem to be holding up well.

USER-FRIENDLINESS: With simple updates (self-tailing winches, roller furling and slab reefing) the boat will be easier to handle.

SAFETY: The cockpit is long and shallow and feels somewhat exposed; the single lifelines could be taller and pulpits a bit beefier. Below, there are good sea berths in the saloon.

TYPICAL CONDITIONS: While most 35s were originally used as club racers, today they are almost always used for coastal cruising. The condition often depends on how far the previous owner has gone in upgrading the boat and how good a job he or she has done.

REFITTING: Although the simplicity of the boat facilitates refit jobs, the lack of original parts and generally older age make them more difficult to work on. A Bristol 35 is certainly a boat that warrants a complete refit, however.

SUPPORT: Bristol Yachts has been in and out of bankruptcy and there is not much information available about its older boats.

AVAILABILITY: There simply are not many 35s on the market, and when for sale they often sell quickly, which leads to a better rating in the next category.

INVESTMENTS AND RESALE: The Bristol 35 is definitely considered a quality boat but it can often be found at an affordable price. Don't place much stock in equipment on the listing sheet unless it is new.

OVERALL 'SVG' RATING

standard with a shower. The shower drained into the bilge and if this has not been rerouted, it will need attention. The forward cabin is a traditional V-berth, with shelves to either side and storage below. Due to an overall lack of volume, the 35 is not long on locker space.

Engine

The good old Universal Atomic 4 30-horsepower gas engine was standard on the 35. And while there is nothing actually wrong with this old workhorse, gasoline engines have simply gone out of fashion. Most Bristol 35s I have encountered have been converted to diesels. *Dragon Lady* has a Westerbeke 4107, which provides ample horsepower. If you find a 35 with a gas engine, this undoubtedly will be reflected in the price. If you can live with it, you will be able to save some money; the market for sailboats with gasoline engines is not strong, to say the least. If you choose to convert to a diesel, Universal makes a 30-horsepower diesel that conveniently uses the same mounts as the Atomic 4, though engine access is not particularly good. Pierce has rectified this problem on *Dragon Lady* by making the sink easily removable. He has also created custom stuffing box wrenches because of the difficulty reaching the stuffing box and swinging a conventional or adjustable wrench. The 25-gallon fuel tank is monel and installed on the bottom of the cockpit sole.

Underway

Backing out of the slip is always an adventure with a long-keel boat and a small two-blade prop. Pierce handled the boat superbly, and although *Dragon Lady* resisted, made a three-point turn and steered for the Intracoastal Waterway. The tide was flooding and although we were bucking a stiff current, we still made good speed.

There was a nice trade wind blowing as we headed out narrow Hillsborough Inlet and made our way toward the Gulf Stream. With the 130 percent genoa billowing and the full main drawing nicely, we ambled south at nearly 6 knots. *Dragon Lady* is a deep-keel 35 and when we hardened up on a tight reach she tracked well. The winds piped up and we shortened the headsail and romped off to weather. Surprisingly, even with a full main, there was little weather helm. The boat felt solid in the water.

Conclusion

If you have a taste for traditional boats and love that classic look, an older Bristol 35—which just seems to improve with age—may be the ideal boat to carry you to those alluring islands.

Ericson 35-II

Vintage racer-cruiser makes a affordable daysailer, club racer and weekender

The Ericson 35-II, designed by Bruce King, is representative of the versatile, racer-cruiser breed of production boats that dominated the American sailboat market from the late 1960s through the mid-1980s. The 35-II, which in 1969 replaced King's original long-keel, CCA-inspired 35, was one of Ericson's most successful boats. More than 600 rolled off the line before the design was replaced by the 35-III in 1983. For more than two decades Ericson was one of the most consistent production builders in the country. The California-based company developed a reputation for producing solid, well-appointed boats that performed well and held their value financially. Ericson, like many other builders, struggled during the 1980s. Pacific Seacraft rescued what was left of the company in 1990, purchasing the name and the tooling for the 24, 32 and 38.

With prices ranging from less than $20,000 for an older 35-II to around $40,000 for a clean, well-equipped later model, the Ericson 35-II is another good example of the sound values that can be found on the used boat market.

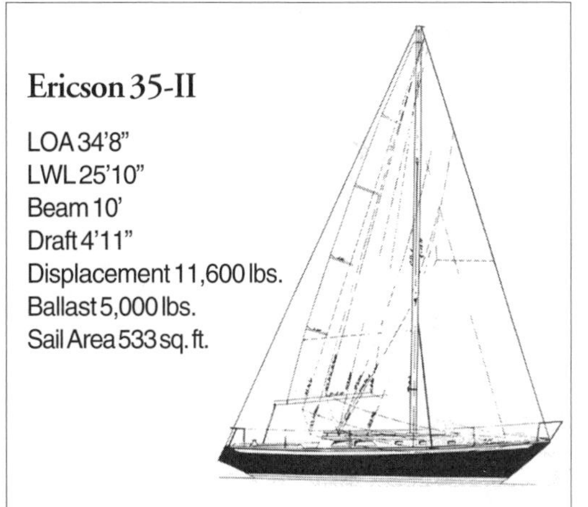

Ericson 35-II

LOA 34'8"
LWL 25'10"
Beam 10'
Draft 4'11"
Displacement 11,600 lbs.
Ballast 5,000 lbs.
Sail Area 533 sq. ft.

First impressions

King's hull designs rarely shock and often please, albeit in subtle fashion. At first glance the Ericson 35-II looks like many boats of her time period. The more you study the boat, however, the more you notice its quiet attributes. The entry is fine with a moderate overhang, and the sheer has punch forward before tapering off aft where the freeboard is quite low. Despite the lack of freeboard, the cabintrunk is proportionate to the hull, not always an easy task to accomplish aesthetically, especially if you hope to maintain adequate headroom below. A long cockpit blends into a springy counter stern with a slightly reversed transom.

The 35-II has a double-spreader rig, which was ample for its day, inboard lower chainplates and decent side decks, despite a beam of just 10 feet. Below the water, a swept-back fin keel and a semibalanced spade rudder gave the 35-II a modern underbody in 1969. Although it won't keep up with today's speedy boats, the 35-II has a sweet motion and still performs quite nicely, especially for family daysailing, PHRF club racing and coastal cruising.

Construction

Ericson built its hulls in halves and laminated them together. Although many boats are built this way,

Ericson 35-II Price Data

		Low	High
BUC Retail Range	1972	$20,000	$22,000
	1976	$23,600	$26,000
	1980	$27,700	$30,800

		State	Asking
Boats For Sale	1972	MI	$25,000
	1976	PA	$34,900
	1980	NY	$26,500

especially overseas, it comes as a surprise to some sailors who instinctively think a one-piece hull is stronger. The 35-II's hulls were joined by 11 laminates of mat and roving, and I have never heard of a problem with a centerline hull joint. The hull is solid fiberglass and is heavily laid up. The 35-II predated Ericson's trademark "Tri-Axial Force Grid" construction technique. There is a lot of talk about the heavy lay-ups of older glass boats, and for the most part it is true. However, glass work was unsophisticated and hulls were often thick with resin. Another reason older fiberglass boats have stood the test of time is the conservative nature of their hull shapes. Low freeboard, narrow beam, slack bilges, sloping ends and short waterline lengths were extensions of wooden boats and far easier to support structurally than today's lighter, wider designs with longer appendages and much higher loads.

The 35-II deck is balsa-cored, and plywood was used in high-stress areas such as under the winch moldings in the cockpit. Molded liners and cabin soles helped support furniture and encapsulated the bulkheads below. I dislike liners on used boats because they can mask serious problems. Additional tabbing or bonding of bulkheads to the hull was not always sufficient.

The lead ballast was cast and then fitted into the keel cavity. The debate over internal and external ballast will never be resolved, but one advantage of internal ballast is that as boats age, you don't have to fret over the inevitable deterioration of metal keel bolts. A close examination of the fiberglass around the keel cavity when the boat is hauled will usually reveal any damage that might affect the ballast. Examining the condition of keel bolts is more challenging.

What to look for

Throughout the 35-II's long production run, there were only a few significant changes. Originally there was an after bridgedeck that supported a small Yacht Specialties pedestal and wheel as well as the mainsheet traveler. The small bridgedeck also divided the cockpit into steering and working stations. Later, a standard pedestal was used and the traveler was moved over the companionway. The vast majority of 35-IIs came from the factory with a wheel. The few tiller boats on the market are likely the ones that were raced the hardest. Late in the production run, around 1979, the interior woodwork was changed from mahogany to teak. Ironically, one reason for the switch was that mahogany was becoming too expensive and hard to find.

Chainplate leaks are notorious problems, and unfortunately these often lead to serious rot in the main bulkhead. In fact, a chainplate pulling right out of the bulkhead has caused the loss of the rig on at least one 35-II. Carefully examine the upper portion of the

Ericson 35-II

Sailing Magazine's Value Guide

PRICE: With prices ranging from $20,000 to the mid-30s, it is likely you can find the 35-II in your budget.

DESIGN QUALITY: Bruce King's designs age well. The 35-II is still a very nice boat to look at and sail.

CONSTRUCTION QUALITY: The initial quality was solid, but the use of liners can mask problems. Chainplate leaks are a real problem.

SAFETY: There is a stout companionway bridgedeck and plenty of handholds below. The two overhead hatches could be dangerous in heavy weather, and the stanchions could be taller and better supported.

USER-FRIENDLINESS: The 35-II is satisfying to sail and responsive to the helm. The helmsman is isolated at the wheel, however.

TYPICAL CONDITION: Avoid tiller boats; most were raced hard. Although condition varies with age, 35-IIs seem well cared for.

REFITTING: The 35-II is not easy to work on. Possible replacement of the main bulkhead, installing opening portlights, swapping the engine are some probable projects.

SUPPORT: Pacific Seacraft is doing a good job of servicing owners. Some parts are available from the factory, including rubrail sections. Call (714) 879-1610, fax (714) 879-5454 or visit www.pacificseacraft.com

AVAILABILITY: With more than 600 boats afloat, there is a wide selection to choose from. Ericson had an extensive dealer network; you will find 35-IIs all over the country.

INVESTMENT AND RESALE: The Ericson 35-II seems to have reached a stable, well-defined place in the market.

OVERALL 'SVG' RATING

main bulkhead where the chainplates are through-bolted. If the wood is delaminated, the chainplates leak and the integrity of the bulkhead should be questioned. Replacing the main bulkhead is a huge project and may require skills and tools that can only be found at a yard. While you're inspecting the bulkhead, check the wooden compression post; it is not uncommon to find stress cracks that may lead to more serious problems.

Early boats were fitted with gate valves on the through-hull fittings. Check carefully any owner-retrofitted seacocks. Look carefully at the tabbing around the forward berths. If it has pulled away from the hull or the liner, or if the liner is cracked, that is a sign of oilcanning or excessive flexing. While forward, check under the V-berth where most 35-IIs have a 25-gallon water tank or a retrofitted larger tank. Make sure the tank is well-supported and secured in place. Remember to check age-related ailments, including the standing and running rigging, and the condition of what may be worthless sails. You should particularly look for cracked swages on the uppers.

On deck

The 35-II has an uncluttered deck and a large, comfortable cockpit. Beginning forward, the stemhead fitting is just that, and typical of boats of this period, there is no provision for anchoring. The deck cleats and chocks are certainly not oversized and the tiny original running lights mounted on the foredeck are comical. The side decks are proportionately wider, and a molded toerail, decent nonskid and several teak grabrails on the deckhouse lend security. There are double lifelines, but the stanchions could be taller. The genoa track is outboard on the rail. The deck-stepped, double-spreader spar is a beefy aluminum section. The boom gooseneck is quite high, the result of reducing rated sail area with a sloping boom.

The cockpit is one of the best features of the boat. "The cockpit is great for a Sunday sail," says Quinn McKenna, who sails a 1980 35-II on San Francisco Bay. "I'm not sure I would want to be caught offshore in a storm," he adds, "and singlehanding is a challenge."

The divided cockpit was trendy in the 1960s and 1970s, and can also be found on C&Cs and Tartans. It was more efficient for handling the mainsail than the later midboom sheeting arrangement. Even with the aft bridgedeck, the cockpit easily accommodates six adults. There is a locker to starboard, large enough for a couple of sails or a rolled-up dinghy, and there's storage in the coamings. The mahogany coaming boards may need replacing.

Down below

Although wood-grained formica surfaces and green-checked settee cushions are a dead giveaway of a boat's age, the 35-II—with its general openness and well-thought-out interior plan—was definitely ahead of its time. Working from bow to stern, the forward end of the V-berth is narrow, the result of the boat's fine entry, and unless a filler piece has been added, the V-berth is not a suitable double. There is a hanging locker to starboard, and although there are clever bins, most storage space under the bunks is lost to tankage. The head is to port and came standard with a fiberglass shower sump. Unfortunately, the shower drained directly into the bilge; be sure to check if a trap or sump pump has been installed. There is a large overhead hatch and many owners have added opening portlights.

The saloon was offered in two versions, standard with two opposing settees and a centerline drop-leaf table, or with a dinette to port. The dinette, which can be lowered to form a double, seems to be the most common. The starboard settee stretches into the hanging locker for extra legroom when sleeping. An advantage of an older model is that the mahogany is easier to paint than oily teak. I examined a 1974 boat that looked great with white painted bulkheads. There is good storage above and below the settees.

The cabin sole is molded with small access hatches and is usually carpeted. There is often another water tank in the bilge, but be forewarned: It is difficult to remove and replace. There is a huge overhead hatch in the saloon. For cross ventilation, however, it's still essential to add side portlights.

The L-shaped galley has ample counter space. The original design called for a three-burner alcohol stove. Most owners have changed to propane, so check the retrofitted gas system carefully. A single, deep sink is tucked behind the companionway. The insulation in the generous icebox is totally inadequate. You will need to fix this before you add refrigeration.

The small electrical panel is behind the icebox, a strange location considering the likelihood of water. The nav station is excellent, with a large chart desk and drawer. A good-sized quarter berth forms the seat for the navigator and is also the best sea berth on the boat.

Engine

The Atomic 4 was the only engine option until 1974. Later, a variety of diesels were available. The most common was the 25-horsepower Westerbeke 4-91. The engine placement depended on the interior plan. Dinette models had the engine under the aft end of the settee. This arrangement gave great accessibility for both the engine and stuffing box and had good balance under sail. The twin-settee models squeezed the engine into a tight space below the companionway.

Even late models that came with a diesel may be ready for repowering. McKenna replaced his Westerbeke with a three-cylinder, 27-horsepower Yanmar. When it comes to repowering, the dinette model makes the job much easier. The original fuel tank was just 14 gallons.

Underway

Like most King designs, the 35-II is a capable boat both on the wind and off, and in a variety of conditions. McKenna notes that he ties in a reef in the main and rolls in the genny to about 100 percent when the wind is steady around 18 knots.

The boat is comfortable, without much weather helm up to 25 knots. At 25, it is time to shorten up again. Although the 35-II is not overly stiff and is easily driven in light air, it has a sweet motion in a seaway and rarely pounds in a chop.

The 35-II is a 5.5- to 6.5-knot boat in most conditions according to Jim Riley, a yacht broker who sails a 1976 35-II out of Ft. Lauderdale. Visibility from the helm is excellent, but the aft bridgedeck makes it tough for the helmsman to do anything other than steer. Some owners report the boat to be a bit squirrely running before large seas. But the 35-II is no stranger to blue water, and was highly successful in several ocean races on the West Coast, taking overall honors in the La Paz, Ensenada and Puerta Vallarta offshore races.

Conclusion

The Ericson 35-II makes us consider what we really want in a sailboat. If serious racing and offshore voyaging are not in your plans, but daysailing, weekend cruising and occasional club racing are, then you should consider the 35-II. As McKenna writes about his 35-II, "It is a solid, well-designed and well-made older boat that can be had at a reasonable price, is pretty to look at and comfortable to sail." Not a bad recommendation for any boat.

Islander 36

Comfortable, attractive, capable 1970s racer-cruiser

The Islander 36 is unique among the myriad of production boats that sprang to life in the early 1970s. It was designed with a good IOR rating in mind during an age of racer-cruisers. But as boats designed closer to the rule soon passed it by, it turned out to be one of the first cruiser-racers.

Introduced in 1971, the I-36 was a result of the combined efforts of designers Alan Gurney and Joe Artese. Gurney, whose most famous design is the Maxi racer *Windward Passage*, was the primary designer and was responsible for the hull and the rig, while Artese fashioned the deck layout and the interior. The I-36 was almost radically beamy for its day. Although the 11-foot, 2-inch beam seems almost sleek by today's standards, the I-36 carried nearly a foot more beam than the Columbia 36 and Ericson 35, comparable designs of the time.

Artese made good use of the beam, and even compared to today's boats, the I-36 interior is comfortable and spacious. From the elimination of a bridgedeck to the use of a clever folding bulkhead table and overstuffed saloon cushions, the Islander 36 was user-friendly from the start. Islander Yachts understood that there were (and still are) a lot of sailors who enjoyed spending the weekend on their boats, even if they never unplugged the shore-power cord. And while traditionalists ridiculed the 1-inch companionway sill, claiming that any green water that sloshed aboard would surely find its way below, a new breed of sailors loved the ease of stepping, rather than climbing, below.

Islander 36

LOA 36'1"
LWL 28'3"
Beam 11'2"
Draft 6'1" (fin) or 4'9" (shoal)
Displacement 13,450 lbs. (fin) or 13,600 lbs. (shoal)
Ballast 5,400 lbs. (fin) or 5,600 lbs. (shoal)
Sail Area 612 sq. ft.

A little history

The irony is that with a powerful underwater profile and more than 6 feet of draft the I-36 is a great boat in a blow and is no stranger to blue water. Two I-36s that I know of have circumnavigated, although this was never the design intent. While you will find Islander 36s all over the country—more than 700 were built before production stopped in 1986—there is something about the blend of modern lines that subtly snubs tradition and about the plush interior that marks the I-36 as a quintessential California boat. In a long-ago review, *SAILING* Technical Editor Bob Perry described the interior as "Southern California Gothic." Not surprisingly, California is where you will find the best selection of used boats on the market; there are about 200 boats in the San Francisco Bay area alone.

Sailors in bars say profound things like: "If a boat doesn't look right, it just doesn't sail right." Well, strangely enough, sailors who review boats say the same thing. Most of the boats that find their way into this column are handsome and the Islander 36 is no exception. While many boats of this era have not aged gracefully, the I-36 is still a striking, well-proportioned boat.

The profile view reveals a racy sheerline that was common in the 1970s, and when blended with the low freeboard, gives the boat sweet lines. The trunkhouse, which is carried well forward, melds nicely with the cockpit coaming astern. The stern is not as pinched as other IOR boats and the raked bow has a moderate overhang.

Below the water, Gurney created a large, classic fin keel and a deep, skeg-hung rudder, which was another feature that doomed the boat as an IOR racer and yet has helped it endure as a cruising boat.

The I-36 is known as a relatively stiff boat, although by the numbers (sail area/displacement and displacement/length ratios) it is moderate in every sense. The double-spreader sloop rig is a bit stubby and sports 587 feet of working sail area. The double spreaders, which were unusual at the time, allow for a narrow shroud base and tight sheeting angles.

Islander 36 Price Data

		Low	High
BUC Retail Range	1973	$27,500	$30,600
	1978	$35,500	$39,400
	1984	$50,800	$55,900

		State	Asking
Boats For Sale	1972	ID	$29,900
	1978	WA	$34,500
	1985	LA	$60,000

Construction

Islanders were originally built by a company called McGlasson Boat Co., which later became Wayfarer Marine. By the time the Islander 36 was ready for production in 1971, the company was well-known as the Islander Yacht Corp. with a plant in Costa Mesa, California. In 1979 it moved to Irvine. Unfortunately, after Islander went bankrupt in 1986, all company records were either destroyed or lost. What we do know about the company has been pieced together from Islander boat owners and former employees. Skipper Wall, who sails *Snow Flower*, hull No. 156, on San Francisco Bay, has compiled a fairly detailed history of Islander Yachts and can be reached through the I-36 Association at **www.paw.com/sail/islander36/**.

The quality of the construction of the I-36 remained remarkably consistent. Boats from the early 1970s still race competitively and occasionally as a class with boats built in the mid-1980s. In fact, it is surprising how few structural changes were made during the production run. The hull is solid fiberglass and the deck is plywood cored. The hull-and-deck joint is on an inward-facing flange and incorporates the aluminum toerail, which is unique in that it runs nearly the entire length of the boat.

What to look for

Like any boat that had a long production run, the I-36 went through many changes. Although by no means complete, here is a list of some of the key upgrades that were offered over the years. Prior to 1975, most I-36s were fitted with gas engines—either the venerable Universal Atomic 4 or the Palmer M-160—and in both cases the boat was underpowered. Although most boats have been retrofitted along the way, old I-36s with gas engines are almost always less expensive than those with diesels. A variety of diesels were used over the years, including Perkins, Volvos and Westerbekes. In the early 1980s, the company switched to Pathfinder, marinized Volkswagen diesels. Many I-36s on the used boat market seem to have these engines, either as originals or retrofits. Late in the production, three-cylinder, 30-horsepower Yanmars were offered.

According to some reports, a lead shortage caused Islander to use cast iron keels on some boats built between 1973 and 1975. In the mid-1980s, a 4-foot, 9-inch shoal-draft version was made available but it was never popular. In 1977 Islander decided to really upgrade the boat, particularly down below, and the standard interior became more elegant. The carpeted fiberglass sole was replaced with teak and holly; galley countertops were changed to oak. Also, if you are looking for an Islander 36, be sure not to confuse the boat with the Islander Freeport 36, the deck-saloon boat designed by Bob Perry and introduced in 1978. In the early 1980s, the L-shaped galley was changed to a U and a new deck mold added slightly more headroom.

Although the I-36 has held up very well over the years, there are some common problems to look for. Frank Burkhart, who sails a 1974 I-36 on San Francisco Bay, advises those looking to buy an I-36 to carefully check the main bulkhead, especially the port side, which comes adrift and often needs to be refiberglassed. Most boats you inspect will have addressed this problem, but check the work carefully to be sure that the fiberglass tape is equally distributed on the bulkhead and the hull and is tabbed on both sides. And don't limit your inspection to the port main bulkhead; check them all. Typically, the tabbing does not come loose from the hull but from the bulkhead itself. As a result of the narrow shroud base, the chainplates can cause delamination in both the side deck and the bulkheads. Frequently, the plastic portlights leak. It is just as easy to replace them as to re-bed them, and if this hasn't been done, consider it a must-do job. Also, the hull-and-deck joint has been known to leak. One last item: Although Islanders are not unique, they seem to be prone to osmotic blistering. Check to see if and when a blister job was done and which barrier system was used.

On deck

One of the most appealing features of the I-36 are the wide side decks which, with the chainplates set well inboard, make it easy to move about the deck. There are long teak grabrails on the trunkhouse and double lifelines. The beefy mast section is stepped through to the keel. The boom, however, is a little light. With a midboom sheeting arrangement that was clearly ahead of its time, the boom can be overloaded. Many owners have replaced their booms with stronger sections.

The I-36 was heavily rigged, including jumper stays; however, swaged terminal fittings were used. If the boat you are considering is more than 10 years old and still has the original rigging, you should think about changing over to mechanical terminals.

The T-shaped cockpit is deep, comfortable and set up for efficient sail handling, as the helmsman can reach both sets of winches without too much trouble. Unfortunately, it is tough to see over the cabintrunk from the helm. Although the boat was originally designed with a tiller, almost all came with a wheel. The aforementioned lack of a bridgedeck provides added cockpit space, but I think it is a poor trade-off. I must confess that after years of wailing about improper bridgedecks in modern designs, I recently read an interesting counter opinion by noted naval architect Ted Brewer. He observed that when a boat is pooped, the water has to drain through small cockpit drains and temporarily rides dangerously out of trim astern. If the water actually flooded below and into the bilge, the boat would not be as far out of trim and would be more stable. He does insist, however, when lacking a bridgedeck, it is critical that stout washboards can be secured in place.

Down below

The open, stylish interior created by Artese was undoubtedly one of the prime reasons the Islander 36 sold in such numbers. There is a V-berth forward with a head just aft to port. The saloon features a fold-away, bulkhead-mounted table, which is a great feature on any boat less than 40 feet. The galley in the early boats was rather basic and the later U-shape was a good improvement. The original boat came with two 27-gallon water tanks housed under the settees. Many owners have added extra tankage, usually under the V-berth. The nav station is tucked under the side deck just forward of the quarter berth, and like many boats of this era, has little practical value. It is interesting that Islander never improved the nav station during the production run.

Engine

The only advantage of older boats with gasoline engines is that they are smaller than their diesel counterparts and offer better working access. The engine can be reached three ways: from behind the companionway, through a hatch in the quarter berth and from below the galley sink. Unless major repairs are to be undertaken, access is adequate. The stuffing box is reached through the cockpit locker.

Burkhart's *IslandGirl* was repowered with a 42-horsepower Pathfinder in 1986. The Pathfinder is a high-revolution engine, with a red line at 4,000 rpms. Burkhart finds that at 2,800 rpms, he maintains 6-plus knots while using around .5 gallon per hour.

Underway

The I-36 is well-balanced under sail, stiff and surprisingly fast. Burkhart's *Island Girl* took PHRF division honors in last year's San Francisco Bay Ocean

Islander 36

Sailing Magazine's Value Guide

PRICE: Prices of Islander 36s can range from as little as $27,000 for a 1973 model on up to $50,000 and more for an '80s model.

DESIGN QUALITY: The handsome hull shape will never go out of style. The interior has shortcomings but was certainly innovative in its day.

CONSTRUCTION QUALITY: Although the I-36 has held up well over the years, it is as much a result of caring owners. Original construction was on the light side.

USER-FRIENDLINESS: From pleasant sailing characteristics, to wide open companionway, to spacious cockpit, to comfortable interior, the I-36 is user-friendly.

SAFETY: The lack of a bridgedeck compromises safety offshore as does the open interior arrangement.

TYPICAL CONDITION: The condition of most boats I have seen on the used boat market is surprisingly good.

REFITTING: Common problems are well-known, so when it comes time to upgrade or refit, there is a lot of information available. The boat is relatively easy to work on.

SUPPORT: With no company records, support is through the active I-36 association and other I-36 owners. There is a newsletter and a Web page: www.paw.com/sail/islander36/

AVAILABILITY: There are many I-36s on the market. The best selection is in California and the Great Lakes.

INVESTMENT AND RESALE: While the I-36 represents a sound value, it loses a little value each year.

OVERALL 'SVG' RATING

Series. Burkhart explains that the boat can carry a full main and 135-percent genoa in a capful of wind. "On the bay, the winds can go from 15 to 40 knots in minutes," he said. "The I-36 is a perfect bay boat." Burkhart also noted that weather helm is never an issue, even hard on the wind with an overpowering headsail, and that he does not tie in the first reef until winds are consistently over 20 knots. The skeg-hung rudder gives the boat excellent control, especially running downwind in big seas. One owner noted that on a passage to Hawaii he encountered 30-foot seas but the I-36 never skipped a beat.

While most people who own I-36s use the boat for daysailing and weekend cruising, the boat does very well under PHRF and carries a rating of 147.

Conclusion

If comfortable daysailing, occasional PHRF racing and coastal cruising accurately represent the type of sailing that you do or hope to do, then the Islander 36, which is considered by many to be a modern classic, is certainly a logical boat to consider. With prices ranging from the mid-20s to the 50s and more, the I-36 is without question one of the best used boat values around.

Columbia 36

This good-performing Crealock-designed cruiser is a bargain in disguise

The Columbia 36 is an interesting boat in that it offers a glimpse into sailing's recent past during the 1960s and early 1970s, when fiberglass boats came to completely dominate the industry. At the time several fledgling sailboat companies were struggling to develop mass-production building techniques while adjusting to a new sailing public that no longer had a sworn allegiance to traditional boats. One of the early companies to embrace both new production methods and innovative designs was Columbia.

Launched in 1960, the company, initially called Glas Laminates, specialized in molding camper tops and shower stalls. In 1961 it turned its focus on sailboats and a year later acquired the tooling for the Columbia 29, a boat that led to the company's name and distinctive logo. By 1964 it was one of the largest sailboat builders in the country. Columbia expanded from its Costa Mesa, California, base by opening a plant on the East Coast in Portsmouth, Virginia. By the time Whittaker Corporation (one of the early conglomerates) bought Columbia in 1967, the former camper-top builder was one of the largest sailboat builders in the world.

Columbia 36

LOA 35'9"
LWL 28'3"
Beam 10'6"
Draft 5'5"
Displ. 12,000 lbs.
Ballast 5,500 lbs.
Sail Area 557 sq. ft.

Columbia's line of boats was diverse and distinct. Bill Tripp designed the company's flush-deck, bubble-top boats, which included the popular 26, 34 and 43. Tripp also designed the Columbia 50, one of the best-looking fiberglass boats of all time. Bill Crealock designed Columbia's 22, 28 and 36, which featured more traditional styling above the waterline. Columbia also built designs by Charley Morgan and Sparkman & Stephens as well as the Coronado line of motorsailers. Alan Payne tried modernizing the fleet in the early 1980s, but over time Columbia sailboats gradually lost their appeal in the marketplace. Complicating the problem, the company added too many models every year, spreading its resources too thin. Columbia was essentially out of business by the mid-1980s.

First impressions

The Crealock-designed 36 was a handsome boat when it was introduced in 1967, and it still is today. The boat remained in production until 1972, and more than 500 were built, although it is hard to say exactly how many. Unlike Crealock's well-known, canoe-stern Pacific Seacraft designs, the 36 was quite modern in its day. There isn't much sheer to the lines, and the cabintrunk has a saucy step and large portlights like the Columbia 50. The entry is fine and the overhangs fairly moderate for the period. Like most production boats of the period, it was considered a racer-cruiser.

Below the water Crealock opted for a spade rudder and the swept-back fin keel that was something of a Columbia trademark. The overall hull shape is very narrow by today's standards, with a beam of 10 feet, 6 inches. The 5-foot, 5-inch draft reflects the boat's West Coast influences. A boat designed for Florida or the Chesapeake wouldn't have been as deep.

The overall sail area of 557 square feet is modest and displacement is 12,000 pounds. The displacement/ length ratio of 261 translates into decent sailing performance for an older boat.

Construction

In retrospect, there is plenty of room for criticism of Columbia's construction techniques. But at the time, they were considered to be well built and most Columbias have stood the test of time and are still sailing.

The 36's hull was solid fiberglass, most likely 24-ounce woven roving and chopped-strand mat held together with polyester resin. The hull-to-deck joint was unique and not particularly effective, as the hull and deck meet on end in a double H-shaped aluminum channel. This does not allow much bearing surface and makes the connection vulnerable during docking mishaps. Judging from the numbers of owners who report leaking hull-to-deck joints, this is not an uncommon occurrence.

The deck is likely cored with plywood and should be carefully checked for delamination. The 36 is less prone to delamination than the company's Tripp-designed flush-deck models, but problems are not unknown. Columbia was one of the first builders to use pans, or molded liners, and the 36 pan is tabbed to the hull to provide athwartship support. I have never liked pans in bigger boats since they are structurally suspect and make accessing the hull virtually impossible. The 36 also has a molded headliner. The external fin keels were reported to be lead, but some owners claim that theirs are iron. Either way, carefully check the keel bolts.

What to look for

According to Mike Witt, who keeps his 36 on Biscayne Bay in Florida, leaks are the most annoying problem with his boat. As mentioned, the hull-and-deck joint is a problem, and if a leak develops it is difficult to repair. Leaks around the ports and hatches are also common. The original boat had poor ventilation so it is likely that hatches and portlights have been added.

The rubber rubrail is not secured very well either, so adding a solid rubrail or strake would be a useful upgrade. When checking for deck delamination be sure to carefully sound the area around the mast and any other areas where gelcoat crazes have widened into cracks. Just walking heavily will usually reveal the telltale cracking sound. Checking the condition of the keel bolts is difficult to do without an X-ray.

Most Columbia 36s were fitted with Atomic 4 gasoline engines, although a few came with diesels. It is likely that most of the Atomic 4s have been replaced, which is a good thing since there isn't much access in the engine compartment and repowering is a big job even in the best of cases. As with any retrofit, be sure to check the installation, and while you're at it, also check the condition of the tanks. The original water tank held 44 gallons and the fuel tank held 29 gallons. Naturally, any boat of this vintage is likely to have problems with its electrical wiring. The molded sections make the wiring difficult to repair and replace so most of it is probably still original.

Columbia 36 Price Data

		Low	High
BUC Retail Range	1968	$18,200	$20,300
	1970	$19,200	$21,300
	1972	$22,100	$24,500

		State	Asking
Boats For Sale	1969	MD	$22,000
	1970	CA	$38,900
	1971	FL	$19,900

On deck

The Columbia 36 has a long, fairly comfortable cockpit, and tillers were standard, although many previous owners have converted to wheel steering. Carefully check this installation. The mainsheet arrangement leads aft, which works with a tiller but not with a wheel. The companionway hatch was poorly designed and the stanchions and lifelines, which on some boats lead to the base of the bow pulpit, are not all that well supported and can be sources of leaks. The pulpits are typical of the era and therefore undersized. The original anchoring arrangement was inadequate and has likely been upgraded. If the nonskid is original it probably doesn't have much life left.

The sloop rig was standard. A yawl version was also offered, but I have never seen one. Witt says he has

Columbia 36

Sailing Magazine's Value Guide

PRICE: With prices ranging from $20,000-$25,000, the Columbia 36 maximizes the boat-per-dollar index. It really is one of the prime reasons for considering the boat.

DESIGN QUALITY: Crealock's design maintains a certain grace after all these years. The boat doesn't look as dated as some of Tripp's flush-deck, high-freeboard boats.

CONSTRUCTION QUALITY: Columbia's building techniques were no better or worse than other production builders of the time. Problems include a questionable hull-and-deck joint, possible deck delamination and the extensive use of molded liners.

USER-FRIENDLINESS: The Columbia 36 is an easy boat to sail and handle. The interior is surprisingly functional. The lack of engine room access is a drawback.

SAFETY: There is nothing unusually unsafe about the boat, but small features could be improved upon. The stanchions and pulpits are undersized, and the companionway hatch is poorly designed.

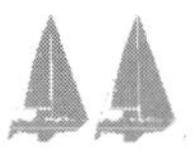

TYPICAL CONDITION: These boats are old—most are more than 30 years old—and have had several different owners. It is really surprising how well the boats have held up.

REFITTING: The construction methods make the Columbia 36 a hard boat to work on. Also the company is long defunct, which makes obtaining parts more challenging.

SUPPORT: There is a large group of Columbia owners out there, and they love their boats. There are a number of different Web sites out there. A good place to start is at the Columbia Owner's Association page at www.columbia-yachts.com.

AVAILABILITY: There are also a lot of used 36s out there, so if this is the boat you want, you have the luxury of being selective. There is a concentration of boats in Southern California.

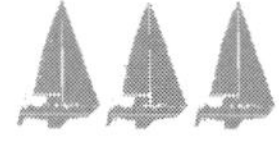

INVESTMENT AND RESALE: It is hard to go wrong with a 36-foot boat for less than $25,000. Like other good old boats, the price seems to have bottomed out. I suspect you could buy a 36 today, sail it a few years, and sell it for around what you paid for it.

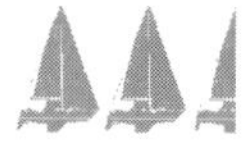

OVERALL 'SVG' RATING

upgraded his boat's sailhandling systems by adding a full-batten main and changing over to a midboom sheeting arrangement. He also added a roller furling headsail, led the halyards aft and replaced the original winches with self-tailing Andersons. The previous owner changed the standing rigging, but that was 10 years ago, so Witt is making plans to swap the swage fittings for mechanical ones. The original spars are still in good condition after 32 years.

Down below

The interior arrangement is an interesting one. A forward V-berth was standard, and it is actually long enough to sleep tall people. Next aft is the head to port with the nav station opposite. The chart table is large and functional and although located in a strange place, allowed Crealock to create room for two full-size quarter berths aft. The galley is in-line along the starboard side and the U-shaped dinette is opposite. Although the molded liners can give the boat a very plastic feeling below, they are practical, easily washed and have worn well over the years.

The boat seems small by today's standards, but for its day, the Columbia 36 was innovative and rather spacious. Witt, who sails with his wife and two small children, likes the arrangement, because each child has a quarter berth. There is plenty of storage, and the 6 feet, 3 inches of headroom and large main portlights add to the sense of spaciousness. The finish work leaves a bit to be desired, and the wood-grain Formica bulkheads date a boat as surely as the rings of a tree.

Engine

The standard power plant was the ubiquitous Universal Atomic 4, and this old workhorse is still a good engine, even though gasoline engines are dinosaurs. If you are considering a boat with an Atomic 4, don't immediately discount it. Parts are readily available and cheap, and it provides plenty of horsepower. Oftentimes diesel refits have resulted in less horsepower. The logical repower route was to swap the Atomic 4 for a Universal diesel, which allowed for the same engine footprint to be used. However, the owners I talked to had a variety of diesels.

Engine access is not good, and I am sure that repowering would be a big job. I would first look for a boat with a diesel, or otherwise plan on being content with the Atomic 4. Witt reports that his 18-horsepower Yanmar pushes the boat along at 5 knots in a flat sea, but still leaves him underpowered. The 30 gallons of fuel give him an effective range of around 200 miles, or as he says, "all the way to Key West and halfway back."

Underway

The Columbia 36 was actually designed to win races in the 1960s. The result is a boat that is still nice to sail in 2000. Witt says he consistently beats a Catalina 30 in casual racing on the bay. The boat has a solid feel in the water and is fairly close-winded. In 15 knots of breeze he sails at around 6 knots upwind and about the same with a cruising chute off the wind. Witt notes that weather helm is a problem in winds higher than 20 knots, but that can be said for almost all boats of this vintage. He ties in the first reef at around 17 knots and shortens up the headsail. He rarely ventures beyond the first reef, but he has sailed the boat to the Bahamas on occasion.

"A few years ago, we ran into a storm, a squall really, in the Gulf Stream. It was nasty but I put the second reef in the main and rolled in the 120-percent genoa to a size of a storm jib and we kept going. I was happy to see Bimini in the morning."

Conclusion

The Columbia 36 is a good example of an old boat that offers good sailing at a fraction of the price of a new, or even newer used boat. For a family that is looking to move up to a larger, more comfortable boat, but wants to spend less than $25,000, the Columbia 36 is a boat to consider.

Tartan 37

Though pricey, this is a well-designed, well-built boat that is a pleasure to sail

The Tartan 37 has an enduring reputation as a high-quality, performance cruising boat. There were 486 T-37s built during a 13-year production run, with the last hull rolling off the line at Tartan's Grand River, Ohio, plant in 1989. Designed by Sparkman & Stephens, the T-37 was not built with a particular rule or rating in mind. The design philosophy was wonderfully idealistic: Tartan wanted a boat that in the last analysis would be a pleasure to sail. With today's ever-widening schism between dedicated performance or cruising designs, 10- to 15-year-old boats like the T-37 don't fit cleanly into either category and therefore often represent excellent values on the used boat market, for there is nothing wrong with a boat that is a pleasure to sail.

First impressions

The T-37 is a good example of what might be called Sparkman & Stephens' modern period. Relatively low and sleek with a modest sheer and pretty reverse transom, the T-37 has a profile that still seems quasi-modern today and doesn't appear outdated like many of the IOR boats of its era. Under the water, it has a long, low-aspect fin keel and full-skeg-hung rudder. The vast majority of 37s were built as keel-centerboarders. While I have never particularly liked centerboard boats, there is no denying that a board-up draft of 4 feet, 2 inches opens up a lot of thin-water harbors, and I should add, the owners I spoke with had no centerboard horror stories to relate. The deep-keel version has a draft of 6 feet, 7 inches. The single-spreader rig was moderately high aspect for its time with a short boom and a working sail area of 625 square feet.

Construction

Although Tartan had some financial woes through the years, the quality of its boats has been surprisingly consistent. By all accounts, the Tartan 37 is a well-built boat incorporating progressive coring techniques and sound workmanship. Tartan recognized early on that the glass-to-resin ratio was important and its layups were not usually resin rich. The T-37 has a balsa-cored hull, and combined with unidirectional roving in high-stress areas, the result is a strong and light hull. Balsa coring in any boat can be a potential problem, especially in the hull, which needs to be carefully inspected for any signs of delamination. The problems with cores usually originate between the core layer and the skin where stress has caused delamination and separation has occurred. A boat with a badly delaminated balsa-cored hull should be avoided like the plague. With that said, however, many manufacturers have used balsa-cored hulls for years.

The 37's hull-to-deck joint is on a wide internal flange, well bedded and mechanically fastened through a husky teak toerail with 1/4-inch stainless steel bolts on 6-inch centers. The centerboard trunk is tucked away neatly below the main bilge and to keep things tidy, the pennant is routed through the mast before exiting on deck. The bulkheads below are securely tabbed to the hull and deck.

What to look for

While most Tartan 37 owners have nothing but praise for their boats, there are a few items to check before buying. The bronze bottom rudder bearing support, especially in the older boats, has been known to sheer, leaving the rudder support to a single top bearing. Obviously, the boat must be out of the water to check for this problem. Hull-and-deck joint leaks are not uncommon; look closely at the toerail to see if it has lifted or twisted slightly from the deck. A bead of caulk along the toerail is usually an indication of a leak. Check below for signs of moisture or water damage caused by a leaky joint. Also, be sure to check the fittings where the centerboard pennant exits the trunk. One last note, carefully inspect the swage fittings on the rig. This should be done with any boat with a rig more than five years old and I do know of one T-37 that lost its rig when the backstay swage let go in a strong blow.

On deck

The deck and cockpit of the 37 are two of its most appealing features. The side decks are wide, the chainplates are well inboard and the nonskid is aggressive, providing a safe working area. The decks could be even wider but for some reason the stanchion bases are set well inboard, wasting valuable space. There are teak grabrails that run the length of the coachroof and plenty of ventilators. Surprisingly, S&S didn't make much of a provision for anchoring the boat. There is no external chain locker, no reasonable way to fit a windlass and the standard bow rollers are a joke. Typical of the quality of the boat, the toerail tapers into beefy aluminum chafe pads near the bow and stern cleats to eliminate any wear and tear on the teak.

The cockpit of the Tartan 37 is surely one of the nicest in its class. Tartan was one of the first builders to go with a T-shaped cockpit that can accommodate five or six adults comfortably. There is an enormous locker to starboard and good-sized lazarette astern, which provides access to the steering quadrant and emergency tiller. The coamings are actually fairly comfortable to lean back against. The standard Edson wheel was a 32-inch destroyer and there is room for a slightly larger wheel if desired. The visibility from the helm is excellent. While most 37s have been retrofitted with at least self-tailing primaries, this still may be a necessary upgrade in the older boats. There is not much of a bridgedeck and, in fact, it is little more than a sill. While this makes it easy for the crew to slide down the companionway, at the first sign of threatening weather, a hatch board should be dropped in place. The mainsheet controls are on the aft coachroof. The winch for the centerboard is also mounted here.

Like almost all aluminum masts, the spar is extruded from 6000 series aluminum and anodized for corrosion protection. The standing rigging is not overly beefy, but it is almost never the wire that fails anyway. It is invariably a fitting like a swage or tang that parts and causes grief. The original main and genoa halyards were wire to rope, and if they haven't been replaced, they should be, with consideration given to low-stretch Kevlar, Spectra or Technora line.

Tartan 37 Price Data

		Low	High
BUC Retail Range	1976	$38,000	$42,000
	1980	$46,900	$51,500
	1984	$60,800	$66,800

		State	Asking
Boats For Sale	1977	NY	$53,000
	1980	WI	$49,000
	1982	NC	$56,000

Down below

The arrangement below is not overly creative. There is a V-berth forward, which could have been a little longer, followed by a head to port. The saloon features a pilot berth to starboard and lockers above the settee to port. Storage throughout is excellent, especially for a boat with a moderate beam. The settees extend to provide two good sea berths. A large drop-leaf table stows vertically to the bulkhead when not in use and this serves to open up the saloon. The arrangement for

Tartan 37

Sailing Magazine's Value Guide

PRICE: While there may be better buys for the buck, the overall quality of the T-37 usually justifies the high asking price.

DESIGN QUALITY: An S&S design with a nice combination of aesthetics, performance and comfort.

CONSTRUCTION QUALITY: The construction standards remained high throughout all of Tartan's financial ups and downs. Tartan never watered down the materials on the 37.

USER-FRIENDLINESS: An easy boat to handle under sail and power, with a very commodious cockpit. A better anchoring system must be devised. The only complaint below is that the forward berth is not very long or comfortable.

SAFETY: While the overall quality is a safety feature, there is still the lack of a bridgedeck to consider. The stanchions could be taller and better supported.

TYPICAL CONDITIONS: Some 37s were raced hard and put away wet. Also, many have cruised extensively. But most boats on the market are in pretty good shape.

REFITTING: Most 37s more than 10 years old will need to be rerigged. Some original parts may be available through Tartan.

SUPPORT: Tartan Yachts is alive and well. It is possible to talk to Tim Jackett, the in-house designer and production manager who has been with the company for 20 years and probably knows the 37 better than anyone.

AVAILABILITY: Although nearly 500 37s were built, they don't change hands that often. There are, however, 37s available all over the country.

INVESTMENT AND RESALE: The Tartan 37 holds it value quite well on the used boat market and, when compared to new boats, represents a sound investment.

OVERALL 'SVG' RATING

securing the table to the sole is rather flimsy and should be upgraded if it hasn't been already.

The galley is to starboard and features double sinks, a three-burner stove and oven and a large icebox. Most owners will have added some form of refrigeration, and if the previous owners did not add extra insulation to the icebox, plan on doing it, especially to the lift-off top section.

Tartan didn't skimp on tankage and the 37 has 90 gallons of water in two fiberglass tanks. The nav station is opposite the galley and has a good-sized chart table and comfortable seat cut into the large double quarter berth. The quarter berth—if you can resist the urge to make it into a garage—is a legitimate double and would be a good place to sleep under way.

Typical of its era, the interior is quite dark. While it is possible to strip the wood down and lighten it up, don't underestimate what a big job it is. The excellent craftsmanship and skilled joinerwork make the darkness easier to live with. Also, there are opening portlights throughout for excellent ventilation. Unfortunately, at some point Tartan went to plastic ports and these have a tendency to crack and the dogs strip.

Engine

The standard engine for most Tartan 37s was the Westerbeke 50, which rated out at 40 horsepower. Some boats were fitted with the ubiquitous Perkins 4108, which has about the same horsepower. Spare parts are readily available for both engines and either one provides plenty of punch for the 15,500-pound T-37 and its easily driven hull. Most owners have upgraded the two-bladed prop into a three-blade, trading off slightly increased drag under sail for more speed under power. Engine access is adequate through a panel behind the companionway steps and panels in the quarter berth and cockpit locker. It is tough to reach the oil dipstick from the front panel. The stuffing box is readily available from the cockpit locker. On many of the older boats, the engine sound insulation was falling off and needed to be replaced.The fuel capacity is 50 gallons in a single tank, which gives the 37 a realistic motoring range of 250 to 300 miles.

Underway

"The centerboard eliminates any weather helm and really balances out the boat," said Bill Strandhagen, owner of the 1977 built *Destiny.* "It obviously also reduces leeway when beating." Strandhagen has owned *Destiny* for six years and has put some miles under her keel with several trips between his home port of Jacksonville, Florida, and the Bahamas. "You'd almost think she was a Hood design," Strandhagen says with a laugh. "She was meant to be sailed from the low side with two fingers on the helm."

Most 37s you will encounter on the used boat market will have a roller furling headsail and if close windward sailing is high on your list of priorities, look for a 37 with optional inboard genoa tracks, most were fitted with them. The 37's performance is lively on all points of sail and it has good motion with its fine entry.

Conclusion

The Tartan 37's prices range from near $40,000 for a 1970s model to near $70,000 for a well-maintained late model. They offer an excellent blend of performance, quality and comfort and remember, any boat that is "simply a pleasure to sail," should be given strong consideration.

Tayana 37

Excellent bluewater cruiser that remains a sure bet for the 'big cruise'

Conventional wisdom in the sailboat brokerage community says, "Sell the dream not the boat." There is no doubt that the traditional look of the Tayana 37 appeals to the dreamer in all of us. When we close our eyes and picture a boat snugly anchored in the shadow of lush tropical mountains, we see a boat like the Tayana 37. What's different about the Tayana 37 is that it has actually been the vehicle for many sailors dreams.

Officially, the 37 is still available as a new boat, although the Taiwanese builder, Ta Yang, is building bigger boats today and does not have the 37 currently in production. While the cost of a new or late-model boat would disqualify it from our self-imposed $100,000 limit for this column, the vast majority of used 37s on the market are priced at, or below, $100,000.

First impressions

Designer Robert Perry freely admits that the Tayana 37, along with some of his other early designs, including the Hans Christian 34, was inspired by the phenomenal success of the Westsail 32. "The Westsail 32 changed everything," Perry said. "Cruising became a lifestyle. I'll never forget seeing a full-page picture of a 32 in *Time* magazine; cruising had gone mainstream and the Westsail 32 was largely responsible. Nobody mentioned that it was not much of a sailboat."

The Tayana 37 incorporates the same handsome profile, sweet sheer and shapely Baltic stern of the Westsail, but the overall design, especially below the water, was much better conceived. Perry, who learned his craft working with Dick Carter and doesn't have it in him to design a slow boat, has always had the unique ability to blend a traditional look above the water with more progressive ideas below the waterline.

While it is quite a stretch to call the 37's hull shape progressive, especially by today's standards, in many important ways it was quite different from the Westsail. Perry cut away the forefoot of the Tayana 37's long keel and included a shapely constellation rudder. The boat was proportionally lighter, with a more moderate displacement and leaner bilges. These features, combined with a good-sized rig and a generous 861-square-foot sail area, translated into a rather nice sailing boat with surprising performance, especially upwind.

Tayana 37

LOA 36'8"
LWL 31'
Beam 11'6"
Draft 5'8"
Displ. 22,500 lbs.
Ballast 7,340 lbs.
Sail Area
Cutter 861 sq. ft.
Ketch 768 sq. ft.

Construction

The Tayana 37 is massively constructed. The hull is solid glass and Perry noted that he specified the same laminate schedule used in the legendary Valiant 40. The deck is balsa-cored with the usual concerns about delamination around through-deck fittings. The cast iron ballast is dropped into the hollow keel section and glassed over. While some cruising sailors prefer an externally fastened lead keel for its impact-absorbing qualities, a properly manufactured, internal ballast keel offers less opportunity to ultimately compromise the integrity of the hull through the failure of a single keelbolt.

The hull-and-deck joint incorporates a substantial hollow bulwark that forms an incredibly strong boxed joint. Early Tayanas reportedly had leaking problems around hawsepipes and scuppers that went through the bulwark. On newer boats, the hollow bulwark is glassed over from the inside, eliminating the problem. Deck hardware is all through-bolted with stainless steel backing plates. Bulkheads are well-secured to the hull, and along with stout floors, offer good transverse support.

Tayana 37 Price Data

		Low	High
BUC Retail Range	1980	$ 63,800	$ 70,200
	1984	$ 78,700	$ 86,500
	1988	$102,500	$112,500

		State	Asking
Boats For Sale	1981	FL	$ 71,900
	1984	MD	$ 92,000
	1985	FL	$ 94,000

What to look for

Something not to look for is the ketch-rigged version of the Tayana 37. Although most boats were cutters, ketch rigs in general were popular in the 1970s but they offer few advantages in a boat this size. The standard boat included a spruce box section, spar and boom. If for no other reason than maintenance, look for a 37 with aluminum spars. Another feature not to look for is teak decks. Most early boats had them, but later owners realized they were more trouble than they were worth. The tanks in most boats were made of black iron, which is a good material especially for fuel tanks, but black iron water tanks will eventually rust. Be sure to check if the water tanks are leaking, and if they are, how big a job it will be to pull them out of the boat and replace them. Speaking of tanks, one of the most common complaints about the Tayana 37 is that the builder decided to move the designed fuel tank from under the settees to the forepeak. This 90-gallon tank, along with a couple hundred feet of chain and several big anchors, can certainly make the boat bow-heavy. Many owners have reverted to amidships tankage, and you should too. Also, be sure to check the bronze rudder heel fitting when the boat is hauled out. This fitting is secured with stainless bolts and often shows serious signs of electrolysis.

In the early days of Taiwan boatbuilding, there were glaring inconsistencies from boat to boat. Faulty electrical wiring and suspect stainless steel were chief among them. If you are considering a Tayana 37 built before 1981, be sure to carefully inspect the wiring and the standing rigging. It is very unlikely that these problems have been corrected by previous owners.

On deck

The small cockpit of the 37 is unquestionably a seagoing cockpit and consequently rather uncomfortable. Although cockpit locker shapes and sizes vary because of many different interior arrangements, most 37s that I have seen have large lockers. The steering arrangement on early boats often featured a Tunis worm gear that wasn't particularly sensitive. The view from the helm is not very good, as most 37s have decks cluttered with boom gallows, butterfly hatches and midboom sheeting arrangements. Indeed, most Tayana 37s that you will find on the used-boat market will be loaded down with cruising gear. However, as you make your way forward, you realize that the substantial bulwark, fairly wide side decks and tall, well-supported double lifelines provide a sense of security. The through-bulwark hawsepipes, complete with cleats, offer a good arrangement for docklines.

I have never liked bowsprits much; structurally, they just don't make much sense and the Tayana 37 does little to change my mind. The argument that a sprit offers a good anchoring platform is not valid because the rode invariably chafes on the bobstay. Also, the lead from either of the two anchor rollers on the 37 is not true back to the windlass. The only good thing about bowsprits is that they are pretty—especially if they are festooned with a lovely figurehead.

Down below

Although there are nearly 600 Tayana 37s afloat, it seems no two are alike down below. Tayana offered custom interiors at no extra charge and owners couldn't resist designing their perfect cruising-boat

Tayana 37

Sailing Magazine's Value Guide

PRICE: Certainly one of the most alluring features of the 37 is the price. Simply put, it is hard to find a better bluewater cruising boat per dollar invested.

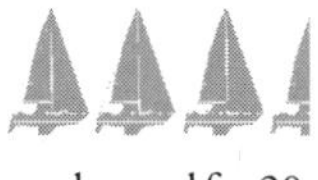

DESIGN QUALITY: It is folly to fault a design that has logged so many miles. The design has remained basically unchanged for 20 years.

CONSTRUCTION QUALITY: There is no disputing that the 37's hull is heavily laid up and construction quality is robust.

USER-FRIENDLINESS: The deck is cluttered. Close-quarter maneuvering under power is always a bit tricky with a long keel.

SAFETY: A substantial bulwark, tall, well-supported lifelines and a seagoing cockpit make the 37 a very safe boat on deck.

TYPICAL CONDITIONS: Most 37s are well-equipped but some are old. Be suspect of brokerage listings until you see the boat.

REFITTING: Although the boat has a few idiosyncrasies that make some aspects of retrofits difficult, there is a lot of communication between 37 owners.

SUPPORT: Like many boats built in Taiwan, factory support is sometimes lacking; however, the strong owners group makes up for this.

AVAILABILITY: With nearly 600 boats afloat, there is usually a good selection of 37s on the market.

INVESTMENT AND RESALE: The Tayana 37 has held its value very well over the years. Demand for the Tayana 37 remains strong.

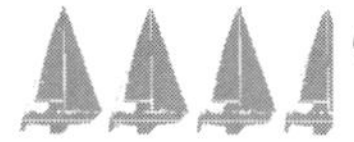

OVERALL 'SVG' RATING

interior. Interiors range from the standard arrangement of an offset double berth forward with a quarter cabin aft, to a single aft cabin with the head forward, to probably the most popular style, a forward pullman berth to port or starboard with large head and separate shower opposite. One 37 owner designed the forward half of the boat around a full-sized dental chair. Obviously, he had plans for working while he cruised.

Despite the variety of arrangements, the interior is undoubtedly the most charming feature of the boat. The quality of the joinerwork is excellent. Tayana could offer custom interiors without pricing its boats out of the market because, in effect, every boat is custom-made anyway. The craftsmen who built these boats shaped every piece of wood while working; there is virtually nothing that is mass-produced. By today's standards, the rich teak finish is rather dark. When you compare the quality of other domestically built cruising-boat interiors, however, the darkness becomes more tolerable.

Engine

Over the years, three primary engines have been used in the Tayana 37: the venerable Perkins 4108, the Volvo MD 17C and the Yanmar 3QM 30. Fortunately, most 37s were fitted with the Yanmar. Access to the engine behind the companionway box and ladder is adequate. It is difficult to get at the back of the engine, and ironically, this is usually where the oil dipstick is located. Some owners have cut access ports through the quarter cabin and others through cockpit lockers. The standard fuel capacity in the older boats was 90 gallons and is 100 gallons in newer boats.

Underway

A couple of years ago, I delivered a 1989 Tayana 37 from Key West to Fort Lauderdale, Florida. Although the wind was light, this short passage of a couple hundred miles confirmed what I had been told: The Tayana 37 is a surprisingly good sailing boat. The cutter rig was well-balanced and the boat had a comfortable motion riding over a pronounced Gulf Stream swell. We encountered a brief but gusty summer squall and I hastily reefed the main and rolled in the headsail, which substantially lowered the center of effort, and we easily rode out the squall.

Bill and Rockie Truxall sail their 37 on Chesapeake Bay. "We sail the boat mostly as a sloop on the bay, with a 130-percent roller furling genoa instead of the yankee. The boat is easily driven. When we go offshore, we revert to the twin headsail rig." The Truxalls head up the lively and informative Tayana Owners Group and publish a most informative quarterly newsletter, *TOG News*.

The 37 is not an overly stiff boat, at least not initially, but that is a characteristic of many cruising boats that carry a lot of weight up high. Designer Perry believes that this initial tenderness is a plus because it eases the snap of the rolling motion. The 37 can develop a mean weather helm, but this can usually be reduced by removing some of the rake out of the mast. One important thing to note about older 37s: Many were originally fitted with inferior Hong Kong sails and they should be replaced.

Conclusion

The Tayana 37, with prices ranging from $60,000 to $80,000 for an older boat to around $100,000 for a 1988 or 1989 model, represents a sound value in a bluewater cruising boat.

Endeavour 37

Florida-bred, strongly built coastal cruiser

The Endeavour 37 was one of many familiar fiberglass production sailboats cloned into existence on the West Coast of Florida during the 1970s and 1980s. The nondescript metal warehouses tucked away in mundane industrial parks may not inspire comparisons to Down East yards like Hinckley and Concordia, but in the last 30 years, more sailboats have been built in the Tampa Bay area than anywhere else in the country. As cruising boats came to dominate the industry, Florida quietly replaced Southern California as production central for sailboats. Endeavour, Morgan, Irwin, Gulfstar, Lancer, Watkins, Island Packet, Caliber, Compact, Sovereign, Nimble, Antigua and Wind Ship—just to name a few—were some of the makes and models that were, and still are, built in the Tampa Bay area.

John Brooks, who was a true gentleman and refreshingly candid, and his partner Rob Valdez launched Endeavor Yachts in 1974 when they acquired the Irwin 32 tooling. The restyled Endeavour 32 was an immediate success and was quickly followed up by the comfortable Endeavour 37. The 37 is usually listed as a house design, and although there is some mystery about who really designed the boat (Creekmore sometimes get credit), there is no disputing the 37's popularity. Nearly 500 boats were built before Brooks sold Endeavour, and the new owners switched the company's focus to larger monohulls and multihulls.

Endeavour 37

LOA 37'5"
LWL 30'
Beam 11'7"
Draft 4'6"
Displacement
21,000 lbs.
Sail Area
580 sq. ft. (sloop)
640 sq. ft. (ketch)

First impressions

The most distinctive feature of the Endeavour 37 is a beefy cockpit coaming that looks like it belongs on a boat 10 feet longer. The coaming makes the cockpit feel secure, and it is a great base for a dodger, although it spoils what would otherwise be a decent profile. There is a moderate sheer and a fair bit of freeboard, especially forward, which helps make the 37 a dry boat when sailing upwind. Below the water the 37 features a shallow, long fin keel and skeg-hung rudder. The 4-foot, 6-inch draft didn't help the boat track better upwind, but it certainly helped sell it to many sailors who prized thin-water meandering more than snappy windward performance.

While most 37s were masthead sloops, quite a few owners chose the optional ketch rig, which increased working sail area from 580 to 640 square feet. Either way the 37 is undercanvassed, especially when you consider the design displacement of 21,000 pounds. By comparison the Ted Brewer-designed Morgan 382, a direct competitor to the Endeavour 37, carries 668 square feet of sail area and displaces 18,000 pounds with a similar LWL.

Construction

The Endeavour 37 was built like many of her Tampa Bay area sisterships—simple and strong. The hull is solid glass and the deck is balsa cored. The ballast is internal, meaning that lead is placed in a molded keel cavity and glassed over. There are no keel bolts to worry about—a distinct advantage when considering older boats. The mast is keel-stepped, and early on Endeavour did a good job of building a step that was well-supported and out of the bilge. The hull-and-deck joint incorporates a molded bulwark flange and a wide teak caprail for a nearly leak-proof boxjoint.

Below decks the 37 is amazingly free of bulkheads. In either the A or B interior plan there is no complete amidships bulkhead, which opens up the cabin but can bring into question the integrity of the structural engineering. The flat areas of freeboard in the forward hull sections are not well-supported and oilcanning, or flexing of the hull, is a potential problem.

Despite these problems, few structural problems have been reported over the years. Endeavour 37s were popular Virgin Island charter boats, and most endured the tough windward slog from Florida down island without mishap. Dick Jachney, who at one time had several 37s in his St. Thomas-based fleet, told me that the boats stood up to the rigorous demands of bareboat chartering.

Endeavour 37 Price Data

		Low	High
BUC Retail Range	1977	$41,700	$46,400
	1980	$50,500	$55,500
	1983	$62,000	$68,100

		State	Asking
Boats For Sale	1978	FL	$55,000
	1980	SC	$52,000
	1983	FL	$77,000

What to look for

Unfortunately, like other boats built during this period, Endeavours were prone to osmotic blisters. This is not the kiss of death it once was for a used boat, but it's certainly a problem that will have to be corrected if you hope to maintain reasonable resale value. Blisters caught the boating industry off guard and forced changes on builders and suppliers that were tough to swallow at first, but have served the industry well in the long run.

Nobody can say exactly what caused the outbreak of "boat pox" in the early 1980s, but it was likely a combination of inferior resins coupled with hasty laminating techniques in a rapidly expanding industry that had little regard for quality control. Today most builders use blister-resistant materials and carefully monitor the laminating process, so that the problem has been almost eliminated.

While I would clearly look for a 37 that is blister-free, or one with a recent epoxy-based bottom job, I wouldn't rule out a boat with minor blisters. The price may well reflect the defect, and the blisters can be repaired for much less than most yards charge if you are willing to do the work yourself.

Other common problems with the Endeavour 37s are faded gelcoats and worn out nonskid surfaces on the decks. Carefully inspect the plastic portlights, which are often cracked and impossible to dog down. Most boats came from the factory with gate valves on through-hull fittings, but most likely these have been changed to seacocks. Check the installation carefully. A surprising number of Endeavour 37 owners have lived aboard at one time or another, and this is a mixed blessing for used boat buyers. Live-aboard boats often have features like air conditioning and generators, luxuries that are great when they work, but they usually don't and their components tend to wipe out a lot of good storage space. The best used boat is one with the least equipment, that way you can add what you want without the hassle of removing rusty old compressors.

There were also a couple of production changes to note. At some point (it is hard to know exactly when), a small bowsprit was added, which was used mostly as an anchoring platform, although on some models the forestay was extended to ease weather helm. A taller rig also became an option late in the production run, which increased the air draft from 46 to 49 feet.

On deck

There is only one way to describe the cockpit of the 37—comfortable. The visibility from the helm is excellent, and there is plenty of storage in two lockers and a lazarette. There is a stout bridgedeck, and although the well is large, it is rather shallow. The scuppers seem more than adequate should an errant

Endeavour 37

Sailing Magazine's Value Guide

PRICE: With prices ranging from $40,000 to $70,000, the Endeavour 37 is a good value but not a great one. Prices seem lowest for boats in Florida.

DESIGN QUALITY: The cockpit, deck and interior are well-designed, but the inefficient nature of the hull shape is a major drawback.

CONSTRUCTION QUALITY: Despite some problems with blisters, most Endeavour 37s have held up pretty well. Look for signs of oilcanning forward.

USER-FRIENDLINESS: The Endeavour is an easy boat to sail and quite comfortable. It does not back well under power, but how many sailboats do?

SAFETY: The cockpit is secure, the side decks are wide, the stanchions well-supported, and there are plenty of handholds below. The nonskid is often worn.

TYPICAL CONDITION: This rating would be higher if only private boats were considered, however, many 37s served in charter fleets and have been well-used.

REFITTING: Most systems on the Endeavour 37 are accessible for working on and upgrading. Fortunately, Endeavour used relatively few proprietary parts so finding replacements is manageable.

SUPPORT: There is not much communication among 37 owners, and the factory has no interest in, or records of, the old boats.

AVAILABILITY: There is always a good selection of 37s on the market. Look for privately owned, blister-free boats.

INVESTMENT AND RESALE: Like other boats of this vintage, the selling price has remained solid for the last several years. When compared to new boats, the Endeavour 37 is a lot of boat for the money.

OVERALL 'SVG' RATING

wave slop aboard. Unfortunately, on early boats the mainsheet is tacked to a fitting on the cockpit sole just forward of the wheel. I would sacrifice space to add a traveler. The sheet winches look lonely and small mounted on the massive coaming boards, and they are hard to reach from the helm.

The side decks are wide, and the molded bulwark provides security when going forward. The stanchion bases are well-supported, and double lifelines were standard. Check the swaged end fittings on the plastic coated lifelines. The shrouds are outboard, and the headsail track is on the caprail. Needless to say tight sheeting angles are not a feature of the boat.

There are large hawsepipes and mooring cleats forward, although the anchoring arrangement on pre-bowsprit boats seems like an afterthought. Originally the halyards were designed to be deployed at the mast, but many owners have opted to lead them aft. This task can be more difficult than it looks, and unless the leads are well designed, it may take a lot of umph to sweat the main up. Personally, I like to pull the main up, hand over hand, standing by the mast.

Down below

The Endeavour 37 came with two distinct interior plans. Plan A was unique because it eliminated the V-berth. The saloon is pushed forward, centered around a large U-shaped dinette. Two large quarter cabins are aft, with the head amidships to port. The galley is a shallow, U-shape to starboard, with the nav station located farther aft. This layout has always been popular for live-aboard couples. Plan B is more conventional with V-berth forward (although there isn't much headroom over the bunk) and a double quarter berth aft. The head is aft of the V-berth, and the saloon usually has a fold-up bulkhead table. A large galley is aft to starboard with the nav station opposite.

Both plans have two Endeavour trademarks, a teak parquet sole and an open feeling. The workmanship is quite good, although in contrast to today's boats, teak interiors seem dark. There is good storage above and behind the settees in both plans, and ventilation is excellent with 10 opening portlights and at least two large overhead hatches. The galley, especially in Plan B, has large counter surfaces with adequate fiddles, deep sinks, and unfortunately, side-opening Norcold-style refrigerators that are nearly impossible to open on the wrong tack.

Engine

The Endeavour 37 came standard with the ubiquitous Perkins 4108 diesel. This workhorse is rated anywhere from 37 to 50 horsepower depending upon whether brake horsepower is measured, i.e. without accessories, or shaft horsepower, which is what the engine will actually deliver after deducting for a water pump, alternator, possible refrigeration and a marine gear box. The 4108 is no longer in production, but parts are still widely available, and any diesel mechanic worth his salt will know the engine well.

Access is good from behind and below the companionway steps. The 4108 is not the quietest engine around, but the 37's sound insulation is excellent. The stuffing box is accessed through the cockpit locker; however, of the three 37s I inspected for this article, two had generators mounted directly aft of the engine, limiting access. A single 55-gallon aluminum fuel tank was standard, although this has occasionally been retrofitted. One owner told me he has a fiberglass tank.

Underway

Robert Pierce, who owned a 1976 sloop for six years, made several passages from Florida to the Bahamas. He noted that the boat never gave him an anxious moment in the Gulf Stream, even during one memorable "norther" when it was really blowing. "The boat is stiff but, she also carries a bit of helm," Pierce said. "Especially in more than 20 knots."

While Pierce acknowledged the many advantages of the 4-foot, 6-inch draft, particularly when cruising the Abacos, he admitted that sailing upwind in any kind of seaway was frustrating because the boat tracked poorly. Upwind sailing in general is not the 37's forte. The sheeting angles are hopelessly wide, the mainsheet arrangement is inefficient, the bow tends to lumber through the water and leeway must be factored in. Many 37 owners resort to motorsailing when working to windward. Off the wind, however, the 37 has a nice motion and carries a decent amount of sail as the wind builds. William Fresco, who sails a 1982 sloop out of New Bern, North Carolina, told me that the boat was ideal for the shallow water and unpredictable winds of Pamlico Sound and the Neuse River. "The boat is very forgiving and easy to handle," he said.

Conclusion

The Endeavour 37 is an ideal boat for coastal cruising and comfortable for living aboard. If I was planning a voyage down the East Coast and over to the Bahamas and had around $50,000 to spend on a boat, I'd look seriously at the Endeavour 37.

Swan 38

A famous pedigree at a fraction of the cost

We were hard on the wind, sailing over a long, low Gulf Stream swell, when I remarked to my young friend and crew that I didn't particularly like the rapid motion of the cruising catamaran we were delivering. My comment triggered a spirited conversation about boats and designers. When I mentioned that Olin Stephens was still my favorite designer, my friend responded with a blank look. I was dumbfounded. *Stormy Weather*, *Dorade*, *Finisterre* aside, he was also ignorant of Stephens' impressive list of production boats, including the Tartan 37 and the classic Swan 44. Fresh from college and clearly infected with the sailing disease, my friend was intrigued by the new breed of multihulls for cruising and anything drawn by Bruce Farr for racing. His concept of the sailing world was neatly divided.

I came of age in an era when the division was not so stark, when a racer-cruiser was not thought of as an unfortunate compromise but as a dual-purpose boat. The early and mid-1970s S&S-designed Nautor Swans, especially the 38 and 44, seemed to be near-perfect boats to me. The Swan 38 was introduced in 1973, and with 116 boats built, it was one of Nautor's most successful production boats before being phased out in 1979. For years I admired Swans from a distance, impressed that, although most people bought them for racing under the IOR rule and in Swan regattas, they always seemed to turn up at the Atlantic crossroads of Bermuda, Antigua, Horta, Panama and Gibraltar. These were definitely oceangoing boats.

Recently, I have delivered several Swans, including a 1975-built 38, which I sailed 1,000 miles from the Virgin Islands to Ft. Lauderdale, Florida. I discovered a few shortcomings, but I also came to admire the weatherly nature of Stephens' Swan 38 design and the quality of Nautor's construction. A top-of-the-line Swan 38 will sell for $80,000, to $110,000.

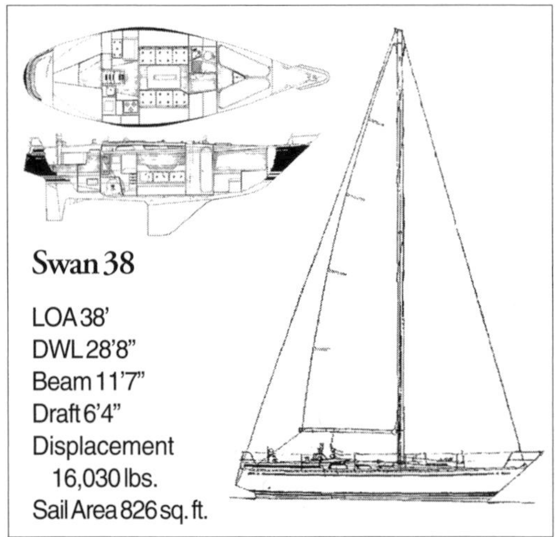

Swan 38

LOA 38'
DWL 28'8"
Beam 11'7"
Draft 6'4"
Displacement 16,030 lbs.
Sail Area 826 sq. ft.

First impressions

The Swan 38 is a handsome boat and a vintage Olin Stephens design. Low-slung, the hull sports a bit of tumblehome, a fine entry and a pinched stern. In profile, the wedge deck and trunkhouse that naturally blend into the cockpit coaming immediately give the boat away as a Swan. The rig is relatively high-aspect, and as with all Swans, the mast section is beefy and the deck hardware is first-rate.

South of the waterline, the Swan 38 features a deep fin keel and full skeg-hung rudder. When you see the boat out of the water you realize that there is a lot more boat below the waterline than above. The 38 has a hull shape that is almost incapable of pounding. Coupled with a high ballast-to-displacement ratio, the 38 is extremely seaworthy and can carry sail upwind when other boats can't. Indeed, like many S&S designs of the period, upwind sailing is the Swan 38's strong suit, although the crew should be prepared to get wet if there is a sea running.

Construction

Nautor, a small division of a parent company that is primarily in the paper business, has been building boats since 1966 at its plant near Pietarsaari, Finland, on the Gulf of Bothnia, just 250 miles below the Arctic Circle. Nautor achieved prominence 30 years ago when it was selected by custom builder Palmer Johnson to be its production yard for the new S&S-designed 43. Nautor has since built more than 1,600 boats, ranging from 36 feet to 112 feet. From the beginning, Nautor created well-engineered and well-executed boats that have stood up to the whims of Neptune and the tests of time. Any used 38s are at least 20 years old and many are 25. Yet from a construction standpoint, excluding the teak decks, most are still in excellent condition.

The hull of the 38 is solid fiberglass, reinforced with several full-length longitudinal stringers. A steel beam is laminated into the hull on the centerline. This forms the base of the maststep and also supports the keel bolts. The ballast is lead. The decks were usually balsa-cored, although some were foam. They are almost always covered in teak. Teak decks are the single biggest source of problems on old Swans, including the 38. To keep the weight down, thin teak was used, only 3/8 inch thick in some cases. After many years of sanding and chemical maintenance, there just isn't enough teak left when the fasteners need taking up and when seams are ever-widening. The hull-and-deck joint is through-bolted, incorporating a nearly full-length aluminum toerail. The joint is also fiberglassed from the inside—it almost never leaks.

What to look for

Start by looking for a Swan 38 with a new teak deck. This will, of course, be reflected in the price, but considering that a new teak deck could easily cost $20,000 and possibly more, avoiding the aggravation of the job might be worth the money. There is nothing older-looking than worn-out teak decks. While subdeck delamination is rare (although by no means unknown), the problem is usually cosmetic. The first sign of deck problems are popped bungs and exposed fastenings, followed by peeled caulking, and finally, lifting teak. If water has permeated into the balsa core, then it can separate from the fiberglass deck skin. The result is delamination and an expensive deck refit project. Before you sign on the dotted line, a competent marine surveyor should carefully examine the decks of a Swan 38. If you choose to tackle redecking an older 38, be sure to specify a type of teak deck that requires a minimum of fastenings. By the way, I have seen a Swan 38 with fiberglass decks and Treadmaster, a synthetic nonskid covering. While it's practical, it just doesn't look right on a Swan.

Swan 38 Price Data

		Low	High
BUC Retail Range	1974	$66,500	$ 73,100
	1976	$74,000	$ 81,400
	1979	$95,100	$104,500
		State	**Asking**
Boats For Sale	1975	FL	$ 89,000
	1976	Greece	$125,000

Other problems associated with the 38 come more from age than engineering flaws. Of course, the standing rigging should be carefully examined, and if original, should probably be replaced. The aluminum toerail may be pitted or corroded; this will not be easy to replace because the joint below is glassed over. Replacing a small section, however, is possible. There is also a good likelihood that some of the portlights may leak and need rebedding.

Down below, the original layout called for pipe berths forward, but many 38s have retrofitted permanent berths. Check this joinerwork carefully. Also, an extra water tank has often been added under the forward berths, so be sure to carefully check this installation.

Checking the sail locker, do not allow a vast sail inventory to impress you. More likely than not, these are tired racing sails.

On deck

The Swan 38 cockpit is functional and deceptively comfortable. The wheel is well aft with a short cable run to the quadrant, which, by the way, is very cumbersome to access from the aft cabin. The helmsperson has a nice perch, level at any angle of heel and isolated from the sail controls. By design the cockpit is divided into steering and working stations. Though many old 38s have been converted to bluewater cruisers, this layout is not as awkward as it may seem at first. My experience is that cruising sailors

Swan 38

Sailing Magazine's Value Guide

PRICE: Prices of Swan 38s can range from less than \$70,000 for one that will require a deck job to approximately \$115,000 for one in excellent condition.

DESIGN QUALITY: This is a classic S&S design. The design pedigree is part of the value in owning a Swan.

CONSTRUCTION QUALITY: The construction of the 38 would warrant a five if not for the problems with the teak decks. Overall, hull construction is simple and solid. The boats have held up well over the years. Top-quality gear was used throughout its production run.

USER-FRIENDLINESS: Although originally designed for racing, the overall sweet sailing characteristics make the boat a pleasure to sail. With its IOR rig, it can be a lot of work cranking in headsails.

SAFETY: The overall quality construction makes the Swan 38 a safe boat. The helm is rather prone to green water that frequently sloshes aboard.

TYPICAL CONDITION: This would warrant a higher rating if not for the deck problems. If the decks have been replaced, used 38s are often in excellent condition.

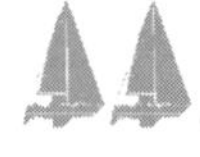
REFITTING: The 38 is not a particularly easy boat to work on. The deck, diesel and rigging are high on the retrofit list.

SUPPORT: Support is through the five Nautor agents located around the country. Because most 38s are so old, there is not much support by agents interested in selling new boats.

AVAILABILITY: The 38 was one of Nautor's largest production runs and many boats were imported into the United States. There seem to be more boats on the East Coast.

INVESTMENT AND RESALE: The Swan 38 is a sound used boat value. When you search for comparable quality in a newer boat, you will be looking at spending much more money.

OVERALL 'SVG' RATING

rarely sit behind the wheel—the autopilot is almost always driving. The 38's cockpit is very efficient for trimming sails.

Double lifelines were standard-issue, although the original stanchions could be taller and the bases better-supported. I like teak decks underfoot, especially in rough conditions. There are teak handrails on the low deckhouse, and if it hasn't been done, consider adding mast rails. Unless the 38 you are considering has been altered for cruising, chances are that the halyards terminate at the mast. I am not a great fan of leading every control line to the cockpit, although the 38's near-flush deck lends itself well to this purpose. Working the deck is an integral aspect of sailing and keeps you in touch with the rhythm of the boat. Moving all the way forward, the stem fitting is poorly designed for serious anchoring and will need to be retrofitted if you are considering cruising.

Down below

A frequent complaint about older Swans is the fire-stationlike main companionways. While steep, the bridgedeck companionway on the 38 is not quite as severe as other Swans. Typical of the times, the accommodations seem cramped by today's standards. The layout features either pipe berths or a converted cabin forward followed by the head to port. The saloon has pilot berths, straight settees and a centerline table with drop leaves. On the 38 I delivered from St. Thomas, one pilot berth had been converted to a cabinet for an entertainment center and it made the saloon seem even smaller. The pint-sized galley is to starboard. The three-burner Flavel stove is sandwiched in place and there is not much counter space. The forward-facing nav station is opposite, with a good-sized chart desk and the electrical panel above. The aft cabin is tucked in under the bridgedeck and cockpit sole and has a single bunk to port and a double to starboard.

Lack of headroom often hurts the 38 on the used boat market. Anyone 6 feet or taller will need to bend his or her neck when moving forward and bend completely over moving aft. Despite the small space, the teak interior woodworking is rich and light, giving the 38 a friendly, homey feel. There are handholds in the logical places, plenty of storage lockers and four excellent sea berths, which reflect the sailing purpose of the Swan 38.

Engine

The standard engine was an underpowered Buhk 20-horsepower diesel. An agile sailor, Stephens figured that the diesel would be used for easing in and out of the slip and little else. He seems to have been right, for most 38s still have the original engine and many have low hours. The fuel tank holds only 30 gallons, which gives a realistic range of about 200 miles in flat seas. Access to the engine and stuffing box is good. I spent an entire day powering on the delivery. Running at 1,800 rpms, which sounded right and vibrated the least, we kicked along at about 5 1/2 knots. With a little assist from the 150-percent genoa, we quickly shot up to nearly 7 knots, although the true wind was probably less than 5 knots.

Underway

We shot out of the Virgin Islands under full sail with a Force 5 easterly just aft of the beam. Although the boat had been in charter service and needed some attention, I was immediately impressed by the way it handled. The steering was tight and true and the boat tracked nicely. The seas built quickly, reaching 6 to 8 feet, but the 38's motion was rock steady. Dropping below, I might have been in a library—needless to say, the off watch slept well. It began to roll a bit when the winds moved further aft and I longed for a spinnaker. Instead, I dropped the main and poled out the headsail, and although our speed dropped to around 6 knots, the autopilot steered the boat effortlessly for the next two days. As a delivery skipper, I have learned that boats with easy motion generally have fewer problems than boats that battle the sea.

After the day of calms, the winds returned from the northwest, a direct head wind, and the Swan 38 was in her element. We rolled in a bit of headsail and sailed close to the wind. At less than 45 degrees, we sliced through the water. We didn't need the autopilot; with the sails trimmed properly, the boat steered itself for long stretches. Our maximum upwind speed was less than 7 knots but the motion was sweet despite a short, choppy sea. Sheets of green water routinely doused anybody in the cockpit. A spray dodger, which we didn't have, should be standard equipment. The winds continued to clock and soon we were reaching again, touching 8 knots occasionally. I spied the condo towers lining Port Everglades on the morning of the sixth day. We had averaged almost 160 miles per day without raising a sweat or losing any sleep.

Conclusion

With prices ranging from less than $70,000 for a boat that needs decks and general upgrading, to around $115,000 for a boat in excellent condition, a used Swan 38 can be purchased for a fraction of its replacement value. Retrofitting may be costly and aggravating. In the end, however, you will have a high-quality boat with a true pedigree, and one that will be desirable if you ever choose to sell. I don't think you will want to sell, for the Swan 38 is an unusually fine sailing boat, capable of crossing any ocean or offering its crew a few hours of solace out on the bay.

Baltic 38 DP

Used models of this high performer sell at a premium—and they're worth it

In 1973, five former employees of Nautor Swan pooled their resources and launched an upstart company in the village of Bosund, Finland, not far from Nautor's plant. The Swan mutineers named their company Baltic Yachts and were committed to applying the latest technology to their boats, while maintaining the high level of engineering and finish that established Swan's lofty reputation.

The sparsely populated western coast of Finland has a disproportionate supply of talented boatbuilders and the new company was quickly on the road to success. In just a few short years, Baltic was producing boats from 33 to 46 feet and had more than 100 employees. Today Baltic Yachts is one of the industry's premier builders, and its distinctive racer-cruisers can be found all over the world, although it now focuses more on large, custom projects.

Early Baltics were designed by the C&C design group and included the 33, 37, 39, 42 and 46. In 1981 Doug Peterson was hired to update the 42, which then became known as the 42 DP. The success of this model prompted Baltic to ask Peterson to design a new 38-footer the following year. The 38 DP was in production from 1982 through 1989. Fifty-five boats were launched during this period, making it Baltic's second largest production run.

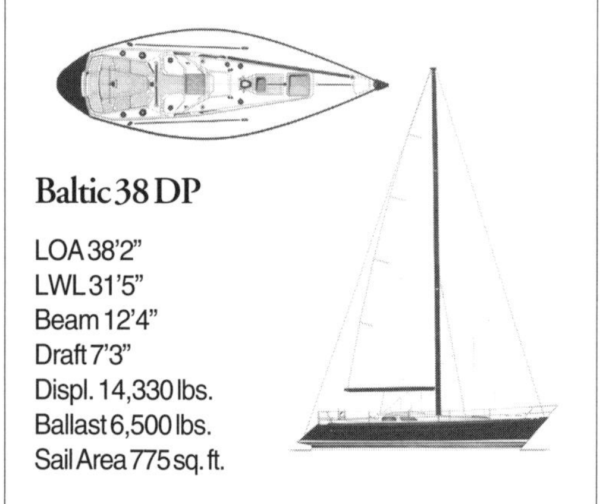

The 38 DP was particularly popular in North America. While it is difficult to track down some Baltic models on our side of the Atlantic, (like the 37 for example) you can usually find a few 38 DPs on the used market. They don't linger long, however, despite their rather steep price tag for a used boat. The 38's blend of sailing performance and quality workmanship holds its own against many new and more expensive cruisers.

First impressions

The older Baltics strike me as a cross between the Swans of the same period and the handsome and lighter boats coming out of C&C's shop in Canada. The lines of the Baltic 38 DP manage to give the boat a powerful yet elegant look. When you examine the line drawings there are a lot of straight edges and sharp angles, yet the finished product seems perfectly balanced in the water.

The low cabintrunk blends sleekly into the foredeck and the flat sheer trails into a broad, rakish transom. The 38 was deceptively beamy for her day at 12 feet, 4 inches, but the hull tapers dramatically as it runs forward and the entry is razor sharp. There is a fair bit of bow overhang by today's standards and the 38 DP was designed to sail with a bit of heel, effectively increasing the LWL.

Below the water Peterson fashioned a high-aspect fin with a draft of 7 feet, 3 inches, which can be a problem for many American sailors as it seems like the water is getting shallower everywhere. The balanced spade rudder is well aft and, combined with full stern sections, offers good steering control downwind. A 45 percent ballast-to-displacement ratio coupled with the deep draft makes the boat stiff upwind.

The Baltic 38 DP, which is built with a balsa-core hull, is comparatively lighter than Swans of similar size. With a displacement of 14,330 pounds, the 38 DP weighs nearly 2,000 pounds less than the old Swan 38 and almost 5,000 pounds less than the Swan 391. The double-spreader, high-aspect rig carries a hefty 775 square feet of working sail area, which is 15 percent more than the Swan 38.

Construction

Like C&C before it, Baltic committed to sandwich construction from the beginning. Most of its boats were balsa-cored and the 38 DP is no exception. Baltic's method of coring involved laminating the end-grain balsa on both sides with unidirectional roving. This provides a stronger and lighter laminate than conventional woven roving. Unidirectional roving also allows more fiberglass to be placed in areas of high stress. In general I'm wary of cored hulls, especially in cruising boats. But the exceptional attention to detail in the initial building process sets Baltics apart. I spoke to a couple of surveyors who have extensive experience with used Baltics, and both told me that they haven't seen or heard of any boats with delaminated cores.

The deck is also balsa-cored with extra reinforcement in load areas, like under the winches and cleats. The hull and deck are joined on an inward flange and double through-bolted on both sides of the aluminum toerail. The lead keel is hardened with antimony and bolted to the hull. There are stout transverse floors throughout the bilge and longitudinal foam stringers.

Baltic 38 DP Price Data

		Low	High
BUC Retail Range	1984	$101,000	$ 111,000
	1985	$107,500	$ 118,500
	1985	$115,000	$ 126,000
		State	**Asking**
Boats For Sale	1985	FL	$ 115,000

The maststep is a galvanized steel plate bolted to the floors to form a bridge and keep the mast base out of the bilge. Overall, the engineering is superb. A prime example is the way the chainplates tie into a longitudinal web that spreads the rigging loads throughout the hull. Another example is the way the teak deck is applied. Although teak decks were optional, the vast majority of 38 DPs have them. The teak takes the place of one layer of fiberglass and is bonded to the molding to be a structural part of the hull, not just an added feature. Also, Baltic went to great lengths to use only vertical wood grains in the teak planking, making it more resistant to rot and subsequent leaks.

What to look for

If you hate teak decks and can't live with 7-foot-plus draft, don't despair. Baltic did make a few boats without teak decks, and other owners have removed them. I recently examined a 1984 model that not only didn't have teak decks, it also had a centerboard instead of the deep fin. This boat, which is for sale, has been sailed all over the world by her Finnish owner and is well equipped for cruising. Considering the miles that have passed under her keel, I was impressed by the overall condition. This is the only centerboard model that I know of.

Most 38 DPs were raced at some point in their lives, although today they are more likely used for

Baltic 38 DP

Sailing Magazine's Value Guide

PRICE: The main drawback to all used Baltics is that they are expensive. But then again, you have to pay for quality and the 38 DP is a high-quality boat.

DESIGN QUALITY: This Peterson design is fast, weatherly and lovely to look at it. It has also aged nicely, which is a key measure of design quality.

CONSTRUCTION QUALITY: Baltics are superbly engineered and beautifully finished. A cored hull is both an advantage and disadvantage, depending on how you look at it.

USER-FRIENDLINESS: It is likely that a more experienced sailor will better appreciate the 38 DP. The boat is not difficult to handle, but the use of runners and a performance-oriented cockpit make it less user-friendly to new sailors.

SAFETY: The excellent construction makes the 38 DP safe, however the stanchions could be taller and better supported. The companionway is very steep and the long bridgedeck makes it tricky moving from the cockpit to the companionway in a blow.

TYPICAL CONDITION: Although many Baltics were raced hard, their owners seem to have lavished care on them. It is rare to find a used Baltic of any size or age that isn't in good condition.

REFITTING: To maintain the resale value of the 38 DP, any refit should be done by a skilled person or yard. Parts and advice are available from Baltic Yachts.

SUPPORT: Baltic Yachts offers support through both its main office in Finland and local dealerships. Baltic USA just completed a move to Newport, Rhode Island, and can be reached at (401) 846-0300. The company's Web page can be found at www.balticyachts.com.

AVAILABILITY: There just were not enough boats built and, because the boats were marketed worldwide, there isn't a concentration in one area. 38 DPs were popular in the U.S. and there are usually a few for sale. There were three boats on the market at press time.

INVESTMENT AND RESALE: Although you pay a premium to purchase a used 38 DP, if you maintain the boat in good condition, it is more than likely that you will get your money back.

OVERALL 'SVG' RATING

cruising with an occasional Wednesday night gig or weekend series race. Naturally the sail inventory needs close inspection, as many old headsails may be ready to be converted into deck awnings. Also the original standing rigging was continuous rod and needs to be checked thoroughly. Although rod rigging holds up well, any 38 DP you are considering is between 12 and 20 years old. Chances are you will need to rerig the boat. If you do, it is worth the extra money to go with discontinuous rod shrouds that are not bent around the spreader tips. Also check the deck prisms for signs of leakage, as they are notorious for letting water seep into the core.

On deck

Ironically the deck of the Baltic 38 DP is the biggest reason why people buy and don't buy the boat: you either love it or hate it. What's not to love about it you ask? Well namely the cockpit. In the same style as many Swans, the 38 DP cockpit features the helm well aft and a substantial bridgedeck forward. The cockpit is efficient for sailing, especially with a crew, but the seats are not very long and it is a bit awkward to make your way to the companionway while under way.

The mainsheet traveler runs across the aft end of the bridgedeck and the mainsheet winch mounts horizontally on a molded form. Unlike some Swans of similar vintage, the genoa sheet winches are located a bit farther aft, within reach of the helmsman, and the view from the helmsman's seat behind the large wheel is excellent. Unfortunately, it is very difficult to rig up an effective dodger or spray hood for the helm and cockpit, and the Baltic 38 DP can kick up its share of green water.

Most 38 DPs have teak decks that provide both excellent nonskid and continual maintenance. Beginning in the bow, there is an adequate double anchor roller, better in fact than most performance-oriented boats of this period. The stemhead fitting also has a twin tack fitting for the jib. Behind the downhaul U-bolt there is a decent-size external chain locker, where a couple of anchors and rodes can be creatively stored.

The deck hardware is of the highest quality. Robust, Skene-style chocks and stout mooring cleats keep dock lines well secured. The aluminum toerail has functional but circular attachment holes instead of rectangular openings that can clip your toes. The stanchion bases are attached to the toerail.

Most 38 DPs will have a nest of winches at the base of the mast. I suspect that many owners will have rerouted halyards and lifts aft to the cockpit, bypassing many of these winches. The boat came with an impressive list of standard sailing gear, from complete spinnaker gear to snatch and spreacher blocks. Baltic builds its own spars, distinctive in most harbors because they are painted with black Awlgrip. While painted spars look nice, they are another item requiring periodic maintenance.

Down below

The only drawback to the 38 DP interior is getting there—the companionway steps are very steep. Erkki Lassonen, who sails his hull No. 49, a 1989 model, in the Gulf of Bothnia, mentions the "long, steep" steps as one of his few complaints with the boat. Once below, you will be charmed by the classic Scandinavian workmanship. The teak interior is rich and snug, without a taste of the ornate, like a Finnish spa. The arrangement is rather innovative.

The bulkheads are cleverly set at an angle providing a feeling of spaciousness that standard, right-angle bulkheads don't permit. Forward is a V-berth, and it is much more tastefully finished than other performance boats of this period. (Most Swan 38s came equipped with pipe berths.) The saloon features a centerline table with a wraparound settee to port and a shallow L-settee opposite. The table folds up and accommodates more people for dinner than anyone should ever have aboard.

The galley is small but functional with deep fiddles. There is plenty of storage, although the large locker spaces might have been more useful if designed in smaller sections. There is however, a slide-out cutting board and a built-in rubbish bin.

The nav station opposite the galley is quite comfortable, although the electrical panel behind the seat makes it easy to accidentally throw a switch. A single head makes sense on a 38-foot boat. It's located aft just to the right of the companionway, allowing it to double as a wet locker.

The most impressive design feature is the aft cabin. Tucked beneath the cockpit, the Baltic 38 was one of the first boats to feature a centerline bunk. Unlike today's bunks that are designed for rolling out of at sea, bulkheads and small leeboards line the 38 DP aft bunk. There are seats to either side at the foot of the bunk and there is ample storage. The only drawback is the lack of headroom in the bunk itself, the limitations of which I will leave to the reader's imagination.

Engine

The standard engine was the Yanmar 3HMF, a freshwater cooled three-cylinder, 30 horsepower diesel. This is a very reliable power plant and by all accounts pushes the 38 DP along smartly even with the small, two-bladed folding prop that came standard. The main drawback is that the hull shape and engine placement required the use of a V-drive transmission. I confess, I just don't like V-drives. As a delivery skipper I know from experience that they are more prone to problems and make getting to the stuffing box difficult.

Access to the engine itself, however, is quite good, as panels can be removed from all four sides. The stainless steel fuel tank carries 30 gallons that provides a realistic motoring range of about 200 miles. Serious cruisers would probably augment this with additional tankage, although there isn't a logical place to add a rigid tank. A bladder tank may be your best option.

Underway

The Baltic 38 DP is a treat to sail, and wonderfully versatile in a variety of conditions. The helm is responsive, there is rarely excessive weather helm, and the helmsperson has a commanding and unobstructed view of the sails. Lassonen especially likes the boat's performance in light air. He notes that his boat consistently out points her competitors in light going. He also notes that the fine entry helps the boat maintain way through chop, and even in heavy going, the 38 DP is unlikely to pound or to get stopped dead in her tracks.

Lassonen usually sails with a furling genoa when cruising and doesn't feel the need to tuck a reef in the main until the wind is consistently above 20 knots. When racing, he flies a Mylar genoa to about 12 knots of apparent wind, at which point he shortens up to a No. 2. Beyond 18 knots he flies a No. 4 in conditions up to 30 knots, then it is time for storm canvas. The 38 DP will easily attain 7 1/2 to 8 knots on a broad reach in moderate breezes, and can claw upwind at nearly 7 knots until the seas really build.

Conclusion

The Baltic 38 DP is an intriguing used boat. Although it will take between $130,000 to $150,000 to buy one, a similar quality new boat would command three to four times as much. For a couple that puts a premium on all around sailing performance and quality workmanship, the Baltic 38 DP actually represents an excellent value.

Morgan 382

Formerly a cruiser-racer, now a do-everything cruiser that is able and strong

There were two distinct generations of the Morgan 38: The much-respected CCA-style centerboarder designed by Charley Morgan in 1969, and unfortunately, only in production for three years; and the popular Ted Brewer-designed 382, which was launched in 1977. In this review, we will look at the 382, which included two slightly modified editions, the 383 and the 384. Morgan built about 500 of the Brewer versions before production was halted in 1986, which was shortly after Catalina purchased the company.

The Morgan 382 sprang to life during the infamous age of the racer-cruiser or cruiser-racer, depending upon your point of view. In comparison to the more specialized boats of today, racer-cruisers of 15 to 20 years ago are often criticized as being unable to perform either task (racing or cruising) well. This is an unfair judgment. Indeed, a versatile boat is in many ways the most enjoyable. Pure cruisers tend to be sluggish in anything but stiff breezes and modern flyers require micromanagement. The virtual takeover of club racing by PHRF confirms that most sailors don't want extreme boats. And while Morgan's original brochure touting, "Two special sailing yachts in one beautiful body," seems to border on the absurd (is there anything older than old advertising copy?), a used Morgan 382, 383 or 384, with prices ranging from the mid-40s to high 70s, often represents a good value. There are, however, several specific items to check before buying.

Morgan 382

LOA 38'4"
DWL 30'6"
Beam 12'
Draft 5' (optional deep draft, 6')
Displacement 18,000 lbs.
Ballast 6,800 lbs.
Sail Area 680 sq. ft.

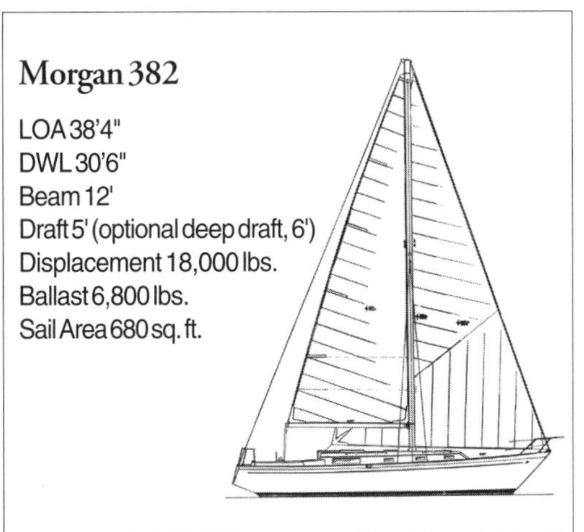

First impressions

I recently spent a lovely afternoon aboard *Sea Dancer*, hull No. 9, a 1978 Morgan 382 owned by Don Childs, a yachtbroker in Ft. Lauderdale, Florida. The 382 is a handsome boat in an understated way and still has a contemporary look. The sheerline is relatively subtle, the bow rake is straight with a moderate overhang and the counter stern has a slightly reversed transom. From abeam, the cabintrunk blends nicely into hull and deck as a result of a substantial 5-inch bulwark and a fair amount of freeboard.

A masthead sloop, the 382 has a 51-foot spar. The 383, which was introduced in 1980, had a taller rig. The underbody of the 382 is a blend of a classic Ted Brewer fin and skeg arrangement with the flattish ends inspired by the IOR rule. The hulls were tank tested at the Stevens Institute and Morgan was proud of the fact that they proved faster than many IOR One Tonners of the day. The standard draft was 5 feet with a high lift, NACA fin keel and an optional 6-foot-deep keel was also available but never popular. In the boat's final evolution, the 384, the rudder was slightly enlarged along with a few additional modifications on deck.

Construction

Throughout many changes in ownership, Morgan Yachts of Largo, Florida, has maintained a well-earned reputation for building strong boats. Most of the 382s, 383s and 384s had cored hulls, but some did

Morgan 382 Price Data

		Low	High
BUC Retail Range	1978	$36,800	$40,900
	1981	$43,000	$47,700
	1984	$54,000	$59,300

		State	Asking
Boats For Sale	1980	FL	$52,000
	1982	CA	$49,000
	1984	FL	$63,000

not. Most used Airex foam in a sandwich construction, but a variety of coring materials were used during the production run. Be certain to verify the type of coring material used in the boat you are interested in.

Morgan was one of the first builders to look closely at the glass-to-resin ratio in fiberglass hulls. The lead ballast is encapsulated in the keel cavity and covered over with fiberglass. The holding tank was also cleverly designed into the keel cavity—no doubt to keep the stench as far away as legally possible. The 382 was generally finished to high standards both on deck and below. However, there are two specific areas of construction to check before purchasing a used 382.

What to look for

Both areas of concern can usually be checked in the head compartment. Early 382s did not have the aft head bulkhead glassed to the hull. This bulkhead helps support the mast partners and keeps the spar from working. In some of these boats, the keel was literally lowered by the compressive load of the pumping mast. To its credit, Morgan recalled these boats and resolved the problem by properly bonding the bulkheads to the hull. Another early problem was the port forward lower chainplate, or lack thereof. Instead of a chainplate, the shroud was secured with a U-bolt, which tended to lift the deck and cause delamination. Many owners retrofitted chainplates and filled the delaminated deck area with epoxy. Be sure to sound the area around the port lower on deck and also inspect the area from below through the locker in the head.

On deck

Like other racer-cruisers of this era, the 382 has a T-shaped cockpit, which I think is quite functional. The visibility from the helm is excellent and the primary sheet winches are within easy reach. Chances are the winches will need to be upgraded to self-tailing winches on older 382s. Check the components of the steering system, including the cables, sheaves and sprocket chain. One recent survey of a 384 revealed that the boat's entire steering system needed to be replaced. There are two cockpit lockers and a lazarette astern. This lazarette has often been converted to a propane locker; check that it is properly sealed and vented. The cockpit scuppers are quite large but the plastic grates, which always break, should be replaced with metal grates.

Morgan always rigged its boats stoutly. Check the swages and turnbuckles, some of the newer boats used closed-body turnbuckles, which have not held up well. The deck hardware is first-rate. One of the changes made between the 383 model and the 384 was to move the mainsheet traveler out of the cockpit and up onto the coachroof. This was one of the first midboom sheeting arrangements. Many owners of older boats have retrofitted this type of traveler bridge, so be sure to check the construction closely.

The side decks are wide and the friendly 5-inch bulwark lends a feeling of security as you make your way forward. Morgan was again one of the first builders to make double lifelines and double pulpits standard. There are massive amidships cleats and there are through-the-bulwark leads that won't let your spring lines wander. The chain locker opens up on deck and most 382s are set up with two anchor rollers.

Down below

Morgan had some progressive styling ideas in the late 1970s. The most noticeable was to mix teak with ash to lighten up the boat. However, when it came to interior arrangements, the 382 series was strictly conventional. The fo'c'sle features a V-berth that discriminates against tall people. Next aft is a huge head with a separate shower and hanging locker opposite. The saloon has an L-shaped settee to port and drop-leaf teak table. To starboard is a settee with a

Morgan 382

Sailing Magazine's Value Guide

PRICE: With prices ranging from low $40s to high $60s, there is enough range to find good values.

DESIGN QUALITY: A functional, nice-looking boat that won't appear outdated anytime soon. It's a good sailing boat in most conditions.

CONSTRUCTION QUALITY: A strong boat, though Morgan was a bit slow on correcting a few flaws of the 382.

USER-FRIENDLINESS: A very easy boat to sail with good accommodations for an aft cockpit design.

SAFETY: Wide side decks and bulwarks make moving around secure, but the double lifelines could be taller. There are good sea berths and plenty of handholds below.

TYPICAL CONDITIONS: While most 382s were used for cruising and not racing, their condition varies widely. Many were sold in Florida so they have had year-round use in salt water.

REFITTING: Although parts are readily available, the 382 is not a particularly easy boat to work on and some of the necessary repairs are rather involved.

SUPPORT: Morgan was purchased by Catalina and remains active as a builder. Customer support is excellent, and for $38, prospective buyers can obtain an 80-page original owners manual. The company still has many parts in inventory.

AVAILABILITY: There are a lot of used 382s, 383s and 384s on the market. Most seem to be located in the Southeast.

INVESTMENT AND RESALE: While the boat seems to hold its value well, the very nature of the design makes it less desirable. People want a cruising boat or a performance boat, not both.

OVERALL 'SVG' RATING

pilot berth above. For some reason, many 382, 383 and 384 owners have converted this pilot berth into cabinets and extra storage. Sometimes, as on *Sea Dancer*, the workmanship is quite good. Even with the pilot berth the 382 has a lot of storage space. In fact, the brochure touts that there are 50 lockers below. I confess, I didn't count them.

The U-shaped galley features two deep stainless sinks. On the older boats, it might be necessary to convert an alcohol stove to propane or natural gas. The nav station is opposite and the chart desk is good-sized. Behind is the quarter berth, under which the batteries are set. The only problem with this arrangement is that the quarter berth usually ends up being the catch-all storage space, which means that you have to move a pile of gear to check the batteries. Bilge access is good through several hatches.

Engine

Sea Dancer is fitted with the original 3QM30, a 33-horsepower seawater-cooled diesel. I must admit, this 17-year-old, three-cylinder engine pushed the boat along smartly. Early on in the production run, however, the venerable Perkins 4108 50-horsepower replaced the Yanmar. Simply because it is a freshwater-cooled engine, I would prefer it over the older 3QM30. Access to the beast is from behind the companionway steps and through a hatch in the quarter berth. Typically, it helps to be a midget with long arms to work on the engine, especially when it comes time to reach the stuffing box.

The boat came originally with a two-bladed prop. Depending on whether or not they still race the boat or just cruise, some owners have opted for a three-bladed prop. Fuel capacity is 41 gallons in either a fiberglass, aluminum or stainless tank, which translates into a realistic motoring range of about 250 miles.

Underway

We had a perfect day to sea trial *Sea Dancer*. The wind was from the east at 15 knots and the seas were moderate. We unveiled a 150 percent genoa and hauled up the main. One of the complaints about the early 382s was that the rudder was too small. I found the helm to be quite light, and although we certainly did not have any conditions to really put her to the test, the boat steered very nicely in moderate to light air with a big headsail. It was quick and also had an easy motion upwind.

We put the boat through a range of wind points, including wing-and-wing while running back toward Port Everglades. We raced a setting sun to the western horizon and lost, but it didn't matter. Easing up the Intracoastal Waterway in the soft darkness, we saluted the crew of another Morgan, a 384 model. They were loaded down for serious cruising and headed for blue water.

Conclusion

Juggling the requirements for speed, comfort, seaworthiness, and cost with any boat will always be a compromise. The racer-cruiser approach to sailboat design and construction, while introducing its own issues, tends to reduce the negative characteristics resulting from this juggling act. The Morgan-Brewer combination found in the 382 goes a long way toward balancing the trade-offs one encounters with wanting a sailboat in the $50,000 to $70,000 range that delivers comfort and performance. For someone looking for a mid-sized cruiser that can also be raced, the Morgan 382 should be considered.

C&C 39

One of the prettiest fiberglassed boats ever built doesn't cost an arm and leg

I admit it, my choice of the venerable C&C 39 was based primarily on appearances. While the old C&C 33 had a larger production run and the C&C 35 is considered a classic, there is no denying it: The C&C 39 is one of the prettiest fiberglass boats ever built. Although the 39 was in production for only three years, 1972 to 1974, and less than 50 boats were produced, the 39 has a loyal following and has not only retained its value, it has also retained a lofty perch among the cult of connoisseurs of early 1970s boats. Designed by Cuthbertson and Cassian, the 39's original manufacturer's brochure brilliantly proclaimed, "The C&C 39 was designed to win races by going fast!" Though there is no doubt that the 39 was built with the IOR rule in mind, it was not a rule-spawned hybrid. *Windquest*, hull No. 2, took two firsts, one second and two thirds in the 1972 SORC. Later that year it took third in class in the Newport-Bermuda Race and was the first boat under 40 feet to finish. However, winning races was just a bonus for owning a boat that garners compliments at every encounter.

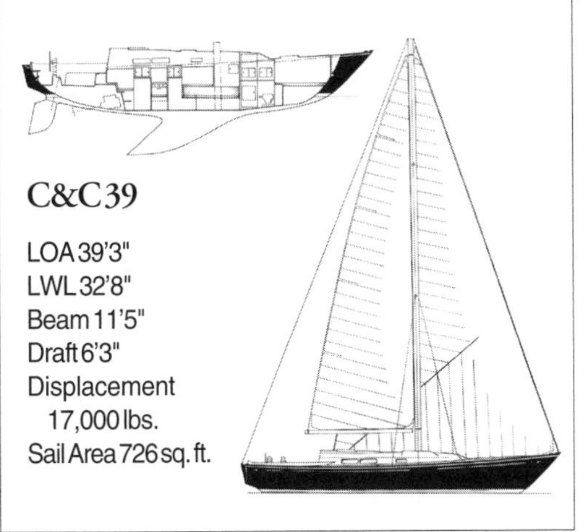

First impressions

While most C&C models maintained a handsome and distinct look right up to the company's last bankruptcy, the boats from the early 1970s somehow seemed sleeker and more elegant than many others of the day. This was the period when C&C established itself as a top-flight production builder.

The 39 has a graceful profile with a subtle sheerline and longish overhangs that disguise what is really a very fast hull shape. The freeboard is modest and the low cabintrunk tapers to the deck just forward of the mast, resulting in a large foredeck that, together with the long cockpit, gives the boat nice proportions. The plan view reveals the pinched stern that IOR favored, and while a narrow stern has little to

C&C 39 Price Data

		Low	High
BUC Retail Range	1972	$38,300	$42,500
	1973	$41,400	$46,000
	1974	$42,400	$47,100

		State	Asking
Boats For Sale	1972	MA	$45,000
	1973	MI	$40,000

recommend from a performance or accommodations standpoint, it sure is pretty.

Below the water the 39 has a moderate forefoot leading to an extremely swept-back fin keel, formerly called a whale-tail fin, and a semibalanced spade rudder. Al-though the 39 was designed to be fast, she wasn't particularly light for her day with a displacement of 17,000 pounds. This was 10 percent more than the Cal 40 and only marginally less than the Tartan 41, both introduced in 1972. The 39 sported a tapered, double-spreader, keel-stepped spar with inboard shrouds and a working sail area of 726 square feet.

Construction

C&C was one of the first production builders to core hulls. The 39 has end-grained balsa sandwiched between inner and outer skins of hand-laminated fiberglass. In the early days of coring hulls, the balsa was usually about an inch thick and the skin layers were anywhere from $^{1}/_{4}$ to $^{7}/_{16}$ of an inch. These hulls were laid up with standard polyester resins and vacuum-bagging technology didn't exist. Consequently, older cored boats may have problems with the bonding between the core and the skins. Older C&C hulls, however, have held up remarkably well and there have been few reports of hull-core troubles. In fact, *Veracity*, a 1972 C&C 39 owned by Carl and Pat Richards, spent 14 years and nearly 100,000 miles on a circuitous circumnavigation after which a survey revealed that the hull was still in excellent condition.

Bulkheads are solidly bonded to the hull and encapsulated by longitudinal stringers. The external lead keel is bolted to reinforced hull sections. The deck is also balsa-cored and should be thoroughly examined for signs of delamination. The hull-and-deck joint is on an inward flange and incorporates the aluminum toerail. While C&C certainly built boats with attention to detail, any 20- to 25-year-old boat will likely have a leaky hull-to-deck joint.

What to look for

I recently had the opportunity to visit with Carl and Pat Richards and spent several hours looking closely at their 39, hull No. 32. The Richards have traveled the world in their boat, and while they have had a few problems along the way, it is amazing how well *Veracity* has held up.

The aluminum toerail was married to the hull with stainless steel fasteners and electrolysis is sure to set in once the insulating bedding compound breaks down. The fasteners should either be replaced with aluminum ones or rebedded. This process will also help relieve any leaks in the hull-to-deck joint. Also, check the deck carefully for delamination, especially around the winches mounted at the base of the mast. In fact, many owners have changed this arrangement and led everything aft to updated self-tailing winches. If the winches have been moved, make sure that the old holes were properly filled and faired. Also, carefully inspect the standing rigging: the terminal ends, the turnbuckles and the condition of the chainplates from below. If the boat has the original swage fittings, rerigging is a must.

Down below, be sure to check the keelbolt backing plates, which are iron. Richards replaced his recently, not because they were leaking but because they were corroded. While you are probing around the bilge, sound the maststep, which spans several floors, and look for signs of corrosion. Also, most 39s have been retrofitted with a diesel engine, replacing the gas Atomic 4. Be sure to look carefully at the installation. Repowering boats is not always a simple, straightforward task. Note excessive vibration or grinding on the sea trial. A slightly out-of-alignment engine can cause excessive wear to the shaft, stern tube and strut.

One last item to be wary of is the listing sheet supplied by either the broker or the seller. Typically with boats of this vintage, much of the gear listed should be considered of little value. Unless the boat has been upgraded recently, look for a 39 with as little equipment as possible. This makes retrofitting easier in that you don't have to tear out the old gear before adding the new. Also, most used 39s seemed to be in the Great Lakes area and a freshwater boat is greatly preferred over one that has lived in salt water.

On deck

The first thing you'll notice on deck is the lack of an anchoring arrangement. The stemhead fitting is certainly not robust and an anchor roller of some type must be retrofitted if it hasn't been already. If it has, check to see that it is securely through-bolted; many of these owner-added rollers are rather feeble. One appealing aspect of the IOR rule was that it encouraged uncluttered decks. The foredeck of the C&C 39, which was clearly designed to be worked, reminds us of what life was like before roller-furling systems conquered all. The C&C 39 had double lifelines, five Barient halyard and sheet winches and a roller-reefing boom as standard deck gear. Fortunately, most 39s have long since been retrofitted to slab-reefing systems.

The 39 came standard with wheel steering and aluminum castings in the binnacle, which should be checked for corrosion. Overall, the T-shaped cockpit is very workmanlike. Another nice aspect of narrow ends is that the genoa sheet winches are easily reached from the helm. The mainsheet traveler spans the cockpit on the bridgedeck and seems inconvenient by today's standards. It is possible to retrofit a mid-boom traveler and sheeting arrangement, but I wouldn't. Part of owning an early 1970s boat is accepting certain limitations.

Down below

The interior arrangement of the 39 was innovative for its day. The forepeak had either sail bins or a double berth, but the owner's cabin was designed to be aft and included the chart table and double quarter berth to port. Unfortunately, the arrangement doesn't work well because there just isn't enough beam aft to work with. Like other IOR boats of the time, the interior is loaded with berths, anywhere from seven to nine, depending upon the height, weight and friendliness of the crew. The standard interior does have a good-sized chart table with a quarter berth behind, a handy wet locker at the foot of the companionway and a seagoing, U-shaped galley.

Although what was left of C&C has been merged with Tartan and Fairport Yachts in Ohio, there is still excellent support service for older C&Cs through South Shore Yachts in Niagara-on-the-Lake, Ontario, Canada.

"We have a great inventory of parts and access to most original C&C vendors," explains South Shore's Rob MacLachlan. "Another aspect of what we do is to design custom interiors for older boats. Typically, an owner loves the way his boat handles, but every time he goes below he has a terrible flashback to the 1970s."

Engine

The 39's standard power plant was the popular Universal Atomic 4 gas engine. While there is nothing wrong with the Atomic 4, it simply went out of fashion as safer and more rugged diesels captured the sailboat market. Used 39s with gas engines sell for about $5,000 less than models retrofitted with diesels. The most common retrofit is the Universal 30-horsepower diesel, which was specifically designed to replace the Atomic 4 using the same mounts. The fuel capacity is 28 gallons in an aluminum tank and there are two 35-gallon water tanks. The stuffing box can be reached from either the cockpit locker or from either quarter berth.

Underway

As a testament to how well the 39 sails, the Richards found that the 28-gallon fuel tank was perfectly adequate for their circumnavigation. "We really didn't motor much," Carl explained. "Unless it was completely calm, we could always coax 4 or 5 knots out of the boat." Richards also told me that it was not at all unusual to race along at 8 or 9 knots in the trade winds, usually with a reefed main and a poled-out genoa. "The boat is so easily balanced that the Aries vane can handle her even in a downwind blow."

Mark Williams, who races a 39 on Lake Ontario, claims that the boat can track upwind with today's fast boats and only loses ground on a reach. The 39, with her fine entry and moderate forefoot, doesn't pound upwind in a chop, although with a relatively narrow

C&C 39

Sailing Magazine's Value Guide

PRICE: Most 39s can be bought for less than $50,000. Finding a boat of similar size and quality is very difficult; the 39 offers a lot of bang for the buck.

DESIGN QUALITY: It is hard to fault the design. A beautiful-looking boat is usually a fine sailing boat—the case with the 39.

CONSTRUCTION QUALITY: C&C built fine boats in the '70s; however, I am wary of balsa-cored hulls. Overall, the construction quality is high.

USER-FRIENDLINESS: The 39 is not laid out for easy short-handed sailing. The interior is not particularly comfortable and needs upgrading.

SAFETY: Although the 39 was one of the first boats to feature double lifelines, the nonskid pattern on most boats is well worn and the small aluminum toerail doesn't offer much support. The cockpit is relatively deep with a stout bridgedeck.

TYPICAL CONDITION: Most 39s seemed to have been raced hard early on, then converted to cruisers. The gear can be dated. Freshwater boats are usually cleaner than saltwater sisterships.

REFITTING: The clever design and construction services offered by South Shore Yachts in Ontario makes refitting and upgrading an older 39 a viable program.

SUPPORT: South Shore offers good service support to owners. Contact South Shore Yachts at (905) 468-4340 or at: www.niagara.com/sailboat on the Web. The C&C Sailing Association, www.cnc-owner.com, is the owner's group.

AVAILABILITY: There were not many 39s produced and they change hands grudgingly. Most owners hold on to them for years.

INVESTMENT AND RESALE: The original price of the 39 was $39,950 in 1972. The 39's BUC Book value is around $40,000 and this won't change for a long time.

OVERALL 'SVG' RATING

11-foot, 5-inch beam and deep 6-foot, 3-inch keel, she does roll downwind. As a family cruiser, the boat still offers good performance, handles well, has an interior that affords privacy for parents and kids and commands attention at the dock. Besides, the 39 passes an important litmus test, when you row out to your mooring you'll be convinced you have the most beautiful boat in the harbor.

Conclusion

With prices ranging from the high 30s for the earliest models with gas engines, to the high 40s for 1974 models with diesel engines, the hard-to-find C&C 39 offers an excellent value on the used boat market. This is a boat I'd like to own.

Valiant 40

The boat that set the standard for bluewater cruisers still good value

It is hard to believe that the Valiant 40 was introduced nearly 30 years ago. Designed by Robert Perry, the Valiant has attained legendary status because as Perry said, "It's been everywhere and done just about everything." The story of how the Valiant 40 came to be will inspire all young dreamers who scribble sailboat designs on napkins. Nathan Rothman, Bob Perry and Stanley and Sylvia Dabney were friends living in Seattle and dreaming of boats and islands. Rothman wanted to build boats, Perry, who lived aboard the Dabneys' Islander 36, wanted to design them, and the Dabneys wanted a more serious boat to cruise the world. What evolved from this friendship was the Valiant 40.

Perry's design, which has been dubbed the first genuine performance cruiser, was a bit of a change for a bluewater cruising boat. Instead of a full keel and attached rudder, the Valiant featured a powerful fin keel and skeg hung rudder. Above the waterline, the Valiant 40 was quite traditional, with a hull shape based on a photo of *Holger Danske*, a lovely double-ender designed by Aage Nielsen. Perry confesses that the famous canoe stern was incorporated into the boat more for its looks than its seakeeping characteristics and because of the surprising popularity of the Westsail 32.

Valiant 40

LOA 39'10"
LWL 34'
Beam 12'4"
Draft 6'
Displacement 22,500 lbs.
Ballast 7,700 lbs.
Sail Area 772 sq. ft.

"The Westsail changed the world," Perry said. "Cruising hit the mainstream when the boat was on the cover of *Time* Magazine. Everybody wanted a double-ender."

Perry's canoe stern had much better hydrodynamics than the sharper-ended Westsail, and his version of the double-ended design influenced the look of serious cruising boats for years.

Rothman contracted with Uniflite, primarily a powerboat builder in Bellingham, Washington, to build the boat because he was unable to find enough resin during the oil crunch years of 1973 and 1974 to build it himself. After tooling up for production, the first Valiant 40 rolled off the lines in late 1974. The boat has been a top choice of cruising sailors for decades, but Valiant's stellar bluewater reputation is also a result of its success in singlehanded ocean races. Francis Stokes, aboard *Mooneshine*, won his class in the 1980 OSTAR. Dan Byrne, a retired journalist and inexperienced sailor, sailed Valiant 40 hull No. 1 in the inaugural BOC Around the World Race. Mark Schrader completed an epic circumnavigation in a Valiant 40 in 1983.

Unfortunately, Valiant's reputation took a hit when Uniflite's construction experienced severe blister problems after it changed resins in the mid-1970s. Rothman sold Valiant to Sam Dick Industries, which later sold it to Uniflite. Valiant was teetering on the edge of bankruptcy when it was purchased by Rich Worstell in 1984. Worstell had been an enthusiastic Valiant dealer in northern Texas, and after building a few hulls in Washington, moved the production to Lake Texoma, near the Oklahoma border. Worstell continued to build the Valiant 40, and the boat remained in production until 1993, when it was replaced by an updated 42. Some claim that the Valiant 40 is technically still in production because the new 42 uses a hull built from the same tooling. The 42 does have a new deck and includes a short bowsprit, adding 2 feet to the LOA. All told, 200 Valiant 40s were built and sold.

Valiant 40 Price Data

		Low	High
BUC Retail Range	1975	$ 80,900	$ 89,000
	1978	$ 96,900	$106,500
	1982	$113,500	$125,000

		State	Asking
Boats For Sale	1975	MD	$105,000
	1976	OR	$109,000
	1978	FL	$ 90,000

First impressions

The Valiant 40 was conceived as a boat for world cruising and ocean passagemaking, and it looks the part. From the handsome canoe stern to the proud bow, the 40 has a sweet sheerline, a fine entry and a relatively long LWL, especially for its day. The cockpit is anything but spacious and the cabintrunk extends well forward, making it a bit boxy by today's standards. Rigged as a cutter, the 40 carries 772 square feet of sail area and is surprisingly nimble for a boat that weighs 22,500 pounds.

This review will focus on the older Valiant 40s built by Uniflite.

Construction

Like most boats of this era, the Valiant 40 hull was a solid but rather thick, hand-laid-up fiberglass laminate. The deck was balsa cored. The hull-and-deck joint is robust and forms a box with the molded bulwark. The top of the bulwark has an inward flange and the deck forms the forward face of the bulwark, joined to the hull with an outward flange. The joint is through-bolted and covered with a teak caprail.

A series of transverse floors are glassed to the hull for athwartship support. Unlike other production builders that use fiberglass liners or pans, the Valiant 40 was traditionally built by fiberglassing bulkheads and furniture faces directly to the hull. The lead keel, which went through three design changes, is an external lead casting bolted to a substantial keel stub. Perry changed the keel at Uniflite's request because it was expensive to build. The second keel lowered the vertical center of effort. The last keel redesign included input from Dave Vacanti and is an improved foil shape. The skeg is a steel piece, encased in fiberglass and externally fastened to the hull; it is not part of the hull mold.

What to look for

You can't mention used Valiant 40s without talking about blister problems. According to Dabney, who not only was one of the founding fathers (and Valiant's vice president and sales manager for the first five years) but has also owned hull No. 8, *Native Sun*, for 25 years, there is a lot of misinformation about what caused the blistering. Dabney, who with his wife Sylvia owns Offshore Atlantic Yachts in Riviera Beach, Florida, explained that the commonly held belief that Uniflite changed to fire-retardant resin, thus causing the blisters, is not quite right. Uniflite had been using fire-retardant resin already, but the blisters were a result of a switch in resin suppliers during the oil crunch of the mid-1970s. The new resin wasn't up to standard.

Dabney sells eight to 10 used Valiants every year, most of them 40s. The blister problem can be traced from 1976 through early 1981. Almost all boats during this period blistered to some extent and some badly, both above and below the waterline. Early boats, which also used fire-retardant resin, have never blistered, and later boats rarely. Worstell solved the problem for good in 1984 when he switched to isophthalic resin. He carefully monitored the catalyzation and included epoxy barrier coats. According to Dabney, there is only one way to properly repair a badly blistered boat. You have to peel the boat down to a mere shell and then refiberglass it. It is a big job. Not surprisingly the market price of the Valiant 40 is directly related to the year built. An early 1975 Valiant 40 in good shape will command more money than a 1979 or a 1980 boat, even if they had only minor blistering. Indeed, a used Valiant 40 that has had only mild blisters can be a great value.

There are a few other common problems to look for when considering an older Valiant 40. The aluminum water and fuel tanks have not aged well and may need to be replaced. The chainplates on early boats were on the light side and should be upgraded. Occasional delamination in the subdeck is a problem, particularly around the chainplates, but this of course is common on any old boat with a balsa or plywood core. Be sure to check the standing rigging and replace any original fittings. Later boats had optional rod rigging, which is harder to check. If it is more than 15 years old, have a rigger inspect the terminal ends. The irony of the blister woes that haunt older Valiants to this day is that they have aged very well, considering that most have been sailed hard and logged thousands of miles.

On deck

The Valiant 40 was designed as a cutter, as opposed to what Perry later called a double-headsail sloop. The mast is located well aft and the boom is not overly long, which makes for a manageable mainsail. Most boats used intermediate stays to support the staysail, although some owners have opted for runners to avoid chafe. Early boats featured end-boom sheeting, which tended to increase the weather helm. Later a midboom sheeting arrangement was added, which opened up the cockpit and eased the helm.

The original molded nonskid pattern, stout bulwark, well-supported stanchions and double lifelines make it easy to move about the deck in any kind of weather. Early boats had a single bow roller. Later a double roller was standard. The dockline leads are hawsepipes through the bulwark and are very strong. Throughout the long production run, Valiant used top-quality suppliers, from Lewmar and Barient to Edson and Harken.

Down below

The Valiant's interior arrangement was also innovative in its day and featured two private double cabins. After dropping below, the aft cabin is immediately to port. There is a small seat and good locker storage. Opposite is a hanging locker, and on some Valiants, a pantry storage area. The nav station is located forward to starboard, with the galley opposite. The galley is U-shaped with double sinks, a three-burner stove and a large icebox. Some boats have upgraded the stove and added a refrigerator/freezer. There is lots of storage space above the stove and under the sinks.

The saloon design is straightforward, with an opposite facing settee that can be a sea berth on either tack. There is a pilot berth to port. The seat backs are a bit abrupt and a centerline table can be cumbersome. The head and shower are to port and there is a hanging locker opposite. The V-berth is good-sized when the filler cushion is in place. Valiant finished most of its boat with white formica that is nicely accented with teak trim and veneers. This is both practical and visually appealing as it brightens the interior. The original workmanship was well-done, not fancy but functional, and the 20-year-old 40s that I have climbed through still look good below.

Engine

The first Valiant 40s came with a Westerbeke 4107, which was a good engine for the boat. Other engines used for the boat were the Perkins 4108, a Westerbeke 50, which was a notoriously fickle engine, and late in production, the Volvo 2003. Engine access is good, from behind the companionway and through the aft cabin. I'm not a fan of V-drive transmissions, but certain hull shapes and interior arrangements dictate their use. The fuel capacity in two aluminum tanks is approximately 100 gallons. A consideration when looking at older Valiants is the prospect of repowering. When the Dabneys recently repowered *Native Sun*, they exchanged the Westerbeke 4107 with 6,500 hours of running time, for a Perkins 4108 that had the same footprint.

Underway

The Valiant 40 has earned its enviable reputation by consistently making fast offshore passages. The cutter rig is well-balanced, with just a bit of weather helm that actually assists most wind-vane steering units. The cutter also offers versatility under sail. Flying a high-cut yankee on the forward headstay allows it to be easily shortened. The staysail can then carry the load as the wind pipes up. Although not particularly close-winded by today's standards, the Valiant 40 tracks well to weather.

A few years ago I delivered a 40 from St. Martin in the West Indies, to Buzzard's Bay, Massachusetts.

Valiant 40

Sailing Magazine's Value Guide

PRICE: The Valiant 40 was originally an expensive boat. However, the blister problem has skewed used boat prices and in many ways made them a good value.

DESIGN QUALITY: The Valiant 40 launched designer Bob Perry's career and the concept of the performance cruiser. The design has stood the test of time.

CONSTRUCTION QUALITY: This would be much higher if Uniflite had stuck with its original resin supplier. Other than blisters, the overall construction quality is high. Valiants have rounded every cape and survived rollovers, reefs and most things the sea can throw at them.

USER-FRIENDLINESS: The cutter rig is easy to sail and well-behaved. The interior is comfortable and offers two private cabins.

SAFETY: A solid design and robust construction make the Valiant a safe boat. The interior has well-placed handholds and the galley is functional in a seaway.

TYPICAL CONDITION: Once again, the blister problem skews the overall results. Some used 40s are really a mess, while others are equipped and ready to sail around the world.

REFITTING: The Valiant 40 is a relatively easy boat to fix. The boat had a long production run and the company is still building them in Texas, which means finding parts is easy.

SUPPORT: Without doubt the best source of information for used Valiants is from Stanley and Sylvia Dabney. You can reach them at (561) 845-9303 or on the Web at www.offshoreyachts.com

AVAILABILITY: With a production run of 200 boats, there is always a good selection of used 40s on the market.

INVESTMENT AND RESALE: Prices for the Valiant 40 have bottomed out. The blister problem is well-known and repairable. I suspect that the value of older, repaired 40s will gradually climb.

OVERALL 'SVG' RATING

The winds were fresh on the first leg and we reeled off consecutive 160-mile days on a beam reach. We ran into a gale in the Gulf Stream on the second leg. I was impressed with the Valiant's easy motion as we gradually shortened sail until we were down to a double-reefed main and the staysail. I was forced to hand steer for days, but the helm was balanced and I was able to tie it off when I needed a break. The sailing characteristics are the prime reason for buying a used Valiant 40.

Conclusion

The Valiant 40 is a genuine bluewater cruiser that can, when purchased carefully, be had for about a third of what it would cost to buy a comparable new boat. Badly blistered old boats can be bought for around $90,000, but be prepared for a major repair project. Those boats with minor blisters sell for at least $100,000. For a blister-free Valiant 40, post-1981 but before construction shifted to Texas, expect to pay around $140,000.

Cal 40

Yes, this racing classic can be a cruiser, one that still offers an exciting turn of speed

For those of us who began sailing in the 1960s and early 1970s, there will always be something mysterious, almost mythical, about the Cal 40. I remember there was a Cal 40 just down the dock from our Sabre 28 on the Clinton River in Mt. Clemens, Michigan. Although I was just a kid, I dutifully led every visitor down the dock, and with reverence in my voice, pointed out the Cal 40. The odd thing was that the 40 was a rather plain-looking boat—at least above the waterline. What was it that created the mystique?

A huge part of it was the extraordinary success of the Cal 40 in virtually every major ocean race in the 1960s. There is no disputing that the 40 was, and still is, a downwind flyer, one of the first big boats to surf consistently, and three successive Transpac wins in the mid-1960s cemented its reputation. But the Cal 40 also dominated the 1966 Bermuda race, a slog with plenty of windward work, and the unpredictable SORC throughout the decade. Many top-notch ocean racers cut their teeth on Cal 40s, including Ted Turner who emerged on the sailing scene in 1966 when his 40 *Vamp X* took overall honors in that year's blustery SORC.

But there was more to the mystique of the Cal 40 than racing success; there was something almost heretical about its design. Designer Bill Lapworth and builder Jack Jensen threw away their copy of **Skene's** and created the first big fiberglass production boat that wasn't somehow modeled on a wooden ancestor. While there was nothing radical about the boxy cabintrunk, nice sweeping sheerline and spoon bow, there were major innovations concealed below the waterline. From the flattened forefoot to broader, flatter bilges, the 40 had a shape more like a racing dinghy. The waterline was extended by cutting down on the stern counter and the displacement was a dangerously light 15,500 pounds. The keel was a long fin and the rudder was freestanding and set well behind the trailing edge of the keel—a naked, dangling

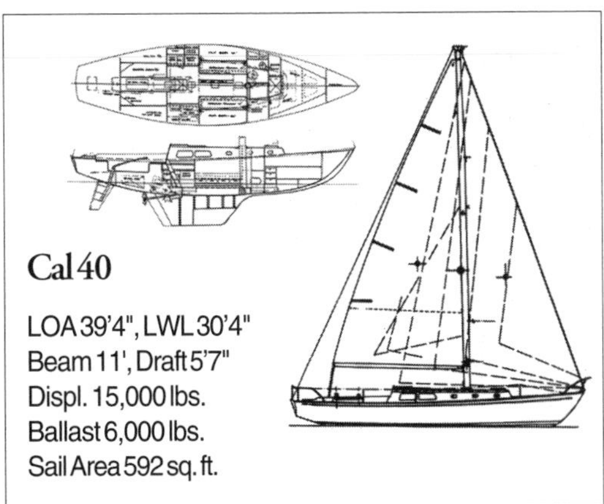

Cal 40 Price Data

		Low	High
BUC Retail Range	1966	$31,700	$35,200
	1969	$32,000	$35,600
	1972	$38,900	$43,300

		State	Asking
Boats For Sale	1965	WA	$44,000
	1968	CA	$36,000
	1970	FL	$30,000

appendage that doomsayers were certain would fall off. In 1963 these were dramatic design changes indeed. They opened the eyes of designers and builders to the true advantages offered by fiberglass construction techniques. *SAILING* Magazine Publisher Bill Schanen enthusiastically described the Cal 40 after its introduction into the American Sailboat Hall of Fame last year as "the boat that changed everything."

First impressions

Ironically, the boat that changed everything seems rather tame by today's standards. Jensen Marine built somewhere around 140 Cal 40s between 1963 and 1972, which means any 40 you consider purchasing today will be at least 25 years old. Chances are most 40s were raced hard, and if the boats have not been upgraded and retrofitted along the way, they may appear tired. The hulls are often dull and chalky, the winches may be outdated and the sails are usually baggy. But don't let appearances deceive you. While it is unlikely that you will ever be competitive with today's performance boats, an older, updated Cal 40 makes an excellent cruising boat and club racer. The value is apparent when you consider that you can usually find a decent 40 on the used boat market for less than $50,000.

Construction

While the design was radical for the 1960s, the construction of the Cal 40 was more in line with the times. Fiberglass boats of this era were robustly laid up. Of course, most hulls were resin rich, so the apparent thickness of the hull may be deceptive. Still, Jensen Marine, which produced almost all of the 40s before Bangor Punta bought the company and moved the production to Florida, built a stout boat.

The hull is solid fiberglass, as is the deck, which eliminates a likely problem with older boats—a delaminated subdeck. Doublers for stress areas were put in during the layup, eliminating the need for metal backing plates that ultimately corrode.

The hull-to-deck joint is on an inward flange and incorporates the bolted-on teak toerail. This type of joint relies heavily on the chemical bond between surfaces to prevent leaking. Any boat 25 years or older is likely to have hardened sealant. While some Cal 40 owners have actually completely redone the hull-and-deck joint to stop the leaks, most just rebed the toerail fastenings every few years.

The bulkheads are tabbed to both the hull and the furniture facings and need to be carefully checked. The mast is stepped to a bridge at the cabin sole, which was also an intelligent innovation, and the chainplates are tied into both a transverse bulkhead and an aluminum fitting that is glassed into the hull. The lead ballast is an internal casting and is glassed over. The construction details of early fiberglass boats can often drive you crazy. From totally inaccessible electrical wiring to the seemingly sheer impossibility of removing engines, refits of Cal 40s can be extremely frustrating.

What to look for

Jim Eddy, a longtime Cal 40 owner on the West Coast, advises potential buyers to carefully check the lower chainplates and the forward bulkheads. The chainplates themselves should be examined for wear, especially at the pre-bend, as well as the wooden bulkheads below. The original tabbing on the forward bulkheads was poorly made and the thin strips of cloth and resin have often cracked and peeled. If the bulkheads have come adrift, it is very important to properly reglass them to the hull. In fact, it is a good idea to check all the tabbings around the forward V-berth, as the athwartships and longitudinal rigidity of this berth is central to eliminating oil-canning in the bow.

As mentioned earlier, look for evidence of hull-and-deck joint leaks as well as leaks around the portlights. If it hasn't been fixed recently, assume you will have to rebed everything in sight. Carefully check the built-in backing plates beneath stanchions, winches and other hardware; sometimes they show evidence of stress cracks. Also, most Cal 40s have had hull blisters to some degree so you should look for a boat that has had a recent blister job. Another warning is to be suspect of the inventory on the listing sheet. The 15 bags of sails and extra sailing gear may seem enticing at first, but the sails and gear usually end up being old, well-used and of little value. Older boats with less gear, especially old electrical and mechanical items, are sometimes more attractive because it is easier to just add new equipment than to have to remove the old stuff first.

On deck

Another innovation of the Cal 40 was to set the chainplates inboard of the rail, which allowed for closer sheeting angles. The side decks are wide, especially for an older boat, and moving about is easy. The decks are often crazed and the nonskid is well worn. Carefully check for any gelcoat spider cracks; most are not structural. It is possible that the deck will need painting with a nonskid element added to the paint.

The cockpit is large and typically uncomfortable with abrupt seat backs and unkind angles. It is, however, seaworthy, with a healthy bridgedeck and low overall volume. Betsy Crowfoot, who sailed a 1969 Cal 40 in the last two Transpacs, always felt secure.

"In the cockpit I felt like I was cradled in the palm of the Cal 40 and was part of her long proud history," she said.

The original steering system was a husky tiller, an unusual feature on a 40-foot boat. While some owners have converted to wheel systems, many 40s still have the original tiller. With the balanced spade rudder, the boat handles well with the tiller and the feel is wonderful. Also, when at anchor or dockside, the tiller can be lifted out of the way, opening up the cockpit area. I would look for a tiller boat. While it is likely that the original single-speed winches have been replaced, much of the sailing hardware may need upgrading.

Down below

Lapworth had run out of fresh ideas by the time it came to designing the interior. The Cal 40 is quite typical of its times. Cal was unduly proud of the fact that the boat could theoretically sleep eight, although forcing crew into the pilot berths and tunnel berths aft would be cruel, indeed. Yet for a couple looking for a capable cruising boat, there is enough room in the boat to be comfortable.

The V-berth forward is good-sized with ample storage below. There is a small bureau to port. The head is just aft, with a hanging locker opposite. The saloon has a drop-leaf table, slide-out settees and pilot berths above. The boats I have seen have resisted the urge to convert the pilot berths into finished cabinets. Most Cal 40 owners, even if they don't race, seem weight conscious and this is a healthy instinct for all sailors. Also, I have noticed that many owners hold the Cal 40 sacrosanct and, few have made major changes.

The galley, to port, is small with a single small sink and gimbaled stove. Counter space is nonexistent. The nav station is opposite with a large icebox below. As mentioned earlier, there are two quarter berths aft, but these narrow, tubelike bunks are not someplace you would want to spend a lot of time. These berths usually end up as storage areas anyway.

Engine

Originally the Cal 40 had either an Atomic 4 or Gray Marine gasoline engine; both were approximately 25 horsepower. It is unlikely that you will find a 40 with an original engine. Over the years several different diesels were used to repower the boat, including Universals, Perkins 4108, Volvo MD2B, Westerbeke 50s and even Volkswagen Pathfinders.

Jim Eddy has a four-cylinder Universal 35 horsepower with a V-drive transmission that was retrofitted some time ago in his 1967 Cal 40 *Callisto*. I am not fond of V-drives for maintenance reasons, but at least with a Universal the gear is easy to service. In fact, the access to the engine from behind the companionway and through the quarter berths and stuffing box is good, which is an unusual feature for boats of this era. Cruising speed is around 6 knots, although several owners noted that no matter what engine was in the boat, there was a lot of vibration while powering.

Underway

"The boat just seems to be made for the Pacific Ocean swell," Eddy said affectionately.

"I remember footing along in real light air just off the Mexican coast," said Steve Maseda, who raced a 40

Cal 40 — Sailing Magazine's Value Guide

PRICE: With asking prices from $30,000 to $50,000, the Cal 40 is a lot of boat for the buck.

DESIGN QUALITY: The original design was so innovative and ahead of its time.

CONSTRUCTION QUALITY: The Cal 40, built in the 1960s, has a heavy layup, the glass work in general is good, with problems with bulkheads and chainplates.

USER-FRIENDLINESS: The boat is relatively easy to handle with a modest rig and good maneuverability under power, but updates to today's standards will be necessary.

SAFETY: Although a capable offshore boat, it may be necessary to add lee cloths below and to better support the stanchions and pulpits.

TYPICAL CONDITIONS: Most boats on the used-boat market have been sailed and raced hard; a quarter century of wear and tear takes its toll.

REFITTING: Refits can be big jobs on Cal 40s, and with the demise of Cal, parts and patterns are not available.

SUPPORT: There is virtually no support from the factory. But there is a fairly active owner's association. Contact: Fin Beven, Cal 40 Association, 1255 S. Grand Ave., Pasadena, CA 91105.

AVAILABILITY: There were less than 140 Cal 40s built. Most are on the West Coast, from Seattle to San Diego. East Coast and Great Lakes boats seem a little cheaper.

INVESTMENT AND RESALE: The Cal 40 has waned and the market is not as strong as it was. There is always an element of risk in buying a 25- to 30-year-old boat. Still, for the money, it is hard to go too far wrong when purchasing a Cal 40.

OVERALL 'SVG' RATING

in the Ensenada race a few years ago. "We closed the coast early and caught a little breeze. It was great to overtake some of the hot boats that were just dying in the calms farther offshore."

"I'll never forget blasting down the Molokai Channel," Crowfoot said. "The boat was really in her element with 25 knots of breeze and big rolling seas. It was exhilarating."

There is no disputing that the Cal 40 is at its best reaching in a stiff breeze. It has always had the ability to get up on top of the waves with its spade rudder in control.

The masthead rig is not overly generous and most owners note that the boat is easy to handle, especially as the going gets rough. With roller-furling headsails and the sail controls led aft, the 40 can be made even more user-friendly.

On the wind, the Cal 40 tends to pound up forward, especially if there is a chop, and it can be wet. A good dodger is a must for cruising. Although the boat was light for its day, it can be slow in light air and good light air sails are a necessary complement. Don't let the Cal 40's legendary racing record deceive you. Although it is a fine sailing boat, it is by no means a thoroughbred by today's standards. With that said, I should note that as recently as 1985 a Cal 40 has won the Transpac race again.

Conclusion

The Cal 40 occupies a unique place in the history of American sailboats; it truly was an instrument of change. And while race-winning days may be behind it, that does not mean that the Cal 40 is ready for mothballs. Anyone looking for a capable and swift cruising boat for less than $50,000 should seriously consider the Cal 40.

Hunter 40

A good sailing cruiser at a very good price

A couple of years ago I was a bit surprised when my Swiss friend, Michel Bonneau, informed me that he was in the market for a used Hunter 40. Bonneau, an experienced sailor, was searching for an affordable boat to take his young family cruising in the Caribbean.

"Hunter has a good reputation in Europe, better than in the States, we think it is a good value in your country," he explained. "Also, we want a boat that will perform upwind. Much of Caribbean sailing is to windward. So many American cruising boats are, well, how should I say it, heavy and old-fashioned."

Like many Europeans, Bonneau found most American used boats divided into two distinct classes, heavy cruisers or light racers. The Hunter 40 appealed to him because it straddled the line on performance and offered excellent accommodations for a family of four.

Bonneau eventually located a clean, reasonably priced ($65,000) 1987 Hunter 40. He spent about a month refitting the boat and then pointed the bow south. For several years, he and his family have spent six months out of every 12 in the Caribbean. Each summer they put the boat on the hard and return home to restock the cruising kitty. They have thoroughly explored the Leeward and Windward Islands and are delighted with the boat.

Hunter unveiled the 40 in 1984 and kept the boat in production for six years. In the late 1980s the Legend Series was introduced, which added a few interior modifications. In 1991 the Legend 40.5 replaced the 40 altogether.

Along with the 34, the 40 signaled a new direction for Hunter in the early 1980s, a direction that was extremely popular with sailors, especially entry-level sailors who appreciated Hunter's sailaway "Cruise Pac." This was also the period when Hunter President Warren Luhrs embraced offshore racing and participated in several singlehanded and crewed bluewater challenges. Although his race results were a mixed bag, his boats were highly innovative. He received considerable press coverage, helping to alter Hunter's once shabby image. By the end of the decade, Hunter was building boat-for-boat with Catalina, as the two companies vied for the top spot among American builders.

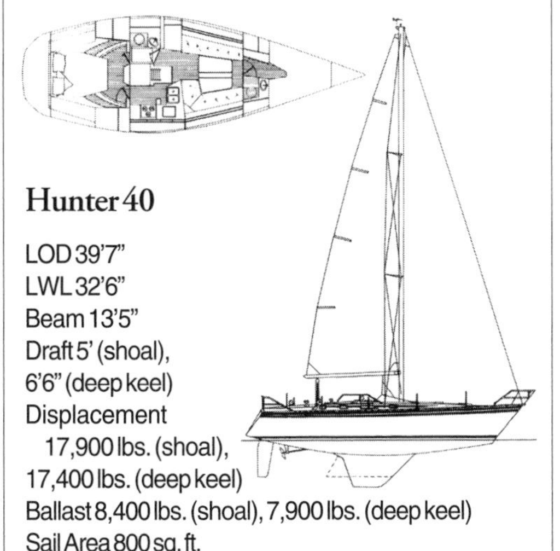

Hunter 40

LOD 39'7"
LWL 32'6"
Beam 13'5"
Draft 5' (shoal), 6'6" (deep keel)
Displacement 17,900 lbs. (shoal), 17,400 lbs. (deep keel)
Ballast 8,400 lbs. (shoal), 7,900 lbs. (deep keel)
Sail Area 800 sq. ft.

First impressions

At the risk of sounding like a fashion designer, the Hunter 40 has a distinct 1980s look. There is a fair amount of freeboard, and the fine entry quickly flares into a beamy midsection that is carried aft to the wide reverse transom. The low, angular trunkhouse blends nicely into the deck, a look I prefer to Hunter's new raised-deck models. The 40 has Hunter's distinctive black plastic portlights, which some feel give the boat even more of a "plastic" look.

The Hunter 40 sports a generous 58-foot rig, featuring 800 square feet of working sail and the B&R staying system with its swept-back double spreaders and diamond shrouds (which can be a challenge to set up and keep tuned). It comes with a choice of a 6-foot, 6-inch deep-draft or a 5-foot shoal-draft keel. Deep

Hunter 40 Price Data

	Year	Low	High
BUC Retail Range	1984	$51,400	$56,500
	1985	$54,800	$60,200
	1986	$58,500	$64,200

	Year	State	Asking
Boats For Sale	1984	FL	$69,900
	1985	FL	$64,000
	1986	MD	$69,000

and shoal models on the used market reflect specific locations: West Coast boats usually have the deep draft, while Florida and Chesapeake Bay boats opt for shoal models. The displacement varies with the draft, with much of the difference coming in the ballast. The shoal model carries 8,400 pounds of ballast compared to 7,900 pounds for the deep-keel version. The rudder is free-standing.

Construction

Hunters were, and to a large degree still are, affordable production boats—and for some sailors that translates into being poorly built. This isn't always true; just ask most Hunter owners. Hunter has an enviable record of owners trading up to larger Hunters, which of course means that they have been pleased with their boats. Production boats do, however, have limitations, and Hunter, especially on some older boats, occasionally cut corners.

The 40 has a solid fiberglass deck and a balsa-cored hull. The hull is supported by interior molded liners, which offer a simple way to add structural support and are ideal from a production standpoint, since once the tool is complete, they can be laid up like the hull and deck and then dropped into place. The problem with molded liners is that it is difficult to access the hull behind them. Several owners report problems with leaks that become trapped between the hull and liner, including leaks from the holding tanks. It is also difficult to make changes in boats with liners, so that simple tasks like running new electrical wires can become quite maddening. Like most builders, Hunter used iron for its fin keels, which require more maintenance than lead keels.

What to look for

Bonneau reports that his biggest problem with the boat is a leaking hull-to-deck joint, especially up forward in the V-berth. He has gone to the trouble of removing the through-hull bolts and rebedding them. He noted that although the boat was just 7 years old when he purchased it, the bedding compound was already hard and brittle.

Michael Wise, who sails a 1985 Hunter 40 in the Florida Keys, warned me that the rudder blade on the shoal draft model is vulnerable because it has the same draft as the keel. Some owners have actually shortened the rudder about an inch and report no adverse effects. Wise also said that his iron keel seems to rust more than usual and needs to be ground down and epoxy-coated during every annual haul out.

The aforementioned leaky holding tanks can be aggravating, but are not a particularly serious problem. Apparently the tanks leak from the top, and the effluvial runoff becomes trapped between the liner and the hull. It is possible for a stuffing box leak to become trapped as well. Fortunately, the Hunter Owner's Association Web page is brimming with information, and several owners have outlined solutions to the above problems.

When considering used 40s, look for boats with propane stoves. Many are fitted with compressed natural gas, which is safe and reliable, but never really caught on and can be hard to find in many areas. Many owners have upgraded to a feathering prop, like Max prop, an expensive but worthwhile addition since the original two-bladed prop is not very efficient. Also, check the plastic opening portlights and fixed Plexiglas ports for cracks. Both are notorious leakers, and the portlights have often been overtightened.

On deck

The Hunter 40 has a clean deck layout and many boats on the used market have routed all sail controls aft. I have mixed feelings about this, since I still like the positive purchase of hauling the main up hand-over-hand or jumped at the base of the mast. Although the side decks are wide, they can become slippery when wet as the nonskid surface is not very aggressive. The

Hunter 40

Sailing Magazine's Value Guide

PRICE: Price is one of the key reasons to consider a Hunter 40. What other 40-foot boat offers modern styling, good performance and a livable interior for about $60,000?

DESIGN QUALITY: The Hunter 40 was quite innovative when new. The aft cabin arrangement and B&R rig are two examples that have stood the test of time.

CONSTRUCTION QUALITY: Hunters are typical of most production boats. However, the 40s have held up adequately and former owners have kind things to say.

USER-FRIENDLINESS: The 40's rig can be a bit difficult to tune, and the boat needs to be set up right to sail well. The interior is quite comfortable.

SAFETY: The nonskid is not effective when wet, and the lifelines and stanchions could be taller and better supported. The interior needs more handholds.

TYPICAL CONDITION: The 40 has held up better than some "experts" predicted. Gelcoat crazing and spider cracks are not uncommon. Also, the keel needs attention.

REFITTING: The use of liners makes certain repairs difficult, and some original workmanship was suspect. Parts are still widely available, and most problems are known and well documented.

SUPPORT: The factory maintains support for used boats, and Jim Bohart has a wealth of knowledge and is ready to share it. Reach him at (800) 771-5556 or on the Web at www.huntermarine.com. The owner's group can be reached at www.hunterowners.com.

AVAILABILITY: The 40 is well represented on the market, but with prices ranging from $50,000 to $80,000 they don't linger all that long.

INVESTMENT AND RESALE: Hunters in general, especially the older models, don't hold their value as well as some other boats. However, as a used boat buyer this can work to your advantage. Of course, as a used boat seller, this works to your disadvantage.

OVERALL 'SVG' RATING

stanchions could also be taller and better supported.

Like many builders, Hunter did not make the anchoring arrangement a high priority. But since most owners today cruise their boats and many live aboard, some 40s have redesigned stemhead fittings or added anchoring platforms. Be sure to check the installation carefully.

The B&R rig has the advantage of single-pod chainplates and eliminates the backstay. However, the extreme swept-back spreaders and extra diamond shrouds present a few problems. Off the wind, the main cannot be paid out very far before it begins to chafe on the spreaders. Also, as mentioned earlier, tuning the rig requires a lot of patience, and the mast needs to be set up properly to keep from pumping. It would likely be money well spent to have an independent rigging survey done when purchasing the boat.

The cockpit is comfortable, and the view from the helm is excellent. There is plenty of legroom at the wheel, offering good support when the boat is heeled. The mainsheet traveler runs in front of the companionway, but the alternative is midboom sheeting, which would be highly inefficient on the 40's large rig. While I admit that sliding around the mainsheet to drop below can be inconvenient, most people really don't go up and down that often while sailing anyway, unless they are on a passage. When at anchor, you can simply shift the mainsheet to one side, freeing up the companionway.

Down below

The Hunter 40 has a terrific interior arrangement—if you are interested in coastal cruising and living aboard. I say that because it needs some modifications for offshore work, including more handholds and better security latches on hatches and cabinets. While the joinerwork of the older Hunter 40s is utilitarian at best, it doesn't really matter when the living space is so well utilized. Hunter was one of the first American builders to follow the European lead and include aft cabins in aft-cockpit boats. The 40 features an island double, tucked under the cockpit, which in 1984 was rather unique, not to mention a huge selling point. Hunter also opted for open, airy interiors, and the 40 is a good example.

The spacious galley is to starboard and double sinks, a large icebox, a three-burner stove and ample counter and storage space makes preparing meals pleasurable. The aft cabin, which includes a hanging locker and a bureau, is accessible through the galley. A head is opposite the galley and can be entered from the saloon and aft cabin. The saloon has a centerline double drop-leaf table and an L-shaped settee to starboard with storage above. A straight settee to port provides the best sea berth aboard and the seat for the navigation station. The V-berth forward is rather tight, but it has worked perfectly for Bonneau's two young children. The second head is just aft of the forward cabin with a large hanging locker opposite.

Engine

Most 40s are powered by four-cylinder 44 horsepower Yanmar 4JH44 diesel engines. While this is plenty of engine for the boat, the original prop was undersized. Access is excellent from four sides, and if you needed to repower or rebuild, lifting the engine out of the boat is straightforward. The stuffing box is serviced from the aft cabin, which is far more civilized than cramming yourself into a cockpit locker. The fuel capacity is 38 gallons, which should give the 40 a realistic range of 250 miles.

Underway

The 40 is at its best sailing upwind in light to moderate conditions. In heavy air the 40 is not immune to pounding. According to Bonneau, it easily points inside of 40 degrees, and more importantly, tracks well. Once the winds reach 20 knots, the mainsail should be reefed to reduce weather helm and flatten the boat out. Like most modern hulls, the 40 sails best on its lines. Bonneau also notes that it balances well and responds quickly to the Autohelm autopilot. Off the wind, Bonneau poles out his roller-furling headsail in moderate breezes and hoists a cruising spinnaker in light air.

The deep-draft model, despite having less ballast, is stiffer than the shoal version, which shows that it isn't so much the weight of the keel but where the weight is located and the keel shape that contributes most to sailing performance. An advantage of the B&R rig is that the mainsail can have a full roach. A way to add horsepower to the 40 and make it easier to sail is to opt for a full-batten, full-roach main and a smaller roller-furling headsail. This arrangement calls for a commitment to an asymmetrical chute for reaching.

Conclusion

The combination of features that made the Hunter 40 a popular new boat are still valid on the used market. Good performance, a great interior arrangement and strong factory and owner support complement the basic fact that Hunters are a lot of boat for the buck.

Bermuda 40

This timeless top-of-the-line cruiser earns a rare five stars for its construction quality

The first Hinckley Bermuda 40 was launched more than 40 years ago. Any doubts that fiberglass would come to dominate the boatbuilding industry were laid to rest when this beautiful yacht hit the market just before John F. Kennedy was sworn in as president. The B-40 was finished with the elegance of a fine wooden boat, and Bill Tripp's shapely design was indisputably handsome. It must have been a low moment for wooden boatbuilders when it became apparent that fiberglass was not only distressingly practical but, in the hands of the right builder, also beautiful.

The B-40 did not spring to life in a fit of inspiration. Instead it was the result of a calculated business decision by Henry R. Hinckley. Hinckley had been toying with the idea of converting his yard in Southwest Harbor, Maine, to fiberglass construction and intended to use his 38-foot wooden Sou'wester Senior as a plug. However, in 1959, before he had a chance, a consortium of eight men approached him with a modified version of Tripp's Block Island 40 design, which they wanted Hinckley to build. Hinckley reluctantly abandoned his plans for the Sou'wester and went ahead with Tripp's redesign. The result was the Bermuda 40, one of the most recognizable sailboats in America today.

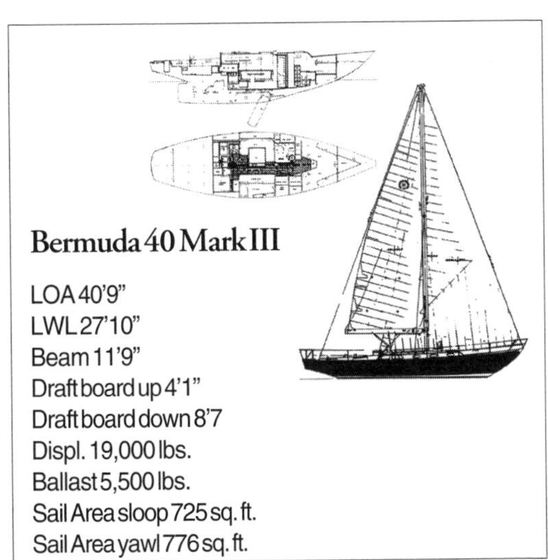

Bermuda 40 Mark III

LOA 40'9"
LWL 27'10"
Beam 11'9"
Draft board up 4'1"
Draft board down 8'7
Displ. 19,000 lbs.
Ballast 5,500 lbs.
Sail Area sloop 725 sq. ft.
Sail Area yawl 776 sq. ft.

Of course, Hinckley quality has never come cheap and there is some merit to the argument that you pay extra for the Hinckley name. Technically, you could still order a new B-40, but the price is prohibitive, which is why a used B-40 makes good sense. In all, only 203 of the B-40s were built in the course of the boat's 32-year production run (the longest of any auxiliary sailboat) and the boats have held their value extraordinarily well through the years. Still older models, pre-1983, can be found for a lot less than a new, comparably sized, off-the-shelf production boat. If you have $150,000 to spend, would you rather have a beautifully reconditioned 1975 B-40 or a new 32-foot ABC production boat? Which boat will be worth more in five years? Which boat would you rather sail?

First impressions

There are other boats, such as the Allied XL 42 and the Block Island 40, that resemble the B-40. Yet there are both tangible and intangible elements that set the B-40 apart. From the recessed, frameless portlights to the custom-made stainless steel deck fittings, to the lovely toerail, the boat drips with quality.

The B-40 design is typical of the CCA rule. The sweeping sheerline accentuates the long overhangs and Tripp's trademark counter stern. The boat was considered quite beamy in its day, and unlike other early fiberglass designs that have very tight interiors, the B-40 has a livable arrangement below.

Under the water, the B-40 has a shoal-draft long keel with a gently curving forefoot and a long straight run aft. One of many reasons for the B-40's enduring popularity is the well-engineered keel-centerboard system that uses a worm gear to raise and lower the

Bermuda 40 Price Data

		Low	High
BUC Retail Range	1964	$ 91,800	$101,000
	1972	$105,000	$116,000
	1980	$149,000	$164,000

		State	Asking
Boats For Sale	1964	NC	$ 80,000
	1975	ME	$159,000
	1980	ME	$200,000

board. Board-up draft is just 4 feet, 1 inch. The barn door rudder is attached to the keel.

Like many CCA boats, all the early B-40s came down the ways with a yawl rig, although some boats have since been converted to sloops by their owners. Naturally the boat won't keep up with today's boats, or even yesterday's IOR boats, especially upwind. Yet the B-40 performs well through a range of conditions, tracks well with the board down and has a forgiving, seakindly motion.

Construction

The B-40's construction evolved over the years, but certain things, like the solid fiberglass hull, never changed. The deck was originally solid fiberglass as well, although in later years it was given a balsa core, and a few of the last boats built have PVC foam cores. Hinckley has always been proud of its hull-to-deck joint, which begins with a stout, 1/2-inch-thick inward flange with a lip that ensures a tight fit once the deck is lowered in place. This joint is then both glassed and through-bolted. Very few boats have reported any leaks. Interior bulkheads are securely tabbed to the hull, although all signs of glasswork are cleverly masked when the boat is complete.

Ballast is forward in an external lead shoe, bolted to the keel with husky stainless bolts. From a safety standpoint, external ballast married to a molded keel shape is the best arrangement since you can damage the ballast without necessarily damaging the hull.

Hinckleys have held up well over the years, in part because of the attention the company paid to detail during the construction process. The bolts that secure the deck fittings, for example, are not only properly backed and fitted with a lock nut, but the deck is tapered to keep the fitting as tight and leak-free as possible.

The trend among today's builders is to assemble components manufactured by others. Hinckley made many of the parts for the B-40 in-house, from stainless fittings to the tapered aluminum mast section, maintaining a strict quality control program.

What to look for

The first thing to consider when looking at B-40s is the differences inherent in the three versions that were offered by Hinckley. The early boats are called Custom Bermuda 40s and include a 47-foot air draft and 725 square feet of sail area. The Mark IIs have an added 2-feet on the mast and slightly increased sail area. And the Mark III, introduced in the early 1980s, is an updated design that attempted to make the boat more competitive with the IOR boats of the day. The Mark III was the first to offer a sloop rig with the mast raised more than 4 feet and moved aft a couple of feet. The increased sail area required 1,000 pounds of additional ballast. The extra ballast dropped the boat lower in the water, extending the waterline a foot, making the Mark III definitely the best performer.

The original boats came with gasoline engines, although Hinckley was one of the first manufacturers to convert to diesel. A Westerbeke diesel was standard before 1970. While it is unlikely that any of the original gas engines are still around, many of the boats that were repowered may need to be repowered again. Although today's engines are smaller, it is still a tight operation on the B-40. If possible, look for a boat with a fairly recent engine and check the installation carefully.

Many Hinckley owners routinely take their boats back to the factory for maintenance and winter storage. Consequently, these boats are usually extremely well maintained. Also, let's face it, most B-40 owners have the resources to update the boats as necessary, so even the really old boats are usually in surprisingly good shape on the used market. Be sure to check all age-related problems, including the standing rigging. Also, Hinckley had its share of blister problems, although the older B-40s seem less likely to have had the pox than the later boats.

On deck

One of the most appealing features on the B-40 is the wide side decks. While this restricts interior space, it certainly makes moving about the deck a pleasure. The Hinckley custom-made stemhead fitting is a work of art, although compared to other 40-foot cruising boats, the anchor rollers are a bit undersized. The winches were often chosen by the owner; the model that I delivered from the Virgin Islands to Buzzards Bay had self-tailing Barients. Overall, however, the deck fittings are top quality and have aged well.

The cockpit seats are long, although the rather straight-backed mahogany or teak coaming boards can become uncomfortable during a passage. Cushion seat backs are a must. The pedestal, which is also a custom fabrication, is located well aft, creating a helming position and a trimming position. Hinckley was one of the first manufacturers to go with midboom sheeting, especially on the yawls. Visibility over the low-slung coachroof is excellent. The mizzen mast is set behind the helm, an advantage of a yawl over a ketch. However, the mizzen standing rigging does clutter up the cockpit. There are two cockpit lockers that can be locked from below.

Down below

Hinckley liked to claim that B-40 interiors were customized to each owner's taste; however, most differences were in the details, not the basic arrangement. The standard plan called for a large V-berth forward with a handsome bureau of drawers just aft of the bunk. The head follows to port with a cedar-lined hanging locker opposite. The saloon has settees port and starboard with pilot berths above. Pilot berths seem quaint and out of date to some, but I love them. They are good sleeping berths and keep you out of the traffic flow.

The table is found on the centerline and makes a fairly tight space even tighter. However, a handhold is always within reach and the table helps you keep your balance. The galley is aft to port and there isn't much working space, while the stand-up nav station located opposite, is on top of the icebox counter. It is not uncommon to find boats with an optional interior, including a small dinette table in the saloon and a sit-down chart table.

What set the B-40 apart when it was first launched was the high-quality finish work below. Hinckley used to claim that it built a wooden boat inside a fiberglass hull. The joinerwork is not ostentatious, just well-executed. Even after 20 or 30 years, the lockers on the boats still open and shut smoothly, bulkheads are still firmly tabbed in place and signs of leaks are rare. The only common complaint with the interior is that there isn't enough of it—and there really is not a lot of room for a 40-foot boat. In fact, that often becomes the overriding question for many when considering a B-40: Can you live with the lack of space below?

Engine

Although the early boats were built with gas engines, a diesel came standard on the B-40 around 1970. Westerbeke seems to be the most popular engine, with the most common model the 4-107. This engine is very similar to the Perkins of the same model number and delivers 35 to 50 horsepower, depending on how you rate it and whom you ask. It is plenty of engine for the boat, however. Boats that have been recently repowered are likely to have converted to a Yanmar, and given the choice, I'd look for one of these boats first. Squeezing the engine in and out of the companionway and into the narrow engine compartment makes repowering a difficult job.

Bermuda 40

Sailing Magazine's Value Guide

PRICE: B-40s are expensive, of course, but you get a great boat. Because of the long production run and high price of new boats, the price isn't as shocking as it once was.

DESIGN QUALITY: This Bill Tripp design has proven itself for more than 40 years. The keel-centerboard arrangement offers shoal-draft options, but there is no disputing the boat's offshore capabilities.

CONSTRUCTION QUALITY: This is what you pay for: Hinckleys really are built to a very high standard. There have been very few five-boat ratings in the Used Boat Notebook. This is only the second one ever given.

USER-FRIENDLINESS: The B-40 handles well through variety of conditions. However, the nature of the design makes some things hard to work on. Also, lack of interior space is a drawback for many.

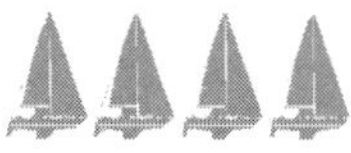

SAFETY: Solid construction, seakindly design, well-supported deck hardware and plenty of handholds make the boat safe. The boat is a bit tender, at least initially.

TYPICAL CONDITION: Most B-40s have been well-loved by their owners. Many East Coast boats have been returned to the factory for maintenance and updates.

REFITTING: Repowering is a common retrofit and not particularly easy. Parts and service are still available but very expensive.

SUPPORT: Hinckley does a good job of offering support to its many used boat owners and offers valuable information about the B-40 online. www.thehinckleyco.com.

AVAILABILITY: 203 boats were built, and they change hands grudgingly. There are definitely more boats on the East Coast, particularly in New England and the Chesapeake Bay area.

INVESTMENT AND RESALE: Few boats have held their value over the years like the B-40s. Financially, I'm convinced you would be better off spending $150,000 on a 25 year old B-40 than a new, off-the-shelf production boat.

OVERALL 'SVG' RATING

The engine is located under the companionway steps. Although Hinckley cleverly located most access and maintenance points on the front end, servicing the engine is still easier for small people. Also, the 50-gallon Monel fuel tank is located in the bilge under the engine. This is great from a weight standpoint but not quite as great if you need to replace the tank.

Underway

I have sailed the Bermuda 40 several times over the years. I really came to know the boat on a 1,500-mile delivery from the Virgin Islands to Massachusetts' Buzzards Bay via Bermuda. My friend Eric Anderson and I met new owner Paul Sullivan and his brother Dan in St. Thomas and were promptly under way on what looked like a typical delivery. We had ideal conditions. The trades were fresh and we reached north, straddling the 65th meridian. With a full main and genoa we rarely dipped below 6 knots and frequently topped 7. The steering was easy and well-balanced and the autopilot controlled the boat without breaking a sweat. With the centerboard down the boat tracked well, and I was surprised with the sweet motion, especially given the large beam seas. We reeled off three 170-mile days, and raised Bermuda on the morning of the fifth day, having averaged nearly 160 miles per day, or almost 7 knots.

Paul and Dan left the boat in Bermuda and Eric and I continued on. We really had a chance to sail the boat because a fried starter rendered the engine useless. We had a variety of conditions, including an ugly nor'easter in the Gulf Stream. With winds of 25 to 30 knots, we had one reef in the main and a partially furled headsail, and we blasted across the stream. Without the engine we had no way to charge the batteries so the autopilot was off duty. Eric and I enjoyed steering, however, and were pleased with the light helm and responsive nature of the boat.

The winds eased as we neared Nantucket shoals and were enveloped in pea soup fog. We coaxed the boat along, gaining way at 3 or 4 knots in extremely light conditions. We finally reached our destination at the Concordia yard in South Dartmouth. Tacking through the many moored boats, we raised and lowered the centerboard to avoid running aground. We sailed into the slip, having completed the 700-mile passage from Bermuda in less than six days.

Conclusion

The Hinckley Bermuda 40 is clearly a genuine classic. The boat was manufactured with skill and pride, and the design has a certain timeless quality. Until recently, however, the price excluded many people from even considering the boat. Today, I think a legitimate case can be made that, when compared to new boats, the B-40 stacks up as a good value. Prices for boats built from 1960 to 1985 range from$80,000 to $200,000. It is quite possible to find a 1975 to a 1980 model in excellent condition for around $150,000. While there is no disputing that this is a lot of money for an old boat, when you compare what you can buy new for the same amount, the value becomes clear.

Morgan Out Island 41

Shoal-draft, spacious, liveaboard cruiser: Still a good buy

In terms of sheer numbers, the Morgan Out Island 41 is one of the most successful big sailboats ever built, with nearly 1,100 hulls built during its two decades of production. While one of the most loved, it also is one of the most maligned. Few sailors are ambivalent about the OI 41. Many cruising sailors rave about its robust construction, extreme shoal draft and spacious accommodations, while others dismiss the boat as too slow, dislike the beamy, raised-deck look and resent the way the OI 41 altered the priorities of cruising boats and helped launch the bareboat chartering industry. One thing is certain: Yachtbrokers just can't list enough OI 41s. With prices ranging from less than $50,000 for an old, walk-over 413 to a little more than $100,000 for a late model, Catalina-built Classic, the Morgan Out Island 41 continues to be a highly sought-after cruising and liveaboard boat.

The inspiration for the Morgan OI 41 was surprisingly the emerging International Offshore Rule. Designer and builder Charley Morgan, on the CCA Rules Committee at the time, was so infuriated by the rule change that he designed the OI 41 to fly in the face of the new IOR. The long-suffering IOR, since blamed for virtually every flaw in boats designed and built in the 1970s, discouraged beamy centerboard boats. Morgan, now 71 and still a vigorous proponent of shoal draft and keelboarders, originally designed the Out Island 41 with a centerboard. But when the boat was introduced in 1971, centerboarders were falling out of fashion. Morgan's dealers insisted that the new boat feature a long, shoal-draft keel sans centerboard. The dealers also disliked the name Out Island. But while Morgan was willing to compromise on the centerboard (for a while it was listed as an option), he wasn't about to change the name.

Most importantly, Morgan brought the boat to market for less than $40,000. When the boat was introduced in 1971 at the United States Sailboat Show in Annapolis, Maryland, it caused a stir. Dealers couldn't take orders fast enough. In the first year of production, Morgan sold 120 Out Island 41s.

Morgan Out Island 41

LOA 41'3"
LWL 34'
Beam 13'10"
Draft 4'2"
Displ. 27,000 lbs.
Ballast 9,000 lbs.
Sail Area 878 sq. ft.

First impressions

The Morgan OI 41 is a classic example of function overriding form—at least from a purely aesthetic point of view. With the raised deck, portlights lost in the dark cove stripe and broad foredeck, it doesn't appear graceful. The irony is that in many ways the OI 41 was simply ahead of its time. The OI 41 was one of the first sailboats to emphasize low exterior maintenance and to consider, right from its inception, the implications of motoring.

Construction

One thing about the Morgan OI 41, even through four company ownerships, is that it has remained consistent: It was always heavily built and a boat that aged well. During its production heyday in the mid-1970s, an OI 41 rolled off the line every day at Morgan's plant in Largo, Florida. The hull is solid laminate and the deck is sandwich construction with plywood coring. Although this is not the best coring material, deck delamination does not seem to be a big

Morgan Out Island 41 Price Data

		Low	High
BUC Retail Range	1973	$46,100	$50,600
	1979	$59,500	$65,500
	1984	$80,600	$88,500

		State	Asking
Boats For Sale	1973	FL	$58,000
	1977	FL	$54,900
	1983	USVI	$85,000

problem with older OI 41s. The internal ballast is glassed-in cast lead. Although Morgan recently told me that he felt the boat could have used more lead, few have complained that the boat isn't stiff enough. The original designed displacement was 24,000 pounds, but that was probably more wishful thinking than reality. Although there is little uniformity in the specs, the 1975 brochures listed the displacement at 27,000 pounds with 9,000 pounds of ballast. The rudder is fiberglass with a core and a beefy $1^3/_4$-inch stainless stock. Bulkheads and furnishings are securely tabbed into the hull, though sometimes you will find cracks and twists where the bulkheads are bonded with the molded deck liner.

What to look for

To understand what to look for first, you have to have a general idea of the evolution of the OI 41. The first model was called the 413 because the company's other 41, the CCA racer-cruiser, was called the 412. The 413s were built from 1971 to 1973 and were all walk-overs, meaning that you entered the aft cabin from a companionway on deck. The 414 was introduced in 1973 and was built until 1976. While early 414s came with a slightly different interior, the big change occurred in 1975 when the first walk-through interior was offered. The 415 models, all of which were walk-throughs, were also the first to be sold in any significant numbers as a sloop. In 1981 Morgan unveiled the 416, which came with dramatically more sail area, and working sail area increased by almost 30 percent. The last major change occurred after Catalina purchased Morgan. While the OI 41 took a production hiatus in 1985, the Catalina design team revamped the boat and introduced the Classic in 1986. The Classic features an updated deck arrangement, comes as a sloop or cutter, and most significantly, has a completely new underbody featuring a NACA-foil keel. There were two generations of the Classic: the MK I and II. Around 150 were built until production ceased in 1991.

There are some specific items to look for when considering an OI 41. The first boats have a hull-to-deck joint that is substantially below the deck level, is covered with a neoprene molding and is used as a rubbing strake. This joint is vulnerable to damage during docking or even when hauled by a Travelift. In 1975 the joint was made where it should be, at the sheer at the edge of the deck. As with any older, mechanically fastened hull-to-deck joint, it's important to carefully check for leaks. Another area to inspect is the maststep. At some point, the isolating material between the aluminum spar and iron step breaks down and electrolysis sets in. Unfortunately, it is hard to look at the bilge because the teak-and-holly cabin sole doesn't have many inspection hatches. Another problem with early boats is the plastic fuel tank. If it hasn't been changed already, the onerous job will fall to you. Most OI 41s carry 170 gallons of water in two aluminum

Morgan Out Island 41

Sailing Magazine's Value Guide

PRICE: Price is undoubtedly one of the most attractive features of the OI 41. Using that ridiculous standard of boat per pound, the OI 41 scores very high. Today's buyer can hardly go wrong financially with an OI 41.

DESIGN QUALITY: Judge the OI 41 for what it is, not what it isn't or ever tried to be. Morgan's design was quite original. The sheer number of boats produced and sold means that a lot of people liked the boat.

CONSTRUCTION QUALITY: There is little to fault with the hearty way the OI 41 was built, but some of the external parts used weren't high quality. The boats have held up well.

USER-FRIENDLINESS: Overall, the boat is easy to handle, although maneuvering under power is usually an adventure.

SAFETY: While the overall strength of construction certainly adds a measure of safety, the lifelines are low, the small aluminum toerail doesn't offer much support and the nonskid is not the best.

TYPICAL CONDITIONS: Many boats went into charter fleets and others were well-used for extensive cruising, so most OI 41s on the market are in average to below-average condition.

REFITTING: The OI 41 is not the easiest boat to refit. Repowering the boat and changing the maststep or water tanks can be big, time-consuming projects.

SUPPORT: Although the boat has been out of production for more than 10 years, Morgan Marine is still quite helpful. Contact Warren Pandy of Morgan at (727) 544-6681.

AVAILABILITY: There are many OI 41s on the market at any given time, but they don't linger. Shoal-draft areas like the west coast of Florida and the Chesapeake Bay have the best selections.

INVESTMENT AND RESALE: Most people who bought early boats actually made money when they sold them.

OVERALL 'SVG' RATING

tanks. I do know of older boats with leaking tanks. A leaking tank is difficult to repair and no fun at all to replace.

On deck

The cockpit of the OI 41 is huge and slightly awkward. The seat on the port side is raised on all walk-through models and is uncomfortable for sitting. The helmsman has a nice perch, allowing visibility over the low deckhouse. There is a decent-sized locker to starboard, but the locker below the helmsman's seat is often converted to a propane locker for a retrofitted stove.

The lifelines seem too low as you make your way forward because the deckhouse is nearly flush. Be sure to check the aluminum double anchor roller for signs of corrosion. For a boat that was designed to spend a lot of time at anchor, a stainless steel stemhead fitting would have been more appropriate.

There have been few if any reports of rigging failures on OI 41s, and this is not surprising. The boat is heavily stayed and the stout chainplates are bolted through the topsides. Of course, if the rig is original, carefully examine all swage fittings. Most riggers suggest replacing any rig after 10 years. While this may not be necessary, be prepared for this possible expense.

Even if the rig is in good shape, the furling system should be updated.

Down below

It is hard to generalize about the interior arrangements because so many different versions were offered. In the walk-over there is usually a V-berth forward with a port-side head, dinette and galley. The aft stateroom has a huge double berth and another head to starboard. As the walk-through model took over, other interior variations were offered. The forward cabin can come with a V-berth or an offset over-and-under arrangement. The head might be found on either side and a convertible dinette might feature a fixed or bulkhead table. Usually, the galley is to starboard and has enormous counter space and storage. The walk-through area sometimes houses a deep-freezer with a chart table and other times houses colossal storage bins and a small, 110-volt icemaker. The aft cabin features a large double berth, a private head and a hanging locker.

One consistent feature of all OI 41s is excellent ventilation. They all feature an array of deck hatches and opening portlights, although the quality is often substandard.

Engine

The OI 41 is one of the first production sailboats to exclusively offer diesel engines. Although some models are fitted with Westerbekes, most of the early boats have Perkins 4107s or 4108s. The 4108 is freshwater cooled. Morgan knew that the design was not going to be a witch to weather and wanted to make sure that the OI 41 had enough power to reach safe harbor before darkness. While the 4108 has a nominal horsepower rating of 50, this is a bit misleading. Perkins used gross ratings that measure horsepower without any load. In reality, when it comes to pushing a boat through the water, you can deduct 15 to 20 percent to get the actual net horsepower. In fact, the later OI 41 Classic, which is powered by a Yanmar 44, has more horsepower than the Perkins 4108 because Yanmar uses net ratings. The 4108 has just enough power and most 416 models have been upgraded to the Perkins 4154, which had a gross rating of 62 horsepower. Some even have the 4236, which has a gross horsepower rating of 85.

Access to the engine, which is perched beneath the cockpit, is excellent through doors in the walk-through. This is a real engine room, although you do have to crawl over the main engine to work on the generator. The stuffing box is easily reached through the sole in the aft cabin.

Underway

I have logged thousands of miles aboard OI 41s. I have delivered several from Florida down to the Caribbean islands, a tough 1,000-mile slug to weather. While I won't tell you that the boat is a great performer, I can say with authority that the OI 41 sails better than most people think. It tends to sail flat, on its lines, and with a relatively long waterline, it's not uncommon to reach along at 8 knots.

It takes a while to adjust to the boat under sail, and unfortunately, it is hard to find and maintain the groove because almost all OI 41s have hydraulic steering. I really dislike hydraulic steering in boats less than 50 feet. Also, the OI 41 makes substantial leeway when hard on the wind in any kind of sea. Morgan's original idea of including a centerboard would have been a nice improvement. The Classic, with a more modern underbody and even more sail area, indisputably performs better than earlier models.

Conclusion

The Morgan Out Island 41 has never fallen out of fashion for one basic reason: It has always represented a solid value to those looking for a well-built, roomy cruising or liveaboard boat.

Whitby 42

Benchmark center-cockpit cruising design gives you lots of boat for the buck

I recently addressed the annual meeting of the Seven Seas Cruising Association. Known throughout the world as the SSCA, this 10,000-member international organization is primarily made up of bluewater cruisers. After my presentation I spoke with many members and naturally we talked boats. As the cocktails and the sea stories flowed, one boat seemed to be mentioned more than any other: the venerable Whitby 42. Designed by Ted Brewer nearly 30 years ago, this sturdy, commodious and affordable ketch is a good choice for anyone contemplating serious cruising and living aboard.

The first Whitby 42 rolled off the ways in 1973, in Kurt and Doris Hansen's Whitby Boat Works in, of all places, Whitby, Ontario. The Hansens also built the legendary Alberg 30 and popular Alberg 37. About 200 Whitbys were built in Canada before production shifted south. From 1983 to 1990, the Ft. Myers Shipyard completed another 32 Whitby ketches. It also built two similar, though more expensive, center-cockpit cruisers, the Brewer 12.8 and the Brewer 44.

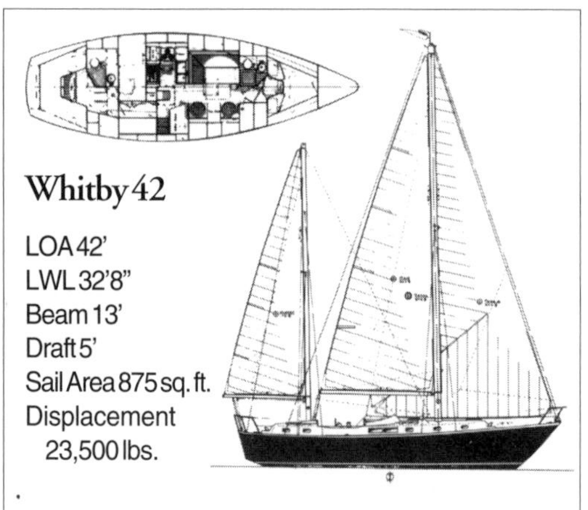

Whitby 42

LOA 42'
LWL 32'8"
Beam 13'
Draft 5'
Sail Area 875 sq. ft.
Displacement 23,500 lbs.

First impressions

Your initial perception of the Whitby 42 will depend on the angle from which you view the boat. If you approach the boat bow on, the Whitby looks anything but graceful. The entry is not particularly fine and the freeboard seems excessive. When viewed in profile, however, or from the stern quarter, the boat looks much better. Brewer's trademark springy sheer blends nicely into the stem, and the fore and aft cabintrunks are well proportioned. The 13-foot beam provides plenty of interior space amidships, and although the hull tapers a bit toward the stern, the roomy aft cabin is clearly one of the Whitby's best features.

Many of the early Whitbys were white, which is practical in the tropics but tends to accentuate the freeboard. Most of the later model boats and some of the older boats, have gone to wide, colored cove stripes and sheer strakes, which is much more pleasing to the eye.

All Whitbys are ketch rigged and carry a generous 875 square feet of working sail. Below the waterline, the modified full keel helps the boat track well at sea but causes it to maneuver poorly in tight conditions near the dock. The relatively shallow 5-foot draft is another reason for the Whitby's enduring popularity with cruisers, and the boats are a common in the shallow anchorages of the Florida Keys and Bahamas.

Construction

When the Whitby 42 first appeared, aside from a few U.S.-made center-cockpit cruisers like the Morgan OI 41 and the Gulfstar 43, traditional designs massively constructed in the Far East dominated the market. While some of these boats were labeled, without affection, "leaky teakys" for their ornate woodworking and skimpy use of caulking, to many they represented what a cruising boat should look like. In contrast, the Whitby was plain looking and didn't appear to be as solidly built. Of course today many of the older Far East boats are in decrepit condition while virtually every Whitby 42 is either out cruising or being prepared for another voyage. The boat has aged quite well, which is an indication of good initial construction.

The hull is balsa cored in the topsides and solid glass below the waterline. Canadian builders of this era, led by the gang at C&C, specialized in cored hulls. Incidentally, among the Whitby owners cult, there seems to be a quiet preference for Canadian-built boats. The deck is also balsa cored, and the hull-to-deck joint is on an internal flange that is mechanically fastened with stainless steel rivets. Through bolts were an option in early boats and later in the production run became standard. The teak-and-holly cabin sole is nicely laid in a molded liner. The main mast is keel-stepped while the mizzen is stepped on deck. The lead ballast is internal.

Like many boats that have been cruised extensively, most of the common problems with Whitbys are well documented. The Whitby 42 Association collects and shares information and puts out a useful newsletter. David Kazen, who has put more than 30,000 miles on his 1978 model *Pathfinder*, advises buyers to look carefully at the water tanks, which are curiously constructed of fiberglass with an aluminum top plate. Leaks can develop along the seal, allowing water to spill when the boat heels. Another problem is the keel fuel tank. The Whitby has three fuel tanks, including two saddle tanks, for a total of 210 gallons. Like any keel tank, the bilge water sloshes around and contaminates the fuel through one of the fittings. Kazen solved this problem by creating a manifold to isolate the tank and adding another filter-separator in the keel tank line.

Another common problem is that the deck-stepped mizzen relies on a partial bulkhead for compression support below. Also, the deck in this area, especially on early boats, was not solid fiberglass. Look for a compressed deck area around the base of the mast as evidence of insufficient mast support. Some owners have added a compression post below. A few Whitbys have rudder problems as the stock is not well supported. Be sure to have the surveyor inspect the rudder carefully when the boat is hauled.

One feature to look for is a Whitby 42 with a bowsprit. According to Ted Brewer, the sprit, which allows for the use of a staysail on a removable stay, helps balance the boat, reduces weather helm and adds to performance. It also provides a handy perch for the anchors.

Whitby 42 Price Data

		Low	High
BUC Retail Range	1974	$68,000	$74,000
	1976	$74,700	$82,100
	1979	$86,300	$94,900

		State	Asking
Boats For Sale	1974	CAN	$85,000
	1976	FL	$65,000
	1979	NY	$95,000

On deck

The cockpit of the Whitby 42 is not only comfortable, but with its stout bridgedeck, it is also quite seaworthy. Either cabin can be entered from the cockpit, a very practical feature for cruising. The view from the helm is excellent. Indeed, if you are used to sailing aft-cockpit boats, you'll be surprised at how short the boat seems when you take the helm of a center cockpit. The mainsheet is led from the end of the boom to a single-point tie down, which is inefficient for hauling the main in for windward work. A small traveler would be a nice upgrade. The port side cockpit locker opens directly into the spacious engine room. This too is quite practical because it allows for ventilation and natural light when working below. Two lockers on the aft deck make up for lost storage space.

Moving about the deck you will appreciate the molded bulwarks, which also support the outboard headsail tracks. The side decks are wide and easy to navigate in spite of a fairly large trunkhouse, although the nonskid surface is marginal. When David Kazen was preparing his boat for a high-latitude voyage he applied Treadmaster decking for more secure footing. Check to be sure that the stanchions are securely installed, since some of the early boats didn't

Whitby 42

Sailing Magazine's Value Guide

PRICE: Compared to a new boat or simply calculate the replacement cost, the Whitby is an excellent value.

DESIGN QUALITY: One of Ted Brewer's most popular designs, the Whitby has not only stood the test of time, it was also a benchmark of sorts for the many center-cockpit cruisers that followed in its wake.

CONSTRUCTION: The initial construction was excellent, as the good condition of most Whitbys on the used boat market attests. Check the rudder and deck area around the mizzen.

USER-FRIENDLINESS: The Whitby has a simple deck layout that is easy to sail, although hydraulic steering limits helm feedback. The interior is spacious, but like all cruising boats, there are a lot of systems to maintain.

SAFETY: A stout bulwark and wide side decks make moving about safe. The nonskid could be improved. There is a good bridgedeck and a husky coaming for a cockpit dodger.

TYPICAL CONDITION: Most Whitbys have been cruised extensively and often require cosmetic upgrades. Structurally they hold up well and osmotic blisters do not appear to be an overly common problem.

REFITTING: The Whitby is an easy boat to work on, primarily because of its overall size and well-designed access ports. Although no longer in production, Whitby used well-known suppliers and most parts are widely available.

SUPPORT: Bernard Boykin, of the owner's association, can be reached by e-mail at beboykin@bcpl.net. Many owners are longtime liveaboards and really know their boats. They are happy to share info.

AVAILABILITY: With more than 230 boats, there's a good selection of Whitbys on the market. Florida, the Chesapeake Bay area and Canada are the best places to look. It is much less common on the West Coast.

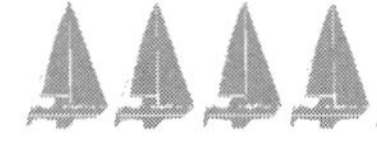

INVESTMENT AND RESALE: It has held its value and has rebounded nicely from the miserable late 1980s.

OVERALL 'SVG' RATING

have backing plates. Whitbys without the bowsprit often have a cast aluminum stemhead fitting with two anchor rollers. Although this piece doesn't appear very beefy, there are few reported problems. The chain locker is accessible through a hawsepipe and most Whitbys have a stout windlass on the foredeck.

Down below

The interior is certainly one of the Whitby's prime attractions. The main companionway ladder is rather narrow, but otherwise it is hard to find fault with the well-designed cabin. Forward, there is a large V-berth cabin with a hanging locker and private access to the head. This forward head does not have a separate shower, but few boats of this vintage did. An advantage of two heads, especially for a cruising couple, is that one can become the designated shower.

In the saloon many of the Whitbys came equipped with two swivel chairs to starboard in lieu of a standard settee. And while the chairs will make traditionalists cringe and are useless under way, it is important to remember that for every day you spend at sea you spend a lot more in port, where having a comfortable place to sit can be a luxury on a boat. I would try the swivel chair arrangement before discarding it, especially since there is also a handy table that drops down between the chairs for a meal or card game. A second feature that most sailors will either love or hate is the fold-down bulkhead table, instead of a fixed table or dinette arrangement. Again, I like the concept because it opens up the saloon.

A U-shaped galley is to port, and with its deep fiddle edges, double sinks, large storage lockers and huge fridge-freezer arrangement, it is everything it should be for a serious cruising boat, while keeping the cook well supported in a seaway. The nav station is opposite with a large desk that can house plenty of charts inside, although the electrical panel is located under the companionway steps, which is not the best place.

The walkway to the aft cabin requires a bit of stooping, which might put off some sailors accustomed to looking at new boats at boat shows. But when the Whitby was designed, the ability to walk through was a major breakthrough.

This aft cabin features a huge bunk and another head. The bunk is designed for sleeping on either tack and makes for a good sea berth. Just for the record, in most offshore sailing situations, the best sleeping is in the aft cabin, unless the aft cabin has an island berth.

The teak joinerwork is workmanlike, and in well-maintained boats, it looks just fine by today's standards. Ventilation is good with overhead hatches and opening portlights. Be wary of plastic portlights. It is easy to overtighten the dogs.

Engine

The standard engine was a Ford Lehman four-cylinder 67-horsepower diesel. This is an old workhorse and provides plenty of punch. Although this engine is no longer in production, parts are still widely available and most diesel mechanics are quite familiar with it. With a total of 210 gallons of fuel, there's a conservative motoring range of 1,000 miles.

Most of the boats that I have seen also have a diesel generator, which is a welcome feature if you plan to run air conditioning, or have a high-output watermaker. However, generators are temperamental, and unlike the old Ford, the likely Onan or Westerbeke generator will probably be a source of much irritation.

Access to the engine room is terrific, which may be one reason why so many Whitbys still have the original engine. The stuffing box is also accessible from the aft cabin.

Underway

Bernard Boykin, who has owned hull No. 156 for 10 years, reports that the boat sails well, although it needs 15 to 20 knots to really come alive. Kazen agreed, adding that the boat is well behaved in a gale. On his passage to Newfoundland, he encountered 40 knots and confused seas in the Cabot Straits. But with reefed sails, he never had an anxious moment.

Boykin said it can take a while to bring the boat through the wind, especially in light air. But he added: "It's a cruising boat, who's in a hurry?" The fact that several Whitbys have circumnavigated with minimal crews speaks well of its sailing characteristics.

One of the features I like least about the boat is the hydraulic steering. There is very little feel or feedback from the helm. The boat is not overly responsive to begin with and hydraulic steering makes the situation worse. Whitby used hydraulics because it is difficult to build a cable and sheave system in a center-cockpit boat without costing a lot of space. Today, most manufacturers of center-cockpit boats use a push-push system, like the one made by Edson. This would be a welcome retrofit on the Whitby 42.

Conclusion

The Whitby 42, with prices ranging from $70,000 for an older, well-used model to over $100,000 for one in top condition, is an excellent value if you are looking for a capable, offshore cruising boat.

PART 2

Ten Great Used Boats to Sail Around the World

Camper Nicholson 35

The British-built Nicholson 35 is a deceptive boat. The Nic 35, as it is called the world over, reminds me of a slightly larger and more comfortable version of the Contessa 32, the diminutive sloop that carried me around Cape Horn from east to west many years ago. "The Nicholson 35 is a handsome boat with a sweet sheerline and well-proportioned overhangs. It is among the best bluewater boats for her size," said Ted Brewer, one of North America's most respected yacht designers. I wouldn't hesitate to sail a Nic 35 anywhere and I can't think of a better boat in which to start this discussion of 10 great boats to sail around the world.

Designed in house by Camper & Nicholson, the 35 isn't a boat that you look at and immediately think, "Wow this boat can sail anywhere." However, the Contessa 32 taught me an essential lesson for offshore sailing. Looks can be deceiving, and no boat can out muscle the sea. In some ways, beefed-up boats are like bodybuilders, nice to look at but not really very strong and often unwieldy to boot. The best that you can hope for is to build a quality boat to a design that limits the pounding that old Neptune dishes out in a sustained blow. The Nicholson 35 is such a design.

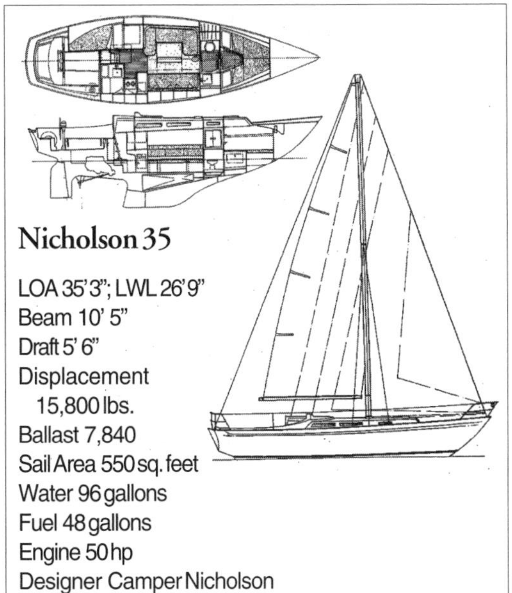

Nicholson 35

LOA 35'3"; LWL 26'9"
Beam 10' 5"
Draft 5' 6"
Displacement 15,800 lbs.
Ballast 7,840
Sail Area 550 sq. feet
Water 96 gallons
Fuel 48 gallons
Engine 50 hp
Designer Camper Nicholson

Introduced by the venerable firm of Camper & Nicholson in 1971, the Nic 35 remained in production through the mid-1980s. The bulk of the more than 200 boats built were launched in the 1970s, and most were originally sold in England. Camper & Nicholson's has been building yachts in Gosport, near Southampton for more than 200 years. Although it builds only exclusive custom yachts today, the 35 was one of its proudest production efforts. For a variety of reasons many Nicholson 35s have turned up on this side of the Atlantic. There was an active dealer-importer in Annapolis, Maryland, for several years, and other 35s crossed the pond during the mid-1980s when the dollar was very strong against the English pound. At any given time there are usually several boats

Nicholson 35 Price Data

		Low	High
BUC Retail Range	1972	$37,800	$41,900
	1977	$43,900	$48,800
	1982	$59,400	$65,300

		State	Asking
Boats For Sale	1976	MD	$47,500
	1978	NY	$55,000
	1979	England	$45,000
	1980	UK	US$50,000

available on the U.S. used boat market, and with today's exchange rates once again favorable, it is worth considering beginning your cruise in Europe after buying a Nic 35 in the United Kingdom. This idea is actually practical, as you can spend time in the Mediterranean and then ride the trades across the Atlantic to the West Indies. I remember the mid-1980s, when the dollar was nearly on par with the English pound, there were plenty of American sailors doing just this. A quick check of online English brokers revealed 10 Nic 35s for sail both in the United Kingdom and in the Mediterranean.

First impressions

The Nic 35 has a low-profile coachroof with long, narrow portlights that blend nicely into the lines of the boat. The entry is fine and the stern fairly narrow. The overhangs are long by today's standards, with a LWL of 26 feet, 9 inches on an 35-foot, 3-inch LOA. However, as the boat heels, it picks up waterline length and speed. The Nic 35 is a very good performer on the wind, and most importantly, it doesn't beat you up when punching into a seaway.

One look at the underbody will tell you why the Nic 35 has such a sweet motion. The long fin keel is swept back from a gently raked forefoot. Yes, there is a bit of wetted surface forward and that does slow the boat down a bit off the wind, but there is no flat forefoot section prone to pounding. The rudder is hung from a husky skeg, a practical arrangement for the vagaries of bluewater sailing. I confess that when I'm doodling on cocktail napkins I always draw sailboats, and the underbody of my scribbled creations invariably looks a lot like the Nic 35.

The Nic 35 is no lightweight, with a displacement of 15,650 pounds, translating into a sluggish displacement-to-length ratio of 365. Let's take a moment to put that number into perspective. Speaking in broad terms, performance cruisers usually have D/L ratios of well under 200. A J/32, for instance, sports a 187. Moderate cruisers fall between 200 and 250, like the smooth sailing Tartan 3800 with a D/L ratio of 240. Heavy cruisers are near or above 300. The Pacific Seacraft 34, a boat comparable to the Nic 35, has a ratio 334. The Island Packet 350, a full-keeled cruiser, checks in with a 283. However, the Nic 35's D/L ratio is deceptive, especially upwind. The ratio is based on waterline length and the nature of a narrow hull shape (the Nic 35 beam is just 10 feet, 5 inches compared to the IP 350's 12 feet) is that it heels early, thereby extending the waterline length and lowering the D/L ratio significantly. On paper the Nic 35 looks slow, but in the water, especially in rough conditions, it performs admirably. Bluewater performance demands that a boat stand up to the elements day after day, and although you can't measure this with a ratio, the Nic 35 is well-proven in this category.

Construction

Many Nic 35s were built to Lloyds Survey specifications. Lloyds has two different certifications. The first, A-1, is primarily a set of guidelines for molding hulls. These include specifications for the hull, deck and bulkheads. The second rating, 100 A-1, requires that a Lloyds surveyor be present during crucial stages of construction and adds a fair bit to the overall price of the boat. *Gigi*, our Contessa 32, was built to Lloyds 100 A-1. If you can find a Nic 35 built to 100 A-1 specs, consider yourself lucky and rest assured that it is a very well-built boat indeed.

Camper & Nicholson has long been known for its quality construction. Ironically, at some point Camper & Nicholson followed the lead of other British builders and farmed the actual hull layups out to a specialized molding firm, while it did the finishwork and commissioning. The 35's hull is solid fiberglass while the deck may or may not be cored, this was up to owner specifications. The lead ballast is internal, encapsulated in the keel cavity. Camper & Nicholson didn't skimp on lead either, the ballast is 7,300 pounds, nearly 47 percent of the displacement.

Nicholson 35

Sailing Magazine's Value Guide

PRICE: In terms of space per dollar, you can buy more boat than the Nic 35 can offer, however, in terms of quality per dollar, the boat ranks quite high.

DESIGN QUALITY: The design of the 35 has aged gracefully and the boat continues to be well suited for ocean sailing. The design limits pounding and tracks well. The engine installation could have been better thought out.

CONSTRUCTION QUALITY: Camper Nicholson built quality boats and the 35 was one of its better efforts. Even after 30 years, most 35s are still capable of sailing anywhere.

USER-FRIENDLINESS: Although the boat is easy to handle under sail and well suited to heavy weather, it is not very spacious. The cockpit is rather uncomfortable and the engine is not easy to work on.

SAFETY: Combine seakindliness and quality construction and you produce a safe boat. Small features like a molded bulwark and plenty of handrails below also make the boat safe under way.

TYPICAL CONDITION: Most Nic 35s seem to have been well cared for by their owners and have stood the test of time quite well.

REFITTING: The Nic 35 is not a particularly easy boat to work on but the high level of initial quality eases the pain of a retrofit.

SUPPORT: Camper & Nicholson does not seem particularly interested in its old production boats, so you are pretty much on your own once you purchase a 35. The boat is considered a classic in the United Kingdom and there is an archival body of literature available from *Yachting Monthly Magazine*.

AVAILABILITY: Just over 200 boats were built. If you include the United Kingdom in your search, availability improves dramatically. By the way, it really isn't a bad idea to take advantage of the strong dollar to buy the boat in England and sail it home.

INVESTMENT AND RESALE: The Nic 35 has held its value well over the years, and considering the high quality of construction, it is something of a value in America.

OVERALL 'SVG' RATING

The mast is keel-stepped just forward of the bilge water tank. There is a deep sump aft of the tank that helps keep bilge water where it belongs, in the bilge.

What to look for

The Nic 35 has aged very well indeed, and there are few if any structural problems to be wary of. Unfortunately, more than a few Nic 35s have suffered from the pox, and you should track down the history of blister repairs from previous owners. Two items not to look for are teak decks and engines with hydraulic drives. A few 35s came from the factory this way, and although teak decks look nice, they are a maintenance headache on older boats and can be expensive to either replace or remove. Hydraulic drives complicate the transmission unduly.

Other items of concern stem from the 35's English heritage. Chances are, if you are buying on this side of the pond, the boat will have been converted to a more familiar American-style electrical system along the way. You should check the installation carefully. Also, few boats came standard with pressure water so many owners have added this system along with hot water. Again, make sure the installations are properly done. As with any older boat, it is likely that items like hoses, running and standing rigging will show wear and need attention. The Nic 35 had a vinyl headliner that has occasionally becomes droopy, especially in southern climes, and is something of a pain to fix.

On deck

The Nic 35's cockpit is designed to go to sea, which doesn't necessarily mean that it's very comfortable. The cockpit seats are relatively short and the seat backs are rather abrupt. Cushions are helpful. There are decent-sized lockers under each seat. The mainsheet traveler spans the cockpit just forward of the wheel, nice for sail trim but not so nice for accommodating more than a couple of people in the cockpit. Not surprisingly there is a stout bridgedeck and two large scuppers: This is after all a seagoing boat. The wheel is placed well aft, making it a bit of a reach to the primary winches, which incidentally are often undersized. There is an excellent molding surround for a spray dodger, an essential piece of equipment as the Nic 35 can be a wet boat.

The side decks are quite wide for a narrow boat, and a small molded bulwark lends security underfoot when moving about the deck and also keeps small items from skipping overboard. The nonskid may well be worn nearly smooth, as many Nic 35s are 25 to 30 years old. Also, as noted above, some boats had teak decks, which probably should be avoided if possible. Teak handrails are well placed on the coachroof and double lifelines were standard. The chainplates, which are simply oversized U-bolts, are bolted through a plate in the deck. We had the same arrangement on *Gigi* and she survived a capsize with the mast standing. The single spreader rig likely includes a gold anodized Proctor spar, usually filled with foam to keep the sound down. The working sail area is nearly 550 square feet.

Down below

The lack of beam becomes apparent the moment you drop below—there just isn't much volume to work with and the designers resisted pushing the living space out to very ends of the boat. The interior arrangement, however, is practical and well executed. While two people can live comfortably enough on a Nic 35 (an important selection criterion for each of the 10 boats in this section), they just can't be overly materialistic.

There is a V-berth forward that does not easily convert to a double, especially on early boats, as the anchor chain hawsepipe ran between the berths. The athwartship head compartment is full width, privacy requires shutting doors to the forepeak and the saloon. This arrangement does allow for a much larger head than if it had been squeezed to one side or the other, and in truth, privacy issues for a couple while cruising are different than when living ashore. The saloon usually has a drop-leaf centerline table with a U-shaped settee to port and straight settee opposite. Most boats came with a pilot berth to starboard, although some owners have invariably converted this space into locker space. Also, models with pilot berths rarely had quarter berths. There is ample storage beneath the settees and room to convert either space into a second water tank. The fiberglass tank below the sole holds 70 gallons. The galley, off to starboard, is not particularly inspired, although like pub grub, it is workmanlike. A two-burner cooker, as they say in the United Kingdom, was standard. A single sink faces aft with the icebox outboard. There is just enough counter space to prepare a meal. The teak fiddles are serious as is the stainless steel grabrail. The nav station is to port and features a large chart desk. The head of the quarter berth serves as the nav station seat with a convenient wet locker nearby. Early boats had white laminate bulkheads with teak accents. Later, Camper & Nicholson switched to a light-grain teak veneer. Ventilation is usually inadequate, making the addition of dorade vents and opening portlights a high priority before you sail south.

Engine

Early boats were fitted with the common Perkins or Westerbeke Model 4107. While these engines are virtually bulletproof and parts are available worldwide, the transmission arrangement is something of a problem. The shaft was designed to exit from the trailing edge of the keel, a questionable notion at best. This required an aft-facing engine with a hydraulic drive unit in the bilge. Around hull No. 135 boats had a strut bearing that allowed for a more conventional V-drive transmission, again, not my favorite arrangement. Some of the last boats were fitted with a Westerbeke L 25, a marinized VW Rabbit engine. The 40-gallon fiberglass fuel tank is located behind the engine and beneath cockpit sole. Access to the engine is adequate, although reaching the stuffing box beneath the V-drive is a challenge.

Underway

Almost all owners report the same sailing tendencies—the Nic 35 needs a breeze to find its stride but it can carry sail while others are tucking in reefs. By all accounts the Nic 35 has a terrific motion in a seaway. "When others are hanging on for dear life in moderate air, you feel as if you are riding in a new Cadillac," said John Staats. Of course, the Nic 35 was designed for the tempestuous waters of the English Channel and

North Sea: It may seem a little out of place on the Chesapeake Bay. However, these attributes are what make it an ideal boat for bluewater cruising. Just ask Roger Molten, who spent five years circumnavigating in his Nic 35. I met the singlehander in Gibraltar several years ago, and was impressed with the simple way he had equipped his boat. "Nothing breaks, at least not very often," he said. "I spend my passages reading and catching up on my sleep."

Like other moderate-aspect sloops of the period, the Nic 35 needs a big overlapping headsail for light air work. It is not fair to paint the boat as woefully slow, however, and the Nic 35 has a faster PHRF rating than heavy cruisers like the Tayana 37. The Nic 35 is also an easy boat to handle. An advantage of limited sail area is that you rarely get caught in a compromising situation. Also, the Nic 35 tracks extremely well and won't exhaust the crew with a herky-jerky motion.

Conclusion

The Camper Nicholson 35 is one of my favorite boats, both from a practical and good-looking perspective. Sure it has shortcomings. It isn't the most comfortable or commodious, but for extended bluewater cruising, it has one feature that overrides all others—the Nic 35 will look after its crew. If you have $50,000 to $60,000 in your budget, and you are serious about crossing oceans, you owe it yourself to consider the Nic 35.

Alberg 37

The Alberg 37 is an ideal namesake for one of sailing's most enduring naval architects—Carl Alberg. In many ways it represents his vision of the perfect offshore cruising boat and he spent a long time nurturing that vision. The 37, like most of his memorable designs, came later in life. Alberg was in his mid-60s when the design was first produced.

Alberg was born in 1900 in the seafaring town of Göteborg, Sweden. He immigrated to the United States in 1925, where he deemed the prospects were better for an aspiring yacht designer. He cut his teeth working in the office of John Alden but he never abandoned his roots. Throughout his career Alberg maintained a great affinity for the simple, spartan Scandinavian folkboat and evoked some aspects of its basic hull form in most of his 56 designs. In the end, more than 10,000 boats have been built to his designs.

Kurt Hansen, who was already building the popular Alberg 30 at his Boat Works in Whitby, Ontario, commissioned Alberg in 1966 to create a larger boat capable of comfortable bluewater sailing and competitive racing under the CCA Rule. The result was the Alberg 37.

The boat was a success from the beginning and enjoyed a long production run, from 1967 though 1988. Hansen was finally forced to close his doors in 1989 as the North American sailboat industry suffered through tough times. Nearly 250 Alberg 37s were launched, although production slowed dramatically in the 1980s. From humble beginnings on the shores of Lake Ontario, many 37s have cruised far and wide, including numerous ocean crossings and at least one circumnavigation. You'd be hard pressed to find a better boat for the money if you're considering bluewater cruising.

Boatbuilding continues in Whitby today, as many of Hansen's former employees work for PDQ Catamarans, which manufactures large cruising cats in the old Boat Works facility.

First impressions

Of course Alberg's vision of the perfect cruising boat may differ from many modern cruisers who have been weaned on today's beamy, bulbous, luxury liners doubling as cruising sailboats. It is not a stretch to claim that there is more interior space in a new Hunter 290 than there is in an Alberg 37. Alberg's design mantra is slack bilges, a cutaway full keel with an attached rudder, low freeboard and narrow beam. And it's safe to say that he abhorred fat boats. The 37's beam is just 10-feet, 2-inches. From the Bristol 27, to the Pearson Triton, to the Cape Dory 36 and Alberg 37, all his boats have a similar profile above and below the water.

The Alberg 37 has a soft sheerline that tends to obscure just how low the freeboard really is. The bow has a fine entry and the counter stern has a springy lift. The overhangs are pronounced, translating into a LWL of 26 feet, 6 inches, which is just 71 percent of LOA. The theoretical hull speed is a whisker under 7 knots, which is about the same as that earlier mentioned Hunter 290. This of course is sacrilegious for today's designers who maximize LWL for boat speed with little respect for motion or comfort in a seaway. The Alberg 37 heels early and heels a lot. The result is that the LWL extends when sailing to weather and the boat tends to gather speed as it claws up wind. Sailing on your ear may get you old, but the trade-off is that you will rarely pound when the going gets rough.

Below the waterline the Alberg 37 features a full keel that is cutaway both fore and aft. The attached rudder is perched quite far forward. (The forward edge of the sloped rudderpost is located nearly under the companionway.) This design premise is the antithesis of the fin keel and spade rudder arrangement that moves the rudder as far aft as possible. The Alberg 37 may tend to pitch or hobbyhorse a bit, and downwind steering in big seas will be challenging, but the rudder will always be in the water responding to the helm.

The shaft and propeller exit the hull near the top of the keel and are exposed through a small cutout in the rudder. The boat came as both a sloop and yawl. Many early boats were often yawls, which added sail area without impacting the boat's rating under the CCA Rule. Also, there was something romantic about a split rig during the early days of the production run. Later boats were almost all sloops as the sailing world plunged into an era of sterile practicality.

Construction

Hansen built solid boats. The Alberg 30 is a legendary cruiser and has sailed around Cape Horn. The Whitby 42 endures as a roomy and popular world cruiser, few linger long on the used boat market. Like those two well-found boats, the Alberg 37 also features a solid fiberglass hull with a balsa-cored deck. About half the boats were built with a small balsa-cored section amidships, just up from the turn of the bilge for better support when the boat rested on a cradle all winter long.

The hull-and-deck joint is on an inward flange. Early boats had a teak toerail, while a small fiberglass molding replaced the wood on the Mark II version. A molded liner was also added during this redesign. The lead ballast is encapsulated in the keel compartment. I prefer internal ballast as opposed to externally fastened keels and shoes on older fiberglass boats because of the difficulty of determining the condition of the keel bolts.

Construction techniques were not fancy, but the 37 was solidly built. Stories of Alberg 37s that have survived hard groundings, or worse, abound. Paul Howard tells a story in *Canadian Yachting* magazine about a singlehandler's 37 that went on the reef near Palmyra Atoll in the South Pacific. After three days of pounding he managed to get off the reef by jettisoning all of his supplies. He then sailed to Tahiti 2,000 miles away to enact repairs.

A hull plug for the depthsounder transducer on a 1969 model I recently inspected was legitimately more than one inch think. Of course fiberglass layups in those days tended be resin rich, still most surveyors agree that Whitby's hull scantlings were among the heaviest in the industry, with the glass work consistent and well-executed.

Alberg 37 Price Data

		Low	High
BUC Retail Range	1974	$36,400	$40,400
	1978	$46,900	$51,600
	1982	$58,400	$64,200

		State	Asking
Boats For Sale	1969	NY	$32,000
	1973	TX	$68,000
	1975	Canada	$48,000
	1977	Canada	$52,000

What to look for

"The first thing to look for is an Alberg 37 with the larger engine, the ones with the Westerbeke 4107 40-horsepower diesel," Doug Stephenson said. The standard engine fitted in most boats was either the 23-horsepower Volvo MD2D or the 27-horsepower MD11C. "Both engines are a bit undersized," he said. "We could barely move against the ebb of the Elbe."

Stephenson, who worked for Whitby Boat Works for many years and also ran a separate sales company that marketed the boats, is an authority on used Albergs and Whitbys. He has practical experience too. Many years ago, Stephenson, Hansen and two others sailed a 37 across the North Atlantic.

Although slight improvements were made throughout the production run, major changes were applied in 1971 when the MK II model was introduced. This version of the Alberg 37 incorporated a molded cabin sole and headliner that streamlined production and made the hull a bit more rigid, though less accessible. The interior was upgraded, more storage was added and the head was expanded. Two noticeable differences occurred on deck. A molded dodger coaming was added and the portlights were reshaped, which is the quickest way to tell the difference between the MK I and MK II models.

Of course all age-related items should be thoroughly checked, including the standing rigging, wiring and plumbing. There is a very active owner's association Web page where many common problems are discussed. Apparently the original wiring was not very well thought out and frequently needs work and updating. Several owners also had complaints regarding the poor quality seacocks. It is a good idea to change them when you retrofit for bluewater sailing. Remember, peace of mind is a vital commodity when offshore, as passagemaking is exhausting enough without the burden of wondering whether the boat's through-hull fittings are in good shape. Also be sure to check the mast tangs, particularly on the forestay. One owner reported that he nearly lost the mast on a transatlantic passage when the tang gave way. Fortunately they managed to limp into Madeira, Spain, under main alone where they had a new tang welded.

Dan Stuart who sails a 1967 Mark I on Lake Erie has made few changes to his boat. He advises buyers to look for a sound MK I not only because it may be less expensive but the absence of the molded liner is a big advantage, especially when maintaining deck fittings. I agree with him on this point. He also thinks the teak toerail looks better than the molded rail as it is more in tune with the boat's overall traditional styling. From a maintenance viewpoint, though, the fiberglass molding will require far less upkeep.

On deck

The Alberg 37's cockpit is long and narrow, making it very seaworthy but not particularly comfortable. Although some early boats were built with tillers, most of the production run featured wheel steering. Some owners have retrofitted pedestals and wheels and these installations should be carefully inspected. The mainsheet traveler on both the yawl and sloop is aft of the helm, running at a slight angle from the end of the boom. This is the logical sheeting arrangement for the 37's long boom. The wheel, however, is quite far forward, between the primary and secondary winches. Although the helmperson is well positioned to trim both the main and the headsail, the cockpit can quickly feel crowded with more than a couple of sailors taking up space.

How many people do you really want aboard when cruising offshore? As few as possible. The 37 is ideal for a couple, or a family with small children. One advantage of a tiller is that it simplifies self-steering arrangements, especially windvanes. One couple who recently completed an Atlantic Circle noted that a Monitor windvane steered their boat 99 percent of the time.

The 37 has wide side decks, although the nonskid might be worn, which is not surprising. After all most 37s on the market are 20 to 30 years old. Teak handrails line the coachroof and the stanchions are well-supported, although there may be extensive spider cracks in the gelcoat around the bases. There is a massive cast aluminum bow fitting with a single anchor roller. Owner-retrofitted anchor sprits are not uncommon, and you should check these installations carefully.

The mast is a stout aluminum section with a single set of spreaders. The standing rigging will likely have been updated, and if it hasn't, you should place this task at the head of the project list before heading offshore. You may curse the yawl rig when it comes to expense of rigging. Approximately, one-third of the boats were originally yawls, which was a fairly expensive option.

Alberg 37

Sailing Magazine's Value Guide

PRICE: With used boat prices ranging from around $30,000 to just over $60,000, depending upon the year the boat was built, the Alberg 37 opens the door to bluewater sailing for many people.

DESIGN QUALITY: Carl Alberg's design is a bit dated, but that doesn't make it any less seaworthy. Many of the Alberg 37s attributes stem from a design created for bluewater sailing.

CONSTRUCTION QUALITY: Whitby Boat Works built stout, well-engineered boats that have stood the test of time. I wouldn't hesitate to retrofit an older Alberg 37 for world voyaging.

SAFETY: The nature of a narrow hull usually translates into good support below and on deck. The 37's cockpit is secure in a blow, and the easy motion and the boat's ability to heave-to are prime safety features.

USER FRIENDLINESS: The Alberg 37 is an easy and fairly forgiving boat to sail. It does develop weather helm and it can be tiring to steer downwind. The interior is adequate for a couple or a small family, but it isn't comfortable by any definition.

TYPICAL CONDITION: Although many Alberg 37s have been extensively cruised, many more have not. There are lots of freshwater boats for sale in the Great Lakes region, and some of these 30-year-old boats look great.

REFITTING: Like many boats of the era, the Alberg 37 is not particularly easy to work on. However, most systems are fairly simple, especially in comparison to modern boats.

SUPPORT: Whitby Boat Works is no longer in business, however there is an active and informative Alberg 37 owner's association. You can find the answer to almost any query about the boat at www.Alberg37.org.

AVAILABILITY: Alberg 37s can be found all over the country and in Canada. The best selection is clearly in the Great Lakes area and along the East Coast, from the Chesapeake to New England.

INVESTMENT AND RESALE: There are boats that may be better buys, but not many if your intent is inexpensive bluewater voyaging. However, because the design is a bit dated and most people don't dream of sailing around the world, the resale market is not as strong as it should be.

OVERALL 'SVG' RATING

Down below

The interior of the 37 is functional for bluewater sailing, although there's no denying it is small by today's standards. However many cruisers have lived aboard quite happily for extended periods of time, and small can also be looked at as cozy. Three design factors limit interior volume: the overall lack of beam, slack bilges and wide side decks that narrow the coachroof. Stephenson, who is an unabashed admirer of the boat, points out that space lost below because of the narrow coachroof is just that, space, air space, not an area that is used very often.

The arrangement is predictable. A double V-berth forward is followed by a small head compartment and hanging locker opposite. The saloon may have either a fold-down bulkhead table or a fixed table, but either way there's an L-shaped settee to port and a straight settee opposite. Storage is ample, with numerous drawers and lockers that are more useful than large open areas where everything ends up in a pile. The joinerwork is workmanlike, but remember, we are looking for boats to sail around the world, not to impress our friends.

The galley is to starboard. A three-burner cooker and oven was standard. The icebox has adequate insulation, although Stephenson noted that if you find yellow dust in the bilge, it might be that the insulation has completely broken down. He suggests trying to repair the problem with spray-in foam before dismantling the galley area. A decent-sized nav station is opposite with a quarter berth located behind it.

Engine

It seems three engine options were available, and by all accounts, the Westerbeke 4107, which incidentally, is almost identical to the Perkins 4107, is the preferred engine. Unfortunately, two smaller Volvos were more common. Spares are available for all three engines, and one advantage of the smaller engine is that there is more space available to work on it. Minimal access is from behind the companionway and through a panel in the quarter berth. Of course, the nature of a narrow, slack-bilged boat requires shoehorning the engine into a small area. The 35-gallon fuel tank is aluminum, although this may have been upgraded if the boat had been fitted out for offshore cruising at one time.

Underway

"The boat handles like an absolute dream," said Dan Stuart, who sails his 1967 sloop *Falcon* on Lake Erie. Stuart, who like most Alberg 37 owners is blinded by love, said the 37 has no apparent bad habits. The 37 is at its best in heavy weather, but in light air, Stuart flies a 150-percent genoa on a Harken roller furling system, keeping the boat moving at a sprightly 6 knots. He also said that the boat balances well and that he can leave the helm for several minutes at a time without a self-steering unit—a forgotten feature on new boats. Although, by most accounts, the Alberg 37 is a bear to handle in reverse when under power, but that's not uncommon for a full-keel boat with the propeller located quite far forward.

Doug Stephenson sailed a 1975 Alberg 37 across the Atlantic 25 years ago. His passage was from Halifax, Nova Scotia, to Falmouth on the Cornwall coast of England. With a crew of four, he completed this nearly 3,000-mile run in just over 19 days, averaging 150 miles per day.

"We really sailed the boat," Stephenson said. "And the boat responded, we kept her moving through gales and calms—the 37 is a great sea boat." Stephenson and Hansen eventually made their way through the Kiel Canal into the Baltic Sea. "For a family looking for a safe, forgiving boat to go cruising in, the 37 is hard to beat," he said.

The 37 is not particularly close-winded but it does track well, and for offshore work, that is far more important. Also, the easy motion is a critical advantage because fatigue is the enemy offshore. The Alberg 37 won't wear you down or beat you up with a fast, choppy motion. The boat can be wet when beating, and a spray dodger should be considered essential. Is an Alberg 37 the boat to sail around he world? Mike Phelps recently completed a seven-year circumnavigation aboard hull No. 42 built in 1968.

Conclusion

Prices for a used Alberg 37 range from $30,000 to $70,000 with most in the $40,000 to $50,000 range. Assuming that you will need to spend an additional $10,000 to retrofit the boat for an around-the-world voyage, you can likely put an Alberg 37 together for the big cruise for around $50,000. At that price, there is no excuse to delay launching your dream.

Shannon 38

It's become a trend for builders to shamelessly tout their boats as offshore cruisers. Most of these boats are impostors and are better suited to marina life, despite the glitzy brochure pictures and ad copy splashed across the magazines. Offshore sailing is incessantly demanding, with rarely a let up. And a boat has to endure the ocean's relentless motion day after day. Even among the builders that produce genuine offshore cruisers, few can lay claim to the impressive track record of Shannon Yachts.

Founded by David Walters and Walter Schultz in 1975, Shannon was committed to building capable bluewater cruisers right from the start. "The plan was simple, I wanted to build the best offshore sailboat in the world," Schultz noted in a recent newsletter. That's a lofty goal to be sure, but some of Shannon owners claim Schultz achieved it with the 38, his first boat. "I can't think of a better boat for the trip we made," Marsh Damerell said. And just what trip was that? A three-year, 32,000-mile circumnavigation by way of the Cape of Good Hope.

Although the Shannon 38 has been out of production for more than 15 years, it is still probably the best known of the Shannon models, and clearly represents the best value on the used boat market. It is possible to find a well-equipped 38 for a little more than $100,000. When you compare those same dollars to what they can buy new, or even 'newer,' the value in an older Shannon 38 becomes obvious. Around 100 Shannon 38s were launched during an 11-year production run. And of that number, many have circumnavigated, including a recently completed voyage aboard hull No. 1.

The Shannon 38 is a genuine semicustom boat. Schultz and his crew were, and still are, receptive to owner ideas and innovations. As a result, there are few 38s that are identical, at least when it come to the interior details.

When the 38 was finally phased out in 1986, it was replaced by the Shannon 37, the model that Beth Leonard and Evans Starzinger sailed during a well-documented circumnavigation. A 39-foot model replaced the 37 in 1994. Shannon is still building boats in Bristol, Rhode Island, and unlike other builders who treat their older, used boats like unwanted stepchildren, Shannon 38 owners report that the factory continues to offer excellent ongoing support.

Shannon 38

LOA 37'9"; LWL 30'10"
Beam 11'6"
Draft 5'
Displacement 18,500 lbs.
Ballast 6,800 lbs.
Sail Area Cutter 703 sq. feet
Water 125 gallons
Fuel 70 gallons
Engine 50 hp
Designer Stadel, Schulz and Associates

First impressions

The Shannon 38 simply looks like a cruising boat, exuding confidence whether viewed dockside or under sail. The sheerline has a comely sweep, accentuated by a pronounced bowsprit. The stern has a springy lift before trailing into a flat, slightly reversed transom, which was specially designed to support a windvane steering device. The trunkhouse is square and solid and the husky bronze portlights seem just right. A handful of 38s were built as pilothouse models. Most early 38s were ketch-rigged cutters, while later models tended to follow the overall shift to the straight cutter rig. The single spreader rig supports 703 square feet of sail area as a cutter, the mizzen ups the total sail

Shannon 38 Price Data

		Low	High
BUC Retail Range	1978	$ 79,200	$ 87,000
	1980	$104,000	$114,000
	1982	$110,000	$118,500
		State	Asking
Boats For Sale	1979	Ketch MD	$129,500
	1980	Ketch Mass.	$139,000
	1981	Cutter, FL	$126,500
	1982	Pilothouse, SC	$121,000

area by seven percent. Either rig option has a sail area/displacement ratio of around 16.5.

The Shannon has a genuine cutaway full-keel hull shape. The keel slopes gently aft and then has a long flat run to a well-protected rudder and prop aperture. This is a good hull shape to run aground in, at least from the standpoint of avoiding structural damage. It may not, however, be the easiest shape to wriggle free from the bottom's clutch.

While the 38 is no lightweight, the design displacement of 18,500 is less than one might expect for such a design. Owners repeatedly stress that the 38 is easily driven and performs more than adequately in light air.

Construction

Although Shannon proudly builds cored hulls today, the 38 has a fire retardant, hand-laid heavy-on-the-glass laminate hull. The deck is balsa-cored. Shannons have been put through the test on all the oceans of the world and few if any have reported any structural problems. Damerell noted that he and his wife, Fran, aboard their 1978 ketch *Invictus*, were nearly knocked down by a rogue wave in the Indian Ocean. "Things flew around that hadn't moved in two years of cruising," Marsh noted. "But we did no damage to the boat."

Schultz has always prided himself on paying attention to details during the construction process. A small feature like beefing up the transom layup to support a heavy self-steering windvane is an item that is not easily recognized and not something that sells boats at boat shows. It is, however, a terrific idea for a serious cruising boat and typical of the engineering mindset at Shannon. The company expects its boats to sail around the world. The hull-and-deck joint is mechanical, bolted on 8-inch centers. A solid ash cleat backs the bolts. There are extra stringers in the forward sections to prevent hull flex when working to weather in heavy weather.

Naturally, given the hull shape, the lead ballast is encapsulated in the keel cavity. Once set in place, the lead is slathered with a casting resin and then sealed with fiberglass. It's a bulletproof method of protecting the keel and also offers the advantage of a deep sump that keeps bilge water where it belongs, in the bilge. The rudder is fiberglass and the stock is stainless steel with a stainless reinforcing plate. A cast bronze rudder shoe is through bolted through the trailing edge the keel and supports the bottom of the rudder. On deck, the chainplates are 1/4-inch-by-2-inch solid stainless, bolted through transverse knees with 1/2-inch stainless bolts.

Shannon 38

Sailing Magazine's Value Guide

PRICE: You can find a boat to sail around the world for less money, but it is difficult to find a better quality boat for less money. With prices ranging between $100,000 and $130,000 the Shannon 38 is very good value indeed.

DESIGN QUALITY: The long-keel design, with a well-protected rudder and prop, has many advantages at sea. However, it is not as fast or nimble as later, cutaway keel models like the 37 and 39.

CONSTRUCTION QUALITY: The Shannon 38 was built to sail around the world, and Shultz and company take that premise very seriously. From the specially reinforced transom for mounting a steering vane to custom interiors, the boat was put together with serious sailing in mind. The only reason this is not a five rating is that some boats have blistered over the years.

USER-FRIENDLINESS: While modern cruising boats are amazingly well engineered for easy handling, sailing the Shannon 38 takes a bit more of a proactive approach. However, the sweet motion, comfortable cockpit and well-thought-out interior make the boat a capable passagemaker and a cozy home while at anchor.

SAFETY: Many of the elements that make a boat safe at sea are incorporated into the Shannon 38. Robust construction and a seakindly motion head the list. The deck fittings are stout and well-supported and there are handrails everywhere. The cockpit can take a dousing and the bridgedeck will keep green water out of the cabin.

TYPICAL CONDITION: This rating is a bit deceptive. Many Shannon 38s have logged thousands of cruising miles, and with a modest refit, are ready to go again. Some boats may be loaded up with cruising gear, much of it, however, will need to be upgraded or replaced, making it more of a bother than advantage.

REFITTING: Shultz did a fine job of considering refits right from the beginning. The engine can be removed without major surgery, so can the water and fuel tanks. Like most well-engineered products, the boat is a pleasure to work on.

SUPPORT: Shannon is unique because unlike most manufacturers in this section, it's still in business, and it also supports the company's older models with information and assistance. The company publishes an informative newsletter and its Web page www.shannonyachts.com is very helpful.

AVAILABILITY: There were just over 100 38s built, and there are usually several available on the secondhand market at any one time. However, a buyer should be prepared to travel to inspect each available boat.

INVESTMENT AND RESALE: While some may balk at paying $125,000 for a boat that is more than 25 years old, I am confident that after spending four years sailing around the world you will be able to get most of your original investment back. That can't be said for many boats.

OVERALL 'SVG' RATING

What to look for

The first thing to look for is the actual model that you want. Fifty-four Shannon 38s came down the ways with a ketch rig and 43 were delivered as cutters. Eight pilothouse versions were launched. Also, if you are sure you want a Shannon 38, you should invest the time and money to look at as many boats for sale as possible simply because the interior arrangements differ greatly. One thing that doesn't differ, however, is the overall high quality of the finish work.

Another thing to consider when buying an older 38 is the level of use. Boats that have spent the most time offshore cruising usually look better on a listing sheet because they're loaded with gear. But while the basic boat is likely ready for another circumnavigation, much of the equipment may need to be replaced. I would first look for one of the few boats that hasn't been equipped for extensive bluewater sailing and then add the gear that you want or need for your specific voyaging needs.

There are few common complaints with the 38. Damerell noted that the stanchion bases on his boat leaked. Deck leaks are common on most old boats, rebedding much of the hardware before shoving off on an extended voyage is a good idea. Other owners have also reported deck leaks, and one had to have the toerail removed and rebedded—an expensive and time consuming job.

Damerell also noted that the diamond-pattern nonskid provides great traction, but if it is a dark color, it can get hot in the sun and increase the temperature belowdecks. Later boats were equipped with a lighter colored nonskid. It is possible to paint and or replace the nonskid. In fact, the synthetic nonskid can deteriorate if the boat has been sitting in the tropics.

I usually recommend replacing the standing rigging as a matter of course for most older boats unless it has been recently replaced. The Shannon 38, however, came standard with rod rigging, which stretches less than conventional wire and has a longer life. The Navtec turnbuckles warrant more concern. Also, it seems many owners opted for Barient winches and replacement parts can be hard to find.

Like other boats of this era, Shannons had their share of blister problems. My friend Carl Wake nearly purchased a Shannon 38 pilothouse that was badly blistered, but the owner would not agree on how much of a price reduction the blister problem warranted.

On deck

The Shannon 38 has a comfortable cockpit, which in itself is something of a surprise. Most builders of this era equated small and uncomfortable with seaworthy. The cutter cockpit is more open without the mizzen mast in the companionway, yet even the ketch has a functional cockpit. Teak coamings are a bit abrupt as seat backs but can be made softer with cushions.

There are decent-sized lockers under the cockpit seats and a dedicated propane locker. Four large cockpit scuppers will move a lot of water in a hurry should the cockpit get doused. An Edson pedestal and wheel was the standard steering system. Two-speed self-tailing Barients were the usual choice for the primary sheet winches.

The synthetic diamond pattern nonskid provides excellent footing on deck, although as mentioned earlier, it can be hot under the tropical sun and it is a bit rough on the feet when barefoot. Still, the purpose of nonskid is to prevent skidding, especially when the deck is wet.

Stout teak grab rails on the trunkhouse offer added security when moving about. Interestingly, Schultz doesn't like the idea of a molded bulwark, insisting that it can trap water on deck. The teak toerail looks quite nice but it makes you a slave to maintenance. The teak rubrail with a stainless guard is very helpful when lying to less than shipshape quays in many parts of the world.

The bowsprit is solid teak and set up with stainless anchor rollers specifically for a CQR and Danforth. I am not a great fan of bowsprits, at least from a structural standpoint, but there is no denying that they make good anchoring platforms. The deck hardware is robust, including bronze deck chocks and oversized mooring cleats.

The mast is a hefty aluminum section factory painted with Awlgrip. Painted masts look nice and offer a bit of resistance to the elements but they also require more maintenance. The standing rigging is stainless steel rod. Schultz is a big believer in twin headstays, and I agree with him. Twin headstays offer flexibility should a furling system cause trouble, allow for double headsails for downwind work and a stay for a storm jib as well.

The mainsheet traveler is set up on a bridge with the control lines led aft to the cockpit. Few 38s came from the factory with all control lines led aft, which I see as an advantage. Many cruising boats not only lead every line aft, they enclose the cockpit like a bomb shelter with full bimini tops, dodgers and side curtains. This is a false sense of security. If the crew has to leave the sanctuary of the cockpit, they can feel completely out of sync on deck. To me this is more dangerous. You need to know your boat, to be able to move about the deck, and of course, feel secure in the cockpit. Shannon supplied a main with two reefs, staysail, mizzen if necessary, yankee, and later in production, 150-percent genoa.

Down below

The Shannon 38 was built as a semicustom boat and the aspect that invited the most owner interpretation was the interior plan. In reality, however, the changes were generally subtle. The arrangement usually includes a V-berth or offset double forward, sometimes with a workbench and sail bin opposite the berth, followed by the head, usually to starboard. Opposite is a large hanging locker. The saloon includes a centerline drop-leaf table, with straight settees and pilot berths. Many owners have since converted the pilot berths into lockers. Some boats feature a double quarter cabin aft, others have a conventional quarter berth and sit down chart table to port. The U-shaped galley is immediately to starboard and usually includes a three-burner stove, deep, double sinks and plenty of storage space.

The pilothouse models differ, of course, and I confess I really like the arrangement. The pilothouse has two berths, a chart table and an inside steering station. There is no quarter cabin below and the head is moved aft. The rest of the plan is similar to the standard boats.

The interior appears dark by today's standards, but the boats were built in the age of teak, and it was used for covering everything. Shannon's joinerwork reflects the New England roots of the company, and it is nicely executed and functional but not ornamental like some boats built in the Orient during the same period.

You really appreciate the quality of Shannon-built boats when you look closely at the components. There are 12 solid bronze opening portlights throughout the boat. The large teak dorade boxes have chromed hoods and deck plates. A solid teak companionway hatch is set on bronze runners that you can slam in shut in a gale and know it will take a pounding. There are three stainless steel water tanks, all self-trimming, totaling 120 gallons. The fact that the tanks can be removed without major surgery reflects the functional nature of the design and construction.

Engine

Most Shannon 38s were fitted with either a Perkins 4108 or similar Westerbeke diesel. Both engines rate anywhere between 37 to 50 horsepower, and with typical honesty, Shannon calls it a 40-horsepower. The engine is quite accessible—an important feature for long-term cruising. It can also be easily removed. In fact, Shannon claims that the engine can be removed in less than an hour. Although both engines are highly durable, it's likely that if it hasn't been replaced or rebuilt it needs to be. If I were purchasing a Shannon 38 for a world cruise and it had an engine with a lot of hours, I would simply replace it with a reconditioned 4108 short block. A short block is an engine without a transmission and other attachments that can be salvaged from the old engine. It is a very cost-efficient way to repower.

A large three-bladed bronze prop was standard, with a standard internal stuffing box. The cutless bearing is in the hull, not on a strut. A 70-gallon aluminum fuel tank is located in the keel. A dipstick is the foolproof method of checking how much fuel is left in the tank. Under normal conditions the fuel should provide roughly a motoring range of 400 to 500 miles. Like most full keel boats, the Shannon is not very nimble when powering in reverse. Speed under power in mild conditions is around 6 knots.

Underway

Fran and Marsh Damerell were in their mid-50s when they began their circumnavigation aboard *Invictus*, hull No. 12 originally commissioned in 1978. They chose the Shannon after a thorough boat search that included other manufacturers like Allied, Cheoy Lee, Valiant and Pearson. They carried five sails, a main, mizzen, staysail, yankee and 125-percent genoa. Unlike modern cruisers, the Damerells disdained motoring and they literally sailed around the world. Through 32,000 miles *Invictus* averaged just over 102 miles per day, less than a 5-knot average while passagemaking. To put that in perspective, you have to remember that sail was often reduced at night to take some stress out of the onwatch and daily runs were not inflated with long stretches of motoring. Crossing the equator in the Pacific skewed the figures downward. Their 24-hour best run was a very respectable 156 miles, which translates to a 6.5-knot during the passage from Ascension Island to Fortaleza, Brazil.

Marsh really appreciated the twin headstays, although he noted that the genoa was occasionally chafed by the hanked on yankee due to inevitable stay slag. As a rule of thumb the Damerells flew the genoa in winds to 18 knots, the yankee up to about 30 knots and the staysail above 30. Marsh says that the boat balanced quite well under mizzen and headsail only, which made life easy for the self-steering windvane. Although the staysail had a reef point, it was never used. "We were never reduced to bare poles and we never hove-to on the entire trip," he said.

Two sailing characteristic that every owner I spoke to mentioned were the balanced helm and the ability to track true. Leeway is not much a factor on a Shannon 38. While modern flat-bottomed hulls with tall narrow rigs point very high, they don't track well, especially if a sea is running. Clawing off a dangerous shore requires tracking ability more than pointing ability. Another wonderful aspect of the Shannon 38 that makes it good for world cruising is the slow, relatively gentle motion at sea. Nothing is more exhausting and uncomfortable than a bouncy, quick motion day after day.

Conclusion

Even if you plan to spend more than $100,000 to $130,000 on a boat, you should consider the Shannon 38. It is an ideal size for a cruising couple, and the boat has been proven on all the world's oceans. From construction and engineering details to the overall seakindliness of the long-keel design, this boat is at home on the high seas. Also, owning a Shannon 38 usually translates into a solid investment. The resale value has remained strong over the years, making the 38 the perfect vehicle for a cruising sabbatical.

Fast Passage 39

I was reluctant to include the Fast Passage 39 in the 10 Best. Not because it isn't an excellent boat for world voyaging. (It is a veteran circumnavigator proven by way of the Great Capes and the Southern Ocean.) And not because it isn't an excellent value on the used boat market. (It represents a sound investment with prices hovering around \$120,000 to \$130,000 for late models.) The reason I was reluctant to include the Fast Passage 39 was because there were only 40 boats built during its first production run. After much consideration, though, I decided to feature the boat for three reasons. Firstly, it is one of my favorite offshore boats, and after all, I am the author. Secondly, it just maybe the best boat, dollar for dollar, that you can buy for passagemaking. And thirdly, if you fall in love with the Fast Passage 39 but can't find a used one or would like a more updated version, it is now back in limited production.

Jeremiah Mitchel and his company Noah Corporation purchased the original tooling, intending to build new custom FP 39s at Padden Creek Marine in Bellingham, Washington. Of course, a new FP39 will put a much deeper dent in your pocketbook, but the new boat is clearly an improved version of the original, benefiting from 20 years of material and manufacturing development and invaluable owner feedback. The fact that the FP 39 is being built again, even in a limited one-off fashion, enhances the value of older boats too. Mitchell is a terrific source of information and can also provide parts and materials for refits on the older 39s.

In many ways, the Fast Passage is better known than it should be, considering the modest number of boats launched. The William Garden design traces it roots to one of his earlier boats, a 40-foot long-keeled sloop called *Bolero* that was built by Philbrooks Shipyard in Sidney, British Columbia. Denny Coverdale, who worked for the shipyard, asked

Fast Passage 39

LOA 39'6"
LWL 33'6"
Beam 11'10"
Draft 5'6"
Displacement 21,000 lbs.
Ballast 7,500 lbs.
Sail Area 795 sq. feet
Water 100 gallons
Fuel 53 gallons
Engine 40-60 hp
Designer William Garden

Fast Passage 39 Price Data

		Low	High
BUC Retail Range	1979	$ 92,000	$101,000
	1981	$106,000	$115,000
	1983	$116,000	$127,500

		State	Asking
Boats For Sale	1979	MD	$130,000
	1980	FL	$129,500

Garden to design a more modern version of *Bolero*, suitable for stock production. The result was the Fast Passage 39, a boat Garden said is the one he would take cruising.

Philbrooks built the first 36 hulls, some of which were sold as kit boats and owner finished. Eventually, Tollycraft Corporation in Kelso, Washington, obtained the molds and built four boats before production stopped in 1985 after a 10-year run.

One of the Tollycraft boats was sold to accomplished ocean racer Francis Stokes. Stokes christened his FP 39 *Mooneshine*, the name of all of his boats, and competed in the first BOC singlehanded around-the-world race. Stokes sailed to second place in Class 2, cementing the sterling bluewater reputation of the Fast Passage 39. The boat was reviewed in 1983 by *Practical Sailor*. "After the trip (Stokes' BOC circumnavigation) the boat looked no worse than it would have after a 650-mile passage to Bermuda," the article said.

First impressions

At first glance the Fast Passage 39 seems like the offspring of a classic Garden design mated with Bob Perry's early work. Discussing boat genetics may land me in trouble, but the boat is an intriguing blend from a design perspective. The FP 39 is often compared to Perry's classic of the same era, the Valiant 40, which incidentally, was the boat Stokes owned before purchasing the FP 39.

The bow is classic Garden—pronounced, with a generous overhang and a bit of flare. All that's missing is a bowsprit, thank goodness. And while this shape may not be the very best for going to weather, it will keep the crew dry. Maximum beam is reached rather far aft before tapering off at the cockpit and quickly narrowing into a canoe stern. A double-ended hull shape with a sweeping sheerline was almost essential in the mid-1970s if the boat was to be considered a bluewater cruiser. For better and worse, the Westsail 32 was the trendsetter, as odd as that might seem today. The FP 39 has a lot of tumblehome in the topsides, which keeps the motion smooth when heeled. The deckhouse is curved on the edges, and it is lower and much less boxy than the Valiant 40's. The curves are a bit unusual, however, and you will either like this look a lot or not at all. To me, the graceful curves are a large part of the FP 39's charm.

Below the waterline is where the FP 39 really shines, which is where the comparisons to Valiant 40 become obvious, and ironically, so do the differences. The vital statistics are nearly identical—the FP 39 displaces 22,000 pounds and has 7,500 pounds of ballast, while the Valiant 40 weighs in at 22,500 pounds with 7,700 pounds of ballast. LOA, LWL and sail area of the two boats are comparable. However, if you look carefully at the underwater sections, the FP 39 hull shape is slightly more refined, with just a tad less wetted surface area than the Valiant 40. The 39's forefoot is cutaway and a bit flatter than the 40's. The cutaway behind the powerful fin keel also bites a little deeper. The FP 39 has a proportionally larger rudder, although both boats include stout skegs and a strut for the shaft.

Construction

As noted earlier, Philbrooks Shipyards in British Columbia built most of the boats. These early boats, which represent the best deals if not always the best boats, are usually found on the West Coast. The hull of the FP 39 is Airex cored, a sandwich construction that when properly executed creates a lighter and stronger hull than a solid laminate. Solid fiberglass is used in areas of high-stress loads around fastenings and fittings. The deck is balsa cored and joined to the hull on an inward flange, through bolted on 8-inch centers. One area that separates the FP 39 from the Valiant 40 is the ballast. The FP 39 ballast is internal, the cast lead is placed into the keel cavity and glassed over. The Valiant on the other hand, has a lead shoe that is bolted to the bottom of a rather hefty keel section. The debate about which ballasting method is just that, a debate. I prefer internal ballast for the simple reason that it eliminates the need for keel bolts. However, with that said, I have actually logged more miles with externally fastened keels.

Stokes reported no structural concerns during his epic circumnavigation, which is pretty impressive for an off-the-shelf production boat. Of course, the overall construction quality is better than most production boats. The bulkheads are securely tabbed in place. The floors are meaty and well supported. The maststep is on a bridge in the bilge, limiting corrosion of the spar end. Also, the many curves in the design, from the tumblehome in the hull to the slope in the cabintrunk, offers inherent form strength. It may not be an easy way to mold a boat but it's a good way.

What to look for

"The two biggies in the older boats are delaminated decks and rudders," Mitchel said. Incidentally, Mitchel uses all synthetic coring in his new boats. Mitchel contacted every owner he could find before he began building his first boat. Their suggestions constitute a what-to-look-for list.

The original rudders were foam, with fiberglass overlay and were not particularly well built. However, this has been a well-documented problem and most FP 39 owners have likely corrected the problem. A friend of mine purchased a 1982 FP 39 a few years ago and the rudder showed no signs of deterioration. The delamination in the deck comes from leaks that have caused the balsa core to rot. This is a more difficult problem to fix, although it doesn't seem to be widespread.

Some owners have reported problems with the steering cables working loose, but this is probably because the boats have been worked hard. All boats originally had swage fittings on the shrouds, and my friend's boat had cracked swages on the aftershrouds. One of the most important things to look for is the quality of the finish. Some boats were owner finished, and the quality can vary dramatically. A lower than usual asking price is generally a tip that the boat is likely a kit boat. Don't be to quick to reject a kit boat, because you really don't buy a Fast Passage 39 for the ornate joinerwork. You buy a 39 for its seakindly nature. And early kit boats can be real bargains.

On deck

The cockpit is a genuine seagoing cockpit, but not so extreme as to be miserably uncomfortable. The seat backs are high and slightly angled for good back support, while the overall volume is small, making it able to withstand a pooping without much trouble. It is a bit tight maneuvering around the wheel, but that is rather common when you marry pedestal steering with a canoe stern. Most previous owners will have redirected the sail controls to the aft end of coachroof. The self-tailing Lewmar primary and secondary sheet winches are reachable from the helm and visibility is good over the low-slung deckhouse. The mainsheet arrangement is a bit awkward on the older boats. It either runs to a traveler that spans the cockpit sole just forward of the wheel or aft, at a bad angle, to the stern deck. Both of these systems allow for end-boom sheeting. New FP 39s have a traveler bridge over the companionway, moving the sheet out of the cockpit. Most used boats will have a dodger and bimini for protection from spray and sun, and if these are well worn, they're not inexpensive to replace.

There is no disputing that the FP 39 is a good boat for singlehanding. Remember, if you are planning to cruise as a couple, you will be essentially singlehanding much of the time. A cruising couple should set their boat up for solo sailing because it is critical for the person on watch to be able to handle the boat without waking his or her partner. The most underrated concern with bluewater sailing is the lack of proper rest. Fatigue is your enemy as sea. I have few rules during long passages, but preserving the sanctity of the off watch is an important one. The FP 39 is ideal for a cruising couple.

A molded bulwark with a wide teak caprail and vertically mounted stanchions with double lifelines offer good security for moving about the deck. Stout teak rails running the length of the deck provide convenient handholds. The only negative is that the side decks are a bit narrow, especially when sliding around the shrouds. There is a stainless steel double anchor roller and an overboard draining chain locker, although the locker is accessed from the forepeak. The deck hardware is robust, from turning blocks to mooring cleats to bow and stern pulpits.

The aluminum mast is most often a Spartech with an air draft just a shade less than 57 feet. The cutter rig was standard and working sail area is 735 square feet. The headsail tracks are sheeted inboard, not on the caprail, allowing for better sheeting angles but cluttering up the side decks. Most boats are set up with slab reefing on the main and furling gear on the headsail, which is usually a yankee. The staysail may be roller furling, or hanked on, and it may or may not be

Fast Passage 39

Sailing Magazine's Value Guide

PRICE: The Fast Passage is not cheap, and is comparable to Valiant 40s of the same era in many ways. Look to pay from anywhere from $100,000 to $125,000 for a late model. An early Philbrooks kit boat can be real bargain, or it can be a homemade special.

DESIGN QUALITY: The Garden design is superb—nice to look at, fast in most conditions and unquestionably seaworthy. Hard to find fault with anything in this department.

CONSTRUCTION QUALITY: The FP 39 was well put together, evidenced by the many successful bluewater passages accomplished. The hull is airex cored, which is more resistant to water than other early coring materials.

SAFETY: Solid construction and seaworthy design are the main contributors to any boat's safety, and the FP 39 scores well in both categories. A small cockpit, large bridgedeck, molded bulwark and other features make the 39 a safe boat.

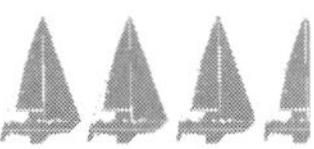

TYPICAL CONDITION: As noted above, there are not many FP 39s that turn up the secondhand market, and when they do, they don't linger long. Most boats have been sailed far and wide, but the several that I have examined were well cared for by knowledgeable owners.

REFITTING: Some aspects of the design make working on the boat a bit challenging. Also, both of the original manufacturers are long out of business.

SUPPORT: Thank goodness for Jeremiah Mitchel, he is a font of information about the boat. His company builds new FP 39s on a limited basis, and he can help track down parts and offer technical advice. His e-mail address is, jmitc723@peak.org, and you can visit the FP on the Web at, www.boatshow.com/thefast passagecompany.html.

AVAILABILITY: This rating is a bit unfair, and lowers the overall rating unduly. However, if you want a FP 39 you must be patient and prepared to move when one comes on the market.

INVESTMENT AND RESALE: The FP 39 represents a sound investment, both as capable world cruiser and a boat that is desirable on the secondhand market.

OVERALL 'SVG' RATING

self-tacking. The FP 39 is a genuine cutter and the staysail is an integral part of the sailplan.

Down below

Dropping below, the aft stateroom is off to port with the nav station and a quarter berth opposite. The aft cabin features a tight double bunk with storage underneath. Access to the engine compartment is through the bulkhead in this cabin. The head is forward of the nav station with the galley opposite. The nav station desk can support a good-sized chart, and if you can resist filling up the quarter berth, it will make a perfect sea berth. An amidships head is typical of the design premise—this is a boat for offshore sailing. Anyone who has tried to attend to business up forward in a rough sea will appreciate the placement of the head in the FP 39. However, some argue that it wastes valuable interior space, and it does seem like the saloon is located quite far forward.

The U-shaped galley has large twin sinks facing aft with the cooker outboard. My friend's boat has a three-burner Force 10 stove and oven. The fridge is forward facing with good counter space above. Not surprisingly the fiddles will actually keep the sliced vegetables from tumbling to the sole in a moderate seaway and there is plenty of room to brace yourself while cooking under way. The saloon is rather straightforward. The table is offset to port with a wraparound settee and there's a straight settee to starboard. Stainless steel water tanks are usually located under the settees. Most FP 39s have around 100 gallons in three tanks, the third tank is usually in the bilge under the saloon sole. The water tank is located under the V-berth on the new 39. There is some arrangement of shelves and cabinets above the berths. Remember, some 39s were finished by their owners and the arrangement and quality of finish can vary. The factory-built boats were finished in teak veneers and are somewhat dark below. The craftsmanship is workmanlike. Handholds are well placed throughout the interior.

The V-berth is forward, usually with storage underneath and shelves along side. The overall arrangement is ideal for a couple with occasional guests or a family with small children. In the real world of cruising, the V-berth and the quarter berth often become storage areas. The problem with fitting everything away in lockers is that every time you need something it becomes an ordeal to find it. You must unpack everything around it, dig out what you need and repack the locker. It is easier sometimes to have larger areas where items can be tossed randomly, especially when in port.

Engine

Most FP 39s were fitted with Perkins 4108 diesels. These good engines are familiar to many sailors. Rated anywhere from 35 to 50 horsepower, they are reliable, rebuildable and all in all perfectly acceptable marine engines. Although no longer in production, parts continue to be widely available. In fact, a quick look online will usually reveal many 4108s in various stages, from rebuilt short blocks to virtually complete new engines. Although Mitchel is using 42-horsepower Yanmars in his new boats, if I were repowering an older FP 39, I'd stick with a rebuilt Perkins 4108. It will cost less than half and will fit onto the same footprint.

The engine is mounted on heavy longitudinal stringers and is well secured. Unfortunately, access is marginal at best. The traditional flax-style stuffing box is difficult to reach and service. The 53-gallon aluminum fuel tank is usually found in the bilge forward of the engine, or all the way forward under the V-berth. It is a safe bet to assume the 4108 will burn one gallon per hour at cruising speed. The FP 39's easily driven hull attains 6-plus knots under power without too much strain, rendering a cruising range of 300 to 350 miles.

Underway

When it comes to discussing the sailing characteristics of the FP 39, who better to reference than Francis Stokes. Stokes wrote about his BOC passage in a book called **The Mooneshine Logs**, published by Sheridan House in 1994. If you are considering an FP 39, by all means buy this book. Stokes was delighted with the boat's performance under the full spectrum of conditions. He liked that the boat was effective in light conditions, despite its genuine cruising pedigree. This is a point often overlooked. A boat must be able to stand up to a severe blow, but the majority of cruising is done in light to moderate air and it is frustrating trying to coax a slow, heavy boat along in the light stuff.

Stokes used heavy sails, heavier than is really needed for most cruising conditions. His largest working sail was a 140 percent genoa. Interestingly, he writes that the moderate draft of 5 feet, 6 inches worked to his advantage when sailing downwind. "Moderate draft allows a boat to slew sideways if caught wrong by a wave instead of tripping over it." He also noted that the boat responded beautifully to self-steering, with both an Aries windvane and Alpha Marine autopilot. It is critical that cruising boats have reliable self-steering.

Stokes compared the Fast Passage and Valiant, having crossed oceans in both boats. He said that he reefed a bit earlier in the FP 39 but maintained similar speeds with less sail area. He also noted that he needed to keep the boat more or less on its lines when sailing upwind to avoid making excessive leeway. He mentions that the boat sailed very well with two reefed headsails. In heavy going he carried a storm jib, staysail and a double-reefed main. His best-24 hour passage was 190 miles.

Conclusion

The FP 39 is a wonderful boat for bluewater sailing. It can stand up to the gales of the Southern Ocean, yet keep moving in the fluky breezes near the equator. The interior is practical and comfortable and overall construction is very good quality. The only problem is that there are not many to choose from on the used boat market. If one does suddenly come available, take a serious look and be prepared to buy it. You won't be disappointed.

Beneteau First 38

Forty feet seems like the magic number when it comes to offshore boats. There are perhaps more 40-footers specifically designed and built for world cruising than any other overall length. The legendary Valiant 40, the classic Hinckley Bermuda 40, the groundbreaking Cal 40 are completely different from one another yet are all very capable of sailing around the world. The list of other great 40-foot world cruisers is long and illustrious—the Bristol 40, the Passport 40, the Island Packet 40, the Nordic 40, the Norseman 400, the Caliber 40 to name only a few. It seems designers and builders have focused their energies on 40-footers. I chose the Beneteau First 38 with a length overall of 40 feet, 2 inches as part of the 10 Best for the simple reason that it's a proven world cruiser, something of a modern classic from a design standpoint and it may be the very best value in this book.

This statement may confuse some readers, especially when you look at the other nine boats in this section. For the most part they are heavy, long-keel types with short production runs. Beneteau, the largest sailboat manufacturer in the world, is a quintessential production builder. But large production numbers do not necessarily translate into poor quality, and Beneteau's early First Series boats were very well constructed. It is safe to say that more Beneteau designs have crossed the Atlantic on their own bottoms than any other brand of boat.

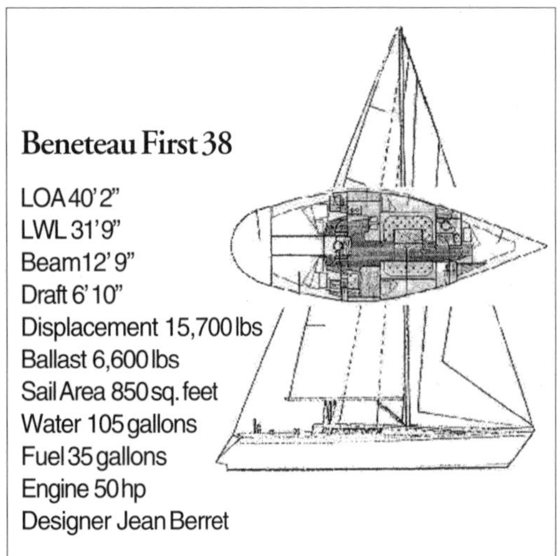

The First 38, designed by Jean Berret, was launched in 1982 and most of the boats were built between 1984 and 1985. Several hundred boats were built. Some were exported directly to North America, while many were sailed across the pond on their own bottoms by new owners during the days when the U.S. dollar was incredibly strong.

The First Series was launched in 1979 with the sleek Berret-designed 30. Beneteau might have coined the phrase performance cruiser with this line of boats. During the next few years Beneteau built three specific boats that stand out as some of my favorites: The First 38, of course, the Frers designed First 42 and the First 456. These boats combine good performance, solid construction, great looks and very livable accommodations. The reason I'm focusing on the First 38 is twofold. The boat is widely available on the used boat market in the United States and Canada and it is possible to find a clean, lightly used 38 for less than $60,000.

First impressions

The First 38 has a modern profile, which may sound quaint given the fact that the design is nearly 20 years old, but the angular, hard-edged looks of this design helped set the stage for the shape of yacht design that continues today. It is a look you either love or hate depending on your politics. I'm partial to the older First Series boats, especially the 38, while I don't particularly like the curvaceous look of Beneteau's Oceanus lineup. I formed my opinions while delivering a 1983 First 38 across the Atlantic, making a swift, trouble-free passage from Cape Verde Island to Antigua, and by singlehanding another 38 from Virgin Gorda to Ft. Lauderdale, Florida.

If you squint while looking at the drawings you will notice a slight dip in the sheerline. The entry is finely raked and the reverse transom is quite wide. The First 38 predates the transom swim step development, but it isn't uncommon to find a boat that has some type of scoop or step arrangement retrofitted, especially on boats that have spent their life in the Caribbean . The cabintop is a wedge-deck type, and the overall profile is low and sleek. The portlights are dark Plexiglas usually in conjunction with a couple of aluminum framed opening portlights. French builders, with their flair for style, just can't resist using colorfully painted or taped racing stripes along the hull or cabin sides to accent the sleek lines.

Below the water, the First 38 steers a different course from most of the boats in this section. The deep fin keel has a standard draft of 7 feet and the shoal version's draft is just over 6 feet. The rudder is a balanced spade, offering good steering control, especially in following seas, although there is no disputing its vulnerability.

A close inspection of the line drawings and a bit of number crunching will reveal why the First 38 is a capable seagoing boat. The forefoot, although flatish, has more bite to it than the modern Bruce Farr-designed First Series boats. The First 38 will occasionally surf down a wave, but more importantly, it can be sailed upwind in a blow without causing uncomfortable motion or making too much leeway.

The design displacement of 15,652 pounds is moderate, while the iron ballast of 6,613 pounds represents a hefty ballast/displacement ratio of 42 percent. The First 38's hull shape can't be overloaded with a lot of cruising gear without quickly dropping the waterline, a disadvantage for long-term cruising. But even assuming a cruising displacement of 20,000 pounds, the ratio is still 33 percent, which is more than most modern boats after the numbers are realistically adjusted for cruising loads.

Beneteau First 38 Price Data

		Low	High
BUC Retail Range	1983	$53,400	$59,000
	1984	$56,900	$62,500
	1985	$61,300	$67,300
		State	**Asking**
Boats For Sale	1984	MI	$59,900
	1984	VA	$72,000
	1985	Caribbean	$64,500

The standard rig is a single-spreader sloop, although a tall rig was also offered. In 1986, the First 38 morphed into the First 40.5, a similar but more elegantly finished boat built from the same basic tooling. The First 38.5 introduced in 1991 was a completely different model.

Construction

Beneteau has always done a good job of blending production efficiencies with time-tested construction techniques. The First 38 has a solid, hand-laid fiberglass hull that includes a partial molded liner. This structural grid system adds hull rigidity and streamlines the manufacturing process. Beneteau's use of liners is quite practical as the hull liner itself is only about 2 feet high, allowing unlimited access to the hull above the liner. There are cutouts through the liner in the bilge area as well. The liner is fiberglassed directly to the hull, in effect creating a rugged system of floors and stringers. The liner does not preclude the more traditional methods of tabbing bulkheads securely to the hull. In fact, the bulkheads are glassed all around and bolted through the molded pan where applicable. Liza and Andy Copeland, who have logged more than 70,000 miles on their 1984 First 38 *Bagheera* have reported that not only has their boat not suffered from structural problems during all their travels but that it never creaks or moans, even in heavy going. Liza's books, **Just Cruising, Still Cruising** and **Cruising for Cowards**, are great references for anyone considering a First 38.

Beneteau First 38

Sailing Magazine's Value Guide

PRICE: Prices range from less than $60,000 to around $80,000. By any measure, the First 38 is a lot of boat for the money.

DESIGN QUALITY: The Berret design includes many features in a small package. The hull shape is easily driven and the accommodation plan is ideal for family cruising. Unlike other modern boats built in the early 1980s, the design doesn't look outdated.

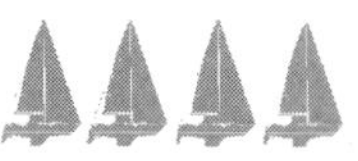

CONSTRUCTION QUALITY: Beneteau's early First Series boats were very well built, better than most people realize. The intelligent use of a low hull liner, heavy layup and good gear add up to a boat that has aged surprisingly well.

USER-FRIENDLINESS: It's an easy boat to handle as the loads are a bit lighter than those found on heavy cruisers. The systems are well-designed. The boat also handles well under power. The galley is small but functional.

SAFETY: The helmsperson is a bit exposed, making a dodger and bimini essential. The deck is easy to navigate but the stanchions could be taller. The hull shape does not heave-to easily.

TYPICAL CONDITION: Although plenty of boats were chartered in the Caribbean and Mediterranean, many were also privately owned. Good original construction has helped the boat hold up.

REFITTING: The First 38 is not the easiest boat to work on, as space is a bit tight. However, the basic systems are simple, especially compared to today's boats. It's possible to find a boat that hasn't been cruised and was lightly used. You can then fit the boat out without having to undo or update old cruising gear and systems.

SUPPORT: Beneteau provides a lot of useful information about its old models and there is an active owner's association. Three good Web sites are, www.beneteau-owners.com, www.beneteau.com and www.beneteauusa.com.

AVAILABILITY: With hundreds of boats built and many exported to North America there is always a good selection of boats available. I would look for a Great Lakes boat that hasn't been outfitted for world cruising.

INVESTMENT AND RESALE: Beneteau's continued success as the largest sailboat manufacturer in the world helps maintain value in its used boats, even if the older boats tend to compete with newer models. The First 38 is well-respected around the world and you should be able to get most of your money back after your cruise.

OVERALL 'SVG' RATING

The deck is balsa cored, and the hull-and-deck joint includes the aluminum toerail. Deck delamination or even mild gelcoat crazing is uncommon. The molded nonskid pattern seems to hold up very well and the overall fiberglass work is finished to a high standard.

The deck molding is very intricate. Beneteau was one of the first builders to include small details like locker drains and handles in the tooling instead of adding them afterward. The iron keel is bolted to the bottom of the boat and nicely faired. It is likely that somewhere along the way most boats have had the keel epoxy coated. The keel bolts are stainless steel and are incorporated into the molded liner. The rudder stock is stainless steel while the quadrant and most components in the steering system are aluminum. The keel-stepped spar has an air draft of 55 feet.

Interior construction of the First 38 includes teak veneers on the bulkheads and fabric headliners. The feel is warm and the engineering clever. Most trim pieces are flat and straight, while the few wooden curves are created in a jig for precision. Most people are surprised at the fine joinerwork and overall high level of finish in the older First Series boats.

What to look for

Beneteaus were hard hit by the bottom pox in the 1980s, and First 38s were not spared from osmotic blisters. The company truly established its well-respected identity in the United States by standing by its boats and paying for the bottom repair jobs. While companies with less wherewithal stonewalled customers, Beneteau paid the tab. The result was that most 38 bottoms have been repaired correctly, and when inspecting a prospective boat, be sure to find out if, when and how a bottom job was completed.

The perception that the First 38 was a lightly built boat vanishes when you begin to examine the boats on the used boat market—most have held up surprisingly well. Be wary of boats that have spent time in the charter trade, or least be aware of it. Although the First 38 was not specifically designed as a charter boat, plenty went into service. Clues that give away a boat's history include high hours on the Perkins 4108 diesel, worn out cabin soles and generic two-sail inventories. A common problem with First 38s are droopy headliners. This is more of an annoyance than a problem, but the foam-backed fabric liner is difficult to re-glue and messy to replace.

Other items to look for include crazing and cracking in the portlights. Most original hardware was Goiot, and it has seemed to have held up well, although the overhead hatches may also be badly crazed. The Perkins 4108 is a workhorse of an engine, but newer models are quieter, cleaner and more efficient. Be on the lookout for a boat with a new engine. Joe Kelly, an Irishman who sailed his First 38 across the Atlantic, said that he had to replace his steering cables twice during his first three years of ownership. Naturally all age-related items, from standing rigging to lifeline terminals and running rigging should be checked and replaced if suspect.

On deck

The First 38's cockpit is deceptively large and quite comfortable. I remember tucking under the dodger and catnapping during a singlehanded delivery. I was able to stretch out and sleep, albeit in 30-minute intervals. Beneteau was a pioneer in molding ergonomics into the cockpit. The seatbacks are angled for support, foot supports on the cabin sole keep you in your seat when heeled and the sheet winches are well placed to be reached by the helmsperson.

The cockpit lockers are restricted in size because of the twin aft cabins below. The cockpit sole actually unbolts, allowing for easy engine removal—a most practical feature in a world cruiser. The large Goiot wheel and steering system is placed far aft, which means that a decent-sized table can be deployed in the cockpit, however the helmsperson can feel a bit exposed.

There is a stout bridgedeck and four large scuppers. The Copelands, who spent six years circumnavigating with their three young sons, further protected the cockpit with a dodger, bimini and lifeline spray panels. They also eventually installed a stern arch for mounting solar panels, a wind generator and the radar dome.

The mainsheet traveler runs just forward of the companionway hatch, keeping the cockpit clear, but this arrangement places a lot of load on the boom, a compromise worth making if you spread the load along the boom. The side decks are wide with the shrouds placed well inboard. The genoa tracks are also inboard, allowing for tight sheeting angles. The aluminum toerail is not really designed for supporting sheet or spinnaker loads, but it's hard to resist snapping a snatch block to the rail for a better lead when flying a cruising chute. The stanchions and bases are a bit light and the double lifelines could be taller. Boats that are rigged for cruising may have added a removable babystay to fly a staysail or storm jib. Be sure to check the installation of the chainplate carefully.

There is a double anchor roller forward, and although it seems a bit undersized when compared to other bluewater cruisers, it's adequate. Remember, a 20,000-pound boat doesn't require the same ground tackle as a 40,000-pound boat. The Copelands carry a 33-pound Bruce as their main anchor and a 45-pound CQR as their second anchor. A 22-pound Danforth is used primarily as a kedge anchor. Still, a custom stainless steel stemhead fitting with beefy rollers would be a nice addition. The external chain locker is quite large and can house a windlass. The mooring cleats and fairleads are aluminum and have seemed to held up to heavy use.

Down below

One of the reasons the Copelands chose the First 38 was the clever three-cabin layout. Of course, they were traveling as a family of five. The boat appeals to me for the same reason—my two daughters would love to have their own cabins. Many cruisers, however, don't want three cabins as it's a waste of space on a 40-foot boat. Although a two cabin model was offered, a quick look at the listings on the Beneteau Owner's Web site shows that the vast majority of boats have three cabins and two heads.

Don't let the interior arrangement put you off the First 38. It is easy to convert one of the cabins and the small aft head into a storage garage, which is very useful item on a cruising boat. There's would be more room than a large cockpit locker and the security is better.

The rest of the interior works well. In the bow there is a standard V-berth cabin with a large bunk and shelves above. The head is to port with a hanging locker opposite. The saloon features a good-sized wraparound table with a settee to port. A straight settee, which makes a good sea berth, is opposite. The original plan also included pilot berths above, but these were small, and most boats that I've inspected have had this space converted into extra storage. The table leaf opens and six people can actually sit comfortably it—a sure sign that the French take their meals seriously. The teak finish may be a bit dark, but it certainly eliminates the plastic feel sometimes associated with production boats.

The nav station is one of the First 38's best features, and you can actually work on a large chart without having to fold it more than once. The chart desk holds a decent supply of charts and nav books and guides fit on an outboard shelf. The seat is very comfortable, with a cushion back located against the bulkhead. The compact U-shaped galley includes two small sinks, a two-burner stove with oven and modest sized icebox. Most boats have 12-volt refrigeration systems, and some previous owners have gone to great lengths to improve upon the original insulation. There is a surprising amount of useful storage, and Liza Copeland claims she never had a problem stowing enough provisions to last for months at a stretch. Counter space is minimal, although deep fiddles will help keep things in place when the going gets bumpy.

There is a double berth in each of the two aft cabins, and both have hanging lockers and shelves along the hull. A tiny head is squeezed between the two. The Copelands converted this head into extra storage. It can also makes a good wet locker. Ventilation belowdecks is only marginal, with several overhead hatches but only a few opening portlights. Fans are an essential addition, especially if you're headed for the tropics. Tankage is usually located under the settees and aft bunks.

Engine

The Perkins 4108 is tucked behind the companionway steps. Access is also gained through the aft cabins and through the cockpit sole when refitting a new engine. It is probably safe to assume that the 4108 has logged more hours than any other cruising diesel, although the four-cylinder Yanmar, which is today's engine of choice, is in close pursuit. Nominally rated at 50 horsepower, the 4108 ultimately delivers far less oomph by the time the prop spins, but it is still plenty of engine for the First 38. There were several days of calms during my singlehanded passage and I easily maintained 6 knots at 1900 rpms. The engine ran smooth—it hardly seemed like it was working up a sweat.

The Copelands have put more than 10,000 hours on their boat's 4108, and my mother, who sailed her Jeanneau *Gin Fizz* that was similar in length and shape to the First 38, easily put more than 6,000 hours on a seawater-cooled 4108. Although the model is no longer in production, parts are widely available. Also, if you choose to repower but don't want to endure the cost of a new engine, you can buy a completely rebuilt 4108 for less than $5,000 or a short block rebuild for less than $3,000. The advantage is that you can use the same engine footprint and accessories like the throttle cables and instrument panels.

A fin-keel spade-rudder hull shape handles much better in reverse than long-keel boats with attached rudders like the Alberg 37, Shannon 38 or Mason 43. You will truly appreciate the First 38 hull shape when attempting to Med moor. Once you have way on you can steer the 38 almost as well in reverse as when going forward. The fuel capacity of 40 gallons is pretty skimpy for a world cruising boat and will likely need to be upgraded. Charging the batteries during a medium length offshore passage will consume much of this fuel. It is safe to assume that a 4108 will burn about one gallon per hour under load.

Underway

I have sailed across the Atlantic many times, in a wide variety of boats, large and small, but my best week's run was aboard a First 38. We reeled off 1,240 miles in seven days for an average of 177 miles a day and an average speed of 7.4 knots. That is good going for any boat, especially for a sustained period of time. The winds were moderate in the 18- to 22-knot range and we sailed with either a poled out genoa or a cruising spinnaker. I came close to a 200-mile day on my solo passage before the trades petered out. The Copelands have averaged 150 miles a day throughout their travels.

The motion of the First 38 is livelier than other boats on the 10 Best list as it tends to sail on top of the water not in it. Still, it isn't as fatiguing as newer, lighter shapes that greet every wave with a bang. The steering is light on most points of sail, in fact, the steering is almost always a fingertip affair as the boat is well balanced. During their travels, the Copelands relied on an Aries windvane (not the most sensitive self-steering equipment), which is another indicator of good balance. I used a small belt-driven autopilot when singlehanding and we hand steered across the Atlantic.

The boat is relatively dry. It's also fastest when sailed flat, avoiding the mistake of overloading the boat and heeling it hard. The first reef should be tied in when the winds are steadily more than 16 knots. The Copeland's recently installed in-the-boom furling on the main, and as proponents of a full-batten, large-roach main, they love the system.

The First 38 tracks well, and unless the seas are large, it makes no more leeway than some of the heavier boats profiled. Some of the 38s are set up to adjust the genoa leads while under load—a great feature. The First 38 is a pleasure to sail even when the wind is light, which sets it apart from many world cruisers. Handling the boat in a gale does requires more management than a heavy boat, though, and the hull shape doesn't lend itself to easily heaving-to.

Conclusion

The First 38 is an economical vehicle for world cruising, especially if you plan to cruise as a family and need the three-cabin arrangement. It can carry you to the watery crossroads with speed and comfort. The boat is widely available on the secondhand market and also maintains good resale value. The maintenance is modest and the systems are not overly complex, making it a fine boat for a sailing sabbatical.

Tayana 42

The Tayana Vancouver 42 just may be the most practical boat in this section of the book. It's an ideal combination of seagoing design, robust construction and livable interior. It is also a sound value, and unlike most of the boats I have profiled, it is still in production, albeit in very limited fashion. Although a new boat hasn't been built in several years, you can, if your heart is set on it, order a new Tayana V 42. I would strongly recommend against it, however. Why spend $300,000 and wait a year or more for a boat to be built when a well-placed $125,000 will buy a nicely equipped used Tayana V 42? Of course some people simply must have new toys, but those folks are probably not reading this book anyway. The fact that the tools are still active is important, because it is nice to be able to purchase parts and retrofit items for a used Tayana Vancouver 42 directly from the manufacturer.

The Tayana 42 was the largest of designer Robert Harris's Vancouver series until a 46-foot pilothouse model went into production recently. These rugged cruisers, most with a signature stair-stepped cabintrunk, include a well-respected 27-foot pocket cruiser that recently carried Englishwoman and singlehander Rona House around the world, and a lesser-well-known but equally capable 36-footer. These boats were originally built by a couple of different yards in British Columbia and later by Northshore Yachts in England. Introduced in 1979, the Tayana Vancouver 42 is the most popular model, with nearly 200 boats launched. It has always been built by Ta Yang in Taiwan.

Ta Yang, located in the boatbuilding city of Kaohsiung, was one of the early yards to build cruising boats in the island nation of Taiwan. Some early boats built by Ta Yang include the Sea Wolf 41, also known as the Yankee Clipper, and the Tanton cat ketch. Tayana, which means grand ocean in Taiwanese, became the trademark of Ta Yang with the introduction of the Robert Perry-designed 37 in 1979. Nearly 600 of these legendary double-enders have been built, making it one of the most popular bluewater cruisers ever. The Tayana Vancouver 42 followed on the heels of the 37 as Ta Yang went on to become one of the first yards to scale up and produce big cruising boats, including the popular Perry-designed 52 and Harris-designed 65. The company continues to build a complete range of boats today, with the 48-foot center-cockpit model being one of its most successful models.

Tayana 42

LOA 41'9"
LWL 33'0"
Beam 12'6"
Draft 5'10"
Displacement 29,147 lbs.
Ballast 11,800 lbs.
Sail Area 1009 sq. feet
Water 150 gallons
Fuel 120 gallons
Engine 44 hp
Designer Robert Harris

First impressions

Your first impression of the Tayana V 42 will depend upon which of the three distinct deck arrangements you're looking at. The original deck plan included a pronounced step in the trunkhouse that actually gives the 42 a pilothouse profile. A later version, the aft-cockpit cabintrunk model, featured a lower trunkhouse that blends naturally into the hull's proud sheerline. This version is the best looking of the three. Approximately one quarter of the production run featured a center-cockpit arrangement that ironically

Tayana 42 Price Data

		Low	High
BUC Retail Range	1980	$ 95,000	$103,500
	1985	$124,000	$135,000
	1987	$152,000	$170,000

		State	Asking
Boats For Sale	1981 Center-Cockpit	FL	$119,000
	1983 Aft-Cockpit	TX	$122,500
	1983 Center-Cockpit	CA	$140,000
	1987 Aft-Cockpit	FL	$159,000

is the least pleasing aesthetically but is clearly the most in demand by world cruisers.

All three deck versions have the same hull shape and specifications. As mentioned above, there is a pronounced sheer, and as a result, a fair bit of freeboard, especially up forward. This makes the Tayana Vancouver a dry boat, but it doesn't enhance its windward performance. The bow entry is clean and fairly raked, with a moderate overhang. The maximum beam of 12 feet, 6 inches is not attained until aft of the middle hull section, accentuating the rather abrupt curvature that forms the canoe stern. Drawing a shapely canoe stern is an art, Perry managed to pull it off with the Valiant 40, ditto with the earlier reviewed Fast Passage 39, and the stern on the Thomas Gilmer-designed Southern Cross 39. I confess, however, that I am not partial to the Tayana Vancouver 42's posterior, although that doesn't diminish my overall admiration for this proven cruiser.

Below the water, the 42 has a long powerful fin keel and a skeg-hung rudder. The draft of 5 feet, 10 inches is a good compromise for a world cruiser, providing directional stability and seakeeping abilities in a blow without being too deep to cross the shallow bars that guard some of the world's best harbors and anchorages like medieval chastity belts. The 42 is no lightweight, with a design displacement of 27,900 pounds. The ballast of 11,800 pounds represents 42 percent of the displacement, of course these figures do not represent actual cruising loads that can easily add another couple tons to the displacement. The cutter rig supports 942 square feet of sail area, a bit more than many comparable boats.

Construction

Following the lead of the salty Tayana 37, the V 42 is massively constructed. "They're built tougher than cobs," said Stan Dabney, who with his wife Sylvia owned and cruised a 42 for a couple of years. Dabney knows a tough boat when he sees one: He was one of the founders of Valiant Yachts back in the early 1970s and continued to work with the company after it relocated to Texas. Today, he and Sylvia operate Offshore Atlantic Yachts, Inc., a cruising boat brokerage in Riviera Beach, Florida. "We sell a lot of used 42s, probably as many as any brokerage in the country, and I am always impressed how well these boats hold up. They usually fly through survey, if anything, they're too heavily built."

There is nothing overly sophisticated in the construction of the 42. The hull is solid fiberglass and the deck is cored. Some of the early decks were cored with plywood, later models with balsa. Most load-

Tayana 42

Sailing Magazine's Value Guide

PRICE: With prices ranging from $115,000 to $150,000 for most used 42s, the boat is well-priced, especially by way of comparison with other cruisers.

DESIGN QUALITY: The design works on many different levels, from seaworthiness to comfort. It will not, however, always be the most beautiful boat in the anchorage.

CONSTRUCTION QUALITY: The construction is robust and tends to hold up well. However, some materials can be questioned, including plywood cores and iron ballast.

USER-FRIENDLINESS: The 42 is a relatively easy boat to sail, although the deck can be cluttered. The boat is also underpowered, limiting its agility in close-quarter maneuvering and when motoring into a head sea.

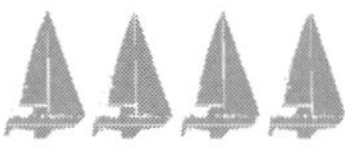

SAFETY: From extra-high lifelines to a very secure cockpit, the 42 is a safe boat. The high freeboard keeps the boat dry, but also makes retrieving an MOB more challenging.

TYPICAL CONDITIONS: Most 42s have been cruised, some extensively, but they have held up well. Engine hours are often high, and teak decks may be a source for problems.

REFITTING: Because of the custom nature of each boat, standard items don't always translate from boat to boat. However, parts are available and the boat has enough elbowroom to make working conditions decent.

SUPPORT: Ta Yang doesn't lend a lot of support to any of its boats, even new ones, and the dealer network is quite loose. Bill Truxall of the Tayana Owner's Group, is incredibly helpful, although TOG is focused mostly on the Tayana 37. Bill can be reached at (804) 453-5700 or visit the Web page at www.tog.org.

AVAILABILITY: Close to 200 boats were built, so there are always a few on the market, however they don't linger.

INVESTMENT AND RESALE: Tayanas in general are sound financial values and this is certainly true of 42. You won't lose money on this boat unless you completely trash it, or spend a fortune outfitting it.

OVERALL 'SVG' RATING

bearing surfaces have plywood cores. Many early boats came standard with teak decks. Teak decks are lovely to look at and provide an excellent nonskid surface, but they're also a maintenance nuisance and sure source of leaks. Many owners have spent a fair bit of money removing them and applying a synthetic or painted nonskid instead. The hull-and-deck joint is through bolted on a standard inward facing flange and usually incorporates an aluminum toerail. The bulkheads and furniture are securely glassed in place—the boat is built the old-fashioned way and molded pieces are kept to a minimum. Surprisingly, the mast is deck stepped, with a stainless steel compression post below. This is a big boat for a deck-stepped spar, and of course, there are advantages and disadvantages. The issue of whether or a not a deck-stepped mast is more prone to dismasting in a knockdown or capsize has never been resolved. One thing is certain, they leak a lot less than a keel-stepped spar, which requires a boot and is always moving no matter how it is supported.

The ballast is cast iron, encapsulated in an internal keel cavity and then fiberglassed over. Lead of course would be a better choice for ballast, but it is not a critical issue in a long-keel design where the ballast is spread out over a large area. Many Taiwan cruisers from this era employed iron ballast, including the Peterson 44, which is included in the 10 Best Boats section of the book.

What to look for

The first consideration is deciding whether you want the aft- or center-cockpit arrangement. The differences between the older Vancouver step-deck and later lower cabintrunk version are minor. The center-cockpit model obviously is a different animal both on deck and below. Once you have zeroed in on a model, look for a boat without teak decks, or at least a late-model boat with modern-style teak decks that limit the amount of fasteners. Ironically, a Tayana V 42 with the step-deck and no teak decks looks a bit sterile, not at all like the image of a Taiwanese "leaky teaky," but it is wonderfully practical. Tayanas have never been overly prone to blisters, although boats built between 1980 and 1985 seem more likely to have had the problem than others. Dabney notes that boats built after 1985 are in general a bit higher quality than the earlier boats.

One of the difficulties in tracking down common problems with the Tayana V 42 is that in many ways it has been a custom boat from the get-go. No two are exactly the same. Just ask Bill Truxall, the cheerful and informative head of the Tayana Owner's Group. "I have been working on assembling an owner's manual for the 42," Truxall said with a laugh. "But it is challenging to say the least. Ta Yang has always been open to owner input, which is great unless you're trying to make an owner's manual." Ta Yang, like many Taiwan builders, considered a folder full of manufacturer's brochures an adequate manual.

Specific items to check on all 42s include the tanks, the standing rigging and chainplates. The tanks, both fuel and water, are black iron, and the water tanks are especially susceptible to rust. It is a good idea to have the tanks pressure tested because removing and replacing them is a major undertaking. Most boats are fitted with three water tanks totaling around 200 gallons. Taiwan stainless was suspect from the late 1970s to the early 1980s, so be sure to carefully inspect the standing rigging. If the standing rigging is more than 10 years old, you should invest a few thousands dollars for the peace of mind and replace it. Deck leaks are not uncommon in most old boats, but 42 owners particularly noted leaks around chainplates.

On deck

The cockpit of the Tayana V 42, especially the aft-cabin model, is a study in seagoing safety blended with comfort. The well is small, the scuppers can easily handle an unexpected pooping or swamping and the bridgedeck is substantial. But unlike the other double-enders, there is still enough room to stretch out or to find a comfortable perch either behind the wheel or tucked near the companionway. Cockpit cushions help soften the angles of the seat backs and coamings. The view from the helm, which is situated well aft, is not terrific in the Vancouver step-cabin model, especially if a spray dodger is in place. It is better on the other two models, particularly the center-cockpit version. In fact, visibility is one of the best design features of center-cockpit boats.

The side decks are fairly wide and the chainplates are situated inboard to allow easy passage around on the outside. The 32-inch tapered stanchions are well-supported and the double lifelines are obviously higher than usual. Most 42s are fitted with husky mast rails, or granny bars, which have many uses in addition to offering safety and support when working around the mast. They are also good for securing lazy mooring lines and fenders. Deck hardware is stout, a single Sampson post handles the stern lines, while oversized skene chocks are used as fairleads forward. A substantial, stainless steel double anchor roller is incorporated into the stemhead fitting. I like the fact that the 42 has genuine cutter proportions without the need to employ a bowsprit.

Unlike many Tayana 37s, the 42 came standard with aluminum spars. The mast is a beefy section with double spreaders. Early boats had a circular jumper spreader to support the inner forestay while later models opted for running backstays instead. The sailplan calls for a high-cut yankee forward, usually set up on furling gear. The staysail was originally designed with a club boom to make it self-tending, but many owners have converted this sail to furling gear as well, often rigging a self-tending triangle sheet arrangement. The main features three different sheeting arrangements, with the best being the direct lead of the end-boom system in the center cockpit. Many older, step-cabin models also have end-boom sheeting, but the lead isn't fair and the tack is a fixed point. Newer cabintrunk models use midboom sheeting and a traveler that spans the forward end of the companionway.

Down below

The interior of the Tayana V 42 is a major selling point when you compare this boat against others for world voyaging. It pushes all the right buttons. Of course, as noted before, no two 42s are identical, and this really becomes apparent when you examine the interior where custom modifications are usually focused. Still, there are basic plans that can be discussed.

The early aft-cockpit boats featured a traditional V-berth cabin forward, while later models went to an offset double. Either way, this is a spacious cabin and includes a large hanging locker and access to the head. There are usually lockers, with louvered teak doors, and access to the chain locker as well. One advantage of the aft-cockpit boats is that they usually have only one head, often with a separate shower stall. The saloon in the aft-cockpit model often has an L-shaped dinette to starboard with two comfortable swivel chairs and a table to port. Serious sailors have mixed feelings about chairs instead of standard settees, but I like them. Remember, many more days are spent at anchor than at sea, and a comfortable, well-supported seat is a wonderful thing indeed. One of the best features of the Tayana 42 is that there are lockers, cabinets and storage nooks all over the boat.

The large, U-shaped galley is usually to starboard with double stainless sinks facing aft, a three-burner stove and oven outboard. The top- and side-opening freezer and fridge faces forward. There is plenty of counter space and good-sized fiddles. The nav station is opposite, sometimes tucked into the aft cabin. The aft-cabin includes a double, which is the best sea berth on the boat.

The center-cockpit plan usually includes a smaller saloon, with the galley in the starboard walk-through, and an athwartships nav station with a swing-out seat to starboard. The forward cabin is essentially the same in either model, but the aft cabin in the center-cockpit features a large double, often angled across the stern, a separate head and or shower and a hanging locker. I have seen a couple of center-cockpit 42s with workrooms tucked into the space beneath the cockpit to port and others that have a bathtub.

The workmanship is superb, with vertical teak slatting the most striking feature in what is a symphony of teak below. It is dark by today's standards, but very warm and cozy, and the joinerwork is terrific. Ventilation includes opening portlights, usually stainless steel, at least five overhead hatches and four large dorade vents. Many cruisers, especially those sailing as a family, prefer the privacy offered by the center-cockpit 42. Either model is extremely livable for an extended cruise.

Engine

I have delivered two Tayana 42s over the years: one an aft-cockpit model that I took from Ft. Lauderdale, Florida, to New York and a center-cockpit model that I sailed back to Ft. Lauderdale from Marsh Harbor in the Bahamas. While I was impressed with both boats under sail, I remember distinctly noting that they could use more power. The most common engine is a three-cylinder, 33-horsepower Yanmar diesel. This is not a lot of power to push a 30,000-pound boat into any kind of head sea. Repowering is certainly an option, although removing the old engine will require a bit of surgery down below.

Typical prop size is in the 18-by-12-inch size range and is usually three bladed. A feathering prop is an expensive but valuable upgrade. Two black iron fuel tanks in the bilge usually hold around 60 gallons each. Three-cylinder Yanmars are certainly stingy with fuel, burning less than a gallon an hour even when throttled up. The range under power is between 500 and 700 miles. Access to the engine is good, although it is better in the center-cockpit model as you can get to the beast from all sides. Overall the mechanical installations in the Tayana V 42 are well done, although early boats may need to upgrade the wiring and charging systems. Most of these boats have been cruised, and it's likely these upgrades have already been completed, so check the work carefully.

Underway

"The boat sails surprisingly well," Dabney said. "It's a 150-mile-a-day boat on passage, and you can't ask for more than that." The cutter rig is well-balanced, and provides plenty of flexibility when the wind begins to pipe up. On our 1,000-mile, nonstop passage up the coast we encountered rough conditions off Cape Hatteras. The wind was from the northeast, a head wind of course, and the seas were lumpy due to the northeast set of the Gulf Stream. We shortened sail, first reefing the main, then rolling in the yankee. We were able to make good progress with a single-reefed main and staysail as long as we didn't pinch. We had a day of headwinds of around 30 knots, but the new owners, an inexperienced young couple, didn't even know they were in heavy weather. The boat has a great motion in a seaway.

The sail back from the Bahamas was one of those magical and memorable nights at sea, and a bit of a strange affair too. I had been dispatched to fetch the boat, called *Lonesome Dove*, for a family from Canada. They had purchased the boat sight unseen, but their deal was still subject to sea trial—not by them, but by me. I was to give them a report when we returned to Ft.

Lauderdale. If the boat sailed well and there were no glaring defects, they would sign the contract, wire funds and launch their cruising dreams.

"Let me get this straight," asked my mate and dear friend, the late Dr. Dave Morrison. "First you don't hesitate to set off across the Gulf Stream on a boat you've never seen before, and secondly, the family is going to trust you to tell them if the boat is right for them or not? Amazing," he said. Soon we had sea room around Hole in the Wall, and made our way west beam reaching with a warm south wind. We reached the edge of the Gulf Stream by nightfall. A sliver of a moon, three fists up in the western sky, was conveniently poised over Ft. Lauderdale. All we had to do was steer toward the moon.

Dave was one of those sailors who never stopped trimming. Even on a cruising boat, performance can always be improved. The wind gradually backed and filled in at 20 knots and we charged along. The sailing instruments didn't work, but by the seat of my pants and from the phosphorescence trailing astern, I knew we were touching 8 knots. The helm had just the right amount of resistance. Dave adjusted the headsail leads to snatch blocks on the rail. The boat was fitted with windvane self-steering gear, but Dave refused to set it. He wanted to sail and so did I. We crossed the Gulf Stream in record time, without any strain on the boat. The only problem was that the passage had been too short.

"What are you going to tell the prospective buyers?" Dave asked as we tied the boat up. "Thanks," I said.

By the way, they bought the boat, spent a year exploring the Caribbean and sold it for more than they paid for it.

Conclusion

The Tayana 42 is really a terrific boat for world cruising. It is ruggedly constructed, an able performer and comfortable both at sea and at anchor. It is also an ideal size for a couple or a small family. The cutter rig is manageable without the need for power winches or other heavy and expensive gear, and at 42 feet, it is not too much of a load when docking or maneuvering in close quarters. The boat adapts well to self-steering and is secure in a blow, it will look after itself and doesn't require micromanagement, a vital design feature.

And, last but not least, the 42 is a sound value, retaining its value when it is time to swallow the anchor.

Mason 43

The Mason 43 is the most traditional boat of the 10 Best and arguably the most beautiful. Al Mason, who worked with Carl Alberg, John Alden, Phil Rhodes and Sparkman & Stephens, not only had an unrivaled resume but also a penchant for drawing lovely boats. His designs invariably reveal the deft hand of a true artist.

The design of the Mason 43 dates from 1978 but its inspiration goes much further back, to the days when boats were crafted from trees, not buckets of chemicals. According to published sources, the Mason 43 evolved, at least conceptually, from the Mason 40, a successful CCA ocean racer. The famous Nevins yawl *Finistere* and the graceful New York 32 were also inspirational. What does all that history mean when it comes to finding a capable world-cruising sailboat? With the Mason 43 it translates into a well-proven hull form that in one guise or another has been gracefully crossing oceans for a long time.

This review will focus on the Mason 43, which was built from 1979 through 1985, with 180 boats launched. The 43 was replaced by the 44 in 1985, and although the boats are quite similar, the upgraded 44 is much more expensive. This book emphasizes sound values on used boat market, and I feel that the 43, which can usually be purchased between $120,000 to $170,000, is a better value than the 44 that is hard to find for less than $220,000.

The Mason 43 was developed by Pacific Asian Enterprises, which specializes in developing and building boats in Taiwan and marketing them in the United States. PAE worked with Ta Shing, which benefited from the relationship to evolve into one of the premier yards in Taiwan. In addition to the Masons, Ta Shing built the Perry-designed Norsemans and Babas and currently produces the Bill Dixon-designed Taswell line.

PAE maintained ownership of its tools and consequently, maintained control of the construction process, a necessity for quality control in the early days of Taiwan boatbuilding. In many ways, the Mason 43 was the showcase for just how far Taiwan yards had come in less than 10 years of active production. The 43 had the look and much of the same quality as a Hinckley or Alden but sold for much less. PAE and Mason had an angry parting of the ways when the company redesigned the 43, creating the 44 and canceling future design royalties. This is an all too familiar story in the saga of Taiwan boatbuilders and naval architects.

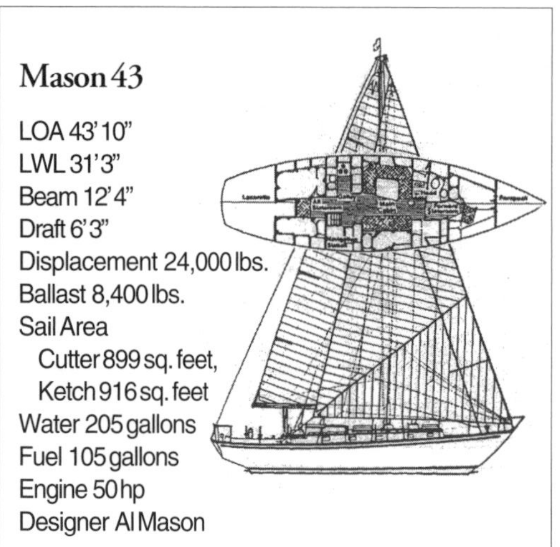

First impressions

The Mason 43 makes a powerful first impression. The pronounced sweep of the sheer, the long cabintrunk, extended overhangs, a graceful stern, relatively narrow beam and fairly low freeboard is a look that might be best described as 20th century traditional. This is a look that Mason might have patented. Although heavily built in fiberglass, the shape of the Mason 43 is a direct bridge to the wooden boats that preceded it. Some may argue that the design is dated, and they are right. The reason that the Mason 43 remains extremely popular and is included in this book is simple: The design still works. I'd sail a well-kept Mason 43 anywhere.

Below the waterline, the 43 has a long keel with just a bit of a cutaway forefoot. The attached rudder extends rather far forward and the post runs on an angled vertical with the shoe forward of the helm. While this hull shape maintains a soft motion in a seaway, it can easily be loaded up with weather helm and also hobbyhorse in a short chop. It is also the type of hull that heels early, to about 15 degrees, before stiffening up. This process extends on paper the 31-foot, 8-inch waterline, creating a working of LWL that is closer to 36 feet. This is a common characteristic of boats with slack bilges, a design trait that Mason shared with Alberg.

The Mason 43 came either as ketch or cutter, with most early boats carrying the split rig. Later models had two headsails and a longer main boom. Sail area of the ketch is just over 900 square feet. With a design displacement of 23,860 pounds, the boat's realistic cruising displacement is closer to 30,000 pounds. The boat is certainly not over canvassed but still carries enough horsepower to keep it moving in light to moderate winds.

Mason 43 Price Data

		Low	High
BUC Retail Range	1980	$104,500	$115,000
	1982	$113,500	$125,000
	1984	$131,500	$144,500

		State	Asking
Boats For Sale	1981	NC	$189,000
	1982	FL	$168,000
	1983	Caribbean	$167,500

Construction

Bulletproof is the way George Day describes the construction of the Mason 43. Day, a former Editor of *Cruising World* and the current Editor of *Bluewater Sailing* magazine, should know, he sailed his 1979 model *Clover* around the world. The hull is solid fiberglass, heavily laid up. The hull is more than an inch thick at the turn of the bilge before tapering off to about a half inch at the deck edge. Like most boats built in this era, especially Taiwan-built boats, the hulls tend to be resin rich, making them heavier than today's hulls that use a variety of techniques to improve the resin-to-fiber ratio. The deck of older Mason 43s had plywood cores while later models were stiffened with balsa. Almost all boats had teak decks, and with the fasteners penetrating into the core, there is always the potential for subdeck delamination.

The hull-and-deck joint on the older boats is typical of the philosophy behind the construction. The joint is on flange, bonded both chemically and mechanically, but it also incorporates a stainless steel flat stock. The through bolts are tapped into this strap to increase the strength of the joint, which is laminated afterward to prevent leaking. This was deemed a bit of overkill, and the steel strap was removed from later boats.

The boat is well-supported with stringers and floors, and the bulkheads are fitted for the long haul. Tank mounts and the engine beds are massive; as unpleasant as it may sound, the Mason 43 would be a good boat to capsize in. Once the floorboards were retrofitted with tie downs, everything would likely stay put while the boat righted itself. The ballast is lead, encapsulated in the wide keel cavity. The rudder is gelcoat and foam built around a stainless frame. It is a known weak spot in an otherwise excellent structural construction process.

The other area of construction that should be mentioned albeit on the aesthetic side is the ornate joinerwork on deck and below. It's no secret that I am not a fan of teak maintenance, however, there is no disputing that a large part of the Mason 43's appeal is the lovely woody feel. From the toerail, dorade boxes and teak hatches on the older boat's decks, to the

Mason 43

Sailing Magazine's Value Guide

Price: The Mason 43 is not cheap under any criteria, however, it does represent a lot of quality per dollar. When compared to a new boat, the value becomes apparent.

Design Quality: Some may argue that the design is dated, and it is, but like a fine wine, some things get better with age. Al Mason was a master and this timeless design still works very well for world cruising.

Construction Quality: Ta Shing's early boats had some flaws, but overall the construction quality is first-rate. The hull is virtually bulletproof and the workmanship very well done.

User-Friendliness: The Mason 43 is comfortable to live aboard and relatively easy to handle. The ketch rig tends to clutter up the stern and most cruisers prefer the cutter.

Safety: The only reason this rating isn't higher is because of the offset companionway and cockpit arrangement. Otherwise, the boat scores high on safety, from the stout handrails and good footing on deck to plenty of handholds below.

Typical Condition: Most Mason 43s have been well cared for, and as a result, boats on the used market are usually in very good condition, even those that have been cruised extensively.

Refitting: One problem with high-quality Taiwan boats is that it is hard to match the original joinerwork. Potential refits and upgrading is rarely factored into the original construction process. Everything is fitted for the long haul, which is great until it is time for refitting.

Support: PAE is still building boats and the factory offers some support for its older boats. There is also an active list at www.Sailnet.com.

Availability: Although 180 Mason 43s were built, they can be hard to find on the secondhand market. The boat is highly desirable and doesn't linger.

Investment and Resale: Few sailboats have held their value as well as the Mason 43. In fact, my current research indicates that the boat is actually appreciating sharply again, evidenced by the asking prices compared to the BUC values. If you take care of the your boat, you will get your money back out and then some.

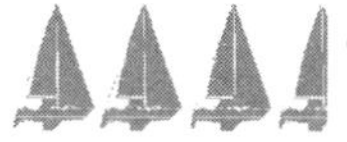

OVERALL 'SVG' RATING

intricate carved panels below, the workmanship is both wonderful and enslaving at the same time.

What to look for

Most Mason 43s are at least 20 years old and many have been cruised far and wide. Naturally some common problems have been exposed that should be carefully checked when inspecting used boats. You may have a hard time finding some of these flaws, because as a group, Mason owners tend to lavish their boats with care and maintenance.

The deck is the first area of concern, especially on older models. The teak decks may need love and might need to be replaced. More and more owners have taken this option to end the maintenance and leaking issues once and for all. Popped bungs, exposed screw heads and black areas are signs that the teak is lifting from the deck. Stomp heavily, especially on the foredeck and around the chainplates. If the deck feels mushy or creaks, the subdeck likely has some rot. Deck delamination, unless it is widespread, should not push a boat off your list, in fact, sometimes it can help you to get a better deal. Day said that he had injected the deck with epoxy occasionally during the five-year cruise, but he never felt that it was a structural issue.

Deck leaks, especially around the chainplates, are common. The original teak hatches may also leak if they have not been replaced with aluminum hatches. This fix would be a must-do project. The teak dorades may be rotted on the bottom, causing leaks.

The rudder is another area to examine closely when the boat is hauled out. It may need to be rebuilt, using a heavier layup. Also, Mason 43s had a minor problem with blisters, try to find out when and if a blister repair job was completed. Some owners have noted that some of the original stainless steel was less than ideal, and many owners have had to replace fittings throughout the boat. The black iron fuel tanks and stainless or monel water tanks should be pressure tested for leaks. Of course, all age-related items like standing rigging, running rigging, lifeline terminals, steering cables and engine control cables should be carefully inspected.

On deck

The Mason 43's cockpit is a bit controversial, and according to Day, the main reason behind the redesigned 44. The main companionway is offset to starboard and located forward of the cabintrunk bulkhead. At first glance this doesn't make sense. A closer inspection reveals that the position of the companionway to starboard allows room for a large aft stateroom, a unique feature in a 43-foot aft-cockpit boat of this vintage. However, this adds extra distance when shifting from the safety of the cockpit to the safety of the companionway steps.

When sailing to windward on a port tack, the companionway is also quite close to water, not an ideal situation to say the least. The mainsheet also runs in front of the companionway, further limiting access and making it difficult to rig a dodger that offers spray protection for the cockpit. Day alleviated this problem somewhat by moving the sheet forward and settling for the inefficiencies of midboom sheeting. Like other boats of this era, the cockpit is not known for its ergonomics, and the seat backs are low and abrupt. The helmsperson does have a nice perch and visibility is good, depending on the amount of the bimini or dodger canvas.

The side decks are wide, and for all the complaints associated with teak decks, they sure offer good traction, especially barefoot. Long teak handrails line the cabintrunk and the lifelines and stanchions are well-supported. Be sure to check the stanchion bases for cracks. The pulpits and deck hardware are oversized and the original anchor stemhead fitting is robust. The windlass is usually mounted on the foredeck.

The mast is painted aluminum and the original rig included swage fittings and Navtec turnbuckles. It is unlikely that the original standing rigging is still on the boat. The mast on older boats, especially the ketch model, is deck-stepped, a feature that I like even on a boat of this size. It is difficult if not impossible to keep a mast boot from leaking, and even if you do, water finds its way into the bilge through mast openings anyway. Some argue that a keel-stepped mast is better supported in the event of a knockdown or capsize, which is true. (There are Mason 43s with keel-stepped spars.) The flip side is that a deck-stepped spar is less likely to tear up the cabintrunk in the event of a dismasting. In either case, dismastings almost always occur well above deck level, in which case how the mast is stepped doesn't matter. The real issue that cruisers deal with on a daily basis are leaks around the mast collar, delamination of the subdeck supporting a deck-stepped spar and metal corrosion at the foot of a keel-stepped spar.

Down below

The interior arrangement of the Mason 43 is ideal for family cruising. Although several different interior plans were offered, the most common arrangement includes an offset V-berth forward followed by a large head with a separate stall shower. The V-berth cabin includes access to the chain locker, a dressing seat and a large hanging locker. The storage throughout the boat is terrific. A single head with a stall shower is a perfect cruising setup—it doesn't waste space trying to squeeze another head into a limited area, offers a good place for wet gear when under way and a civilized way to wash up at anchor. Ventilation includes an overhead hatch in the forward cabin and several opening bronze portlights.

The saloon features a wraparound dinette to port and a settee with pilot berth to starboard. There are plenty of berths without needing to convert the table into a double. I like a pilot berth as a sea berth, although it is hard to resist the temptation to fill it up with gear that doesn't fit neatly into a locker. On many boats you may find that this area has been converted to lockers and shelving. Behind the table, there are additional bookshelves and lockers. Most interiors feature vertical teak panels and solid bulkheads. There are well-placed handholds below the portlights and a stout post in the galley. The headroom gives the boat a more spacious feeling than a 31-foot, 3-inch waterline might otherwise suggest.

The galley is to port and it is a classic U-shape that is very functional. Two deep sinks face aft and the cooker is outboard with a safety rail in front. The poorly insulated fridge and freezer compartment faces forward. The surfaces might range from butcher block Formica to small, hard-to-clean tile. There are fiddles with openings for cleaning and plenty of storage above and below. The nav station is opposite, which almost feels like a separate compartment squeezed next to the companionway ladder. The chart desk faces aft, a situation that's a pet peeve of mine as I have a hard time orienting my simple brain to navigate when I am sitting backward. The electrical panel is located in the nav area, and although it was state of the art in the late 1970s, it may need upgrading to support today's plethora of electronic systems.

"The aft cabin is one of the best ever built," Day said. "It really works." The cabin includes a double bunk to port with a single sea berth opposite—a good arrangement for two children. There is ample storage above the berths and a hanging locker. Some Mason 43s have an arrangement that tries to squeeze a second head in this cabin.

Engine

One of the reasons that the interior plan uses the limited volume so effectively is that the engine is hidden away beneath the sole of the saloon. Long experience as a delivery skipper had shown me that this is not a good place for an engine. Although the sound insulation is excellent, the low position makes the engine vulnerable to bilge water, and more importantly, back siphoning. An advantage is that the transmission and prop shaft are horizontal and more efficient. Access is average, especially on the front end, and changing belts can be challenging.

The most common engine found in the Mason 43 is the Perkins 4108 or the comparable Westerbeke model. Day notes that in flat water *Clover* moved along at close to 7 knots, but motoring into a chop quickly dropped the speed below 5 knots. That is a function of a short waterline and a hull shape that hobbyhorses. Owners who have repowered seem to have opted for a four-cylinder Yanmar, rated from 52 horsepower and up, depending on the model. Maneuvering under power is a bit of challenge, especially in reverse, the bane of all long-keeled boats. A feathering propeller is a great addition. The iron fuel tanks carry a little more than 100 gallons.

Underway

The performance of the Mason 43 is surprising, and the boat sails well on all points of sail, routinely knocking off 150 miles a day at sea. Day and his family logged 32,000 miles aboard *Clover*, and their best 24-hour run was 194 miles. *Clover* was ketch-rigged, and like me, Day is a proponent of the mizzen staysail. This often overlooked sail has several advantages. It is easier to set and douse than a spinnaker, doesn't challenge the self-steering system and can be carried in more wind than a spinnaker. When set properly it allows the ketch rig to outperform the cutter when sailing off the wind. Heavier boats tend to do well when reaching in the trades, even when the winds suffer through a light or variable period as momentum tends to keep the boat moving when a lighter boat might slow or stop.

As noted earlier, the Mason 43 heels early before stiffening up at around 15 degrees. "We rarely heeled the boat more than that," Day said. "It is definitely happiest at that angle and should be reefed accordingly."

Day also noted that the cutter rig performs better to windward, with both rigs, the boat makes a fair been of leeway, at least 5 degrees when hard on the wind. This must be factored into the heading. Day observed that the boat tacked through 85 degrees, but in real cruising terms with leeway factored in, 95 to 100 degrees was more accurate. This, by the way, is about average for most genuine cruising boats.

The Mason 43's full keel section is rather wide as well, further hampering upwind performance. In heavy going upwind, the boat can develop a pitching motion and be stopped up by steep head seas.

The Mason 43 adapts well to self-steering, in fact, *Clover*'s Sailomat windvane did most of the helming on their voyage and Day never installed an expensive belowdeck autopilot. A simple, belt-driven Autohelm 3000 was able to steer the boat when under power in light air. When reefed early, weather helm doesn't seem to be an issue. Overall, the Mason 43 has a very nice motion, an important factor for offshore passagemaking.

Conclusion

The Mason 43 is a fine choice for world cruising. It may not be as practical as the other boats in this section, but world cruising is not an altogether practical pursuit. There has to be some romance in the equation. Rowing out to an anchored Mason 43 can make your heart stir. You can buy a boat that is just as capable for less money, but it will be hard to find a boat that is as lovely to gaze at and as well-constructed for any less money. Also, after a five-year sabbatical and circumnavigation, Day sold his Mason 43 for more than he had put in her, and that is an unmistakable sign of a quality boat.

Peterson 44

Some boats and perfect anchorages occupy a coveted spot in your mind's hard drive, ready to be recalled whenever you need a remedy for tropical fever, or actually the lack thereof. For me, the setting is Galle, a once-thriving colonial outpost and now overgrown Third World port town perched on the southwest corner of Sri Lanka. The harbor is anything but picturesque. It is crowded, dirty and unbelievably hot. It is also exotic—the place where West meets East. It's a place that would have inspired a story by Maugham and a verse by Kipling. When I close my eyes I see dark-eyed women in vivid saris and elephants hauling massive logs down the middle of the street. Oxcarts, rickshaws and native sailboats called *oruwas* complete the picture. And what boat do I see anchored in the harbor? You might guess a traditional copra schooner or an Arab dhow, but you'd be wrong. I see a Peterson 44 in full cruising regalia.

Although it was 15 years ago, I remember clearly helping a middle-age couple secure their Peterson 44 to a mooring in Galle's stifling harbor. Although they had just completed a difficult passage from Penang in Malaysia, they invited me aboard to show off their new decks. It seems they had detoured to Malaysia to have new teak decks put on, and their stories of watching a teak tree hewn into planking and then painstakingly installed on their boat fascinated me. The boat, which was about 10 years old, looked great, and the couple was already halfway through their second circumnavigation!

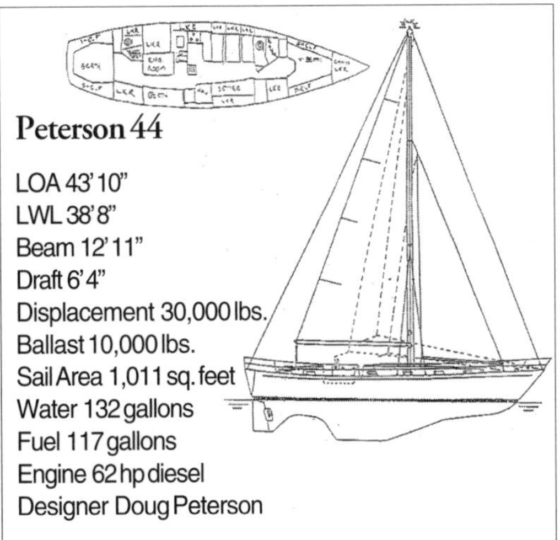

To many sailors, the Peterson 44 is the ideal long-range cruising boat. A center-cockpit cutter designed by Doug Peterson, the boat is a nice blend of comfort and performance. Conceived by Jack Kelly, a yacht broker in San Diego, California, approximately 200 original Peterson 44s were built in Taiwan during a six-year production run. The original 44s were built by Yu Ching Marine in Kaohshing. Later, Formosa Yachts built an updated version called the Kelly-Peterson 46. There have been other copies and knockoffs, but this review will focus on the original Peterson 44s. These boats are admired by cruising sailors everywhere and can be purchased near or even below $100,000—making the boat a terrific value.

First impressions

Even confirmed aft-cockpit sailors grudgingly admit that the Peterson 44 is a fine looking boat. Peterson, a talented and versatile designer, drew a sweet sheerline and kept the freeboard and overall cabin profile low.

Peterson 44 Price Data

		Low	High
BUC Retail Range	1976	$ 96,500	$106,000
	1979	$106,000	$116,500
	1982	$124,500	$136,500

		State	Asking
Boats For Sale	1976	CA	$135,000
	1977	Caribbean	$119,000
	1979	FL	$ 99,000
	1979	CA	$104,000

The bow's entry has a moderate rake—the overhang ratio is 12 percent based on an LWL of 38 feet, 8 inches. Overhang ratios between 12 and 15 percent are ideal as they allow for a clean entry and soft forefoot that won't pound in a chop yet maintain a long waterline for speed potential. A fair bit of beam is carried aft to maintain room for the aft cabin. About the only design feature I'm not crazy about is the abrupt, vertical cut transom—the boat would be more handsome if it were a few feet longer.

Below the waterline, the Peterson 44 has a long fin keel with a cutaway forefoot and husky skeg-hung rudder. The prop is completely protected in an aperture just forward of the rudder. By today's standards, there is a lot of boat in the water, creating a lot of wetted surface. However, my instincts tell me that the Peterson 44 will maintain a sweet motion in almost any sea state, and as I have often noted, motion is a vital element of a cruising boat's design. The powerful, double-spreader rig serves up more than 1,000 square feet of sail area, and the Peterson 44 is famous for completing swift ocean passages. With a design displacement of 30,000 pounds, which translates into more than 35,000 pounds when loaded for cruising, the Peterson 44 was made for tradewind sailing.

Construction

The Peterson 44 might be considered a second generation Taiwan-built boat. Introduced in late 1976, the numerous yards on the island were gradually shedding their "leaky teaky" reputations. The old guard of teak laden, poorly constructed boats like the Sea Wolf 41, which was also called the Yankee Clipper and CT 41, were being replaced by better quality boats like the Robert Perry-designed Baba built by Ta Shing. Taiwan boatbuilders deserve more credit than they have received. In a very short span of approximately 25 years, they went from building some of the worst hulks afloat to crafting some of the finest fiberglass boats ever built.

The Peterson 44 has a typical Taiwan construction. The hull is very heavily laid up, with mat and roving and polyester resin. The hull is nearly an inch thick at the turn of the bilge. The layup is resin rich, as were most boats built during that time, but the Peterson 44's hull is undeniably strong, which has been proven on all the world's oceans. The iron ballast is encapsulated in a keel cavity. Lead would be better, of course, but iron is cheaper, and in an internal ballast arrangement, it's adequate. The rudder is solid fiberglass and the stock stainless steel.

The deck and trunkhouse are cored with plywood, and although this is not an ideal coring material, delamination does not seem to be a terrible problem. The hull-and-deck joint incorporates the bulwark, forming a box joint that is strong and dry. The only way this joint leaks is from the genoa track bolts. The stainless steel chainplates are mounted through the deck, instead of outboard and bolted through the topsides—a design and construction feature found on many early Taiwan-built boats. Many Peterson 44s came with teak decks, although it is hard to find boats that still have the original decks as most have been removed and replaced, sometimes with painted or synthetic nonskid.

What to look for

The first thing to look for is a Peterson 44 without teak decks. Sue Holt and Larry Hamilton, columnists for **Sailnet.com**, detailed the process of removing the teak and applying Treadmaster, a synthetic nonskid on their Formosa 46, which is a stretched out Peterson 44. It was not a casual undertaking. Also, as noted above, the original decks were cored with plywood, and even if the teak decks have been removed, check the subdeck for any evidence of delamination.

Tanks were often another problem with Taiwan-built boats of this vintage, and the Peterson 44 is no exception. The original water tanks were made of questionable stainless steel and were known to develop cracks, creating hard-to-find and hard-to-repair leaks. Fortunately, leaky tanks are also hard to live and cruise with, so it is probable that if the tanks had developed leaks they will have been replaced. If this task falls to you, be prepared for a big job because the Peterson 44 came standard with four water tanks for a total of 132 gallons. If you replace one, you might as well replace them all. The fuel tanks were made of black iron, however, and the anti-corrosive nature of diesel fuel usually has helped to preserve these tanks.

Jack Kimble, who with his wife, Sandy, circumnavigated in the 1980 Peterson 44 *Zorona*, has written a detailed report about how the boat fared during their nine-year, 45,000-mile voyage. Among other items, Kimble suggested that the steering cables be inspected and the genoa track bolts be checked for leaks and corrosion. Naturally, all age-related items need to be checked, especially the rigging. Most boats came from the factory with Navtec turnbuckles, and if these have not been replaced, they should be. The original wire was a beefy 3/8-inch on the headstay, backstay and upper shrouds, and you may consider lightening the rig to reduce weight aloft when adding new standing rigging.

Another item to inspect carefully during the survey is the bronze heel bearing on the rudder, which may be corroded from the original stainless steel bolts. Several owners reported that the original tack plate for the staysail was not well supported.

On deck

The cockpit was one of the features that many cruisers first appreciated in the Peterson 44: It was actually comfortable. Remember, this boat was designed and built when many old salts still considered large cockpits to be inherently dangerous, and small, miserable footwells masquerading as cockpits (the Westsail 32 springs to mind) were thought to be truly seaworthy. The Peterson 44's cockpit has two 6-foot-plus seats that are perfect for open-air napping, or just stretching out while on watch or at anchor. Many previous owners have fashioned some type of helm seat, often incorporating the seat into a propane locker. There is a good-sized locker to port and four large coamings, which gobble up a lot of gear. There are cockpit companionways for both the main cabin and the aft cabin. Depending on the size of the wheel, it can be a tight squeeze around the pedestal. The cockpit has a substantial dodger molding, and I have seen some boats fitted with hard dodgers, although this seems more common on later Kelly-Peterson 46s and Formosa 46s. Almost every boat you look at will have a bimini top, a vital piece of gear for tropical travels, although it takes a bit of getting used to sailing without being able to view the mainsail.

The Peterson 44 has a substantial molded bulwark that provides security when moving about the deck. The lifelines and stanchions are well-supported, although the Taiwanese stainless hardware is old and may need to be replaced. Teak grabrails on the coachroof may or may not have been replaced, and I wouldn't hesitate to change them to stainless steel rails that can be purchased reasonably at most marine stores. The chainplates are set on the outside of the side deck and inside the bulwark, yet there is plenty of room to slip around the stays. The boat came from the factory with substantial anchor rollers and a manual windlass, which has likely been updated, especially if the boat has been cruised extensively. The original deck hardware was robust, although most boats will have been refitted at some point. Common upgrades include self-tailing winches.

The main spar is 60 feet above the waterline, give or take an inch or two, and has double spreaders. The stays are beefy: The lowers and intermediates are 5/16-inch, the inner forestay 9/16-inch and the uppers 3/8-inch. The factory installed swage terminal fittings, and if these are original, they should be replaced. It is likely that somewhere along the line the fittings have been upgraded to swageless fittings.

Down below

While the interior finish may seem dark by today's standards, the extensive use of richly oiled teak was considered elegant in the 1970s and early 1980s. However, it really isn't the ornate Oriental joinerwork that makes the Peterson 44 interior attractive, it is the layout. There is a traditional V-berth forward, usually with a large hanging locker to starboard and drawers underneath. Access to the chain locker is from the V-berth. On many 44s the furniture faces are finished in white formica that is both practical from a maintenance standpoint and helps brighten the interior. Teak trim pieces accent just about everything. Aft of the V-berth, a fairly large head is located to port with access from both the forward cabin and the saloon.

The saloon often features a dinette arrangement to port with a settee opposite. Although this type of

Peterson 44

Sailing Magazine's Value Guide

PRICE: While it is possible to find P44s for less than $100,000, expect to pay around $115,000 for a well-equipped model. That is still a very good price for a boat to sail anywhere with speed and comfort. Just compare it to a new boat of the same size for a sense of perspective.

DESIGN QUALITY: Doug Peterson's concept was original in its day—a comfortable center-cockpit design, with a long keel and skeg hung rudder and enough sail area to move ably in most conditions. Ultimately, designs are proven on the water, and the P 44 has lived up to its premise.

CONSTRUCTION QUALITY: There is no disputing that the P 44 is robustly constructed, however, some of the materials might have been better. In a perfect world lead is better than iron for encapsulated ballast. Some of the metals, the stainless water tanks for example, were not high-quality. Also a plywood core with a teak deck is not usually a good combination. Still, the boats have held up well while being sailed hard.

USER-FRIENDLINESS: The Peterson 44 may not have the modern sail control systems of newer boats like a furling main and electric sheet winches, but the systems are simple and robust. The interior is comfortable although some of the original engineering is classic early Taiwanese.

SAFETY: From the molded bulwark to the secure cockpit to an abundance of handholds below, the Peterson 44 is a very safe boat. The ultimate safety feature is a soft motion in a seaway and sense of strength in a gale, both of which the boat has in abundance.

TYPICAL CONDITION: Most Peterson 44s on the used market are equipped for cruising. However, old gear can be more of a hassle than a boat without much equipment, so be wary of paying a premium for outdated gear. As serious cruisers, the boats may appear a bit weatherworn but often a close inspection of systems reveals good maintenance.

REFITTING: Although the boat is no longer in production, and hasn't been for many years, there is a lot of good solid information about refitting the boat for bluewater cruising. Much of the original gear and many of the systems will already have been the byproduct of a refit, so you may be looking at a second or third generation project.

SUPPORT: The Peterson 44 is a well-known commodity among the tightknit world of bluewater cruising. Two excellent Web sites are: www.KP44.org and www.yachting.net. There is also plenty of printed information about the boats.

AVAILABILITY: With just over 200 boats built there are always several 44s on the market, although you may have to travel to find one that fits your specifications. California seems to be the place to find the best selection, although the boats on the East Coast and in the Caribbean are priced better.

INVESTMENT AND RESALE: The Peterson is an excellent value and will continue to be in the future as new boat prices rise and production is reduced. The used market is lively, and clean, well-equipped boats do not linger long.

OVERALL 'SVG' RATING

table is small, I prefer a dinette in a boat because it's a good use of space without having a table to climb around as you move fore and aft. Of course, this advantage is somewhat negated on the P44 by the keel-stepped mast, which is just next to the table. Above the starboard settee are bookshelves and storage lockers. Water tanks occupy most of the bilge area. The forward facing nav station is to starboard at the foot of the companionway. The large desk has chart storage located below, but the bookshelf just above it is too small for much useful storage. The galley is opposite the nav station and is a typical U-shaped arrangement that works well both at sea and at anchor. The large double sinks face aft and the stove is outboard. Most P44s are fitted with a large three-burner cooker with oven. There are usually two iceboxes, one under the companionway steps, which is an inconvenient arrangement. The other is located to port. This is a good arrangement for setting up a separate fridge and freezer system, however. There is a lot of usable counter space and ample storage located above, behind and below the counters.

The aft cabin is accessible from either the cockpit via a companionway or a starboard walk-through below. It's a pity that few boats allow for cockpit entry into the aft cabin anymore. This not only creates good ventilation, it is an important safety feature. Communication with the watch is easier, and in the event of a fire, there are two ways in and out of the boat. The walk-through is tight, especially by today's standards, but it was considered a design innovation in the mid-1970s. Engine access is terrific through sliding doors in the walk-through. Outboard in the walk-through on most 44s is a second fuel tank and battery storage. Sometimes the top of this area has been converted to a tool bench or a berth, and sometimes there is a half-sized wet locker.

The aft cabin features a large double berth that can be used either fore and aft or athwartships, which is a comfortable way to sleep in lumpy seas. There is a large hanging locker with drawers and lockers underneath and next to the bunk. There's no lack of storage on the Peterson 44. To port is the second head which may have been converted to a dedicated shower, unless, of course, that fate has already befallen the forward head. Either way, few genuine offshore cruising boats of this size need two heads. There is a large hatch above the bunk and opening bronze portlights, which are just part of an overall excellent system of ventilation.

Engine

Most Peterson 44s were fitted with a Perkins 4-154 four-cylinder 62-horsepower diesel. This was a workhorse of an engine, and I have spent many hours in communion with this beast, trying to cajole it back into action after some ailment or another. That being said, I wouldn't hesitate to buy a boat with a 4-154. Parts are still widely available and others can be made to work. For example, many parts from the Leyland 154, an old London taxicab engine converted to marine use, will fit the Perkins 4-154. Some P44s came with a six-cylinder Ford Lehman as well. It's likely that many boats have been repowered, and the most common new engine is the four-cylinder Yanmar that's rated anywhere from 52-horsepower for the naturally aspirated model to almost 100-horsepower for the bored out, turbocharged version.

Engine access is great, and an engine that is easy to work on usually receives better maintenance than one that requires contortions. Actually, a real advantage of a center-cockpit design for serious cruisers is that engine access is invariably better than in an aft-cockpit model. Although I shouldn't admit this, the dirty little secret of cruising is that we motor far more than we ever admit, making engine maintenance a vital aspect of a happy voyage. Tanks are iron, with most boats carrying around 130 gallons in two tanks. This translates into a cruising range of at least 500 miles, and possibly more if conditions are light and the engine is throttled back. An advantage of the Perkins 4-154 is that it was usually matched with a Borg Warner Velvet Drive gearbox, which is smooth and reliable. The 44 drivetrain features a long 9-inch shaft and two bearings. Several owners report using a Max prop, or other types of feathering propellers, with much success.

Underway

The Peterson 44 is a fine sailing boat, indeed, it is one of the best performers in its class. Jack Kimball reported occasional 180-mile runs and consistent 150-mile days when sailing in the trades. Shirley Kaplan, who sailed with her late husband, Leonard, aboard *Serenata*, noted that 7 to 7.5 knots was the average boat speed in most conditions.

"Beating down the thorny path from Florida to the Caribbean, we tended to sail with just the main and yankee," Kaplan said. "Once we began reaching more in the islands, we used a 135-percent genoa, again going without the staysail quite often."

Kaplan, who recently delivered a Hylas 49 between Florida and New England, didn't hesitate to rank the Peterson as the better performing boat. "In light air especially, the Peterson is quicker," she said. One feature both boats share is that they never pound in a seaway. "During the 15 years we lived aboard *Serenta* I don't recall her ever pounding," Kaplan said.

I won't go into my standard lecture on the merits of a hull shape that doesn't beat you up, but it sure makes life aboard more pleasurable. Owners universally report that the Peterson 44 balances extremely well under sail and responds nicely to both windvane self-steering and electronic autopilots.

The Kaplans reefed the main when the wind approached 20 knots. "We tended to undersail the boat a bit, always handling it with just two of us," Kaplan said. "What we found was that we rarely lost any speed when we reefed." Jack Kimbal said in his report that the boat rarely gave them an anxious moment through a variety of gales around the world. He noted that during a couple of blows in the Tasman Sea and in a passage between Tonga and New Zealand, the Peterson 44 came through unscathed while some other cruisers took a beating.

Conclusion

The Peterson 44 just may be the best value available in a roomy center-cockpit cruiser that really sails well. The boat is an excellent combination of design, construction and aesthetics. The downside is that any boat you purchase will be at least 20 years old, but most have been consistently upgraded. I would steer clear of the bargain boats and zero in on well-maintained, updated boats that are ready to head off toward the South Pacific.

Stevens-Hylas 47

When three cannibalistic weather systems converged off the New England Coast to create the perfect storm as Sebastian Junger named it in his monumental best-seller, I had just cleared Maryland's Chesapeake Bay Bridge. It was late October 1991, and like the crews of the sword-fishing boats working the Grand Banks in the North Atlantic, I was carefully monitoring the progress of Hurricane Grace. I was skippering a Hylas 47 sloop on an offshore navigation training voyage between Annapolis, Maryland, and Nassau, Bahamas. When we learned that Grace was heading north and east, well clear of our intended path, we headed offshore. The seas, spawned by the distant storm, were majestic and terrifying, the largest I have encountered in 25 years of bluewater sailing. For four days we literally surfed south, riding enormous breaking waves that at times took our breath away. The speedo was frequently buried at 12 knots, and yet you could still feel the boat accelerate as one wave after another leveled out with a crescendo. I was impressed with how capably the Hylas 47 handled those wild conditions, a boat that was supposed to be at its best sailing upwind, not running before monster seas.

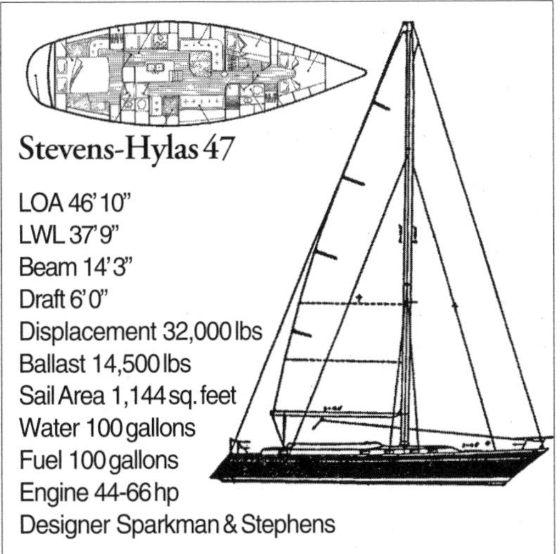

Steering required both concentration and strong arms. We were exhausted, exhilarated and well ahead of schedule as we logged successive 200-mile-plus days. We decided to slip into Marsh Harbor in the Abacos for a good night's sleep before carrying on to Nassau. I lined up the approach bearings on Fish Hawke Cay to thread the reef at North Man-O-War channel and proceeded under power. Soon it became clear that the breaking waves would make negotiating the pass too dangerous. It was a classic rage condition. However, before I could turn the boat around, a steeply curled wave lifted the stern and hurled us forward. I screamed for the crew to hold on. I honestly thought we might pitchpole, or at the very least broach and roll over. The 32,000-pound boat was thrown forward like a toy in a bathtub as water crashed over the length of the boat. I held the wheel and somehow the Hylas 47 kept its feet. Miraculously nobody was washed overboard. Once I started breathing again, I swung the boat around and powered offshore as fast as the Perkins would push us. On another boat this could have been a disaster.

The Stevens-Hylas 47 is a proven offshore thoroughbred, and although it's the most expensive boat in this book, it is still an excellent value for a three

Stevens-Hylas 47 Price Data

BUC Retail Range		Low	High
	1982 Stevens 47	$138,000	$152,000
	1985 Stevens 47	$171,000	$198,000
	1988 Hylas 47	$165,000	$192,000

Boats For Sale		State	Asking
	1981 Stevens 47	FL	$ 195,000
	1985 Stevens 47	FL	$ 224,000
	1989 Hylas 47	Caribbean	$ 185,000

cabin, center-cockpit bluewater cruiser. The Stevens 47 was an unusual commission for the venerable design firm of Sparkman & Stephens. Queen Long, a Taiwan boatyard already building the Peterson 44 for Jack Kelly, had approached the firm. The yard wanted to build its own boats, and for the most part, left the design to the brain trust at S&S. For Rod Stephens and crew this was a dream come true. According to Paul Bennett, the former President of Stevens Yachts, Rod Stephens became personally involved in project. "He took me under his wing and became my mentor in the boatbuilding business," Bennett said.

Bill Stevens, the founder of the Stevens Yacht Charters, had been buying Peterson 44s for his Caribbean fleet. When he saw the new S&S 47, he told Queen Long he'd take all they could build. He slapped his name on the boat and the Stevens 47 was born. Approximately 56 Stevens 47s were built before Stevens sailed into financial difficulty. Dick Jachney of Caribbean Yacht Charters took up where Stevens left off and began selling the boats into his fleet, and together with Queen Long, they renamed the boat the Hylas 47. In 1992, Jachney and Tony Siebert redesigned the deck and added a swim platform, along with many other interior upgrades, creating the Hylas 49.

I have logged 27,000 miles aboard different Hylas 49s, including 10 round trip passages between the East Coast and the Caribbean Islands. I have also logged another 10,000 miles aboard Hylas 47s. I have only sailed the Stevens 47 a few times, although I did deliver a boat from Antigua to Ft. Lauderdale, Florida, recently. Although the Hylas 49 is certainly one of my favorite boats, this chapter will focus on the Stevens-Hylas 47. Why? Because at this moment these boats are better values. "You can find a Hylas or Stevens 47 in good condition for under $200,000," said Ft. Lauderdale broker Rob Jordan. "It is difficult to find a 49 under $300,000." Of course the Stevens-Hylas 47 will likely be 10 years older, but because the basic hull shape is unchanged and the original construction bulletproof, the difference in asking price can equal the same amount of money spent for a three or four year circumnavigation.

First impressions

At first glance, the Stevens-Hylas 47 doesn't look like a boat that has six documented circumnavigations, seven more in progress and has won just about every offshore cruising rally there is. It doesn't have that clunky, overbuilt, hey-look-at-me-I-am-a-cruising-boat look. A closer inspection, however, reveals a powerful, yet fine entry for efficient windward work, a subtle sheerline, generous though not excessive beam carried aft and a flat broad transom designed to power before ocean waves. The 20-percent overhang ratio may seem out of step with today's blunt nosed flyers, but to my eye it is hard to design a better looking entry. The center-cockpit cabintrunk maintains a low profile, although the cockpit coaming looks a bit out of place.

The real secret to the 47's great sailing nature is found below the water. The forefoot is deep and there is enough deadrise to eliminate any tendency to pound in a seaway. The long fin keel provides the directional stability that had kept the boat under control during my wild approach in the Bahamas, and the rudder is mounted on a full skeg. The design displacement of 32,000 pounds incorporates 14,000 pounds of ballast for a ratio of nearly 44 percent. This hull shape, coupled with a powerful sloop rig capable of carrying enough sail to keep the boat moving in light air yet stand up in a blow, translates into an ideal world-voyaging boat.

Construction

Paul Bennett is very proud of the solid original construction of the Stevens 47, but he admits it was always a challenge to build high-quality boats in Taiwan. The 47's hull is solid fiberglass, heavily laid up and supported with four full-length longitudinal foam stringers on each side. The floor timbers include 12 transverse members and six longitudinals. I have weathered three different hurricanes in Hylas 47s and 49s, which have the same hull scantlings, and I have never felt a hull flex. The deck is cored with rigid PVC Airex foam, and although deck leaks are distressingly common, deck delamination is rare. The hull and deck are joined on a flange, and after being set in 5200, fiberglassed together from below. "There is no substitute for a fiberglass joint," Bennett said. "It's a monocoque construction like a metal boat." The aluminum toerail is bolted through the joint as well.

The ballast is internal lead, encapsulated in the keel cavity. The bulkheads are securely glassed in place, both to the hull and deck. The mast is keel-stepped, although a bridge keeps the butt of the mast above the bilge water. The interior joinerwork is extraordinary.

What to look for

The first thing to look for is whether or not you prefer a Stevens or Hylas, or whether or not it matters. Are there really any differences? Naturally Bennett is biased toward the boats he built. "We built the first 56 boats," he said. "And after about hull No. 30, they were all custom boats and no two were exactly alike." Bennett changed the direction of Stevens Yachts after it sold off the charter business. "After that we built boats for private individuals, not the charter trade. We imported top-quality rigs and fittings and went to great lengths to make sure they ended up on the boats."

Queen Long built another 82 Hylas 47s before phasing out the boat in 1991. Most of the Hylas 47s went into the CYC fleet and endured the hard life of a Caribbean bareboat. However, many on the market today have already been refitted and converted into cruising boats. The lowest priced boats have usually not been fitted out for cruising. And while some may just need cosmetic upgrades and new cruising gear, others may need new power plants, sails and rigging. Try to determine if the cost and aggravation of a complete retrofit is worth it. If you are ready to cruise now it might be better to a buy a boat that is all ready to go. If you spot a Stevens on the market for well above $200,000 chances are it has been restored to almost new condition by Bennett's' Bennett Brothers Yachts in Wilmington, North Carolina. These retrofitted beauties are expensive, but ready to explore the world.

On my many delivery passages I have been well acquainted with some specific and common problems with the Hylas 47. Unfortunately, almost every boat I have sailed has leaked through the ports and hatches. It seems Queen Long was stingy on bedding compound. The Hylas 47 came standard with 14 opening portlights and six deck hatches. Fortunately, the Airex-cored decks are not prone to delamination, but the teak veneers below certainly are. You should consider rebedding the ports and hatches if hasn't already been done. Also, check the push-pull steering cables and replace them if the steering is stiff and they show signs of corrosion. Pressure check the fuel and water tanks. Some early boats had questionable stainless tanks and have developed pinhole leaks that are hard to find and frustrating to repair. If the original Taiwanese batteries are still in the boat don't hesitate to replace them. Also, consider paying extra for a boat that has already been repowered, especially if it has a new four-cylinder Yanmar.

On deck

The cockpit of the Stevens-Hylas 47 just may be its least desirable feature. I know I am being harsh on the boat, but only because I truly admire it and know it well. The coamings are too low and it is difficult to brace your feet when steering. These two problems were addressed in the new deck design of the Hylas 49. The bridgedeck is just a small sill, meaning that the bottom hatch board will need to be in place when sailing in heavy weather. The center-cockpit design does allow for excellent visibility, which is especially helpful when handling the boat in close quarters. The mainsheet traveler is aft of the cockpit, allowing for efficient end-boom sheeting. Some of the earlier boats had a single point attachment instead of a traveler. Most boats had self-tailing Barients as standard sheet winches and overall the quality of the sailing hardware is excellent.

A stainless steel stemhead fitting includes a double-anchor roller, and many boats seem to have vertical capstan electric windlasses. Stout pulpits and double lifelines make moving around the deck secure. The nonskid pattern is passive, however, and while it is comfortable on your feet and when lounging on deck, it can be slippery when wet. Well-placed teak handrails line the trunkhouse. Mooring hardware is robust and includes four forward cleats and two aft.

Stevens-Hylas 47

Sailing Magazine's Value Guide

PRICE: Okay, the price is steep, at least by the standards set down in this book. However, when compared to new boats, or other similarly sized cruisers, the value becomes more apparent.

DESIGN QUALITY: The 47 delivers in so many ways. It is a great sailing boat, capable of 200-mile days. It can stand up to dirty weather, and with an innovative three-cabin layout, it is comfortable to live aboard.

CONSTRUCTION QUALITY: The original construction is robust and intelligent, with a solid fiberglass hull, airex-cored decks and a beautiful teak interior. It is just a shame so many were abused in the charter trade.

USER-FRIENDLINESS: Although the rig is powerful, it is simple. With the right gear it is easy to control. Most systems are well thought out. One advantage of a charter boat is that the mentality is to keep everything simple, build it ruggedly and have an alternative if one system should fail.

SAFETY: The nature of the hull shape and seakindly motion make the boat extremely safe. The lack of a bridgedeck and questionable nonskid keep the rating from being higher.

TYPICAL CONDITION: This rating is a bit misleading. A Stevens 47 recently refitted by Bennett Brothers would receive a five. However, some of the Hylas 47s coming out of charter need love and lots of attention.

REFITTING: You won't be the first sailors to refit a Stevens-Hylas 47 for a world cruise, and Paul Bennett specializes in it. Typical projects include repowering and rerigging, both big jobs, but the high quality of the boat makes them less of a hassle.

SUPPORT: Although there is little support from Hylas Yachts, Bennett Brothers closely monitors the Stevens class and offer a concierge service for boats out cruising that needs parts and advice. Reach them at www.bbyachts.com.

AVAILABILITY: All together there are more around 130 Stevens-Hylas 47s afloat, and there are usually a handful for sale. You may need to travel to different parts of the county to look at more than one boat.

INVESTMENT AND RESALE: The 47s have held their values extremely well over the years and will do so into the future. With sailboat production way down, a great sailing, comfortable boat will be a valuable commodity.

OVERALL 'SVG' RATING

Although many boats are rigged as cutters, most are sailed as sloops. Be sure to check the staysail chainplate for signs of leaking.

Long headsail tracks run down the middle of the side decks, making for good sheeting angles but also another obstacle to avoid when moving about. Fortunately the side decks are wide, and the low profile trunk is an easy step up and down. The chainplates also fall in about the middle of the side deck. Sheets are usually led from the fair lead to a massive turning block aft and then back to the cockpit winch. One safety tip to remember is that a flogging headsail sheet is much more dangerous on a center-cockpit boat because the crew is well-positioned to be thwacked. The boat came standard with chromed dorade vents and plugs for rough weather sailing.

The standing rigging is massive, although if the original swages or mechanical terminals are still in place, be sure to check them carefully. If the rig is more than 10 years old, it is worth spending the money for a rigging survey. Most boats that have been retrofitted for cruising have redirected the halyards and other sail controls back to the cockpit. Although the Stevens 47s may have a variety of headsail furling systems, some of the Hylas 47s were fitted with the Hyde Stream Stay system. Chances are this inferior, solid aluminum rod system has been replaced, and Hylas later switched to the excellent Furlex gear.

Down below

The well-thought-out, beautifully finished interior has always been a prime attraction for the Stevens-Hylas 47. The joinerwork is first-rate, blending solid teak with veneers and occasional bits of Formica. Hand-carved trim pieces give the boat an old-world feeling, and yet, the boat doesn't have the excessive, ornate decorations that festooned the first generation of Taiwan-built boats. Some of the Stevens 47 refits by the Bennett Brothers have lightened up the interior.

Although many Stevens 47 had custom interior plans, the last boat the company built became the model for the Hylas 47s to follow, and in one form or another, continues to be copied by other builders today. This arrangement includes a large V-berth forward, complete with cabinets above and a hanging locker. Immediately aft to starboard is a head with a quarter cabin opposite. This cabin, with either an upper and under, or slide-out double, is popular with families that need private accommodations for the kids.

The saloon includes an L-shaped settee to port with a fold up table. Some early boats had a pilot berth above the settee on the starboard side and others had cabinets and shelves. The tanks are usually located in the bilge, but extra water tanks maybe located under the settees. The galley is located to port in the walkway and includes a three-burner stove with oven and a large fridge and freezer compartment that serves as counter space when closed. Double stainless sinks are cleverly located under the companionway in the box covering the engine compartment, which puts them close to the centerline. Food storage is in Formica-faced lockers located above the counter. The fiddles also serve as handholds when moving into the aft cabin. Once you get used to having the galley located in the pass through, you realize it is quite practical. There is nowhere to fall, and you can brace yourself clear of the stove without needing a harness. I have managed to prepare hot meals during the worst conditions, of course, the boat's seakindly motion is a big help too.

The nav station is opposite and not particularly big for a 47-foot boat. Charts need to be folded. The electrical panel is outboard and the battery switches are below the seat. It is easy to accidentally throw a breaker when perched in the nav seat on the port tack. Behind the nav station is a second head that also functions as a second access point into the aft cabin.

The owner's stateroom is located aft and usually features a centerline queen berth and a dressing area to port. A hanging locker is opposite and there are plenty of drawers below the bunk and shelves along the hull sides. I have stuffed six people aboard a Hylas 47 for a 10-day passage between Newport, Rhode Island, and St. Thomas, U.S.V.I., and we managed to find room to stow everybody's gear and five shopping carts worth of provisions. The merits of a centerline queen on an oceangoing sailboat are hard to find, however the bunk can be made more useful by splitting the mattress and rigging a lee cloth down the middle.

Engine

It is hard to speculate about engines in the Stevens-Hylas 47, short of saying they all have a diesel. A quick look at three Stevens 47s on the used boat market shows one boat with an original 80-horsepower Ford Lehman, another with a 66-horsepower Yanmar and a third with a refit 44-horsepower Universal. The Perkins 4-154 diesel was the most common engine in the Hylas 47 until late in the production run when Queen Long switched to the 62-horsepower Yanmar. With the Perkins, the boat was a bit underpowered (it was a struggle to motor into a head sea), and even in flat water, the boat topped out at 6 knots. Regardless of what engine was used, a feathering propeller is a great help when handling the boat, especially when in reverse.

The engine is located beneath the cockpit well, with a framed box that housed the galley sinks above it. Still, access is good with hatches from both sides and the front. Although it isn't an easy task to pull the engine out of the boat, it can be done without major reconstructive surgery. Most boats came standard with 100 gallons of fuel in either one or two stainless tanks located in the bilge. Boats that have been retrofitted for serious cruising often have increased tank capacity. Many of the Hylas 47s that were in the charter trade have high-hour engines, and it may be practical to factor repowering into your cruising budget. Also, most of the Hylas 47s came with a zinc casting throttle control switch that is notorious for failing at just the wrong moment.

Underway

If you are considering long-distance cruising and have a $200,000 boat budget, you should consider the Stevens-Hylas 47 for one reason above all others: It is a great sailing boat that can handle almost anything Neptune can throw at it. The 47 is one of Rod Stephens favorite designs, according to Bennett. It's a boat where he felt he put it all together. I couldn't agree more.

For all the nit-picking I've done about certain features, I can lavish an equal amount of praise on the boat's overall performance. The nature of the hull shape is well suited to tradewind sailing because the long fin gives good directional stability and the wide transom is fast in a following sea. Naturally being an S&S design, the boat sails well upwind too. The 47 responds well to self-steering systems, both autopilots and windvanes, and best of all, does not need to be micromanaged. You can get caught in a squall without being knocked down. You can reef long after you should have and get away with it. Maybe this isn't perfect seamanship, but it's the reality of ocean sailing for most of us.

I have pored over the logs from my many voyages aboard Hylas 47s, 49s and the 1,200-mile delivery of a Stevens 47. The results are impressive. On the six deliveries from Ft Lauderdale to St. Thomas, a 1,000-mile upwind slug, my average passage time was exactly seven days, or 143 miles per day, and that was sailing upwind and up current. On four different deliveries on the reverse trip, the average shot up to more than 160 miles per day. Sure there was always a bit of motoring involved, but the 47 is not a good performer under power so we sailed whenever possible. On five round trips between the East Coast and Antigua, roughly 1,500-mile passages, I've averaged 158 miles per day. These figures include gales and calms, but they speak volumes about the Stevens-Hylas 47 as a seagoing boat.

Bennett, who has built many other fine boats over the years, is partial to the Stevens 47. He has personally delivered new boats from Annapolis to New York for commissioning and remembers many ugly nights beating up the Jersey shore.

"The boat never gave me a problem," he says fondly. "She was in her element." Bennett also recalls logging plenty of 200-mile-plus days, an impressive feat for a boat with a 37-foot, 9-inch LWL. "The key is that the boat never slows down," he said.

Conclusion

Some readers may wonder how I can consider a $200,000 boat an affordable boat for a circumnavigation. I confess, the Stevens-Hylas 47 is a different animal than most of the boats in this book. I view it more as a legitimate alternative to the madness of new boat pricing. What does $200,000 buy new these days? Most likely a production-built 35-footer, if you can drive a good deal. When viewed in that light the value becomes obvious. The Stevens-Hylas 47 is a one-of-a-kind S&S design that can be your magic carpet to the world.

Gulfstar 50

This choice as a 10 Best may surprise some readers, but ironically, it was one of the first boats I penciled in when forming the list of 10 great boats for this section. While many boats were scratched out, and then scribbled back in, and then erased, and then reconsidered, the Gulfstar 50 remained a rock solid member of the list. Some people still associate Gulfstar with the wide-bodied motorsailers the company produced in the early 1970s, and there is little to recommend about those floating bathtubs. The Gulfstar 50, however, is a completely different animal. I know. I delivered a 1979 ketch from Ft. Lauderdale, Florida, to Japan, a 12,000-mile sea trial. It is a surprisingly capable offshore boat, comfortable on deck and below, nice to look at and a terrific value. In fact, this is a boat I would seriously consider purchasing to take my family on a circumnavigation.

Gulfstar, like its founder, Vince Lazzara, was constantly reinventing itself. Lazzara was one of the pioneers in the fiberglass boatbuilding industry, and left his mark on several companies. Before he became a boatbuilder, however, he was an engineer and owned a foundry. In fact, he is credited with inventing the first snap shackle. After selling his business, he followed his dream to build boats. He teamed up with Fred Coleman to produce the legendary Rhodes-designed 41-foot Bounty II. Lazzara, who early on believed that fiberglass would dominate the industry, went on to become one of the founders of Columbia Yachts. Columbia rapidly grew into one of the largest sailboat manufacturers in the world before Lazzara finally sold out. A two-year noncompete clause forced him to bide his time building houseboats before founding Gulfstar Inc. in 1970.

Gulfstar jumped into the market with low-priced, incredibly commodious boats with hulls that were virtually interchangeable as trawlers and sailboats. If you wanted a sailboat you were given a mast. The trawler lacked a rig but had a larger engine. Lazzara understood the need for production efficiency and tapped into the floating RV mentality of some boaters. However, by the mid-1970s, he began to sense a change in the mindset of boat buyers. Cheap boats were losing market share to higher quality products as consumers began to view boats, even fiberglass production boats, as long-term investments, not toys. Once again Lazzara shifted with the times and Gulfstar suddenly became a builder of high-quality, handsome yachts.

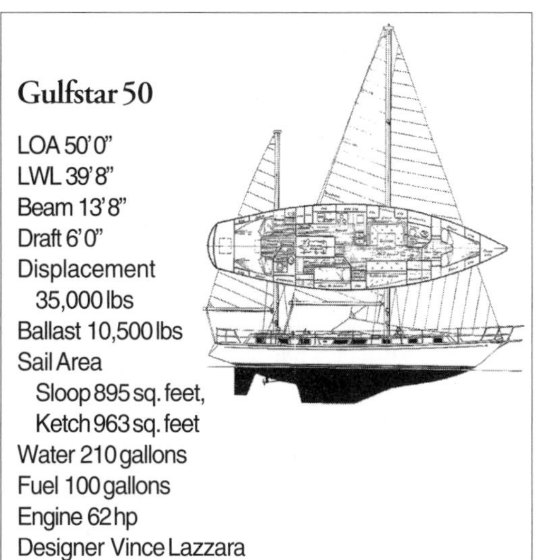

Gulfstar 50

LOA 50'0"
LWL 39'8"
Beam 13'8"
Draft 6'0"
Displacement 35,000 lbs
Ballast 10,500 lbs
Sail Area Sloop 895 sq. feet, Ketch 963 sq. feet
Water 210 gallons
Fuel 100 gallons
Engine 62 hp
Designer Vince Lazzara

Gulfstar 50 MK II Price Data

		Low	High
BUC Retail Range	1975	$109,000	$120,500
	1978	$122,000	$138,500
	1980	$134,000	$150,000

		State	Asking
Boats For Sale	1975	MA	$ 85,000
	1975	NJ	$111,000
	1978	FL	$ 99,000
	1978	FL	$ 86,000
	1980	FL	$149,000

First impressions

The Gulfstar 50 MK II is Vince Lazzara's design, through and through. Although he wasn't a naval architect by training, he had sound instincts and production savvy. He knew how to design a handsome boat that could still be manufactured efficiently.

The 50, which is a scaled up version of the Gulfstar 41, is moderately proportioned, which used to be a compliment when describing a design. The hull has moderate sheer, the bow entry is soft and the reverse transom has a springy lift. Although the beam is 13 feet, 8 inches, the boat appears long and lean as the ends taper. The long cabintrunk, divided by a center cockpit, blends unobtrusively into the overall linear flow of the deck. The Gulfstar 50 design was a long way from the bulbous deck-saloon boats of today. Lazzara was more inspired by the shapely look of low-slung center-cockpit boats like the Bowman 46 than by his own earlier designs. He wanted to create a boat that would have a legacy and he succeeded.

The Gulfstar 50 has an appealing underwater profile. The forefoot has just enough bite to keep the boat from pounding without creating unnecessary wetted surface. The long fin keel is cut away aft and the rudder is protected by a full skeg. The prop is mounted on a strut. The LWL of just less than 40 feet translates into an overhang ratio of 20 percent, which works better in a 50-foot boat than in a 40-footer. 10,500 pounds of lead ballast is encapsulated in the keel and the on paper displacement is 35,000 pounds. *Country Girl*, the boat I delivered to Japan, weighed more than 40,000 pounds when we hauled her before the voyage. Although the boat was offered as a sloop, most were ketch rigged with 963 square feet of sail. Lazzara resorted to his old efficient ways in tooling up for both rigs. The main mast is the same size in the same place for the ketch and the sloop, you simply added a mizzen to create the ketch and lengthened the boom for the sloop. Both models have an air draft of 54 feet, 5 inches.

Construction

The hull layup of the Gulfstar 50 is robust, to say the least, and Lazzara worked hard to maintain a high glass-to-resin ratio, aiming for 45 to 50 percent, which was unheard of in those days. The fact that he was even concerned about this in 1974 indicates his sophistication with laminating techniques. Many tout the strength of old glass hulls, and for the most part they are strong. But old boats like the Pearson Triton are resin rich, with very thick hulls. But the strength is in the fibers not the resins, so boats with lots of resin needed extra thickness for strength. It is true that early fiberglass builders were unsure of the material's strength, so they tended to make hulls extra thick.

The Gulfstar 50 layup schedule included seven layers of mat and roving at the turn of the bilge, tapering to five layers at the gunwale. The hull is solid fiberglass, although, according to a few published reports, late in the production run a handful of boats were built with balsa-cored hulls. The decks were balsa cored, and although deck leaks are a frequent complaint, deck delamination is not a commonly noted problem. The hull-and-deck joint includes an overlapping lip on the deck and a hull flange. The joint is both bolted through the teak toerail and glassed over from underneath. The bulkheads, which on early boats are solid teak, are securely tabbed to the hull. The mast was originally stepped on an iron plate in the bilge, which often resulted in a fair bit of corrosion caused by bilge water mixing with dissimilar metals. The ballast is cast lead, fitted into the keel cavity and glassed over. It is difficult to inspect this part of the boat because tanks take up most of the bilge area. The skeg and strut are actually bolted on, and the bolts can be examined from beneath the sole in the aft cabin.

The 50 marked a change in Gulfstar's finish and joinerwork. Instead of copious use of Formica, the 50s were symphonies of teak and mahogany, and great pains were taken to match grain patterns in each boat.

The company boasted that its craftsman used a patented process to form curved trim pieces, and even after 25 years, the quality of the interior woodworking is impressive. For the most part the detailing was ahead of its time. The electrical system was first-rate and most mechanical installations well-done.

What to look for

It is not exactly clear when the Gulfstar 50 became the 50 Mark II and what precise changes accompanied the name change, with 1977 being my best estimate based on company literature. Gulfstar was constantly tinkering with the boat, upgrading it. It was one of the company's most successful models. Company brochures list four different drafts, ranging from 5 feet, 6 inches to 6 feet. It is safe to assume a 6-foot draft. Ballast is either listed at 10,000 or 10,500 pounds, and printed displacement figures range from 33,000 to 35,000 pounds. The discrepancies in these numbers point up the risk in trying to evaluate a boat based on performance formulas. And when you factor in additional weight from cruising gear and alterations over the years, it is very difficult to come up with precise data. My hunch is that most 50s on the market tip the scales at around 40,000 pounds.

There are several different items to look for when you start examining used 50s. First, there are two different interior plans; one with two private cabins fore and aft and one with a third captain's cabin amidships to starboard. Ironically, the three-cabin boats that were developed for the charter trade have become more popular today. The 50 is one of the few affordable three-cabin, center-cockpit boats on the market. Most boats originally came with a Perkins 4-154 60-horsepower diesel, and surprisingly, given Gulfstar's experience with motorsailers, the boat is underpowered. Some came with an 85-horsepower diesel, which definitely gives the boat better performance under power. A quick glance at the boats for sale today reveals that many have been repowered with four-cylinder turbo Yanmars, a wonderful upgrade. Most 50s also came with Onan generators, which are notorious troublemakers. I would look for a boat without a generator or one that has had the Onan replaced. One more note, the standard tankage varied over the years, early boats had 60 gallons of fuel and more than 200 gallons of water in a single tank. Later in the production run fuel capacity was increased to 100 gallons. Also hull numbers 124 through 143 had an additional 65 gallons of water.

Deck and hatch leaks are common on the 50, according to Steve Maseda. An experienced sailor, he took his family on a yearlong Caribbean sabbatical on a 1974 sloop. Areas around the turning blocks and stanchion bases are prime leak sources. The wooden framed hatches over the forward and aft cabins on older models are also leak sources. Changing these out for aluminum hatches is a terrific upgrade. Late model boats had alloy Atkins and Hoyle hatches that were standard. The plastic opening portlights are often cracked and leak down onto the interior teak veneer, causing discoloration and delamination. Today's plastic ports are much better than they were in the mid-1970s, although the best move is to replace them with aluminum models. An important item to check is the steering system. The original Yacht Specialties systems had problems with the sprocket chain, and some owners have reported problems with the cable leads and sheaves. The chain parted on *Country Girl* while running before large Pacific rollers and it nearly caused a broach. Not only was it difficult to repair, I discovered that the emergency tiller is designed to be used from inside the aft cabin while I was working upside down in the engine room.

Finally, Gulfstars were hard hit by the blister pox that shook the industry in the 1980s. This problem was most severe with the late model 50s and boats built after 1976. Try to find out if and when a blister repair job was done on the boat and what barrier coating system was used.

On deck

The Gulfstar 50 has a comfortable cockpit, and unlike many center-cockpit boats, it is actually situated fairly far aft. This positioning is subtle but it makes for dry upwind sailing and good visibility for sail trim. There is not much of a bridgedeck—it's just a small sill—and some 50s are set up with swinging hatch doors instead of drop boards. These handsome, louvered doors look great but are not very secure in heavy weather. There is a small cockpit seat locker and a large lazarette astern. The mainsheet traveler is aft of the cockpit, allowing for an efficient end-boom sheeting arrangement. The mizzen sheet is tacked to a double block on an eyebolt astern and the mizzen boom tends to ride up when sailing off the wind. A block-and-tackle vang would be helpful. Early on, Barlows were the standard sheet winches, but soon Gulfstar switched to Barient 32s and many owners opted for the self-tailing option as soon as it became available.

Gulfstar 50 MK II

Sailing Magazine's Value Guide

PRICE: The Gulfstar 50 is one of the best-priced big cruisers on the market, especially if you are a looking for a rare three-cabin boat. What else compares at just over $100,000?

DESIGN QUALITY: Vince Lazzara was not a trained naval architect, yet he managed to create some lovely boats. The Gulfstar 50 was one of them. Although he readily admits the 50 was scaled up from the less-desirable 41, the design works.

CONSTRUCTION QUALITY: The real test for construction quality is how well the boats have held up. Most 50s are going strong today, even those that were chartered for years. Blisters and old outdated mechanical items are the biggest problems.

USER-FRIENDLINESS: This is tough one to rate, the 50 is easy to sail but it is a big boat with big loads, making it more demanding than a smaller boat. However, the ride is comfortable and the interior plan very livable.

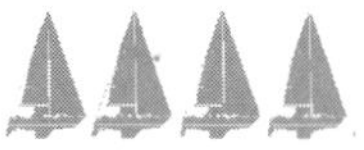

SAFETY: There is a certain element of safety that comes with size that can't be denied. The stout construction and wide side decks and well-placed handholds above and below deck lend security. The cockpit is a bit open.

TYPICAL CONDITION: Remember, even the youngest 50 is more than 20 years old and some are nearing 30. Most boats that were chartered have been converted back to private use. There may be a lot of outdated gear to deal with.

RETROFITTING: Gulfstar is long out of business, consumed by Viking Yachts in the 1980s. Unlike other U.S. production builders, Gulfstar was not big on using proprietary parts, so finding refit items is not impossible. Chances are yours will not be the first retrofit project.

SUPPORT: Irene Meinch, who with her late husband Jack, were long time Gulfstar brokers, operates the Gulfstar Owner's Club. You can reach her at (727) 825-0757, or at www.gulfstarownersclub.com.

AVAILABILITY: With 172 boats built, there is always a decent selection of boats on the market. The 50 seems to be more of an East Coast boat. The best place to look for boats is Florida.

INVESTMENT AND RESALE: The 50s are affordable but still hold their value well. The original price in 1978 was $69,000. A well-known boat, most 50s don't linger on the used market.

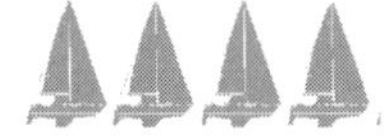

OVERALL 'SVG' RATING

The molded diamond nonskid pattern was originally fairly deep, so even if the deck has been painted once or twice over the years, it should still offer secure traction. Teak handrails line the cabintrunk. The double lifelines, stanchions and pulpits are stout, although be sure to check the condition of the lifeline terminal ends. Gulfstar used beefy deck hardware, especially toward the end of the production run. Mooring cleats are 12 inches and toerail chocks are substantial. I remember the pilot complimenting me on our deck hardware when we transited the Panama Canal. An anchoring platform and bowsprit unit supports double rollers and has a small bobstay. This is a clever arrangement. It helps keeps the rodes clear of the topsides, but it's not a structural bowsprit, and the forestay is securely tacked to the stemhead fitting that is heavily bolted to the hull.

The genoa track leads are usually mounted on the toerail. Efficient windward sailing is not the 50's forte, with wide spreaders set straight and the chainplates set nearly on the deck edge. The masts will likely be painted white, probably with Imron or Awlgrip. Painted spars look great when new, but eventually the paint blisters and peels and the end result is another maintenance item. Many 50s have been retrofitted with roller-furling mainsail systems, and you should be wary of behind the mast systems. The original booms were round and came standard with a worm gear for roller reefing, although a fixed gooseneck was offered on later boats.

Down below

The interior of the 50 is without question one of its prime attractions. "The amount of space and the way it was broken up worked perfectly for a family of four," Maseda said. "We specifically wanted a boat with the third captain's cabin so that our younger daughter could have a cabin amidships, close to mom and dad, and located in an area with less motion than up forward." Maseda, who is nearing early retirement and will cruise full time, is considering buying another Gulfstar 50 even though the kids are grown. "That way, when the kids come, they'll have a bit of privacy." On our delivery to Japan, we either had two or three aboard and the sense of spaciousness was overwhelming.

Both arrangements feature a large, comfortable cabin forward. There is a V-berth, bureaus for storage and a hanging locker. The chain locker is accessed through a door at the foot of the bunk. The head is to port with a private door from the forward cabin. Cruising couples, who didn't need two heads, have converted this head into a dedicated wet locker or a laundry and storage room. The saloon is not huge, but it's functional, both under way and at anchor. Most boats have a wraparound dinette to port than can comfortably seat four, and the table usually folds out for additional seating. A straight settee with a pilot berth above is to starboard. If the boat does not have the captain's cabin, either of these bunks makes a good sea berth. The 50 has the capacity to store enough provisions for a nonstop Pacific crossing. With the tanks in the bilge, the space beneath the settees is freed up for storage, although some boats use this space for air conditioning compressors and piping. The headliner is white vinyl held in place with teak battens, and the original cushions were four inches tall with tufted upholstery.

The L-shaped galley is to port and occupies the walk-through to the aft cabin. Lazzara was one of the first designers to use the area for the galley, a concept that has become common on almost all center-cockpit cruisers. Double stainless sinks face forward and are close enough to the centerline to drain on either tack. A top-loading icebox and refrigerator is outboard from the sinks. Standard equipment included a three-burner propane stove and oven. I remember making a huge Thanksgiving Day feast rolling before a stiff trade wind breeze. Many boats came from the factory with a freezer. Be sure to check the condition of the refrigeration and freezer unit components. Many of these compressors are 20 years old, inefficient and difficult to find replacement parts for. The same can also be said for the air conditioning units.

The two-cabin model includes a huge engine room and a huge, wraparound nav station with a swivel chair to starboard. This is a great arrangement for both chart and office work for liveaboard sailors. Here you'll find the custom aluminum electrical panel and the battery switches. Gulfstar was proud of its electrical system. It used top-quality components, and the 50 came standard with 110-volt shore power. The three-cabin model compresses the nav station and cleverly squeezes the third cabin to starboard. Amazingly, a third head was included as well. This cabin is not for the claustrophobic, but compared to many European three- and four-cabin boats, it seems downright spacious.

The aft cabin includes an enormous bunk that can be slept on in a variety of angles depending on the boat's angle of heel. There is another bureau to port and a hanging locker as well. The aft head includes a separate stall shower and washbasin—a very civilized arrangement. Overall, the Gulfstar 50 interior is a wonderful blend of comfort and practicality, a liveaboard sailor's dream setup.

Engine

Most 50s came standard with the Perkins 4-154, 62-horsepower diesel. This is a fine, reliable engine, but just doesn't provide enough oomph for the boat. "It was always a struggle to motor into a head sea, tough to make 5 knots," Maseda said. Later models offered the 4-236 Perkins, rated at 85 horsepower and a better power plant for the boat. Part of the problem is that Perkins rated its engines before the gear box, meaning that a 62-horsepower engine actually delivered less that 50 to the prop. The standard shaft is 1 1/4 stainless steel and the standard prop is a fixed three-blade. One simple but expensive way to improve engine performance and performance under sail is to opt for a feathering propeller.

The most common size fuel tank seems to be 100 gallons, made of either fiberglass or stainless steel, and located in the bilge just forward of the engine. One problem with tanks located low in the boat is that the fuel pump has to work hard to lift fuel to the injection pump, especially when the fuel level is low. A valuable upgrade would be to install a day tank in the bilge that allows gravity to work with the engine. Of course you need to monitor this tank and have a means of filling it from the main tank, but checking the day tank also forces you to check the engine more frequently, which is forced medicine for many sailors. With either engine, 100 gallons of fuel should translate into a realistic motoring range of about 500 miles.

The engine room, especially on the two-cabin models, is downright amazing. There is room to work and store all your tools. Of course if the boat is fitted with an Onan generator (most were), you'll become very familiar with the engine room indeed. Access is through the double half doors in the walkway. The three-cabin model allows access through the captain's cabin. At first glance the engine room can be intimidating, with a plethora of hoses, bronze seacocks and wiring conduits running in every which direction. Once you become familiar with the engine you'll find that Gulfstar's engineering practices are very sound.

Underway

The most surprising feature of the Gulfstar 50 is how well it sails. On the delivery to Japan, we had one 10-day stretch sailing in the trades where we reeled off 1,710 miles, which breaks down to 171 miles a day at an average of more than 7 knots for 240 consecutive hours. That is good going for any boat. What makes that even more impressive is that the main autopilot had died early on and we had to rely on a belt-driven Autohelm 3000, a unit designed for boats about one third of the 50's size, forcing us to reef early and under sail just to keep the pilot happy. Overall, we averaged 148 miles from Ft. Lauderdale to Japan, a 12,000 mile voyage by way of Panama, Hawaii, Guam and Okinawa.

Maseda, who these days campaigns a Melges 24, has raced many different boats and is one of the most knowledgeable sailors I know, was determined to improve the basic sail control systems. "We added a new Garhauer ball-bearing traveler and new genoa turning blocks. But the best move we made was a solid vang, which helped control the boom. The sloop rig has a very long boom."

The previous owner had installed a new Harken headsail furling system that performed well with a new 130-percent genoa. Maseda, who beat down the thorny path to the West Indies, finally concluded that it wasn't worth pushing the boat closer than 45 degrees apparent. "It is best to sacrifice a few degrees and keep moving." Sound advice for most cruising boats.

The Gulfstar 50 rolls off the wind, a nature of the hull shape. We found that by trimming the mizzen fairly flat we could dampen the rolling. Also, the mizzen can help take the strain off the autopilot. Maseda and family flew their cruising chute often on the return trip, often pegging double digits in moderate conditions. "The boat handles well with the chute, and because it doesn't have a big stick, the sail isn't unmanageable," Maseda said. The Gulfstar 50 looks like it should sail well, and it does. It can take a capful of wind. The final, wintery approach to Japan was tough going and we had a week of 40-plus knots on the nose. We were anxious to conclude the passage and pounded into mean seas day after day. It wasn't comfortable, but the boat never gave us a nervous minute. We also hove-to during a mid-Pacific storm, easily riding out the 55-knot gusts.

Conclusion

The Gulfstar 50 is a sleeper on the market and worthy of serious considerations if you need and or desire a large boat. It is a serious cruiser that can be purchased for around $100,000. A well-placed $15,000 to $20,000 retrofit project will produce a fine-sailing, good-looking, comfortable boat that can carry you across oceans. By the way, the boat won't linger when you decide it is time to sell after your sabbatical.

APPENDIX 1

Dimensions Defined and Performance and Safety Indicating Ratios

Sailboat Dimensions

LOA – Length overall, excluding bowsprits, boomkins, davits etc. Sometimes, and more accurately described as LOD, length on deck. Linear measurements in the book are in feet and inches.

LWL – Load waterline, sometimes called length waterline, or DWL, design waterline. This is the length of the boat as it floats, literally measuring where it touches the water forward and aft. LWL can increase when boats are loaded, or heeled excessively.

Beam – The maximum width of a boat. Beam WL is the maximum width at the waterline, a more useful figure when applying to ratios.

Ballast – Weight, usually lead or iron, measured in pounds and carried in the keel for stability.

Displacement – The amount of water measured in weight that a boat displaces. This amount is equal to the boat's weight, (that's why boats float). This figure is usually noted in pounds although occasionally large boats may have displacement listed in tons. Displacement ratios often use tons, a long ton is 2240 lbs.

Draft – The amount of water required for a boat to float, or the depth of the deepest part of the vessel, usually the keel, below the waterline measured in feet and inches. Some boats will list different drafts depending on the model (i.e., deep, shoal, centerboard).

Sail Area – The square footage of working sails that a boat sets. Usually the sail area is the mainsail and the foretriangle, or normal jib.

Air Draft – The height of the rig, at its highest point, above the waterline, measured in feet and inches.

Performance and Safety Indicating Ratios

These ratios are based on design figures, actual numbers may vary considerably. Use these ratios only as part of a range of factors for selecting a boat, don't over-exaggerate their value

Ballast/Displacement $\dfrac{\text{Ballast lbs}}{\text{Displacement lbs}}$

This ratio indicates the percentage of ballast to the overall displacement of the boat. A high ratio—above 45%—usually translates into a stiff boat. Modern hull shapes, with deep bulb keels have lessened the importance of this ratio.

Displacement/Length $\frac{\text{Displacement in long tons}}{(\text{LWL}/100)^3}$

This ratio is used to compare the displacement of different hull shapes. Ted Brewer explains concisely that the lower the number, the smaller the waves that will be generated by the hull through the water, and the smaller the wave making resistance. In other words, the smaller the number the faster the hull. Of course, like all of these ratios, there are caveats. Displacement can be calculated in different ways, and LWL changes when a boat is heeled or loaded. Just remember, like any good statistic, these numbers can be tweaked. In broad terms, ultralight boats will have Displacement/ Length of under 100, light boats in the 100 – 200, moderate 200 – 300, heavy displacement 300 – 400, and over 400 is considered a sumo wrestler of a sailboat.

SA/Displacement $\frac{\text{SA}}{(\text{Disp}/64)^{2/3}}$

This ratio gives an indication of how much sail area is available to push the weight of a boat. Higher numbers translate into faster boats. This figure can be adjusted based on how you measure the sail area, usually it is the main and 100% of the foretriangle. Again, in broad terms, a boat with a SA/D of over 20 can be considered high performance, 18 – 20 is a good range for ocean racers and performance cruisers, 15 – 18 for cruising boats and under 15 for boats that need a stiff breeze to move at all.

Overhangs $\frac{(\text{LOA}-\text{LWL})}{\text{LOA}}$

Developed by Roger Marshall in his excellent book, *The Complete Guide to Choosing a Cruising Sailboat*, this is a simple and useful way to look at the percentage of overhang. Modern boats are extending the LWL at the expense of overhangs. This makes for a faster boat in smooth water, but overhangs are important in a cruising boat because you need reserve buoyancy at the bow and stern. Marshall recommends that a pure cruising boat should have an overhang ratio of 15 – 20%.

Capsize Screening Factor or
Capsize Screening Value (CSV) $\frac{\text{Beam}}{(\text{Displ.}/64)^{1/3}}$

Developed after the 1979 Fastnet Race disaster, this calculation attempts to determine a boat's tendency for capsizing. This ratio is based on the assumption that boats with wide beams are hard to capsize initially but also difficult to right. Heavier boats have less initial stability but are ultimately harder to capsize. The lower the number, the less prone to capsize. 2.0 is a standard of sorts as the maximum acceptable number for offshore boats, under 2.0 is better.

APPENDIX 2

Glossary

This glossary is not intended to be a complete guide to sailing and sailboat terms. Instead, it is a short list of specialized terms scattered throughout the book and used to describe certain design and construction features.

Aft cockpit – A boat with the primary steering station and sail control area located aft, near the stern, as opposed to a center cockpit boat.

Athwarthships – Across the boat, at a right angle to the centerline.

Auxiliary – The engine in a sailboat, or a boat propelled by both sails and/or an engine.

Balanced rudder – A rudder mounted independently of the keel or a skeg, supported only by the rudderstock. Sometimes called a free standing or spade rudder.

Bobstay – Usually stainless steel wire but sometimes chain, that runs from the stem to the outboard end of a bowsprit.

Boom gallows – A frame, usually over the companionway, used to support the boom without the need for a topping lift. Usually seen on traditional boats only, a solid or rigid vang achieves the same result and is also an important sail control.

Boomkin – A frame or spar extending off the stern to support a backstay or sheet.

Bridge deck – A structural member in the cockpit that helps prevent water from going down the companionway. It can be part of the cockpit seating or just a small sill. Offshore boats need a stout bridge deck.

BUC Guide – A widely accepted private service used by brokers and surveyors providing used boat pricing guides since 1961.

Bulb keel – A fin keel with a rounded flair at the bottom for increased stability, often used on shoal draft keel configurations.

Bulwark – An extension of the topsides, above deck, to form a toe rail.

Camber – Athwartship curve of the deck.

Canoe stern/double ender – A rounded, or in some cases, sharp stern, as opposed to a more common flat stern.

Center of effort (CE) – The center of the sail area.

Center of lateral resistance (CLR) – The center of the underwater plane of a boat. The CLR and CE work in conjunction for balance. If the CLR is ahead of the CE, weather helm will develop.

Center cockpit – A boat with the steering station and most sail controls well forward of the stern, with an aft cabin behind.

Clipper bow – Taken from the clipper ships, a bow entry that has a reverse S shape, or a bow with a concave stem profile.

Club-footed jib – A jib, or often times a staysail, with a boom. Not popular anymore with the advent of roller furling headsails.

Coachroof (trunk cabin, deck house, etc.) – The part of the cabin raised above the main deck.

Coaming – The raised sides of the cockpit.

Compression post – A support, usually tubular but not always, that supports a deck-stepped mast from below.

Cored construction – A method of saving weight and adding strength by using a core material between two thin layers of fiberglass. Most commonly used on decks, with balsa wood as the core. Also used in hulls. Other common cores are PVC and Airex foams. Sometimes called sandwich construction.

Counter stern – A stern that slopes aft as it rises, opposite of a reverse transom.

Delamination – This is usually caused when the core between the fiberglass layers has become wet. The core can rot, or delaminate, and without proper support the actual fiberglass is stressed and can also delaminate.

Dorade vent–A clever type of vent that allows air to pass below but not spray. First used on the S&S designed classic, Dorade, in 1931.

Electrolysis – Electrochemical reaction between dissimilar metals in a saltwater environment.

Fiddle – The edge on a table or counter to prevent spillage when underway.

Flare – The forward part of the hull as it bends outward.

Floors – The athwartship frames (not ribs) that support the hull, located below the cabin sole.

Forefoot – The forward section of the hull below the waterline, the area from the steel to the keel.

Freeboard – The distance from the waterline to the deck.

Gelcoat – A trade name introduced by Glidden in the 50s, it consisted of a flexible polyester resin that allowed a boat to be easily removed from the mold and gave a shiny, smooth finished hull.

Gooseneck – The fitting that joins the mast and boom.

Gunkhole – A shallow, out of the way anchorage or harbor. Gunkholing is the practice of exploring such places at a leisurely pace.

Gunwale – Pronounced gunnel, it is the railing where the deck and topsides meet.

Heave-to – The process and result of bringing a boat into the wind to back the sails and put the tiller down. Boats with long or moderately long keels will be able to ride out gales and even storm conditions. Modern hull designs don't heave-to effectively.

Hull speed – The theoretical maximum speed of a non-planing hull. Quickly obtained by multiplying 1.35 by the square root of LWL.

Hydrodynamics – The study of the flow of liquids around solid objects.

IOR–International Offshore Rule, a much-maligned rule of measuring and rating boats for offshore racing. Gained prominence in the early 70s and inadvertently influenced sailboat design well into the 80s.

Joinerwork–The fine woodwork, specifically in a boat's interior.

Jumper strut–A tubular support system on the forward side of the mast, often to support the staysail stay instead of running backstays.

Longitudinal stringer – Supports that run fore and aft to stiffen the flat surfaces in a hull.

Mast step – A member that supports the base of the mast in the bottom of the boat. Sometimes a bridge spanning a couple of floors is used to support the step.

Mold – The form in which fiberglass is applied to create hulls, decks and molded liners and parts.

One-design – A racing boat that forms a class with other identical boats. Strict controls ensure that the boats have uniformity in construction and outfitting.

Osmosis – Blisters caused by osmosis between the layers of fiberglass. Known as 'the pox' blisters were common in the 70s and 80s when manufacturers used polyester resins almost exclusively. The switch to vinylester resin and strict temperature and environment controls while laminating have greatly reduced the blister problem on newer boats.

Overhang – The distance between the bow and stern and the waterline.

Profile – The view of a boat from a distance amidships, a side view.

Raised deck – A deck without a coachroof or trunk, sometimes called a flush deck, which is used on smaller boats to create room below, although not headroom.

Ratlines – Rope or solid rungs, strung between the stays to form a ladder up the mast.

Rubbing strake – Nowadays more commonly called a rub rail, a protective wood or metal piece, fitted to the hull for protection from scrapes.

Rudder stock–The rod, usually metal but occasionally synthetic, that the rudder is attached to. It may enter the boat through a stuffing box or a rudder tube above the waterline.

Running backstays – Movable or temporary stays set up to support the headsail or staysail. Usually just the weather stay is tensioned.

Saloon – The main non-sleeping cabin in a boat, often and mistakenly called salon.

Scantlings – The structural dimensions and standards of a boat.

SCRIMP–Acronym for Seamann Composites Resin Infusion Molding Process, a laminating technique used by Tillotson-Pearson and others, that is similar to vacuum bagging. Boats are layed up dry, without resin, which is added, or infused later in the process. The system allows for cleaner and more environmentally friendly laminating and also eliminates voids and uneven hand layups.

Seacock – A valve that connects some aspect of a boat's plumbing to the sea, usually used below the waterline where a positive closing action is paramount.

Section – Cross section of a hull plan. Many designers work with 10 sections, each designated as a station.

Settee – A horizontal seat usually found in the saloon that can be converted into a berth.

Sheer/sheer line – The curve of the deck line, or gunwale, as observed from the side, or in profile. Traditional boats usually have more pronounced sheer lines than modern boats. Some boats actually have reverse sheer, where the deck is higher in the middle than the ends.

Side deck –The deck space between the coachroof coaming or side and the gunwale.

Skeg – Part of the aft underbody of the hull designed to support the rudder. A skeg hung rudder is found on many ocean cruising boats, as opposed to the more performance oriented spade or balanced rudder.

Sister ship – Boat of the same design, usually by the same manufacturer.

Spreaders – Supports extending outboard from the mast to spread the shrouds out sideways, increasing the angle the shroud makes with the mast. Depending on the rig, boats can have one or more sets of spreaders.

Stability – There are different types of stability. In general, stability is measured as the force necessary to return a boat to upright from a variety of heeled positions.

Stemhead fitting – The metal fitting that covers the very forward section of the bow, and is supported down the stem. It is generally used to support the forestay and the set up to facilitate anchoring.

Stuffing box – A metal unit used to prevent water from leaking in around the propeller shaft and rudderstock. Old style units are packed with flax, newer units are dripless.

Swage fitting – A terminal end rolled under pressure onto wire, commonly used in standing rigging and lifelines.

Swageless fitting – Mechanical terminals that are applied to wire without swaging, also used in standing rigging applications.

Tabbing – Fiberglass that bonds a wooden bulkhead and furnishings to the hull. Ideally bulkheads should be tabbed on both sides with several layers of glass overlapping several inches.

Tabernacle – A fitting on deck that supports the mast and acts as a hinge for lowering and raising. Usually seen on small boats or sailboats that spend a lot of time in canals passing under low bridges.

Toggle – Part of the standing rigging, a cast fitting, usually bronze or stainless, that connects the turnbuckle to the chainplate, allowing for some rig movement without bending the turnbuckle.

Transom – The furthest aft athwartship surface of a boat. The name and hailing port are usually posted on the transom.

Tumblehome – The curvature of the hull, first extending outboard from the deck and then inward toward the waterline.

Turn of the bilge – The point of the hull where the topsides curve inward to form the underbody.

Underbody – The hull shape below the waterline

Wetted Surface – The surface area, measured in square feet, of the underbody.